England's Elizabeth

John Hassall (1868–1948), *The State Entry of Queen Elizabeth into Bristol, August 14, 1574* (*c.*1910). Hassall's large-scale depiction of a white-clad, fairy-tale Elizabeth on a white horse, receiving an ecstatic civic welcome from her West Country subjects, aims at the same effects of idealized and exhilaratingly reanimated history as the pageant-plays in vogue at the time. An accomplished contributor to children's books, Hassall had earlier developed his Art Nouveau-influenced vision of Elizabeth's England as a lost paradise of freshness, light, and national unity in his illustrations to Brenda Girvin's *Good Queen Bess, 1533–1603* (1907).

England's Elizabeth

An Afterlife in Fame and Fantasy

MICHAEL DOBSON

NICOLA J. WATSON

OXFORD

UNIVERSITY PRESS

OXFORD
UNIVERSITY PRESS

Great Clarendon Street, Oxford OX2 6DP

Oxford University Press is a department of the University of Oxford.
It furthers the University's objective of excellence in research, scholarship,
and education by publishing worldwide in

Oxford New York

Auckland Bangkok Buenos Aires Cape Town Chennai
Dar es Salaam Delhi Hong Kong Istanbul Karachi Kolkata
Kuala Lumpur Madrid Melbourne Mexico City Mumbai Nairobi
São Paulo Shanghai Taipei Tokyo Toronto

Oxford is a registered trade mark of Oxford University Press
in the UK and in certain other countries

Published in the United States
by Oxford University Press Inc., New York

© Michael Dobson and Nicola J. Watson 2002

The moral rights of the authors have been asserted
Database right Oxford University Press (maker)

First published 2002
First published in paperback 2004

All rights reserved. No part of this publication may be reproduced,
stored in a retrieval system, or transmitted, in any form or by any means,
without the prior permission in writing of Oxford University Press,
or as expressly permitted by law, or under terms agreed with the appropriate
reprographics rights organization. Enquiries concerning reproduction
outside the scope of the above should be sent to the Rights Department,
Oxford University Press, at the address above

You must not circulate this book in any other binding or cover
and you must impose this same condition on any acquirer

British Library Cataloguing in Publication Data
Data available

Library of Congress Cataloging in Publication Data
Data available

ISBN 0-19-818377-1
ISBN 0-19-926919-X (Pbk.)

1 3 5 7 9 10 8 6 4 2

Typeset in A. Caslon
by SNP Best-set Typesetter Ltd., Hong Kong
Printed in Great Britain
on acid-free paper by
Ashford Colour Press Limited,
Gosport, Hampshire

To the most rewarding of our joint projects, viz.

Elizabeth Anne Watson Dobson
and
Rosalind Sarah Watson Dobson

❦ Contents ❧

❧ List of Plates ❧

12. Cate Blanchett as Elizabeth in Shekhar Kapur's film *Elizabeth* (1998). Channel Four/Ronald Grant Archive.

13. Judi Dench as Elizabeth on a poster for John Madden's film *Shakespeare in Love* (1998). Miramax/Ronald Grant Archive.

❧ List of Figures ❧

INTRODUCTION

The Queen is Dead,
Long Live the Queen

I am one of her owne countrie, and we adore her by the name of *Eliza.*[1]

Long Live the Queen

She has never been anything less than the most glamorous of English monarchs. Familiar as her image has remained from a thousand reproductions of her dazzling official portraits—from the solemn woodcut engravings published immediately after her death in 1603 to the profusion of unlikely artefacts available today in the National Portrait Gallery gift shop—Elizabeth I yet retains a powerful mystique of the unknown, her aura escaping the attempts of every successive generation of biographers, antiquarians, and purveyors of historical fiction to explain and to categorize her. As the author of the Elizabethan Settlement and victrix over the Spanish Armada, she is perhaps the nearest thing England has ever had to a defining national heroine, but neither the years of official Anglican veneration down to the twenty-first century nor our own period's growing scepticism about thrones and altars alike have succeeded in reducing her to a simple, two-dimensional lesson in moralized national history, to be simply embraced or simply repudiated. Whether represented as Anne Boleyn's orphaned, bastardized, suffering daughter or as the implacable nemesis of Mary, Queen of Scots, whether depicted as learned stateswoman or frustrated lover, near-martyred heretical princess or triumphant warrior queen, Elizabeth somehow remains in enigmatic excess of all the stories and images which have sought to define her. Indeed, she has become more fascinating partly as a result of the sheer number of stories that she has generated; mutually incompatible, they have made her into a figure that is greater than the sum of all the disparate parts of her mythos. As a subject she has been the career-making of an extraordinary range of writers and performers: she made the respective pioneers of the historical stage weepie and the historical novel, John Banks and Sophia Lee, into best-sellers in the seventeenth and eighteenth centuries, and took David Starkey to the top of the paperback charts early in the twenty-first; an expertise in her painted likenesses earned Sir Roy Strong his directorship of the National Portrait Gallery; success at impersonating her on the screen won Dame Judi Dench her Oscar and helped get Glenda Jackson elected to Parliament. Even so, Elizabeth remains apparently inexhaustible as an inspiration, forever returning to haunt the imagination of Anglophone culture in yet another variant or context. Though compulsively discussed by historians, she remains above all a figure of romance.

This book is not one more attempt to produce the definitive history of the 'real' Elizabeth Tudor, but a history of English-speaking culture's perennial, forever-mutating investment in a queen who even today is still engaged in a posthumous progress through the collective psyche of her country. The chapters which follow thus set out to investigate not Elizabeth I *per se* but memories of her, offering a history less of the life she lived from 1533 to 1603 than of the many lives she has lived since, in drama, poetry, historiography, propaganda, fiction, and the cinema, from the aspiringly epic to the frankly kitsch. In the course of examining Elizabeth's changing status and meanings over the last four hundred years, we will trace part of the cultural history of English nationalism, of which Elizabeth's marriage to her country—glorified by Solomon J.

Solomon's impressive painting in the House of Lords, 1911 (Plate 1)—remains one of the primal scenes. In the process we will explore the different ways in which the figure of Gloriana—here celebrated as a founding patroness of constitutional monarchy, but elsewhere vilified as a wilful despot—has variously enabled and blocked both consensus and debate about the relations between state, nation, and crown from the seventeenth through the twenty-first centuries. We will consider in particular the changing meanings of that familiar nostalgia for an imagined Elizabethan golden age which has been a recurrent feature of British and even American public life. The playwright Sidney Carroll pondered the phenomenon in his prefatory remarks on 'the general English admiration, which amounts to worship, of the part played in English history by Elizabeth' in *The Imperial Votaress* (1947):

People like to think of her as associated with and responsible for the rescue of England from poverty and depression, from the threat of Spanish invasion. They look upon her also as responsible for the exaltation of England not only into literary and artistic brilliance but the amazing commercial prosperity which laid the foundations of the British Empire as we knew it in the time of Queen Victoria. The very name of Elizabeth arouses recollections of intellectual giants and poetic geniuses, wise statesmen and daring seamen adventurers. Her share in the religious reformation of England can never be forgotten. But lastly to the average Englishman Elizabeth's chief claim to reverence is the poetic illusion she conjures up of a Virgin Queen.[2]

In dealing with such texts as Carroll's, this book will chart, too, the literary history of this 'poetic illusion', as successive chapters look at the modes of imagining Elizabeth central to a whole series of literary and dramatic genres which have made a speciality of narrating her: pageant-play, secret memoir, sentimental novel, psychologized biography, cinematic costume drama. This is a study of the Elizabeths of Spenser and of Shakespeare, of Sir Walter Scott and of Virginia Woolf, of Bette Davis and of Quentin Crisp, of *Westward Ho!* and of *Blackadder II*. We have been enabled to write it because we live at a historical moment in which the partial unravelling of certain notions of Englishness and Britishness alike—still very much in place for Carroll half a century ago—has n the processes by which they once coalesced available for interrogation as perhaps never before. Why and how has the figure of this anomalously powerful unmarried woman been so central to the making (and unmaking) of Anglo-British national identity and Anglo-British culture? What can the successive stories told about Elizabeth since her death reveal about the changing desires and assumptions shared by their makers and their consumers?

Even during her own lifetime, Elizabeth's image was multiple and contested, her different aspects and the different aims of her poets and painters and their courtier patrons producing what Edmund Spenser in *The Faerie Queene* called 'mirrours more then one' in whose reflections she might have seen herself and in which others might have seen her. Spenser himself, for example, indicates that two quite different characters in his poem are to be understood as versions of Elizabeth, the magnificent empress Gloriana and the private, chaste huntress Belphoebe, and this duality is only appropriate to a Renaissance prince whose public role was understood to be double, incorporating both the body politic of the state and, mystically united with it, the body natural of the monarch.[3] Endorsing her father's ecclesiastical reforms, Elizabeth personified the English Church into the bargain, and as such she lies behind at least two more figures in Spenser's allegorical romance, the holy maiden Una and the militant female knight-errant Britomart. This Elizabethan multiplicity has persisted in the range of different names and titles by which the Queen is still remembered—Eliza, Gloriana, the Fairy Queen, Cynthia, Good Queen Bess, Astraea, the Virgin Queen— and the different traces which survive both of Elizabeth's earthly life and of her impact on her contemporaries have provided ample scope for the subsequent metamorphoses of her reputation.[4] Her successive biographers, fictioneers, and scriptwriters have worked with a body of writings, artefacts, and hearsay which has itself continued to fluctuate and vary over time, with different anecdotes and texts achieving currency and prominence in different eras, some to be forgotten, some utterly to change their meanings, and some to be discredited, as different contemporary and near-contemporary documents have successively entered the public domain and different views of past and present alike have become dominant.

Despite her motto 'Semper Eadem' (ever the same), Elizabeth's posthumous metamorphoses have extended to the most canonical and sacrosanct of her recorded utterances, since on inspection little of the evidence concerning even the most famous and often-retold episodes in Elizabeth's career is completely unambiguous or uncontroversial. The Westminster Palace painting referred to above, for example, showing a radiant, saintly Elizabeth raptly indicating the ring on her finger to an awestruck Parliament, illustrates what had by the time of its installation been one of Elizabeth's most famous rhetorical *coups de théatre* for more than three centuries, the climax of her reply, soon after her coronation, to the Commons' petition that she should marry:

'To conclude, I am already bound unto an husband, which is the kingdom of England, and that may suffice you. And this,' quoth she, 'makes me wonder that you forget, yourselves, the pledge of this alliance which I have made with my kingdom.' And therwithal, stretching out her hand, she showed them the ring with which she was given in marriage and inaugurated to her kingdom in express and solemn terms. 'And reproach me so no more,' quoth she, 'that I have no children: for every one of you, and as many as are English, are my children and kinsfolks, of whom, so long as I am not deprived and God shall preserve me, you cannot charge me, without offence, to be destitute.'

So runs the speech in the English version of William Camden's *Annales*, printed in 1625 and much republished thereafter, words which are still part of Elizabeth's legend and which for the Victorians and Edwardians were a crucial part of her political legacy. But what was true about what Elizabeth said to Parliament in February 1559 for the nineteenth century is not what is strictly true for the twenty-first. Historians, both scholarly and popular, have since pointed out that reliable contemporary manuscripts of this speech contain no such reference to Elizabeth's marriage to her country, nor do they cite the stage direction that goes with it. Although the Queen is indeed reported to have resisted pressure to marry by invoking the notion of being already married to her kingdom two years later—not in a speech to Parliament but in conversation with the Scottish ambassador Maitland—the claim that so far from being barren she could boast all the English as her honorary children is clearly one which was embroidered on to this idea only retrospectively, after her childless death.[5] But even without such pointed, memorability-enhancing elaborations, the documentary record of Elizabeth's life and times can yield very different interpretations according to how any given writer chooses to sketch its context or fill in its lacunae, and that goes for the authors of reputable historical studies no less than for those of screenplays or popular novels. Card-carrying modern historical scholars, although professionally denied the licence to improve Elizabeth's speeches, can look scrupulously at the same contemporary evidence and still produce mutually contradictory versions of the Queen's views and character. Hence, for example, the very different verdicts on the Queen's attitudes to her parents recently espoused by Philippa Berry and by David Starkey, both working in the absence from Elizabeth's recorded utterances of any direct reference to her mother. Berry argues that Elizabeth's early appointments to her court and her choice of coronation iconography show that she saw herself as Anne Boleyn's daughter no less than as Henry VIII's, and knowingly allowed her father's dynasty to die out: Starkey suggests that Elizabeth hero-worshipped her father uncritically and would have remembered her mother's death primarily as a temporary impediment to her acquisition of new clothes.[6]

Our aim in citing these examples is not to 'debunk' one popular image of Elizabeth by accusing Camden of dishonesty, or to take sides with either Berry or Starkey, but to point out that for the purposes of this study what matters about Elizabeth is not what scholarship currently thinks is true about her career but what has entered her mythos, and when, and why, and which different aspects of that mythos successive generations have felt they needed to argue about. Camden's text, depicting Elizabeth as a loving national mother, belongs to a nostalgic Jacobean boom in remembering Gloriana as everything her successor was not; Berry and Starkey, depicting her instead as either an angrily Germaine Greeresque daughter or a dutifully Thatcherian daddy's girl, disagree over questions practically unasked by many earlier historians. Their work participates from different standpoints in distinctively late twentieth-century debates about how to understand gender roles and the family both in the Renaissance monarchy and in present-day society. Throughout what follows we are much more interested in how successive accounts of Elizabeth vary from each other than in how they vary from what today's historians offer as received fact about her life—though for our readers' convenience, and as a homage to the forever-doomed quest for definitive authentic knowledge of the Virgin Queen which is one part of our subject, we have supplied a chronology of those facts as an appendix to this introduction.

Despite the presence of this sober, empirical chronology, in fact, we will be working more with the spurious, the apocryphal, and the brazenly fictitious than with the verifiably well attested. The clearest indications of what cultural work the figure of Elizabeth has performed for periods subsequent to her own are often provided by popular drama and fiction more readily than by academic history, and we have repeatedly found the most useful keys to successive understandings of the Queen's life in accounts of incidents unknown to history. Narratives about the past are always by their very nature in excess of the fragmentary, intermittent, and sometimes unstable documentary traces that they are designed to supplement and to interpret, and this is particularly obvious around Queen Elizabeth I, given that some of the most arresting and prominent evidence of who and what she was is provided not in written language at all but in successive portraits, elaborately symbolic icons which at once invite and repel the making of explanatory stories about their sitter. It is in those genres of writing that accept their supplementarity to the hard evidence with the blithest imaginative licence that the plainest outlines of successive Elizabeths are usually to be discovered, though this quality of going beyond the documentary record is necessarily common to all historical narrative. If the various kinds of published writing about Elizabeth were to be placed on a sliding scale between pure antiquarianism at one extreme (the facsimile republication of contemporary documents, for example, pioneered by the Camden Society in the nineteenth century) and pure romance at the other (Michael Moorcock's *Gloriana, or, The Unfulfill'd Queen, A Romance* comes to mind as an example, a would-be erotic 1978 fantasy which is sense 'about' Elizabeth but which uses no recorded incidents of her actual reign at all), then most of the genres involved could be shown to combine both elements, albeit in different ratios.[7] Nearest to the antiquarian might be specialist academic history, most at home in the learned journal article; a little further along would be academic narrative history, synthesizing the conclusions of many such articles in its chronological interpetation of the historical evidence; next would come popular narrative history, refining several such denser accounts in pursuit of a less heavily annotated, more streamlined and page-turning central story with a visible kinship to the novel.[8] A sometimes blurred but nevertheless important line is crossed towards pure romance where such popular histories give place to historical fiction proper (though the historical novel is sometimes just as closely preoccupied with the documentary record as its more reputable cousins, however willing to add imaginary dialogue as a mode of interpreting it); parallel with the historical novel, though inclined to be pushed further towards the extreme of sheer fiction by the formal time-limits which require it to compress events more ruthlessly into narrative patterns, would be theatrical and cinematic costume drama. Even these latter genres, though, usually retain some tincture of the antiquarian, if only in their habit of recreating particular real portraits in the design of actresses' outfits. Equally, even the editors of Elizabethan documents may betray some affinity with romance, consciously or unconsciously arranging their materials in such a way as to fit whichever story is currently being told about the Fairy Queen in the culture at large. In fact it has often been our experience that the preoccupations, assumptions, and narrative structures of historical novels and plays about Elizabeth have been identical with those of more reputable histories composed at the same time, and that this is rarely just the result of novelists and scriptwriters popularizing in condensed, debased form the conclusions of their more scholarly colleagues. Still, for our purposes, many periods' views on how to understand and judge Gloriana have been more vividly and succinctly crystallized by the requirements of literary and dramatic form than in meticulously researched annals and, just as usefully for us, such popular, creative works have usually dated much more quickly and spectacularly than history books proper, to be symptomatically replaced by new 'takes' on the Queen.

It is a central premiss of this book, in short, that the queen who has been of such enduring and multiple importance in English national mythology has been a creature as much of imaginatively reshaped legend as of meticulously verified fact, and accordingly we will be looking closely at a body of texts which have usually caused fastidious dismay in historians and literary scholars alike. Undaunted by the epigraph to Caryl Brahms's and S. J. Simon's celebrated comic novel about Elizabeth and her court, *No Bed for Bacon* (1941)—'WARNING TO SCHOLARS * *This book is fundamentally unsound*'⁹—the chapters which follow take historical fiction and costume drama perfectly seriously, not as either pure history or high literary art but as major indicators of, and participants in, Britain's evolving relationship with its Elizabethan past. History, as Sellar and Yeatman pointed out in 1930, 'is what you can remember',[10] and it is still in some important sense 'true' for British culture that the young Elizabeth, sent to the Tower under suspicion of high treason during the reign of her Catholic elder half-sister Mary, at first refused to disembark at Traitors' Gate, but eventually did so with the words 'Here landeth as true a subject, being prisoner, as ever landed at these stairs', thereby inspiring a spontaneous demonstration of support from the soldiers who reluctantly took her to her dungeon. (As David Starkey points out in *Elizabeth: Apprenticeship*, Elizabeth actually landed at Tower Wharf and entered the building on foot over a drawbridge, and she was kept not in a dungeon but in the ample state apartments: none the less his 1999 television documentary narrating this incident, bowing to the same costume-drama conventions that had shaped the depiction of the canonical, apocryphal tableau in the popular series *Elizabeth R* in 1971, showed images of Traitors' Gate to support its voice-over narrative.)[11] It is culturally 'true' in the same way that Elizabeth greeted the news of her accession in 1558, under an oak tree, by falling to her knees and quoting from Psalm 118, 'A domino factum est et mirabile in oculis nostris' ('This is the Lord's doing; it is marvellous in our eyes');[12] that she once walked across a puddle on Sir Walter Raleigh's outspread cloak; that when she spoke at Tilbury in 1588 about having the body of a weak and feeble woman but the heart and stomach of a king she did so while riding a white horse and wearing armour (however sceptical some scholars with access to early eyewitness accounts of the event may now be about both the oration and the armour);[13] and that after the execution of the Earl of Essex she remarked to the Countess of Nottingham, supposedly guilty of withholding a message that would have induced the Queen to pardon him, 'God may forgive you, but I never can' (a sentence still attributed to Elizabeth in the *Oxford Dictionary of Quotations*). It is not irrelevant here that the screen portrayal of Elizabeth most widely praised for its 'truth' should have been that of Dame Judi Dench in *Shakespeare in Love* (1998), where the Queen is depicted in a personal relationship with William Shakespeare for which there is no documentary evidence whatsoever.

The sections in which we chart and examine such reimaginings of Elizabeth are arranged in a broadly chronological fashion, with each organized around the emergence into the mainstream of her legend of a different, sometimes mutually contradictory set of anecdotes, tropes, or tableaux—some rising into more upmarket genres and contexts, some descending into the shadowy hinterlands of children's fiction or the broadside ballad or even pornography. Broadly speaking, the narrative spine of our account lays out the changing relations of monarchy, state, and nation over the last four hundred years as expressed in the mutations of Elizabeth's mythos. At its inception, Elizabeth's posthumous legend insisted on the identification of her monarchy with both state and nation, but her representations have outlived this particular version of royalism, and at times she has been associated more closely with one or other of these terms. These changes correspond with her relocation within different dominant genres, which have depicted her in such a range of modes and contexts that some of the represented Elizabeths we will be describing may be barely recognizable as such to modern readers. The apparently disparate and mutually contestatory ways in which successive generations have sought to make sense of a national icon who has remained of such crucial importance to all of them—which we hope gives this study an appealing scope and variety—are themselves part of our point. For this astonishing diversity is not incidental to a study of

Elizabeth's afterlives, but is an index both of her power as a repository of potential meanings and of the extent to which, as a Virgin Queen, she has profoundly inconvenienced and unsettled available cultural formations and systems of belief.

Our chapters, largely based on these successive ideological and generic shifts, discuss, in turn, the emergence of a nostalgic cult of Elizabeth during the seventeenth century, particularly in stage plays about her accession and about the Armada; the emergence of a counter-story to this image of a Protestant epic heroine in later seventeenth- and eighteenth-century sentimental memoirs, plays, and novels determined to separate Elizabeth's womanhood from her royal power; the retrospective marriage of Elizabeth to her kingdom's culture achieved by a series of apocryphal narratives which cast her as affectionate, beef-eating patroness to the national poet Shakespeare; the disavowal of Elizabeth as old and sterile carried out in the shadow of Victoria's very different mode of queenship; the invocation of Elizabeth, particularly in the later nineteenth century, as the presiding spirit of imperial adventure and naval supremacy; and the twentieth century's various reinventions of Gloriana as icon of perversity, as frustrated would-be Elizabeth II, as disowned proto-Thatcher, and as mass-media celebrity. This last chapter concludes with some reflections on the persistence of Elizabeth's legend despite the problems which currently beset both the British monarchy and the idea of British national identity, which have hitherto appeared to be inseparable from her fame; this persistence is superbly demonstrated by the pivotal success of Judi Dench's Elizabeth in John Madden's film *Shakespeare in Love* (1998), an impersonation of the Queen which neatly combines many of the tropes we will by then have described. We then append an afterword outlining Elizabeth's posthumous fortunes in the United States, where a long standing, nationally constitutive emancipation from the British monarchy has done little to diminish Elizabeth's glamour, however differently that glamour has been understood.

None of these chapters, we should stress, is exhaustive: we simply do not have the space to discuss or even to mention all the texts we have read in the course of researching this book. It is probably true, indeed, that no one who walked into the relevant section of the Bodleian Library's over-spill depository out at Nuneham Courtenay (an immense, meticulously catalogued limbo of currently unwanted books) and saw the sheer mileage of the densely shelved area devoted solely to historical romances about Elizabeth I would want us to do so. Nor do we claim to describe every feature of interest of those texts we do discuss, generally confining ourselves to their distinctively new contributions to Elizabeth's legend and affect; nor do we deal with many Continental representations of the Queen (despite the temptations presented by Donizetti and his ilk), apart from those which had a notable impact in Britain. Each chapter, however, takes as broad and various a survey as it can of the particular phase of Elizabeth's afterlife which it discusses—bearing in mind that by the present day, with the cumulative build-up of all these possible stories about her and their dissemination by means which now include the internet as well as the printed book, that afterlife is being lived along a very broad cultural front. (See, for example, www.elizabethi.org and www.goodqueenbess.com.) This said, this book is not intended merely as a survey: it takes the form of a narrative cultural history, but for us, as for the texts we describe, to narrate the past is also to interpret it. Like our subjects, too, we are ourselves fascinated by Elizabeth and share the deep emotional investment she has long elicited from her latter-day English subjects. Perhaps another way of describing her as a figure of national romance would be to admit that, given this investment and the potential for cliché opened up by the long history of her representations, Elizabeth I is someone about whom it is hard to write without sounding either sentimental or sarcastic. We have done our best to avoid both.

The Queen is Dead

Elizabeth died at Richmond Palace on 24 March 1603, after a month-long illness, and from that day onwards her legend was set free from physical constraint. Death released her into the agelessness to which her portraits had aspired all along; the whole of her long life and reign and her extensive virtual body (a composite of representation and rumour) suddenly and simultaneously became available for selective remembrance. Contending versions of the Queen's death have been supplementing rival accounts of the Queen's life ever since 1603, each of them determined to fix Elizabeth's end into a single particular meaning, and, by way of prologue to the chapters that follow, we will conclude here by examining a cross-section of Elizabeth's represented deaths.

The wide variance of manners of death attributed to Elizabeth by later writers—some agonized and guilt-stricken, some reconciled and peaceful—results in part from the suspicion which attaches to the accounts of her deathbed given out at the time. These are transparently dictated by reasons of state, retailing a story presumably agreed upon by those figures on the Privy Council most closely involved in stage-managing the passage of the crown to James VI of Scotland—notably Elizabeth's small, crooked-shouldered chief minister Sir Robert Cecil, son of the long-serving Lord Burghley. Cecil had already sent James a draft of his proclamation as King of England at least two days before Elizabeth actually died, and a range of early seventeenth-century manuscripts purporting to give eyewitness accounts of the Queen's death agree only in stating that one of her last acts was to indicate that James was indeed her chosen heir. Some of these accounts are rendered especially suspect by convincing reports that Elizabeth completely lost the use of her voice for the last two days of her life: it is very unlikely, for example, that those clustered around her deathbed heard her say 'I told you my seat has been the seat of kings, and I will have no rascal to succeed me; and who should succeed me but a king? Who but our cousin of Scotland?' (Elizabeth is equally unlikely to have pronounced these words at any time beforehand, given her well-documented and politically understandable reluctance to discuss the succession at all).[14] A number of supposed eyewitnesses take this inconvenient symptom into account, however, suggesting that the dying Queen, questioned about the succession and unable to reply verbally, made the shape of a crown with her fingers, and then held them up to her head. All the manuscripts which report this odd, ambiguous gesture (or versions of it) concur, remarkably or unremarkably enough, in taking it as an explicit and unmistakeable sign that Elizabeth intended James Stuart to replace her on the English throne.[15]

The matter of the succession apart, a number of further anecdotes from Elizabeth's last illness have been elaborated down the centuries, in varying combinations, to shape or adorn images of the deathbed itself. These include, principally, the sawing off of her coronation ring, by now embedded in the flesh of her finger, and its eventual despatch towards Scotland as a token of her death; and the Queen's much-quoted rebuke to Cecil's insistence early in her illness that she must go to bed: 'Little man, little man, the word *must* is not to be used to princes' (or, in more elaborate form, 'Must! Is *must* a word to be addressed to princes? Little man, little man! thy father, if he had been alive, durst not have used that word'). This exchange is reported by Robert Carey as the sequel to an incident which took place soon after the funeral of the Queen's old friend the Countess of Nottingham at the end of February, when Elizabeth was found seated on cushions in a withdrawing chamber in deep melancholy, and refused to go to bed for four days:[16] the two are sometimes crushed together with the eventual death itself to support a story retailed by the French ambassador, who reports that Elizabeth refused to stay in bed during her last days but met her end fully dressed, silently staring at the floor with one finger in her mouth, standing up or propped on cushions. The overwhelming majority of more freely fictionalized accounts, furthermore, moralize the Queen's death by replacing mourning for the Countess with alternative causes for Elizabeth's final depression. Some insist that she really died of grief over the execution of the Earl of Essex two years earlier (hence the tying-in of the innocent Nottingham to the stories about Essex's downfall which we will be exploring in Chapter 2);[17] some that she languished from belated remorse over the beheading of Mary, Queen of Scots (a diagnosis already being insinuated by Carey, who says of Elizabeth's sorrow over Nottingham that 'in all my lifetime before, I never saw her fetch a sigh but when the queen of Scots was beheaded'); some prefer to believe that she perished out of long-term regret that she had not been more receptive to the courtship of the long-dead Earl of Leicester. These readings in their turn are sometimes hybridized with a story reported by one of the Queen's last ladies-in-waiting, the especially imaginative Lady Southwell, to the effect that the ailing Queen was frightened by the vision of a luminous spectral figure of herself in a dream and with the story that one of the other ladies-in-waiting saw the Queen's ghost pass down a corridor before she died (both anecdotes figuring the imminent divorce of body politic and body natural). Hence in drama and fiction Elizabeth I's deathbed is sometimes as well peopled with accusing ghosts as Richard III's tent the night before Bosworth Field.

Southwell supplies a further lurid story about the immediate aftermath of Elizabeth's death, reporting that the Queen's disembowelled, putrefying body exploded in its casket, bursting through the lead sarcophagus and wooden coffin. This story, though eagerly seized upon by contemporary Catholics as the final literalization of Elizabeth's Protestant corruption,[18] is contradicted by other witnesses (including the courtier John Chamberlain, the Venetian ambassador, and the law student and diarist John Manningham) who state that the Queen's corpse, in accordance with her own express wishes, was not disembowelled for embalming at all, but was wrapped uneventfully in cerecloth just as it was. But even this likely absence of any posthumous adventures to Elizabeth's body natural has sometimes served the interests of Elizabeth's later romancers: why should she have insisted on forbidding any post-mortem dissection, ask some, unless worried that such an examination might have either confirmed contemporary rumours of her gynaecological deformity ('she had a membrana on her which made her uncapable of man, though for her delight she tryed many', as Ben Jonson put it),[19] or revealed that she was not a Virgin Queen at all, perhaps even that she had borne children?[20] Just as the historical evidence frustratingly fails to supply the definitive, authoritative record of Elizabeth's private subjectivity, so the Elizabeth of romance is always concealing a secret, and it is often one which her death may at the very last reveal.

Even at the time, Elizabeth's persona as an eternally youthful queen regnant who, *semper eadem*, had defied time, never giving herself in marriage but insisting on being courted to the last, inclined some commentators on her death to view it as a long-overdue exposé, if only of her mere mortality. Royal elegies are conventionally in two minds about their subjects—on the one hand celebrating the immortality of the dead monarch's memory and soul, on the other invoking death's, time's, and even God's indifference to all human distinctions—but in the case of those published on Elizabeth this polarity is unusually marked. Some, it is true, present her death as a triumphant passage into undying legend, the completion of her own regime's imaginative propaganda: as Roy Strong observes, few of those lamenting her death 'seemed able to refer to her as a human being', instead weeping that the phoenix had been consumed in her pyre, the moon had gone into eclipse, the rose had withered on the briar, the pelican had spent itself in giving its life-blood to its young, the maiden-goddess Astraea had fled back to Heaven.[21] One of these celebrants of Eliza's apotheosis, presciently, feels moved to apologize that James's accession is being upstaged by memories of the late queen, asking the new king for forgiveness 'If in our mouthes, and eares now after death | *Queene* oft doth sound, and oft *Elizabeth* | In stead of thy more due, no lesse sweete name': this was a state of affairs with which James would grow increasingly familiar as his reign progressed, as we will see in Chapter 1. Others, however, insist that Elizabeth is being forgotten already: 'Scarce one is found to sing her dying praise | Whom all admir'd and honor'd in her daies'; 'Now is the time that we must all forget, | Thy sacred name oh sweet Elizabeth.'[22] More pointedly, some see her death as the nemesis, above all else, of that long-preserved virginity ('Shepheard remember our *Elizabeth*, | And sing her Rape, done by that *Tarquin*, Death'),[23] or at very least are grimly willing to present it as an ignominious fall from the vainglories of queenly power, a rebuke to female vanity along the lines of the lecture against cosmetics for which Yorick's skull had provided the occasion in Shakespeare's *Hamlet* not so long before. Thomas Newton's *Atropoion Delia*, for example, gloats over the decay of Elizabeth's bathetically mortal corpse in the imagined voices of the worms who are about to devour it:

> For whats her body now, whereon such care
> Was still bestow'd in all humilitie?
> Where are her robes? Is not her body bare,
> Respectles in the earths obscuritie?
> Now where's her glory and her Majestie?
> Her triple crowne, her honour, state, and traine?

The stanza ends with the worms' declaration that 'we in life too filthy for her tooth, | Are now in death the next unto her mouth.'[24] For Newton, Elizabeth may be in Heaven but she is also at supper, not where she eats, but where she is eaten: not for nothing is *Hamlet* associated with the mood of those who welcomed Elizabeth's passing, as we will see in Chapter 1.

Even a striking early visual representation of passionate mourning for Elizabeth, produced just after the death of her successor (when uncritical nostalgia for Gloriana had already become a fact of English cultural life), incorporates this levelling perspective, despite being otherwise committed to the deification of the Queen pioneered by her own poets. The illustrated title-page to Samuel Purchas's 1625 compilation of the annals of English exploration and colonialism, *Purchas His Pilgrimes*, includes a panel depicting the tomb which James I had built for Elizabeth in Westminster Abbey in 1606 (Fig. 1). Sitting on the tomb in a posture of deep grief (complete with a skull as a prop) is 'H.P.', Hakluytus Posthumus, the spirit of the Elizabethan proponent of overseas enterprise whose work Purchas has republished and expanded. H.P.'s foot underlines the end of a quotation from Virgil's *The Aeneid*: 'O quam te memorem virgo!' ('O, how am I to speak of you, maiden?'). These words—which had first been applied to Elizabeth by Spenser at the close of his first great hymn to the Queen, the April eclogue of *The Shepheardes Calender* (1578)—are those in which the archetypal colonist Aeneas greets his divine mother Venus when she appears to him disguised as a huntress near Carthage, and in Spenser they are completed by the exclamation which follows, 'O dea certe', a goddess indeed.[25] Elizabeth is here being lamented as the lost mother of British imperialism, divine patroness of Virginia: but this deification is qualified by another epigraph, this one altogether more egalitarian: above the tomb is a citation from Psalm 82: 6–7: 'I have said ye are gods; and all of you are children of the most High. But ye shall die like men, and fall like one of the princes.' Elizabeth may have been hailed as a goddess, but, alas, she was only mortal after all.

This tension between denying and celebrating the Queen's mortality

Fig. 1. Elizabeth mourned as the lost divine patroness of English imperialism: a detail from the 1625 title-page of Samuel Purchas's polemical collection of voyages and travel memoirs, *Purchas His Pilgrims*. The book was published under the nominal authorship of 'Hakluytus Posthumus', shade of the Elizabethan advocate of colonial exploration Richard Hakluyt. Other panels depict James I's providential escape from the Gunpowder Plot, and the accession of Charles I, but as far as Hakluytus Posthumus is concerned Elizabeth is still more important than her Stuart successors, even twenty years after her death. She is the subject of two vignettes: one depicts the defeat of the Armada in 1588, while this one shows the Queen being forever mourned by the deceased author in person (if that is the word). The Hamlet-like Hakluytus Posthumus is sitting inconsolably on the Westminster Abbey tomb which had been built for Elizabeth by her successor, James I, in 1606.

becomes all the more visible when, nearly two centuries later, a fashion for depicting decisive vignettes from national history encouraged visual artists to foster their careers by representing Elizabeth's deathbed itself. In 1796 Robert Smirke painted a tableau of her last minutes (disseminated as an engraving through R. Bowyer's Historic Gallery of Pall Mall): it is entitled *Queen Elizabeth Appointing Her Successor* (Fig. 2). Smirke's recumbent queen—hollow-eyed but completely unwrinkled—would not necessarily be recognizable without this caption. Her royal status is signalled by the ermine trimming of her costume (part robes of state, part dressing-gown), rather than by any historically obsolete farthingale or ruff; her hair, a lustrous ageless black, is bound with pearls in the neoclassically inspired fashion of Smirke's time rather than Elizabeth's. The death of this queen is no longer a matter simply of her uncrowning on earth to be perhaps crowned in Heaven; the monarchy, by this stage in the Enlightenment, is in a quite different relationship to the state, the queen answerable to a national constitution (albeit an unwritten one) rather than solely to God. The effect of this print is at once of personal pathos and of quiet constitutional triumph: though laid low Gloriana retains all her royal dignity, solemnly attended by two handsome, grieving, dark-dressed ladies-in-waiting, watched over by a clergyman, and anxiously pressed for the still-unknown identity of her chosen successor by the respectfully kneeling figure of Cecil. With a last heartbreaking effort she turns her head towards Cecil, performing her final task of state, giving up her last mortal breath in assuring the stable continuation of the monarchy—and the greater future glory of the nation, securing the creation of Britain through the union of England and Scotland initiated by the passage of her throne to James. Elizabeth's death is here conceived as a solemn, Burkean moment: the picture is clearly designed with another more recent royal death very much in mind—the guillotining of Louis XVI in Paris three years earlier—and it retrospectively identifies Elizabeth as a self-denyingly constitutional monarch. Smirke's picture varies from subsequent sympathetic British accounts of the Queen's death only in stressing the pain which this renunciation of life and power costs her; J. E. Neale's influential popular history *Queen Elizabeth* (1934), for example, takes precisely the same

Q. ELIZABETH APPOINTING HER SUCCESSOR.

FIG. 2. Robert Smirke (1752–1845), *Queen Elizabeth Appointing Her Successor* (1796). Smirke depicts Elizabeth as a constitutional monarch before her time, here seen performing her last painful duty to the crown and to her people. The imputed modernity of her political ideals is reflected in the depiction of her dignified and handsome face, which is not noticeably aged, and which is surmounted by a distinctively 1790s hairstyle and fillet.

view of Elizabeth's deathbed as essentially a site of patriotic duty, but by recourse to the diarist John Manningham's mellifluous phrase on the occasion Neale allows her regrets to be succeeded by complete peace:

She wanted to die, and the last service she could render her beloved country was to die quickly. . . . Having performed her last royal duty by nominating James as her successor, she centred her mind on Heavenly things, rejoicing in the ministrations of her spiritual physician . . . Archbishop Whitgift. And then she turned her face to the wall, sank into a stupor, and between the hours of two and three in the morning of 24 March 1603 passed quietly away 'as the most resplendent sun setteth at last in a western cloud.'[26]

Smirke's celebratory picture, however, would in the meantime be contested by a far better-known and more widely reproduced work which at once reverses its composition and inverts its meaning. Not coincidentally, it is by a French artist, one who would make a career of painting scenes from Walter Scott and William Shakespeare, together with the few canonical tableaux from British history which those two between them hadn't covered: Paul Delaroche. This was the painting that made his name, the immense *The Death of Queen Elizabeth* (1827), which now hangs in the Louvre (Plate 2). Its violent chiaroscuro is such that even in the many cheap prints in which it circulated in nineteenth-century England something of its hostility towards its subject shines through. Smirke's dignified renunciation is refracted through a pervasive, heightened atmosphere of horror and melodrama; respect is replaced by a rather vengeful sense of the indecorum of the red-faced, broken queen's abjection and death. The attendant counsellor is not hanging on the queen's dying breath, anxious for the future of her realm, but is imperatively thrusting out an arm, perhaps to demand the ring which will carry the news of her death to Scotland, perhaps to command in vain that the queen take to her bed. This Elizabeth is pointedly imprisoned in the full panoply of historical dress, and indeed is marked not just as historically obsolete but as personally so, by Delaroche's insistence on her physical ageing. It is a post-absolutism vision of Elizabeth, or at least post-Divine Right—a notion modernized by Burke, which Smirke's picture, with its reverent hush as the mystical aura of monarchy passes from Elizabeth's vulnerable body to that of the offstage James, is clearly designed to invoke. An age is passing, and Delaroche isn't sorry to see it go; *Queen Elizabeth Appointing her Successor* may be about continuity, but *The Death of Queen Elizabeth* is about a dead end. If the future of the crown matters at all in this picture, then what is important is not that it will go to someone who will seek to unite Scotland and England as Great Britain, but that with perfect poetic justice it will go to the son of Elizabeth's rival and victim, Mary, Queen of Scots. Paradoxically, this painting's vindictiveness is at once democratic and Jacobite.

The affect of Delaroche's painting is usefully glossed by two other nineteenth-century commentators on Elizabeth's death, both of them equally inclined—in a fashion characteristic of their time, as we will see in Chapter 4—to prefer Elizabeth's voluptuous, maternal victim to the politic, childless Gloriana. Anna Jameson, writing in *Memoirs of the Loves of the Poets. Biographical Sketches of Women celebrated in Ancient and Modern Poetry* (1829) and, subsequently, *Memoirs of Celebrated Female Sovereigns* (1832), takes the opportunity of the death scene to draw the contrast once more between these two rival national heroines. By now the key test of a monarch is the kind of emotional investment he or she has inspired, and according to Jameson the obsolete absolutist Elizabeth has elicited only the empty signs of devotion rather than the real thing:

The picture of Elizabeth, the renowned and feared, the idol at home, the terror abroad, lying on her palace floor, with her finger in her mouth, seeking no support from religion, no consolation from affection; friendless, helpless, hopeless, comfortless; and thus gradually wasting into death, is such a lesson in the nothingness of power, and the miscalculations of selfishness, that history affords not one more terrible and impressive. . . . I would rather have been Mary than Elizabeth; I would rather have been Mary, with all her faults, frailties, and misfortunes,—all her power of engaging hearts,—betrayed by her own soft nature, and the vile and fierce passions of the men around her, to die on a scaffold, with the meekness of a saint and the courage of a heroine, with those at her side who would willingly have bled for her,—than I would have been that heartless flirt, Elizabeth, surrounded by all the oriental servility, the lip and knee homage of her splendid court; to die at last on her palace floor, like a crushed wasp.[27]

This sense of Elizabeth's disgracefully unfeminine end as the exemplary 'bad death', the agonized extinction of an ego clinging to the last to vanities it has seen through too late, is shared by Jameson's great successor as a purveyor of moralized biographies for girls, Agnes Strickland. Strickland's enormously influential *Lives of the Queens of England* (1851) explicitly shares the perspective adopted by Delaroche, and indeed provides remarkable testimony to the authority his painting had by now achieved as the canonical version of Elizabeth's end, since Strickland supplies a description of the picture as the best available account of its subject-matter:

It is almost a fearful task to trace the passage of the mighty Elizabeth through the 'dark valley of the shadow of death.' Many have been dazzled with the splendour of her life, but few, even of her most ardent admirers, would wish their last end might be like hers . . . Paul Delaroche . . . has treated the subject with all the tragic power of his mighty genius. The dying queen is reclining on the floor of her presence-chamber, among the fringed and embroidered scarlet cushions apparently taken from the throne for that purpose; we see it in the background, empty and denuded of its trappings. Elizabeth is represented in her royal robes, and loaded with her usual profusion of pearls and jewels, but evidently impatient of their weight. Her elaborately braided periwig, with its jewelled decorations, is disordered and pushed back from her feverish brow. The grey, corpse-like tint of her complexion, and the glassy fixture of her expanded eye, where wrath and latent frenzy appear struggling with the weakness of sinking nature, are finely expressed . . . The terror and concern of her ladies, the youth, beauty and feminine softness of the two who are bending over her, afford a pleasing contrast to the infuriated countenance of the queen, and the diplomatic coolness of the lords of the council.[28]

Even this grim, tormented vision of the Queen's death, however, might be transformed in time by new artists and indeed new media. To performers, Elizabeth's presentation via 'the tragic power of [Delaroche's] mighty genius', her transformation here into an unalleviated tragedy queen, looked more like an opportunity than a condemnation. She had been pining away for love of the lost Essex in the theatre since the seventeenth century, but in the twentieth her fate would be taken up by a medium with an even closer relationship to the visual arts, namely film. In 1912 appeared the first ever cinematic costume drama with Elizabeth as its heroine, a silent French 'historical photo play' (adapted from a drama by Emile Moreau) called *Elisabeth*. The film depicts the Queen's infatuation with Essex; his alleged treason; the machinations of the jealous Earl of Nottingham which trick Elizabeth into signing Essex's death-warrant; her hysterical sorrow over his body; and, as the grand finale, the Queen's subsequent death, after a passionate outburst against Nottingham, from grief. The *mise-en-scène* for Elizabeth's death (Fig. 3) is clearly heavily influenced by Delaroche—here again are the cushions, the throne, the beautiful ladies-in-waiting, the dark-clad diplomatic courtiers. But the central figure has been utterly transformed by the film's casting. Elizabeth is being played by Sarah Bernhardt, tragedy queen *par excellence*, and so Delaroche's pitiless taunting of the old queen has been replaced by something that is instead all grand, stylized pathos, less crushed wasp than dying swan. The crumpled, historical farthingale has given place to white, clinging robes that are only nominally Elizabethan, with hanging sleeves to enhance the eloquent gestures of the queen's arms; the hair is again dark and lustrous, the face a smooth mask of lovelorn womanliness; above all the undignified posture of the dying queen has been translated into something positively balletic, the dismal withering on the cushions replaced by a magnificent, yearning swan-dive from the throne on to them. Elizabeth's death here almost becomes a romantic suicide, a chosen escape from history into an operatic triumph of camp self-dramatization.[29] For some in the early twentieth century, Elizabeth's immortality was an artistic achievement as much as a political one, a matter of performative personal style. Drama is always inclined to reimagine Elizabeth in its own image, as above all a star performer, and generations of actresses have responded eagerly to all that is self-consciously larger than life about Elizabeth's own personae—after all, even in life she was 'thought something too Theatricall for a virgine Prince,' as Francis Osborne remembered in 1658.[30] Hence the divine Astraea could have made no more appropriate or auspicious debut on the screen than in the person of the divine Sarah. Subsequent actresses too have made her death into a set-piece display in which the Queen is triumphantly herself (and them) to the end, among them Glenda Jackson, for whom a long, silent tableau in close-up, finger intermittently in mouth, provided a virtuoso culmination to an entire six-part television series (*Elizabeth R*, 1971),

FIG. 3. Elizabeth's first impersonator on the silver screen was the great French tragedienne Sarah Bernhardt in the 'historical photo-play' *Elisabeth* (1912, also known as *Les Amours de la reine Elisabeth*). Although influenced by Paul Delaroche's famous painting in the Louvre (Plate 2), the film's depiction of Elizabeth's death utterly transforms its meaning into a triumph of immortal self-dramatization. Horrified at having been manipulated into signing her beloved Earl of Essex's death-warrant, Bernhardt's tragedy queen—like Smirke's, wearing clothes that are only notionally Elizabethan—plunges from her throne on to the waiting cushions, a romantic, operatic, all-but suicide.

deliberately allowing its viewers to take a long, last, regretful farewell of what was for its time a definitive impersonation of Elizabeth.

Jackson's finally silent, defiant Elizabeth is carefully preserving an enigma, and in this too she is characteristic of twentieth-century versions of the Queen, both more and less historical. Lytton Strachey's best-selling *Elizabeth and Essex: A Tragic History* (1928), for example, presents Elizabeth's death as a final escape from her servants' attempts to pluck out the heart of her mystery: 'She continued asleep, until—in the cold dark hours of the early morning of March 24th—there was a change; and the anxious courtiers, as they bent over the bed, perceived, yet once again, that the inexplicable spirit had eluded them.'[31] Other modern Elizabeths, too, die preserving their secrets, though not always willingly. Comyns Beaumont, for instance, subscribes to so many paranoid theories about the Elizabethans at the same time that his *The Private Life of the Virgin Queen* (1946)—part novel, part soi-disant historical essay— almost defies summary. Beaumont's Elizabeth is, like so many others of his time, not a virgin but the ex-partner of the Earl of Leicester—a figure who returns dramatically to the centre of Elizabeth's mythos in the mid-twentieth century, as we will see in Chapter 6—and in this version they were even secretly married. At the end of her life she has to be actively prevented from naming their unacknowledged son as the true heir to the throne: and as in some other unlikely stories keen to identify Elizabeth as the mother of the national culture by association with the national poet (which we will be looking at in Chapter 3), her son turns out to be Sir Francis Bacon, who, cheated of the crown, will encode his bitter life-story in the plays he will subsequently pass off as Shakespeare's. Beaumont's book ends with a sort of hybrid between Delaroche's painting and some dark fantasies about the role played by Cecil in organizing the Stuart succession, with the Queen's death not just stage-managed but actually hurried on by her most trusted minister:

In her last days she reaped as she had sown in a situation more macabre and terrible than any novelist would dare to portray, and so, perhaps, we may regard with a feeling of pity that last picture of the lonely old woman, propped on a stool, who had outlived her age, afraid to eat or drink, fearful of being murdered, jabbing at [the] arras with a dagger lest an assassin was lurking behind it, suffering agonising physical pain and mental torture, unable to profit from any spiritual aid, racked with remorse, and finally, to her knowledge, strangled by the hand of the even more pitiless little sadist hunchback, who, of all men, she had believed to be her one devoted and most faithful servant.

THE END[32]

A year later Sidney Carroll's 'chronicle play in twelve scenes with nine changes of scene', *The Imperial Votaress*, produces what is in effect the sympathetic, Smirke version of this modern reinvention of Elizabeth as a doomed guilty mother. His Elizabeth has also borne the late Leicester a son in secret, the short-lived Arthur, and on her deathbed she is visited by his angry ghost. The spectral Arthur reproaches her with sexual hypocrisy ('When you die, no-one will believe in *me*. You will always be the Virgin Queen'), with killing Mary, Queen of Scots ('most unforgettable of crimes'), and with betraying Christianity in favour of nationalism ('You have made patriotism the religion of the English'—'I'm proud of it'). Carroll, though, as this last exchange may suggest, regards Elizabeth's commitment to the nation as quite sufficient to redeem these sins, and after Arthur has vanished she is allowed to die in the more reassuring company of the Archbishop of Canterbury, her last words entirely consonant with her status as a genuine national heroine:

> Pray not for me, Archbishop. Pray for England. I am dying. Tell my people my last thoughts, my last words were for them.
> [SHE *dies and the Play finishes.*]

CURTAIN[33]

The return to Heaven of an eternal goddess; the smothering in the ground of a rotting, violated corpse; the last duty of a self-sacrificing constitutional heroine; the despairing extinction of a vain, guilt ridden monster; the final grand performance of a star tragedy queen; the burial of a sexual secret. One last mode of imagining Elizabeth's death deserves comment here, perhaps the aptest from the point of view of this study, and that is its depiction as a passage from biography into legend, from life into afterlife. This motif, too, has had both its euphoric and its dysphoric exemplars within recent memory. At its most simple-minded, such apotheoses may imagine Elizabeth translated into a romantic

27

Elysium in which all an author's fantasies for her—denied full expression in her lifetime by the intransigence of the historical record—can at last be realized. This approach to Elizabeth's death is taken, for example, by a book that was seized upon when it appeared in 1985 as the definitive specimen of middlebrow women's fiction, Susan Kay's novel *Legacy*. The subject matter of Elizabeth's reign, by then associated in the popular mind with memories of Glenda Jackson and paperbacks by the likes of Jean Plaidy, had come a long way downmarket since Virginia Woolf had published *Orlando* in 1928, and this long, laborious novel was the first winner of the Betty Trask Prize for Fiction, an award—specifically invented as a counterpart or complement to the more intellectual Booker—from which 'experimental fiction' was excluded. The judges clearly understood the terms of Trask's bequest as a rubric for acknowledging the otherwise disreputable genre of the best-selling historical bodice-ripper, and so it was that Kay's almost heroically unpretentious and saccharine account of Elizabeth's relations with the Earl of Leicester won the prize. Described in its quaintly retrograde publicity materials as 'the story of a woman in search of a master', *Legacy* is in most respects as conventional as Trask could have wished, its heroine a Queen Elizabeth who, like many others described earlier in the 'New Elizabethan' period, would much rather have had a husband and family in the mode of her latter-day namesake than have astonished the world as a Virgin Queen. When it comes to Elizabeth's deathbed, though, Kay is prepared to take unusual imaginative liberties in depicting this frustrated longing as at long last fulfilled. By the late twentieth century the monarchy had ceased to be the locus of any real state power, its function solely to focus and embody national feeling, and hence Kay's Elizabeth has no final thoughts about her duties of state whatsoever but instead escapes into a solely affective eternity. On the novel's very last page, the dying Elizabeth finds herself 'no-where', at the boundary between her world and the beyond, and from the far side of a dark gulf she hears the voice of her beloved Leicester:

'No, you're not dead.' The voice paused, sighed, seemed to consider. 'You may return even now if you wish. Or you may come with me. But if you go back now, I shall not wait for you again.'

She took another step towards the engulfing abyss and stretched out desperate hands.

'But I can't see you!' she cried. 'How do I know this isn't a dream, or some trick of the Devil's? How do I know you are really there?'

'You don't know', he said quietly. 'This is the final test of your love, you see—to take me on trust in death, as you never did in life.'

For a moment she was silent.

'What must I do to reach you?' she asked at last.

'You must step off the edge,' he said.

Instinctively she recoiled from the prospect and drew back from the emptiness.

'Will you not do that for me, even now?' he asked sadly. 'Are you still afraid to fall?'

She smiled amd flung up her head with pride.

'I'm not afraid of anything—in this world or the next.'

'I don't believe you,' he said with soft challenge. 'Prove it to me.'

She walked alone into the void.

The corridor was gone and the light at the end of it; the darkness around her was absolute. She mastered a scream and held out one hand.

'*Robin?*'

'*I am here.*'

Joyfully, triumphantly, he took her hand and pulled her forward into infinity.[34]

And so the story ends, with Elizabeth and Leicester united forever, rather in the manner of the transparent ghosts of Cathy and Heathcliff who rise from their respective graves and run away over the moors together at the end of the 1971 film adaptation of *Wuthering Heights*. More highbrow works, however—and especially those less committed to an idyllic vision of heterosexual domesticity—have instead treated Elizabeth's apotheosis as the essence of her tragedy. In Benjamin Britten's opera *Gloriana* (1953)—its libretto (by William Plomer) closely based on Strachey's *Elizabeth and Essex*—Elizabeth's passage from life into legend is presented not as a glorious liberation from her responsibility to the state but as a tragic, anticlimactic fall into it. The bulk of the opera dramatizes Elizabeth's largely apocryphal affair with the Earl of Essex, but its heroine is at the end removed from the romantic, passionate life of legend—and, indeed, of opera itself—and reinserted into received history. After she signs Essex's death-warrant near the close of the last act, Elizabeth is increasingly deprived of the ability to sing, like the dying Violetta at the end of Verdi's *La Traviata*. As a soprano she is already dead: the last words she is permitted to utter musically are 'mortua, sed non sepulta'—I am dead, but not yet buried, words Elizabeth is reported to have spoken soon after Essex's execution, and which here follow a rendition of Lady Southwell's anecdote of the ailing Queen seeing a death-like phantom of herself. In place of feeling, lyric song, Elizabeth is reduced to speaking passages from the final pages of her own recorded history: there is nothing left to her except the duty to be remembered as the history-book figure the audience already knew before the opera began. Her tragedy is precisely that in 1601 she cannot be a constitutional monarch, free to pursue her own personal emotional fulfilment. '*The Queen signs the warrant,*' reads the stage direction in 3.3, '*. . . the room becomes dark and the Queen is seen standing alone against an indeterminate background. Time and place are becoming less important to her.*' Elizabeth fades out into quotations of herself, dwindling into the discontinuous icon of the public archives: 'I can by no means endure a winding-sheet held up before my eyes while I yet live . . . I count it the glory of my crown that I have reigned with your love . . . the word 'must' is not to be used to princes', and so on through the last of her canonical sayings. At the end she is silent and isolated, outside life and history alike, as the offstage chorus quote from the masque of Time's truce with Concord which had celebrated Elizabeth as an evergreen rose in act 2:

> (*Cecil disappears. The Queen is alone.*)
> CHORUS (*unseen*).
>> Green leaves are we,
>> Red rose our golden Queen,
>> O crowned rose among the leaves so green!
> (*As the sound fades the Queen is slowly enveloped in darkness*)[35]

So Britten's Elizabeth vanishes from life into the posthumous afterglow of collective memory—and there our study will trace her, down the long years between her still-unforgotten death and its four-hundredth anniversary. What is perhaps most striking about Britten's opera, though to us it may seem its most obvious and predictable (even congenial) feature, is the mood of regret and nostalgia with which the composer evokes the dead Queen, lovingly recreating Elizabethan pageantry and Elizabethan cadences as he does so. In 1603, however, as Elizabeth's state funeral ritually un-performed the ceremonies by which she had been crowned forty-four years earlier, it was by no means obvious that the 'late queen of glorious memory' would become the focus of this enduring national sentiment of loss and veneration. So it is the Jacobean period's increasing compulsion to re-enact not just Elizabeth's coronation but her christening and her military successes, founding the nostalgic cult of Gloriana in the process, which will be the subject of our first chapter.

❧ Chronology ❧

This list of what posterity has regarded as the events and utterances of defining importance in Elizabeth's life is designed to distinguish the verifiable from the traditional and apocryphal. The principal primary sources for Elizabeth's biography available in the twenty-first century are the *Calendars of State Papers*, together with the diaries and correspondence of statesmen and ambassadors who left eyewitness accounts, and the memoirs of retired statesmen put together in the years afterwards. Also included here, as primary sources for subsequent reinterpretations of the Queen, are dates for the painting of those portraits which have become canonical, and dates for the first appearances of literary and dramatic works important to the development of Elizabeth's image. For full bibliographies of primary sources, and amplification of the details of her life, see the many and various popular and scholarly twentieth-century biographies of Elizabeth I: J. E. Neale (1934), Elizabeth Jenkins (1958), Neville Williams (1967), Paul Johnson (1974), Alison Plowden (1980), Carolly Erickson (1983), Jasper Ridley (1987), Christopher Haigh (1988), Christopher Hibbert (1990), Maria Perry (1990), Anne Somerset (1991), Wallace MacCaffery (1992), Alison Weir (1999), and David Starkey (2000). For the most extensive scholarly treatment of portraits of Elizabeth, see Roy Strong, *Gloriana: The Portraits of Queen Elizabeth I* (1987). For the texts and dates of her speeches, poems, and letters, see Elizabeth I, *Collected Works*, ed. Leah Marcus, Janel Mueller, and Mary Beth Rose (Chicago, 2000). (All dates are given in New Style.)

1533   7 September: born to Henry VIII and his second queen, Anne Boleyn, and proclaimed heir to the throne. State christening. Put under the charge of Margaret, Lady Bryan. Since Henry's first queen, the steadfast Catholic Catherine of Aragon, is still alive, Catholics will always regard Henry's marriage to Anne Boleyn as bigamous and Elizabeth as illegitimate.

1536   Death of Catherine of Aragon. Ann Boleyn found guilty on charges of multiple adultery and incest and executed. Henry VIII marries Jane Seymour, by whom he fathers a son, Edward. Elizabeth declared illegitimate and no longer heir to the throne.

1544   Mary and Elizabeth restored to the succession, after Edward.

1544/5   *The Family of Henry VIII*, a group portrait, commissioned and painted about now. *Princess Elizabeth*, attributed to William Scrots, painted some time around now (up until 1547, opinions differ); it portrays the young woman as a learned Protestant princess.

1546   28 January: death of Henry VIII, accession of Edward VI.

1547   Thomas Seymour marries the Queen Dowager, Catherine Parr, and soon begins a flirtation with her stepdaugher, the adolescent Elizabeth.

1548   Catherine Parr sends the princess away from her household. 7 September: Catherine Parr dies following childbirth.

1549   17 January: Thomas Seymour arrested on charges of treason, which included plotting to marry the princess without the consent of the Council. Elizabeth and her household subjected to interrogations and 'shameful slanders'. 20 March. Seymour executed. Elizabeth resident at Hatfield.

1553   6 July: Edward VI dies. 10 July: Jane Grey is proclaimed queen. 11 July: Mary proclaims herself queen and is swept to power on 19 July. 8 September: under increasing pressure from the Queen, Elizabeth attends Mass.

1554   25 January: Wyatt's rebellion breaks out in the North in protest at the marriage negotiations between Mary and Philip of Spain; very nearly successful, it is put down, resulting in the speedy execution of Jane Grey and her husband, and the subsequent imprisonment and interrogation of Elizabeth in th

Tower, 17 March. There she spends the next few weeks (almost certainly *without* contact with Robert Dudley) until mid-May, when she begins her journey north to Woodstock. She remains under house-arrest here in the charge of Sir Henry Beningfield until the following year.

1554   25 July: Philip of Spain and Mary marry.

1555–6   Dudley conspiracy, which aimed to exile Mary, marry Elizabeth to Courtenay, Earl of Devon, and enthrone them as consorts. Philip instrumental in aborting enquiry into Elizabeth's complicity.

1556   18 September: death of the exiled Courtenay, Earl of Devon, in Padua. Around Christmas, renewed marriage negotiations are opened on Elizabeth's behalf with Emmanuel Philibert of Savoy, though they are strongly resisted by her.

1558   17 November: Mary dies, childless. Elizabeth is proclaimed in London on the same day; the news is delivered to her at Hatfield. Accession Day will become a major annual festival as part of the cult of Elizabeth, characterized by tournaments at court and bonfires, bell-ringing, etc., across the country: in 1576 it is added to the official list of Anglican holy days, with its own special set of prayers. (This festival revives over the course of the seventeenth century, rivalling Guy Fawkes' Day as a popular anti-Catholic event, and dies out only in the eighteenth.)

1559   14 January: eve-of-coronation procession through the City. 15 January: coronation. Publication of *The Queen's Majesty's Passage Through the City of London to Westminster*, an eyewitness account of the eve-of-coronation procession, complete with the important story of her receiving a gift of a sprig of rosemary from an old woman. Coronation portrait painted [survives only in an early seventeenth-century copy]. 10 February: replies to House of Commons' petition urging her to marry ('in the end, this shall be for me sufficient that a marble stone shall declare that a Queen, having reigned such a time, lived and died a virgin'). Nevertheless, marriage negotiations are opened variously with Philip of Spain, Archduke Charles of Austria, and Prince Eric of Sweden, but Elizabeth's principal emotional investment appears to be in her relationship with Robert Dudley. 23 April: Dudley dubbed Knight of the Garter. Gossip hots up.

1560   8 September: death of Amy Dudley neé Robsart, Leicester's wife. Leicester banished from court pending the inquest. Although the coroner returns a verdict of accidental death, many (including, apparently, William Cecil) suspect Leicester of having her murdered in order to be free to marry the Queen, possibly with Elizabeth's connivance.

1561   Lady Katherine Grey, a principal claimant to the throne, secretly marries Lord Hertford (treasonously, i.e. without royal consent), and falls pregnant. The marriage is declared void, the child illegitimate. The lovers are imprisoned in the Tower, where Katherine conceives and bears a second son. They are separated; Hertford will not be released until after Katherine's death in 1568. (A similar fate would overtake Katherine's sister, Mary, who married the Queen's Serjeant Porter, Thomas Keys.) June: the Spanish ambassador, Archbishop de Quadra, records how Elizabeth and Dudley, sharing a boat with him on the Thames, joked that he himself might conduct a marriage ceremony for them on the spot.

1562   October: Queen dangerously ill with smallpox. From now on she is under renewed pressure to marry from her Council and the Commons.

1563   Elizabeth suggests the marriage between Dudley and the principal claimant to the throne and to the succession, the young widow Mary, Queen of Scots. First English edition of John Foxe's violently partisan *Actes and Monuments of these latter perrillous dayes, touching matters of the Church*, popularly known later as *The Book of Martyrs* (the Latin edition had come out at Strasburg in 1559). This includes an account of Elizabeth as a Protestant near-martyr, entitled *The Miraculous Preservation of the Lady Elizabeth*, which is the source for many dubious stories, including her speech in the rain at Traitors' Gate, an anecdote of her receiving flowers from a child while in the Tower, and the story that she yearned to be a milkmaid in her captivity at Woodstock. Much reprinted and amplified, it is made an obligatory possession of all English cathedrals.

1564   The Scots ambassador, James Melvile, visits the English court. His account of his conversations with the English queen concerning the rival accomplishments and looks of Mary, Queen of Scots lays the foundation for some of the later stories of the rivalry between the two. He witnesses Dudley's investiture as Earl of Leicester, during which the Queen fondles Leicester's neck.

1565   July: Mary, Queen of Scots, marries Henry Darnley. Renewed marriage negotiations between Elizabeth and Archduke Charles of Austria. Leicester and Elizabeth fall out; Elizabeth turns to another favourite, Thomas Heneage, and Leicester begins a clandestine affair with Lettice Knollys.

1566   June: Mary, Queen of Scots, gives birth to a son, the future James I of England. November 5: indignant speech rebuking Parliament's desire to regulate the succession ('I am your anointed queen. I will never be by violence constrained to do anything. I thank God that I am indued with such qualities that if I were turned out of the realm in my petticoat, I were able to live in any place of Christendom').

1567   Negotiations with the Archduke collapse. February: Darnley is murdered, possibly with the connivance of Mary, Queen of Scots, who subsequently makes an unpopular marriage with the Earl of Bothwell, almost certainly responsible for the murder of Darnley. Rebellion breaks out, and the defeated Mary is imprisoned in Lochleven and forced to abdicate in favour of her son.

1568   Mary escapes to England and is promptly put under house-arrest, under which she will remain for the next nineteen years as a focus for every Catholic conspiracy against the crown.

Leicester begins a liaison with Lady Douglas Sheffield, and flirts with Frances Howard.

1569   Northern Rebellion quashed. Discovery of the Ridolfi Plot leads to the execution of the Duke of Norfolk in 1572.

1570   A French alliance in the shape of marriage to the Duke of Anjou, a brother of the French king, is mooted; Anjou is then replaced as a candidate by his younger brother Alençon. Pius V publishes a bull, 'Regnans in Excelsis', excommunicating Elizabeth and absolving English Catholics from their allegiance to her.

1570s   Sir Francis Drake makes privateering raids in the Spanish Main with quasi-official support from the Queen.

1571   Rise of Elizabeth's new favourite, Sir Christopher Hatton. Elizabeth composes the poem 'The doubt of future foes', which refers to Mary, Queen of Scots as 'the daughter of debate'.

1572   24 August: Massacre of St Bartholomew in Paris initiates a purge of the Protestant Huguenots throughout France: Elizabeth suspends marriage negotiations with Alençon (who in 1574 inherits the title of Anjou).

1573   Sir Francis Walsingham is made Principal Secretary of State, and begins to develop an elaborate intelligence network.

1575   Leicester entertains Elizabeth lavishly at Kenilworth, perhaps in a final bid to marry her. Contemporary account of these festivities published by Robert Laneham as *A Letter, wherein part of the Entertainment unto the Queen's Majesty at Kenilworth Castle in Warwickshire in the Summer's progess, 1575, is signified*. The Darnley portrait (Plate 3), attributed to Federigo Zuccaro, is probably painted this year: it emphasizes for the first time the dual nature of the sitter as both lady and sovereign. The face pattern was to set the depiction of the Queen into the 1590s.

1578   Leicester marries Lettice Knollys secretly. Edmund Spenser publishes his first major hymn to the Queen, the influential 'April Eclogue' in *The Shepheardes Calendar*.

1579   Elizabeth discovers the marriage of Leicester to Lettice Knollys. 17 August: Alençon arrives in England incognito, and his courtship prospers. The portrait of Elizabeth known as the Sieve portrait is painted by George Gower, the first allegorical representation of her as an exemplar of (perpetual?) chastity. In a distinctively Petrarchan symbolic language the painting alludes to the Roman vestal virgin, Tuccia, who demonstrated her maligned virginity by carrying water drawn from the Tiber in a sieve. Two other versions appear to coincide with the years of the Alençon courtship, and a second series was to appear between 1580 and 1583.

1580   Alençon courtship made the more necessary as a defence against Spanish aggression. September: knighting of Drake at Deptford on his return from a three-year voyage circumnavigating the world (and robbing the Spanish) in the *Golden Hind*. John Lyly publishes *Euphues and his England*, which contains a eulogy of the Queen's virginity as mystically constitutive of her success as a ruler.

1580s A mysterious youth appears in Spain, claiming to be Elizabeth's son; claims investigated by Philip but adjudged fraudulent.

1581   Alençon arrives at court, but despite favourable appearances to the contrary Elizabeth eventually tells Alençon that she will not marry him. Alençon is persuaded to depart in February 1582. Elizabeth composes the poems 'On Monsieur's Departure' ('Since from my self another self I turned . . .') and, now or within this decade, 'When I was fair and young . . .'. Execution of Edmund Campion, one of a number of Jesuit missionaries now being sent across as part of the Catholic Enterprise of England. Winter: Walter Raleigh makes his debut at court (anecdotes of his laying a cloak before her feet or scratching couplets with a diamond on a window-pane, first recorded in Thomas Fuller's *History of the Worthies of England*, 1662, are probably apocryphal), and begins his meteoric rise to ten years of favour.

1584 George Peele's *The Arraignment of Paris* is performed at court; Paris is saved from his mythic dilemma by awarding the golden apple not to any of the three goddesses contending for it (Aphrodite, Athene, and Hera) but to Elizabeth herself. *Leycester's Commonwealth* published, an attack on Leicester by an anonymous Catholic propagandist, which claims that in September 1560 Leicester had his wife murdered by one Richard Verney.

1585 The Babington Plot, which aimed to assassinate Elizabeth and put Mary, Queen of Scots on the English throne, is discovered. Raleigh is knighted. The son of Lettice Knollys and stepson to Leicester, Robert Devereux, Earl of Essex, appears for the first time at court. The Ermine portrait is painted, possibly by William Segar, a Petrarchan allegory of chastity which identifies Elizabeth with a crowned ermine, a creature which according to folklore would rather die than soil the whiteness of its pelt. The assassination of the Dutch Protestant leader William the Silent obliges Elizabeth to send troops under Leicester to fight against the Spanish in Holland.

1586 Death of Leicester's nephew Sir Philip Sidney fighting in Dutch wars. October: trial of Mary, Queen of Scots.

1587 1 February: Elizabeth signs the death-warrant. 8 February: Mary, Queen of Scots is executed at Fotheringay. Elizabeth claims her secretary Davison sent the warrant without her consent.

1588 12 July: the Spanish Armada sets sail. 9 August: Elizabeth addresses her troops at Tilbury ('I know I have the body but of a weak and feeble woman, but I have the heart and stomach of a king and of a king of England too . . .'). Armada fails to rendezvous with the Duke of Parma's army, which it is supposed to ferry across the Channel from Holland, is dispersed by English fireships off Calais, and returns to Spain without landing, suffering heavy losses in storms on its way back around the British Isles. Thanksgiving at St Paul's. Death of Leicester; after her own death Elizabeth is discovered to have labelled the final message she ever received from him as 'His last letter'. The Armada portrait by George Gower, an allegory of imperial claims; Elizabeth's hand rests on a globe of the world, in the background the defeated Armada is wrecked.

1589   Publication of first three books of Edmund Spenser's *The Faerie Queene*. (Books 4–6 published in 1596.)

1590s   Tyrone campaigns against the English in Ireland throughout this decade.

1590   Essex secretly marries Frances Walsingham, widow of Sir Philip Sidney, and confesses this to the Queen in the autumn.

1591   Death of Sir Christopher Hatton. Essex leads an abortive expedition to besiege Rouen in support of French Protestants.

1592   Raleigh marries the pregnant Bess Throckmorton and is imprisoned in the Tower for his pains. The Ditchley tournament is held, the culmination of the tradition of the Accession Day tilts. The elaborately allegorical (and enormous) Ditchley portrait by Marcus Gheeraerts the Younger (Plate 4), probably commissioned around this time to commemorate the tilts, shows the Queen dressed in virginal white, standing on a map of England, and depicted as controlling the elements.

1595   William Shakespeare's comedy *A Midsummer Night's Dream* first performed; it refers to Elizabeth as 'a fair vestal thronéd by the West', an 'imperial votaress', but contains a highly equivocal pair of portraits of an Amazon Queen and a Fairy Queen.

1595–6 Ill-fated expedition of Drake and Hawkins to the Caribbean to attack Nombre de Dios. Deaths of Drake and Hawkins.

1596   20 June: Sack of Cadiz under Howard and Essex as joint commanders, with Raleigh in tow: Essex grows increasingly popular.

1597   Lettice Knollys, now the wife of Sir Christopher Blount, finally, if briefly, countenanced at court. William Shakespeare's comedy, *The Merry Wives of Windsor*, first performed; it contains allusions to the Garter ceremonies revived by Elizabeth as part of her chivalric cult and culminates in the appearance of a fraudulent Fairy Queen.

1598   Death of Philip of Spain. Essex throws a tantrum over having his nominee for the post of Lord Lieutenant of Ireland refused, and receives a box on the ear from Elizabeth in front of the entire Privy Council. 4 August: death of Burghley (the elder Cecil).

1599   March: Essex takes a force into Ireland on a disastrous campaign, culminating in a truce with Tyrone. September: Essex returns precipitately in an effort to outride his disgrace and surprises the Queen in her bedchamber. Put under house-arrest for the best part of the year; freed, but out of favour and stripped of certain incomes by the Queen, he retires to the country to brood on his imminent bankruptcy. Combines with others, including Earl of Southampton and Mountjoy, in planning a *coup d'état*. Thomas Dekker's *Old Fortunatus* first performed; also Ben Jonson's *Every Man Out of His Humour,* which includes a controversial impersonation of the Queen when played at the Globe.

1600–3   The Rainbow portrait, attributed to Marcus Gheeraerts the Younger, which allegorizes the Queen as (amongst other things) all-seeing and all-hearing, wise, prudent, and chaste as Diana, and sun-like.

1601   7 February: Shakespeare's acting troupe, the Lord Chamberlain's Men, revive his *Richard II* at the instigation of Essex, apparently in a bid to accustom the London citizenry to the idea of deposing a monarch. Elizabeth, recognizing the parallel being drawn, is later reported to remark 'I am Richard II, know ye not that?.' 8 February: Essex's rebellion goes off at half-cock, and Essex is sent to the Tower (as is Southampton). 25 February: Essex executed. 30 November: Elizabeth, forced to back down over the monopolies against which Parliament has protested, makes what becomes known as her Golden Speech

('For it is my desire to live nor reign no longer than my life and reign shall be for your good. And though you have had, and may have, many princes more mighty and wise, sitting in this state, yet you never had, or shall have any that will be more careful and loving . . .').

1603   February: Elizabeth falls ill, soon after the funeral of her old friend the Countess of Nottingham. Some time in March the coronation ring is filed from the Queen's hand. 24 March: death of the Queen at Richmond Palace. 28 April: funeral of the Queen, Westminster Abbey.

I

Gloriana Revives

She was and is (what can there more be said?)
On earth the chief, in heaven the second, maid.[1]

Apart from their occasional vengefulness, which we looked at in our introduction, one further unexpected impression given by the elegies written for Elizabeth, such as this widely circulated couplet, is of a slight sense of relief. Many of these poems give off a definite feeling that their writers are almost pleased that they can now safely kick the old Queen upstairs as Protestantism's next best thing to the Virgin Mary, glad that death has removed her from power before she has had the chance to tarnish her image any further. Little, on the face of it, could have been less likely than that the earlier seventeenth century would none the less make Elizabeth the centre of a posthumous cult which has survived in recognizable form into our own day—and not only because its founders were, like this anonymous poet who saw the late Queen as the second-blessed Virgin, preoccupied with Elizabeth's role as author of what has come to be known as the Elizabethan Settlement, Anglicanism's compromise between Catholicism and Puritanism. Though they were a matter of life-and-death urgency in the era of the Civil Wars, the debates about Church and State, monarchy and parliament, which provide the context for these seventeenth-century reimaginings of Elizabeth are liable to seem remote now, when the present-day British monarchy appears as eager to disown the Church of England as vice versa. However, Elizabeth's continuing status as a national heroine, or at very least as one of Anglo-American popular culture's most resonant historical icons, remains profoundly indebted to the writers who first looked back to Elizabeth during the century which followed her death. For one thing, despite the disappointments expressed by their forebears during Elizabeth's lifetime, it was militant Protestants who first made Elizabeth the focus of an intense and unprecedented nostalgia, a nostalgia which continues to suffuse her mythos, long after its original stimulus— disquiet at her successor James I's pacific, ecumenical policy towards Catholic Europe—has been forgotten. For another, Elizabeth remains the prime, defining, and founding central character of the new sub-genre which Jacobean and Caroline playwrights invented in order at once to express and to capitalize upon this nostalgia—a sub-genre which we, after Hollywood historical epic and the BBC classic serial, would call costume drama. The story this chapter tells is of how and why historical drama about Elizabeth emerged over the decades following her death, and of how it remained of crucial importance in her retrospective refashioning as an icon of lost national and theological wholeness over the remainder of the seventeenth century—not only on the London stage but in pamphlets, pageants, and poems. Part of this story is about how Elizabeth's womanhood, a disabling problem for her popularity at the end of her reign, became an opportunity for her chroniclers after her death, often helping their refashioned, much-desired Elizabeth to exceed her official role in or as the state and to serve as a figure for Church, crown, City, and country all at once. As we will, see, though, her femininity had again begun to compromise or at very least complicate her status as an epic heroine by the time her anticlimactic successors the Stuarts had been supplanted on the British throne by the still more bathetic Hanoverians early in the eighteenth century.

Costume Drama

The process of selectively remembering Good Queen Bess was at the same time a process of selective forgetting. None of the plays we will be describing in this chapter, for example, depicts the Elizabeth her elegists could most readily remember, the ageing, parsimonious, debt-ridden, stepmotherly queen of the 1590s, stalemated in the long endgame of the succession crisis—a woman who had all but outlived the imaginative hold of her own earlier propaganda, and who now clung to life and power for just long enough to execute her last and most popular favourite, the Earl of Essex, in 1601. By the end of her reign, for all the intervening years of mythologizing which have often denied it, Elizabeth was widely unpopular, even among playwrights. Despite the long tradition, most recently exemplified by the film *Shakespeare in Love*, of representing the Queen as Shakespeare's affectionate patroness (which we will be examining in Chapter 3), the otherwise politically tactful Shakespeare was already exhibiting forms of encoded distaste for this waning national matron during her own lifetime.[2] It has been argued, for example, that his savage depiction of the fraudulent amazon Joan of Arc in *Henry VI Part 1* vents his frustration with Elizabeth's handling of Baron Willoughbie's French expedition of 1589–90 and the Earl of Essex's Rouen mission of 1591–2;[3] that this hostility is further expressed by the bestial humiliations to which Shakespeare subjects her fellow Faerie Queene, Titania, in *A Midsummer Night's Dream*;[4] that Shakespeare may have been actively complicit in the revival of his *Richard II* sponsored by Essex as propaganda for his attempted coup against Elizabeth in 1601, a coup in which Shakespeare's patron the Earl of Southampton also participated; and that the writer's animosity surfaces again in the treatment he metes out to another post-menopausal queen at the centre of a succession crisis, Gertrude in *Hamlet*.[5] Whether or not we are prepared to read Gertrude as a response to Elizabeth, it does seem fair to say that *Hamlet* records something of the mood which, when Elizabeth finally died in 1603, would prompt not only ambivalent elegies but openly triumphal bonfires and relieved masculinist cries of

'We have a king!'.[6] None the less, the stage was to become one of the most important sites of Elizabeth's posthumous rehabilitation and glorification, and even one of Shakespeare's own late plays—*Henry VIII*, originally entitled *All Is True*—would get in on the act.

The theatres' growing nostalgia for Elizabeth, furthermore, developed in defiance not only of her own latter-day unpopularity but in defiance of the new king himself. It is true that James paid due reverence to the late queen—stressing his legitimacy as her successor, for example, by spending an unprecedented £17,000 on staging her funeral, and having her death described in the 1611 dedicatory epistle to the King James Bible as 'the setting of that bright *Occidental Star*, Queen *Elizabeth* of most happy memory'. However, the same text makes it clear that James wished to upstage her completely—if her death is merely the setting of a star, his accession is a far more dazzling event, the appearance 'of the *Sun* in his strength'—and in practice the official view of Elizabeth promulgated by her successor and his court was, even at its most positive, very guarded. In 1606, for example, James installed an admittedly magnificent tomb for his *de facto* political mother Elizabeth in Westminster Abbey, but it is pointedly matched by an equally magnificent one for his natural mother, Mary, Queen of Scots, whom Elizabeth had of course executed. Furthermore, James appears to have had Elizabeth's corpse moved on this occasion from under the altar in the chapel built by the founder of the Tudor dynasty, Henry VII, and placed in the same vault as that of the Catholic half-sister who had come within an ace of having her executed for treason, Bloody Mary. An almost taunting inscription states that the two sisters, though divided in life by religious discord, are now united in death.[7] According to this reorganization of the Abbey, the Tudor monarchs since Henry VII had been a mere digression, the childless, squabbling Mary and Elizabeth a pair of dynastic dead ends: it was James, descended from Henry VII not via Henry VIII but via Margaret of Scotland, who was the true heir, and who would in time occupy the now vacated space under Henry VII's altar accordingly.[8] James thus maintained careful control over Elizabeth's real remains, and, as far as he could he managed her representation in historical narrative too, with the clear intention of sidelining both. Anxious that recent political

history might be written to his disfavour, he dissolved the Society of
Antiquaries in 1607 and thwarted an attempt to revive it in 1614:
although he supported its leader William Camden's desire to continue
writing the *Annales* of Elizabeth's reign which he had laid aside in 1598,
James was primarily concerned that Camden should produce a carefully
vetted, sympathetic account of the life and death of Mary, Queen of
Scots, which would vindicate James from the charge of tacitly consent-
ing to his mother's execution. He actively blocked the publication of the
Annales' final, post-Fotheringay instalment, which, though completed in
1617, did not appear until 1627, two years after James's death, and would
not be published in English translation until 1630. Fulke Greville, meanwhile, one-time school-fellow and hero-worshipper of the glamorous
Elizabethan courtier, writer, and soldier Sir Philip Sidney, was successfully prevented from writing a life of Elizabeth by the King's minister
Robert Cecil. Cecil denied Greville access to state papers so as to prevent
him researching this book on the grounds that such a work about
Elizabeth's reign might be 'construed to the prejudice of this.'

Elizabeth, though, however carefully reburied, just wouldn't lie down.
The more anxious English commentators became about the loss of
national sovereignty that came with the arrival of a Scottish king and his
entourage of hungry Scottish courtiers, and the more concerned about
his attempts to act as a peacemaker between European Catholics and
Protestants instead of as a champion of the latter (especially after the
death of James's more militant eldest son Prince Henry in 1613), the more
Elizabeth was retrospectively flattered as his antithesis. Despite the
King's careful supervision of the *Annales*, an English translation of
Camden's first three books was entered in the Stationers' Register during the controversy over James's plans to marry his son and heir Charles
to the Spanish Infanta, and it was finally published in 1625, its title-page
adorned with vignettes celebrating precisely the half-legendary late
Elizabethan golden age of Protestant triumph which James didn't want
remembered—Drake's circumnavigation, the defeat of the Armada,
the Cadiz expedition, the lot. A magnificent *Apotheosis of Elizabeth I*
serves as its frontispiece, complete with a poem deliberately hymning
Elizabeth as everything James wasn't: 'in this Maiden-Queene Story, |

Admire and view Englands Glory, | Beauties Mapp, DIANAS Mirror: |
Who built up Truth, banisht Error . . . | POPE exiled, SPAINES Armado
| Confounded with their Bravado . . .'⁹ Meanwhile Fulke Greville had
taken his revenge on the court's censorship by inserting a long hagio-
graphic digression about Elizabeth's times into his biography of Sidney,
clearly designed to be understood as a rebuke to her successor.[10] The
mythology which had been built around Elizabeth during her own reign
was somehow too large for James simply to take over and inhabit himself, and her womanhood in particular left a sort of residue which could
gradually be reactivated against him. In particular, the kind of apocalyptic Arthurian romance which Spenser's *Faerie Queene* had embroidered
around Elizabeth's image—in which she is hymned as Gloriana,
Arthur's destined bride, the once and future queen destined to return in
Britain's hour of need, and is also shadowed by Una, the holy maiden
who personfies the true English church—was very hard to adapt to fit a
pacifist bisexual ecumenical Scotsman, and it wouldn't go away. *The
Faerie Queene* was republished in folio in 1611, 1612, 1613, and again in
1617, and this epic poem continued to be read as an important political
and religious allegory well into the eighteenth century.[11] Nor was this
sense of Elizabeth as an apocalyptic champion who cannot really die but
will return to fight for Protestantism in the Last Battle—a role no one
could seriously imagine for James—confined to Spenser's literary epic:
it is vividly exemplified, for example, by an altogether more robust
Jacobean popular ballad:

> She never did any wicked act
>   To make her conscience prick her
> Nor ever would submitt to him
>   That calld himself Christs Vicar.
> But rather chose couragiously
>   To fight under His Banner
> 'Gainst Turke and Pope & King of Spaine
>   And all that durst withstan her.
>
> In Eighty Eight how she did fight
>   Is known to all and some
> When the Spaniard came, her courage to tame

But had better have stayd at home.
They came with Ships, filld full of Whipps,
   To have lasht her Princely Hide
But she had a Drake made them all cry Quake
   & bangd them back and side

  .   .   .   .

And now if I had Argus eyes
   They were all too few to weep
For our good Queen Elizabeth
   That now lyes fast asleep.
A Sleep she lyes, and so shee must lye
   Untill the day of Doom
But then shee'l arise & pisse out the Eyes
   Of the proud Pope of Rome.[12]

Appropriately to this genre, one commentator on the progressive supplanting of the old queen's remembered unpopularity by this sort of enthusiastic retro-Elizabethanism—Godfrey Goodman, writing under the Commonwealth in the 1650s—describes it in terms of an actual resurrection. To Goodman, the increasing public celebration of what became known as 'Queen Bess's Day' (17 November, the anniversary of Elizabeth's accession, which by the later seventeenth century would rival the anniversary of James's preservation from the Gunpowder Plot, 5 November, as a popular anti-Catholic festival) seemed to mark Elizabeth's second coming:

[I]n effect the people were very generally weary of an old woman's government. . . . But after a few years, when we had experience of the Scottish government, then in disparagement of the Scots, and in hate and detestation of them, the Queen did seem to revive; then was her memory much magnified,—such ringing of bells, such public joy and sermons in commemoration of her, the picture of her tomb painted in many churches, and in effect more solemnity and joy in memory of her coronation than was for the coming in of King James.[13]

'The Queen did seem to revive', 'such public joy . . . in memory of her coronation.' If there were cheerleaders to this uncanny chorus of posthumous rejoicing, some of them were playwrights, for Goodman's account corresponds remarkably well with precisely what happened on the

London stage, where the young Elizabeth did indeed seem to revive in the body (often in ways specifically designed to refute or supplant the hostility directed towards her in her later years), and on which her coronation, in particular, was repeatedly celebrated.[14] A whole batch of chronicle plays—by Samuel Rowley, Thomas Heywood, Thomas Dekker, William Shakespeare, and John Fletcher—reconstituted Elizabeth's damaged iconography, re-enacting the stages by which it had developed around her over the course of her long reign. These plays make particular use of another aspect of Elizabeth's reign and its imagery which could not easily be assumed by her successor: her dresses. Tudor dress—particularly the styles associated with Elizabeth's official portraits—would soon become one of the Jacobean theatre's most important markers of historical difference, and the late queen would become the defining heroine of a new sub-genre, costume drama. In this first phase of the form's life, Elizabeth is never herself ambiguous or conflicted, and she always functions as a solution rather than a problem.

In fact of the five plays produced about Elizabeth during the first decade of James's reign (the first four all produced between 1604 and 1607) it would be technically true to say that only two present 'Queen' Elizabeth at all: instead the majority share an overwhelming interest in her uncrowned youth. The Elizabeth who first revives in the theatre, so far from being an embodiment of absolute power, is more often a helpless victim, an exemplary persecuted Protestant cheated of full martyrdom only by special providence. Precisely the figure depicted in John Foxe's *Actes and Monuments of the English Martyrs* forty years earlier—the book which defined Elizabethan Anglicanism, its illustrated account of the sufferings of Protestants under Elizabeth's predecessor Bloody Mary kept in all English cathedrals and treated with almost as much reverence as the Bible—this rejuvenated Elizabeth makes her first appearance in Jacobean drama in the form of a Protestant text of her own.[15] In Samuel Rowley's play about Henry VIII, *When You See Me, You Know Me* (1604, printed 1605), Elizabeth, though Rowley refrains so soon after her death from actually bringing her on to the stage, plays a crucial role in the action as an eloquent absence. Prince Edward is debating the great issues of theology when he simultaneously receives letters from each of his half-sisters, Mary and Elizabeth:

> What sayes my sister *Mary?* she is eldest,
> And by due course must first be answered,
> *The blessed Mother of thy redeemer, with all the Angels & holy Saints be*
> *intermissers to preserve thee of Idolatrie, to invocate the Saints for helpe.*

Elizabeth's letter, read at once in a compare-and-contrast exercise not unlike Hamlet's with the portraits of his father and Claudius, is of course written in a different style altogether:

> *Sweete Prince I salute thee with a Sisters love,*
> *Be stedfast in thy faith, and let thy prayers*
> *Be dedicate to God only, for tis he alone*
> *Can strengthen thee, and confound thine enemies,*
> *Give a setled assurance of thy hopes in heaven,*
> *God strengthen thee in all temptations,*
> *And give thee grace to shun Idolatrie,*
> *Heaven send thee life to inherite thy election,*
> *To God I commend thee, who still I pray preserve thee,*
>   Thy loving Sister *Elizabeth.*

Absent from the play's action, and thus uncompromised by any personal role in the political intrigues it depicts, Elizabeth stands for pure, uncorrupted Protestantism, an ideal towards which Rowley's account of Tudor history will henceforward move with renewed purpose. 'Loving thou art, and of me best beloved', says Edward,

> Thy lines shalbe my contemplations cures,
> And in thy vertues will I meditate,
> To Christ Ile onely pray for me and thee:
> This I imbrace, away Idolatrie.[16]

Thus inspired by his sister, the prince duly goes on to intercede decisively for Catharine Parr and Thomas Cranmer when they are each accused of treason, reconciling them with the ageing and mellowing Henry, and Rowley's chronicle can conclude in the peaceful anticipation of a Protestant succession. As a play produced within little more than a year of Elizabeth's death, *When You See Me, You Know Me* is a remarkable response to the passing of the Tudors: the death of the old, compromised Queen, ceremonially uncrowned by her state funeral rites, here provides the occasion and opportunity for her complete reimagining as absent, uncompromising princess, a figure for an unspotted, disembodied future rather than an all too embodied past.

The legacy of *When You See Me, You Know Me* was soon taken up by a play whose title deliberately echoes Rowley's, Thomas Heywood's *If You Know Not Me, You Know Nobody: or, The Troubles of Queen Elizabeth* (1605).[17] As the title-page of its first edition suggests (Fig. 4), with Heywood Elizabeth arrives in costume drama proper, although the woodcut here provides a less accurate indicator of the play's content than the subtitle: Elizabeth only becomes queen in the very last scene of *If You Know Not Me*, which re-enacts her pre-coronation procession into the City, and does indeed finally present her in this outfit and under this canopy when she receives an English Bible from the Lord Mayor of London.[18] The bulk of the action is instead concerned with her 'troubles' during the reign of Mary. Like Samuel Rowley, in fact, Heywood sets about unwriting Elizabeth the unwanted past queen by giving us instead Elizabeth the desired future queen, her status as Protestant saint confirmed by a vision of angels, vouchsafed to her in a dream:

> *A Dumbe show.*
> Enter *Winchester, Constable, Barwick* and *Fryars*: at the other dore, 2. *Angels*: the *Fryars* steps to her, offering to kill her: the *Angels* driue them back. *Exeunt.* The *Angel* opens the Bible, & puts it in her hands; *Exeunt Angels*: shee wakes.

The vision is designed as a premonition of the City's contribution to her coronation, the presentation of the Bible with which the play closes. A parallel text suggests that Heywood's choice to depict the young, near-martyred Elizabeth was a conscious strategy for rescuing Gloriana from the subsequent decay of her reputation. In 1607 Christopher Lever published a substantial poem, much of it in the form of dialogue, called *Queene Elizabeths Teares: or, Her resolute bearing the Christian Crosse,*

If you knovv not me,

You know no bodie:

Or,

The troubles of Queene ELIZABETH.

AT LONDON,
Printed for Nathaniel Butter. 1605.

FIG. 4. The title-page to the first edition of Thomas Heywood's pioneering costume drama, *If You Know Not Me, You Know Nobody: or, The Troubles of Queen Elizabeth* (1605). As the engraving suggests, this play offers Jacobean audiences another look at 'the late Queen of glorious memory', but its Elizabeth only acquires this signature costume and regalia at the very end of the play: instead of representing the remembered crises and conflicts of Elizabeth's maturity, Heywood nostalgically dramatizes her uncrowned youth. Returning to John Foxe's depiction of Elizabeth in his *Actes and Monuments* (otherwise known as *Foxe's Book of Martyrs*, 1563), Heywood shows Elizabeth as one of the English people—an oppressed subject of Bloody Mary, persecuted for her Protestant faith.

inflicted on her by the persecuting hands of Steven Gardner, Bishop of Winchester, in the bloodie time of Queene Marie. Lever covers exactly the same events as *If You Know Not Me*, part 1, and supplies his poem with an address 'To the Reader' explaining that its purpose is twofold. It is designed 'to please the well affected' by glorifying the memory of Elizabeth, 'whome all the best in the world do honour with admiration, which thou also wilt doe, if thou beest either honest or truely English': Lever wishes to remind the world of Elizabeth's youthful near-martyrdom specifically to confound her latter-day detractors, thereby

giving Envie and her sonnes a morsell to bite upon; wishing that all the depravers of her princely name, may either reduce themselves to some degree of honestie, or perish with their envious and evill breath.[19]

For Heywood and Lever, apparently, the antidote to hostile comments about the old queen Jacobeans could remember was the deliberate idealization of the young princess whom they couldn't. As Heywood would put it in the preface to his later prose account of the same events, *England's Elizabeth* (1631), by comparison with other chroniclers of Elizabeth,

they have shewed you a Queene, I expose to your view a Princesse . . . they the passage of her incomparable Life from the Scepter to the Sepulchre, as shee was a Soveraigne; I the process of her time from the Cradle to the Crowne, as she was a sad and sorrowful Subject.[20]

So much is Heywood's young Elizabeth a 'subject', in fact, that at one point in her captivity she dreams of an alternative career as a milkmaid (another anecdote drawn from Foxe). The crucial first step towards the renewal of the queen's fame is the replacement of a memory of Elizabeth as oppressive bad mother with an image of Elizabeth as oppressed good daughter, a sister in suffering. By the end of Heywood's *If You Know Not Me*, Elizabeth has been spectacularly rehabilitated as a divinely sanctioned personification of true Protestantism, a representative of the English people rather than merely of the court, and a true friend of the City of London.

This play was one of the biggest hits of Heywood's career, and in 1606 duly appeared *The Second Part of, If you know not me, you know no bodie. With the building of the Royall Exchange: And the famous Victorie of Queene Elizabeth, in the Yeare 1588.* It is a play which is nowadays cited, if at all, as an example of how the history play declined as a genre after the accession of James, theatrically sabotaged by its own uncritical nostalgia: according to this line, *If you know not me*, part 2, merely demonstrates how difficult it is to write anything very dramatic about Elizabeth as queen if one wishes to present her in a continuously good light. Since for Heywood the story of Gloriana's reign must be the story of how she was always continuously right, the argument runs, to look for psychological insight or political depth in Elizabeth's scenes of *The Second Part of, If you know not me* is about as rewarding as looking for the same things in *Margaret Thatcher: The Downing Street Years.* Heywood must silently suppress all the topics which might produce dramatic conflict within Elizabeth and her court, so that his play merely depicts someone who, having been providentially crowned, providentially survives Catholic assassination attempts, and then providentially survives an attempted Catholic invasion (after which nothing further happens at all). Deprived of anything risky like interiority or agency, complain the critics, Heywood's Queen Elizabeth spends nearly as much time offstage as the epistolary Princess Elizabeth of *When You See Me, You Know Me*, reduced to a minor supporting role in a citizen comedy much more at home with Sir Thomas Gresham and the jolly burghers of the Royal Exchange.

This is fair enough as far as it goes, but it tends to misread the ways in which Elizabeth is represented in *If you know not me*, part 2, which work not by dramatizing her as a character but by showing her as a figure. In Jacobean costume drama the late queen both enables and embodies unity, completely untroubled by the perceived discrepancies between her womanhood and her queenship which will energize later dramatizations of her reign (as we shall see in Chapter 2). There is no conflict here between the private and the public: instead Elizabeth is animated and explained by dramatic proxies. In this latter respect Heywood copies another strategy from Rowley's play, the one indicated by his title. In *When You See Me, You Know Me*, although our first assumption is that this titular phrase will appear in the script as a line spoken by the self-evidently recognizable royal protagonist, Henry VIII, the nearest we hear to it is instead uttered *to* the King by a character who doesn't recognize him at all: the criminal Black Will, whom Henry meets and fights when spending a night incognito around the streets of his capital.

KING. I carry a sword and a buckler ye see.
BLACK. A sword and buckler, and know not me,
Not *Blacke Will*?

(Rowley, D3r)

Black Will, stealing what apparently ought to be Henry's line, sharing his swaggering sense of his own unquestionable fame and power, and matching him in single combat, is in effect pointed out as King Henry's alter egotist; and Heywood appoints just such a double for Queen Elizabeth in the same manner, and in nearly the same words. For Heywood, however, Elizabeth is not an honorary gangster but an honorary merchant citizen, her role as protagonist deputed both to Sir Thomas Gresham (whose bourse she graciously opens) and, more comically, to the rich haberdasher Hobson, whom she meets during the ceremony:

HOB. God blesse thy Grace Queene *Besse*.
QUEEN. Friend, what are you?
HOB. Knowest thou not mee Queene? then thou knowest nobody.[21]

This punchline may appear to demote Elizabeth to a stooge, but in fact it signals and cements the idealized reciprocity between monarch and citizen which Heywood's whole play celebrates. According to Heywood's dramatic logic, the entire economic life of the City operates under the sign of the Queen and on her behalf—hence the Royal Exchange—so that a merchant subject such as Hobson, filling her coffers on demand, is less her vassal than her proxy. The play hereby supplants recollections of the old Queen's actual debts with what one historian terms a 'nostalgic memory of Queen Elizabeth's special bond with her London citizens.'[22]

Objections to the comparative plotlessness of the Queen's scenes, furthermore, ignore the fact that they remain in every sense costume drama, their principal work not that of telling a royal story but that of restoring a royal icon. Rather than interrogating Elizabethan history, *If you know not me*, part 2, renews the political impact of Elizabethan pageantry: while in 1606 King James, notoriously shy of making personal appearances, was probably away hunting somewhere, his predecessor was back on display in London, her theatregoing former subjects pleasantly enough diverted by Hobson and co. while eagerly awaiting her facsimile progresses on to the stage. The fact that Elizabeth isn't fully treated as a character in a history play, distanced from us by an anxious preoccupation with her own personal story-line, so far from being a disastrous artistic accident, is half the point: she arrives in Heywood's city comedy as herself, revived, graciously rewarding its actors in her habit as she lived. We know that some of Elizabeth's own dresses were used after her death in Jacobean court masques, occasions which required extensive collaboration between court and professional theatre: it would be very interesting to know where the squeaking Elizabeth who boyed her greatness in *If You Know Not Me* got his outfits from, especially as we also know that given the relative costs of costumes and of scripts it was much more common for Jacobean theatre-managers to commission plays to match clothes than to obtain clothes to suit newly written plays. At very least the illustrations used on this play's printed title-pages suggest some expertise about the royal wardrobe at different dates in the Queen's career:[23] it would be only appropriate if it were the players' acquisition of some of the late Queen's dresses—precisely that aspect of her mantle which her male successor could not assume—which gave rise to Elizabeth's return in Heywood's play.[24]

Elizabeth is staged in this play, then, by a series of tableaux vivants separated by costume changes: once again, as in part 1, she becomes a unifying emblem for the crown, the Church, the people, and the City of London. One last costume change, however, certainly the most important of her career on the seventeenth-century stage, extends her signifying repertoire still further, and makes her an even more powerful emblem. After we have seen her process on to the stage in the dress of her queenship to open the Royal Exchange, visually identified as the patroness of mercantile patriotism, and have seen her in full splen court, frustrating Parry's assassination attempt, she subsequently changes her robes in favour of something rather more dashing for the play's final movement, in which she is fully identified with the nation itself:

> QUEEN. Oh had God and Nature,
> Giuen vs proportion man-like to our mind,
> VVee'd not stand here fenc't in a wall of Armes,
> But haue been present in these Sea alarmes
>
> .   .   .   .
>
> A March, l[ea]d on: wee'le meet the worst can fall,
> A mayden Queene will be your Generall.[25]

If you know not me, part 2, finally takes Elizabeth out of her capital and sends her to Tilbury: and there it leaves her as Drake reports her navy's victory, frozen in the audience's collectively revised memory in a permanent idealized tableau of the famous Victory of the year 1588. The sartorial transformation involved is made explicit in the fuller version of the oration she makes at Tilbury, supplied by the later quartos of Heywood's play:

> Be this then stil d our Campe at *Tilbery*;
> And the first place we haue bin seene in Armes
> Or thus [accoutred]: heere wee fixe our foot,
> Not to stir backe, were we sure heere t'incounter
> With all the Spanish vengeance threatned vs,
> Came it in Fire and Thunder, Know my Subiects
> Your Queene hath now put on a Masculine spirit,
> To tell the bold and daring what they are,
> Or what they ought to be . . .
>
> .   .   .   .
>
> Oh I could wish them landed, and in view,
> To bid them instant battaile ere march farther
> Into my Land, this is my vow, my rest,
> Ile paue their way with this my virgin brest.[26]

Elizabeth's heroically defended virginity is here used once again as a sign for the invulnerability and integrity of her island realm, her eternal vitality (since none of these plays admits she ever grew old) a facet of the tri-

umphant emergence of Protestantism. The merely obsolete Elizabeth of
the everyday political past was an old woman: the timeless Elizabeth of
legend becomes instead, over the course of Heywood's play, an exemplary embodiment of national prosperity, national righteousness, and
national machismo. (In this she is a worthy successor to Heywood's earlier cross-dressed heroine Bess Bridges in the two-part *Fair Maid of the
West*, who defeats a man in a duel while in male disguise, commands a
privateer against the Spaniards, and is explicitly compared to Elizabeth
herself.) The canonical version of the celebrated speech which Elizabeth
really had delivered at Tilbury in 1588 ('I know I have the body but of a
weak and feeble woman . . .'), together with the historically dubious
assertion that the Queen was dressed as 'armed Pallas' as she delivered
it, would not reach print until the 1650s:[27] but by the time that it did
Elizabeth had already been long enshrined in the popular historical
imagination as a valiant national cross-dresser, repeatedly staged as such
by a boy player from 1606 onwards.

This visual transformation of Elizabeth into the stuff of patriotic
legend is even more obvious in a play which, a year later, rewrote this one
in a consciously iconographic register, even more clearly calculated to
offset or displace the misogynistic attitudes towards the old Queen visible at the end of her reign. Thomas Dekker's *The Whore of Babylon* (1607)
covers the same chronological ground as *If you know not me*, part 2, and
the ending of part 1—it opens with a dumb-show of the coronation, and
closes with the Queen victorious at Tilbury—but whereas Heywood's
processions and shows provide a costume-drama frame for a London
comedy, Dekker branches out into a more fully spectacular and apocalyptic dramatic form. *The Whore of Babylon* is less a history play than a
staged historical allegory, somewhere between *The Faerie Queene* and
Thomas Middleton's anti-Spanish drama *A Game at Chess*. Dekker's celebration of Elizabeth's resistance to Catholic Europe is cast in the form
of a moralized pageant depicting how Fairy Land successfully held out
against Babylon. The play's characters, usually identified with historical
figures, are given fanciful names, many of them drawn from Spenser, and
so one might expect the Queen of Fairy Land to receive the given name
of Spenser's Faerie Queene, Gloriana: but instead Dekker's heroine goes

by the name of a different fay entirely, hitherto associated only with an apparent pejorative sideswipe at the stepmotherly old Queen of the 1590s—'Titania, the Fairie Queen, under whom is figured our late Queen Elizabeth.'[28]

One noticeable way in which *The Whore of Babylon* seeks to rescue Elizabeth from the slights of her last years is by its provision of a female villain. After attracting such sympathy as Bloody Mary's victim in *If You Know Not Me*, part 1, Elizabeth risks acceding to Mary's role as well as her throne for part 2, when the job of signing traitors' death-warrants falls to her; but Dekker neatly avoids this pitfall by supplying her with a new antagonist for her reign proper, no mere Philip of Spain but 'The Empress of Babylon, under whom is figured Rome' (98). Pitted as Una against this all-powerful Duessa, Elizabeth can remain the play's good woman even after becoming queen, all lingering misogyny concentrated on the grotesquely maternal Whore, self-described as 'the mother of nations, the triple-crowned head of the world, the purple rider of the glorious beast, the most high, most supreme, and most adored Empress of Babylon' (232). By comparison with this exotic and terrifying double—who in the play's mightiest dumb-show blesses the troops boarding the Armada galleons while mounted in state on a pantomime many-headed Beast of the Apocalypse (233)—Titania, fairy or no, is always going to look like one of us, and her comradeship with her subjects is underlined when, duly appearing for the grand finale, she makes her oration at Tilbury (allegorically renamed Beria): 'We come with yours to venture our own blood. | For you and we are fellows . . .' (268). This female Henry V enjoys her righteous victory through an even more lavish closing tableau than that of *If you know not me*, part 2: accompanied by Truth, she is raised aloft with her counsellors, and allowed, by the special intervention of Time in person, to witness the discomfiture of the Whore and her kings and cardinals, as they gnash their teeth over the destruction of the Armada. This is one of the dramatic gains Dekker achieves by promoting Elizabeth out of history and into apocalyptic romance: untroubled by details of chronology or practicality, his play can concentrate on building up to this refurbished visual image of Elizabeth as supreme championess of militant Protestantism, a role which in life

she had neither quite sought nor quite earned, but which Dekker retrospectively affirms.²⁹ *The Whore of Babylon* surely influenced, for example,
one of the best-known seventeenth-century nostalgic images of
Elizabeth, Thomas Cecil's print *Truth Presents the Queen with a Lance,*
*c.*1625 (see Fig. 5). Here again are Truth, the many-headed beast, and the
bird's-eye view of the Armada, just as in the play, and, just as in the play,
this valiant Tudor Britomart is clearly intended to shame her less belli-
cose successor.³⁰ The infinitely larger-than-life Elizabeth of this image
is, crucially, at once England as damsel in distress and the Crown as
knight in shining armour coming to its rescue, at once naked protestant
Truth and undying armoured King Arthur: no single successor could
possibly occupy as many positions for the state and the nation at once.

These popular costume-drama representations of Elizabeth—oper-
ating in one area of the public realm over which James either could not
or would not exert the same level of control as he could over the writing
of official history—became part of the Jacobean cultural landscape.
Although Dekker's extravagant and extreme play does not seem to have
been reprinted after 1607 (though it wasn't forgotten, as Cecil's print
suggests), those of Rowley and Heywood, no less visual but confining
their spectacle within the terms of historical costume and dumb-show,
remained very much in circulation: *If you know not me*, part 2, was
reprinted in 1609 and again in revised and expanded form in 1633, while
part 1 went through at least eight editions by 1639. As if to stress the
importance of the visual element in these plays—their titles' promise to
their audiences of another look at Queen Elizabeth—all these editions
feature portraits of Elizabeth on their title-pages, and Rowley's *When*
You See Me, You Know Me followed suit with a post-Holbein likeness of
Henry VIII when it reappeared in a second edition in 1613. In the same
year even one of Elizabeth's former (implicit) critics made his own contribution to this newly prominent form of Tudor costume-drama, when
Shakespeare returned to the subject-matter of Tudor history for the first
time since the ending of *Richard III*, enlisting his apprentice John
Fletcher to co-write the play published in the 1623 Folio as *The Famous*
History of the Life of Henry Eight.

Appropriately, *Henry VIII*, sharing Rowley's subject-matter and

FIG. 5. Thomas Cecil (fl. c.1625), *Truth Presents the Queen with a Lance* (c.1625), sometimes known as *Queen Elizabeth in Armour*. This apocalyptic vision of Elizabeth as heroine of 1588—which, faithful to the Tudors' Arthurian mythology, sees her conflict with the Spanish Armada as a type of the Last Battle—casts its idealized Queen both as damsel in distress (embodying invasion-threatened England), and as Spenserian knight in armour (the crown, or at least the Tudor Rose-crowned royal helmet, coming to the rescue). Truth's book recalls the English Bible accepted by Elizabeth during her pre-coronation procession through the City in 1559, while Elizabeth's horse tramples on the many-headed Beast of the Apocalypse (from the Book of Revelation), understood by Protestants as a symbol of the corrupt Catholic Church. Taking up one suggestion implicit in the Queen's rhetoric on the occasion, this print identifies Elizabeth's impregnable island with her impenetrable body.

influenced by his dramatization of the fall of Wolsey, is the most thoroughgoing exercise in the visualizing of history in the Shakespeare canon.[31] As drama, *Henry VIII*, for all its pervasive scepticism about the relations between shows and truth, aspires to the status of historical re-enactment or reconstruction, and it says much about the play that it remains the only Shakespearean history of which there has never been a fully modern-dress production: even Howard Davies's would-be Brechtian version for the RSC in the early 1980s only went so far as to show Henry putting on his Holbein robes of state, instead of cutting the robes entirely. This was and is costume drama, and it follows Rowley and Heywood too in presenting Elizabeth as the ultimate miraculous solution to all England's problems. The play associated with Elizabeth's own succession crisis, *Hamlet*, is here comprehensively rewritten: in this later play about a dynastic imbroglio, in which Henry (like Claudius) has incestuously married his brother's widow, all can ultimately be saved from tragedy by the next generation. The play's last scene is not a funeral but a christening: after the agonizing business of Henry VIII's divorce from Catherine of Aragon and remarriage to Anne Boleyn has been poignantly, if tactfully, dramatized, the new heir—represented on stage almost entirely by costume, a state christening gown—is resoundingly named:

> GARTER KING OF ARMS. Heaven, from thy endless goodness send prosperous life, long, and ever happy, to the high and mighty Princess of England, Elizabeth. (*Flourish*)

$$(5.4.1–4).$$

Of all the scenes in the play, this is the one which goes furthest beyond its sources in Holinshed's *Chronicles*, slipping suddenly from mere costume drama into the discourse of religious prophecy when the princess's godfather, Archbishop Thomas Cranmer, is moved to speak a few words on the occasion:

> Let me speak, sirs,
> For Heaven now bids me; and the words I utter
> Let none think flattery, for they'll find 'em truth.
> This royal infant—heaven still move about her!—

> Though in her cradle, yet now promises
> Upon this land a thousand thousand blessings,
> Which time shall bring to ripeness: she shall be—
> But few now living can behold that goodness—
> A pattern to all princes living with her,
> And all that shall succeed . . .[32]

Elizabeth, played on stage by an inanimate doll, takes her place alongside Shakespeare's other redemptive royal infant daughters, such as Perdita in *The Winter's Tale*,[33] Marina in *Pericles*, and the three-year-old Miranda remembered by Prospero from his earliest days of exile in *The Tempest*. She here provides a space where the audience's nostalgia can meet its precise counterpart in Cranmer's optimism, the desire that the Elizabethan past should have been perfect finding itself reflected in his remembered promise that the Elizabethan future would be so. Each interrogates the other; the question the prophecy begs of an audience hearing it ten years after Elizabeth's death is whether her reign actually did live up to Cranmer's vision.

> In her days every man shall eat in safety,
> Under his own vine, what he plants; and sing
> The merry songs of peace to all his neighbours:
> God shall be truly known; and those about her
> From her shall read the perfect ways of honour,
> And by those claim their greatness, not by blood.
>
> (5.4.33–8)

Did all this prove true or not? In leaving us wondering, *Henry VIII* manages to position itself just at the edge of the growing nostalgia cult in which it partakes, even while potentially offering all the melancholy pleasures of that cult. But its profound wistfulness about Elizabeth completely upstages Cranmer's subsequent flattering prophecy about James. James gets only 15 lines of the speech compared to Elizabeth's 35, and despite the chronology of the two reigns these are merely inset: Cranmer closes not with his praise of Elizabeth's successor but with his foreseeing of her death, a sad decade-old memory for this play's first audience:

But she must die—
She must, the saints must have her—yet a virgin,
A most unspotted lily shall she pass
To th'ground, and all the world shall mourn her.

(5.4.59–62)

The Jacobean stage was far more interested in the remembered future of Princess Elizabeth, whether at her christening, her coronation, or her apotheosis at Tilbury, than in the official agenda of her heir.[34]

Doll, Statue, Ghost

The determination of the early seventeenth-century stage to remember Elizabeth, and to do so via clothes—whether christening gowns, ruffs, or breastplates—has been bequeathed, as a governing metaphor, to those modern historians who seek to analyse her memory. So much is costume drama still a constitutive part of Elizabeth's posthumous realm that even professional historians—male ones, at least—often understand the development of her reputation in just this genre's terms. Christopher Haigh, strikingly, argues that by about 1610 'Elizabeth was dressed up in clothes she would hardly have recognized, to pose as a model for her successor . . .',[35] while Wallace MacCaffrey sees the development of her mythos as the making of a doll:

Elizabeth, well before her death, was already enshrined in a myth that heavily veiled the historical personage. Posterity has made liberal additions to it, from the seventeenth century down to our own times. These embellishments have so encrusted the actual person as to create a kind of historical doll as richly and stiffly artificial as the figures shown to us in her portraits.[36]

David Starkey, similarly, describes the Elizabeth of popular memory as a 'monstrous mannequin.'[37] Doll she may have retrospectively become, literally for Shakespeare and Fletcher and figuratively for their successors, but this fantasy Elizabeth remained a doll with a great deal of presence and signifying power for the 1620s and 1630s. Despite James's best efforts, the mourning-cum-deification of Elizabeth would by the e his reign spread even to the Westminster Abbey monument which he had apparently designed in the hope of setting her memory firmly to one side, likenesses of which, as Goodman remembered, were painted in some parish churches. (As we have seen, the title-page of the 1625 edition of *Purchas his Pilgrims*, a book designed to urge the English to renew their long-overdue colonial enterprise, provides another example, with its image of 'Hakluytus Posthumus' weeping inconsolably at the tomb of the dead queen, Fig. 1). In the playhouses, meanwhile, this renewed veneration of Elizabeth and her times never stopped, at least until the English Revolution transposed the arguments over whether she should best be remembered as a bulwark of royal and ecclesiastical privilege against the Puritans or of true Protestantism against the Spanish to the theatre of war. By the 1630s Elizabethan plays were being reprinted in quarto editions which made, for the first time, a positive selling-point of their own archaism, their long-obsolete boasts to have been 'Acted before the Queen's Majesty' pointedly left intact: even comedies as apparently outmoded as John Lyly's could be marketed by association with Gloriana, as is demonstrated by the appearance in 1632 of *Six Court Comedies. Often Presented and Acted before Queen Elizabeth*. (A reprint of Lyly's *Sappho and Phao* from the same year makes the same boast.)[38] In 1631, when Charles I had already assumed personal, parliament-free rule, the King's Men produced Philip Massinger's *The Emperor of the East*, a tragicomedy set in Byzantium much as *The Whore of Babylon* is set in Fairy Land, but with an equally recognizable version of Elizabeth—the chaste, ideal empress Pulcheria—at its centre. Her successor, the weak-willed Theodosius, is a thoroughgoing Stuart, flattered by his favourites into a dangerous belief in the divine right of kings. A more domestic version of the theatre's customary pro-Tudor and anti-Stuart version of nostalgia appeared in 1641, on the very eve of the civil wars, in the form of the Duke of Newcastle's *The Varietie*; here the rich Lady Beaufield is won not by one of the fashionable Caroline courtiers who pursue her but by Manly, a character so obsessed with the lost heroic virtues of the Elizabethan age that he likes to dress up as the Earl of Leicester, Elizabeth's most persistent and enduring suitor and favourite. Meanwhile, Lady Beaufield's daughter Lucy is underwhelmed by the foolish Simpleton, who makes the idiotic mistake of trying to emulate Manly's success by dressing up in Jacobean retro-would-be-chic instead of Elizabethan.[39]

Although the civil wars, by closing the playhouses (already much interrupted by plague), temporarily put a stop to the dramatic representation of Elizabeth, the collapse of Caroline censorship unloosed a flood of discussion about her in print. Her image, encompassing crown, country, court, Church, and City alike, was by now far larger than any of the factions into which the state had split, and its residues haunted them all. For many of its leaders, not least Cromwell, the English Revolution was an attempt to restore the supposed constitutional balance of the Elizabethan age (just as many Cavaliers felt that they were above all defending the Elizabethan Settlement),[40] and politicians on all sides debated her legacy throughout the twenty years' conflict. Pamphlets obsessively revisited her dealings with Mary, with Rome, and with Puritanism. One of Cromwell's chief propagandists, John Milton, voiced the scepticism of some of his colleagues in *The Ready and Easy Way to Establish a Free Commonwealth*: better informed about the Virgin Queen than many, he records that 'Queen *Elizabeth* though her self accounted so good a Protestant, so moderate, so confident of her Subjects love would never give way so much as to Presbyterian reformation in this land . . .'[41] Others were less diffident, fuelling a continuing demand for the laudatory biographies which were printed and reprinted, among them Sir Robert Naunton's *Fragmenta Regalia* (1641), Sir Francis Bacon's *The Felicity of Queen Elizabeth*, and Francis Osborne's *Historical Memoires on the Reignes of Queen Elizabeth and King James* (1658). In particular, Elizabeth's 'Golden Speech' to her last Parliament was endlessly reissued, complete with its poignant farewell that 'This I count the glory of my reign, that I have reigned with your loves.' No wonder that Samuel Pepys, who grew up during the Commonwealth, was keen to see a play about Elizabeth as soon as one was revived after the Restoration, in 1667, remarking as he did so that he had 'sucked in so much of the sad story of Queen Elizabeth from my cradle.'

Such physical representations of Elizabeth, however, would in practice develop in completely new directions during the later part of the century, not least as a result of the replacement of the boy-player by professional actress in 1660. The two great Elizabeth stories of the Jacobean stage—of her providential accession and of her victory over the Armada—were destined to migrate into other media, both upmarket and down. It was not that the new theatre audiences of the Restoration were not as interested in Tudor spectacle as ever: after the Duke's Company first revived *Henry VIII* in 1663 it became one of the most popular plays in the Shakespeare canon, and in 1667 the rival King's Company decided to try reviving Heywood's *If You Know Not Me* plays, conflated into a single entertainment. But the role of Elizabeth as written for a boy, and conceived as an emblematic figure from providential history, no longer seemed to fit the criteria for proper drama in the more visually high-tech and literal-minded playhouses of the 1660s. Pepys, for one, found that in the Restoration context Heywood's drama looked strangely dated:

[August 17 1667] to the King's playhouse . . . to see the new play, *Queen Elizabeths Troubles, and the History of Eighty-Eight.* I confess I have sucked in so much of the sad story of Queen Elizabeth from my cradle, that I was ready to weep for her sometimes. But the play is the most ridiculous that sure ever came upon stage, and endeed is merely a show; only, shows the true garbe of the queens in those days, just as we see Queen Mary and Queen Elizabeth painted—but the play is merely a puppet-play, acted by living puppets.[42]

The women now playing Mary and Elizabeth were here disappointingly reduced for Pepys to mere costume exhibits, not active performers but passive clothes-horses. Historically interesting as their clothes remained, they failed to compensate Pepys for what he had learned to expect from actresses—the display of a female interiority identified with the female body itself. The actress in the cast to whom Pepys did respond positively was the one wearing the minimum of clothes—and those not coded as museum pieces at that:

Only, I was pleased to see Knipp dance among the milkmaids, and to hear her sing a song to Queen Elizabeth—and to see her come out in her night-gown, with no locks on, but her bare face and hair only tied up in a knot behind; which is the comeliest dress that ever I saw her in to her advantage.

It is unfortunate that the altered script used on this occasion has not survived, as neither the milkmaids' dance routine nor the song in which Mrs

Knipp showed to such advantage appear in Heywood's original script. Both are characteristically Restoration uses of the actress as sexual spectacle, and it is worth remembering here that Mrs Knipp was one of Pepys's mistresses as well as one of his favourite stage performers. But what is much more indicative of what Queen Elizabeth still had in store for her on the later seventeenth-century stage is the way in which the displayed Knipp, who presumably played the waiting-woman and confidante Clarentia, seems to deputize for the woman's body now concealed underneath Elizabeth's stage costume. What for Heywood had been a rhetorical gesture towards the status of Protestant martyr—Elizabeth's wistful remark that she would rather be a milkmaid—had now become the occasion for a sexy song and dance about her suffering womanhood. It was the full, unifying force of her emblematic royal costume that had waned: monarchs, apparently, their ability to unify the nation and the state forever called into question, could no longer be construed as internally unified, especially if their imputed private selves were female. If the Jacobean and Caroline stage had been interested in piling costumes on to Elizabeth to make her a triumphantly public and active hermaphrodite, the Restoration stage would soon display far more interest in taking them off, so as to expose Elizabeth's queenship as something only precariously superimposed on her vulnerable, physical, and private femininity. The immediate future for Elizabeth as a character in mainstream drama lay in the representation of apocryphal love plots, more interested in depicting Elizabeth's affairs of state as affairs of the heart than as victories for the true Church, a development charted in our next chapter.

Versions of Elizabeth which Heywood would certainly have recognized, however, survived as vigorously as ever for at least the next seventy years, some on admittedly less respectable stages than those of the Theatres Royal, some in epic poetry, and some in the fresh waves of political pamphlets which accompanied the various constitutional crises which haunted the later Stuarts. The 'Popish Plot' scare of 1678–9 and the subsequent Exclusion Crisis, for example, when Whigs campaigned for Charles II's Catholic brother James to be debarred from inheriting the crown, saw the topic of Catholic assassination plots against

Elizabeth endlessly revisited in the popular press, in publications such as *A Bull sent by Pope Pius, to encourage the traytors in England, pronounced against Queen Elizabeth* (1678), *The Act of Parliament of the 27th of Queen Elizabeth, to preserve the Queens Person, and Protestant Religion, Queen Elizabeth's Speech to her last Parliament, after her delivery from the Popish Plots . . .* , and *The Jesuites ghostly ways* (all 1679). As on the stage, this now oppositional Elizabeth was frequently identified by her signature clothing: 'A Tudor a Tudor! Wee've had Stuarts enough; | None ever Reign'd like old Besse in the ruff', cried one 1678 squib ('A dialogue between the two horses'), attributed to the ex-Cromwellian poet Andrew Marvell.[43] Two new biographies, heavily indebted to Heywood's *England's Elizabeth*, followed: *A Pattern or President for Princes to Rule By . . . ('A Lively Character of the most renowned Queen Elizabeth')* (1680) and Samuel Clarke's *The History of the Glorious Life, Reign and Death of the Illustrious Queen Elizabeth* (1682). Elizabeth reappeared even more forcefully during the popular demonstrations elaborately stage-managed during this episode. On Accession Day in 1679 a grand procession culminated with the burning of an effigy of the Pope beneath her statue at Temple Bar (donated to the City on the occasion of the opening of the Royal Exchange, as dramatized in *If you know not me*, part 2),[44] and for a similar, more elaborate demonstration on the same occasion the following year her likeness was 'adorn'd with a Crown of Laurel, and a Shield, on which was inscrib'd Protestant Religion and *Magna Charta*.' An immense procession including nine floats depicting the wickednesses of the Catholic Church culminated at Temple Bar, where, after the effigy of the Pope from the seventh float had been ritually burned (and a great deal of wine distributed to the crowd), the 'Protestant' on the last float, who had been bound at the stake 'for Reading the Scripture', was released. He immediately addressed a speech to Elizabeth's statue, beginning

> Behold the Genius of our Land!
> England's Palladium! may this Shrine
> Be honour'd still, and ever stand,
> Than Pallas' Statue more Divine.[45]

In between these two instances of street theatre, scripted by the Whig dramatist Elkanah Settle, Elizabeth had returned to the popular stage in the late summer of 1680, in one 'J.D.''s faithfully post-Heywood drama *The Coronation of Queen Elizabeth, With the Restauration of the Protestant Religion: or, the Downfal of the Pope. Being a most Excellent Play, As it was Acted, both at Bartholomew and Southwark Fairs, This present year 1680. With great Applause, and Approved of, and highly Commended by all the Protestant Nobility, Gentry and Commonalty of England, who came to be Spectators of the same* (London, 1680). In this rough, populist sketch, however, Elizabeth remains a figure rather than a character, as much an icon of herself as the Temple Bar statue. This play probably owes a good deal to the compressed version of *If You Know Not Me* which disappointed Pepys, and J.D. may even have read Dekker's *The Whore of Babylon*: in any event, the drama begins with Elizabeth, freshly crowned, banishing Rome's cardinals back to the Vatican and concludes, seemingly only minutes later, when the Pope, miraculously transported to England by 'the Devil in the habit of a Jesuit', is captured by the rabble celebrating Elizabeth's victory over the Armada, who obtain the Queen's permission to burn him, so long as they 'do it with discretion, without Riot or Tumult' (22). Elizabeth doesn't make any version of her Tilbury speech, but the play takes the point of her having the heart and stomach of a king regardless, albeit in comic mode: Tim, the tinker who leads the English mob (very much the character corresponding to Hobson in *If You Know Not Me*), refers to her as 'King *Elizabeth*' throughout. As in Heywood's second Elizabeth play, and as in the Accession Day pageants, the Queen herself displays no interiority, appearing only intermittently to perform ceremonial functions while the drama is filled up with other business (here, the Pope's nefarious dealings with the Devil and a nubile nun, and the rabble's patriotic stave-wielding brutality to any fellow citizens they can find still loyal to Bloody Mary's religion). Here as elsewhere, the Protestant tradition is little interested in representing Elizabeth as a woman, least of all a mortal, self-conscious or self-divided one: she is more frequently an honorary king, or a non-Papist saint, or a goddess, a figure for a unanimous national identification with the true Church.

The crown would in due course attempt to reappropriate this heroine and her iconography once more, once the reigning monarch was again unambiguously Protestant and female. Elizabeth would receive more officially sanctioned veneration from the later Stuarts, Mary and Anne, after their Catholic father James had been exiled, with their consent, in 1688. Their writers promoted her to heights undreamed of since the elegies composed immediately after her death, but they tend to leave her even more unrealized than does J.D.'s play. Both Mary II and Queen Anne were more than happy to be identified with their glorious predecessor as queen regnant; when Edmund Bohun published *The Character of Queen Elizabeth* in 1693, for example, he supplied it with a frontispiece placing portraits of Elizabeth and Mary side by side under the same heraldry, labelled 'ELIZABETH & MARY *Queens of England*'. The happy coincidence that the Glorious Revolution took place exactly a century after the defeat of the Armada was seized upon by many writers equally keen to depict William and Mary as the vindicators of Elizabeth's vision of the Reformation. Queen Anne, in her turn, sought to appropriate both her elder sister and her Tudor precursor, adopting Elizabeth's preferred motto, 'Semper Eadem', modelling the robes in which she appeared before her first Parliament on one of Elizabeth's official portraits,[46] and duly receiving blessings from both Mary and Elizabeth in the loyal Edmund Arwaker's poem *An Embassy from Heaven, or, The Ghost of Queen Mary* in 1704. Here Mary descends from Elysium to pass on her congratulations on her younger sister's recent victories in the Wars of Spanish Succession, events which she, moreover, has not been watching alone:

> The Blest *ELIZABETH* Her Skies forsook,
> To praise great *Ormond*, and encourage *Rook*;
> With *Drake* and *Rawleigh*, She beheld the Seas,
> And Troops of Her Old Worthies wond'ring gaze
> To see a *Spanish*, and a *French Armado* blaze.

Elizabeth embarks alone on a similar errand in the pamphlet *Queen ELIZABETHS Ghost: or A Dream* ('By Paleophilus Anglicanus', 1706), where in a frank interview she confers the sort of condescending approbation on her chosen successor that Mrs Thatcher used to offer to William Hague, though expressed with a surprising modesty:

I fancied *Queen Elizabeth* (to whose Memory I always bore a profound Respect) Appeared to me, and talked to me very freely about our present Affairs. She had an Awfulness however in her Countenance, but that seemed to go off whenever our Queen was named. She told me, She was mightily pleased, that Her Motto, *Semper Eadem*, was taken up in this Reign, and that Queen *Anne* was Her Daughter of Fame . . . She said, the Battels in Her Reign . . . compared with those of Queen *Anne*, make but a Poor Figure.[47]

Dr King's poem 'Britain's Palladium; OR, My Lord Bolingbroke's Welcome from France' makes the same point. 'Whatever in *Eliza*'s Reign was seen, | With a re-doubled Vigour springs again', it promises: 'Imperial *ANNA* shall the Seas controul, | And spread her Naval Laws from Pole to Pole.'

This adoption of Elizabeth as at very least the presiding ghost behind Anne's successes reaches its apogee in a poem by the Queen's own physician, Sir Richard Blackmore. The most elevated of all accounts of the Tilbury rally, Blackmore's full-scale epic poem *Eliza* (1705) outsoars even Dekker's *The Whore of Babylon* in its depiction of 1588 as a climactic date in the calendar of England's Protestant destiny. Although it is written in heroic couplets, the poem aims at the diction of Milton's *Paradise Lost* and even presents itself as its sequel: Philip II's dreams of Catholic world domination are represented as Satan's first really big initiative since he managed to tempt Adam and Eve, but this time he will be defeated. Elizabeth is rewarded for her heroic loyalty to the true religion not with a mere ringside seat at the Armada's sinking, courtesy of Truth, but with a guided tour of Heaven conducted by the Virgin Mary herself—so that the First and Second Maids can establish the cosy familiarity they will enjoy after Elizabeth's death. Needless to say, the Queen is also delighted to be granted a prophecy of the still greater victories that will be won in the future by her daughter of fame, Anne. In *Eliza*, in fact, the first and only literary text explicitly to promote Gloriana to the status of an eponymous epic heroine, Queen Elizabeth gets everything except a self: massively elaborate and baroque as the poem is, fully equipped with historical insets and eschato

---

prophecies, it is completely uninterested in what elsewhere was beginning to preoccupy the Queen's chroniclers, namely her subjectivity. Blackmore's Eliza, like Heywood's, is in the end only interested in her place in official Protestant history, content to be enshrined in her nation's annals as something altogether emblematic and statuesque. From being revived as a facsimile of herself in her own dresses, the Protestant Gloriana was by 1700 beginning to recede into a figure in an ancestral portrait, her representations growing ever more inert.

It is only appropriate that a generation later, during the wave of anti-Spanish feeling and renewed Elizabethan nostalgia which preceded the War of Jenkins's Ear in the 1730s, quarrels about which political faction best represented the true Elizabethan tradition should have revolved no less around literary or dramatic representations of the Queen than around two rival statues. These were Rysbrack's bust of a thoroughly Dekkerian Elizabeth enshrined in Lord Cobham's 'Patriot' monument the Temple of British Worthies at Stowe (Fig. 6), and the likeness of Elizabeth included in Queen Caroline's Spenserian grotto, the Cave of Merlin at Richmond.[48] Just as elsewhere in this decade Elizabeth might practically vanish into abstraction, as the monarch who in a mysterious way 'ruled by the love of her people' held up as a bloodless ideal in Bolingbroke's *The Idea of a Patriot King* (written in 1738, though not published until 1749), or might seem condemned endlessly to repeat the tropes in which she had featured in the pamphlet controversies of the previous century (as in *The Merchant's Complaint against Spain*, 1738, in which Elizabeth is still being used as a rod with which to lash James I in 'A Dialogue between King Henry 8, King Edward 6, Prince Henry, Queen Mary, Queen Elizabeth and Queen Anne [of Denmark, James's queen]'),[49] here, in the controversy over these rival statues, Elizabeth is a costumed figure only residually dramatic. Cobham's statue sees her as a Britomart, clad at once in the ruff that had become her personal signature and in the breastplate with which Heywood, Dekker, and the engraver Cecil had equipped her at Tilbury (an apocryphal costume that was the focus of such national desire that by the 1770s it could allegedly be viewed, for a small fee, at the Tower of London).[50] Queen Caroline, however, has Elizabeth wearing a less militant and more time-bound

Fig. 6. Elizabeth's status as a key member of the newly invented Britain's national pantheon was ratified in the 1730s, when William Kent designed the Temple of British Worthies at Stowe for the 'Patriot' statesman Lord Cobham. The only female member of this distinguished club, she occupies a niche between Edward the Black Prince and William of Orange. Her glorious reign is further represented by Raleigh, Drake, Shakespeare, Bacon, and Sir Thomas Gresham, so that six Worthies out of the total sixteen are Elizabethans. Michael Rysbrack's stern bust, representing Elizabeth as the Protestant heroine of 1588, gives her the ruff of a weak and feeble woman, but the breastplate of a king.

farthingale, associated less with the military side of Britomart than with the dynastic future prophesied for her by Merlin, and less with 1588 than with the Golden Speech. The meanings of these two statues were thoroughly debated in contemporary periodicals, but the discussion remained oddly theoretical: the rise of costume drama may have helped enshrine Elizabeth in the national pantheon as an intensely desired figure for the lost unity of the English Church and the English nation, but as a genre it risked relegating her to the status of an immobile waxwork.

Furthermore, by the 1730s the very femininity which had enabled Elizabeth to be promoted as her country's emblematic Protestant maiden was beginning to be understood as a potentially dangerous or disruptive excess to that status—as is intriguingly demonstrated by another 1730s controversy about a statue of Elizabeth. In 'Queen Elizabeths Ghost, or the humble remonstrance of all the Free-Women of the City of Bristol, shewing why a late order of Council for erecting an Equestrian Statue to the Glorious Memory of his Majesty William the 3rd should for sometime at least be laid aside' (Bodleian Library MS Eng poet e e 45, 16–21), this (imagined?) female pressure group first makes a serious, reasoned argument as to why Elizabeth, heroine of 1588, should be commemorated before the hero of 1688. This third-person poem, however, then gives place when Elizabeth herself steps down from the portrait in the council chamber to harangue the city's governors for their ingratitude in not erecting a statue to her long since, given her generosity to Bristol and her loyal support of its trade against Spain. So far all is zealous earnestness, but the poem ends in flippant, mock-heroic bathos when Elizabeth, in just as grave a tone of voice, begins to display a stereotypical, if fierce, female vanity, appointing named councillors to superintend different details of her statue. One is to take responsibility for her hairstyle, one for her farthingale, one for her whalebone corset, and so on. In the eighteenth century, clearly, it was no longer possible to imagine Elizabeth as a venerated costume-drama statue or epic heroine without also imagining her as a woman preoccupied unbecomingly with her wardrobe, and the two did not necessarily go comfortably together. It is with the drama involved in trying to reconcile the idealized national goddess with contemporary ideas about naked personal femininity that our next chapter will be concerned.

Epilogue

Before turning to such dramatizations of the more womanly Elizabeth imagined as occupying the costumes by which her immediate successors had remembered her, however, we would like to consider one instance of the survival of the Protestant tradition we have just outlined—albeit a rather vitiated one. Some, at least, of the tropes which the Jacobean history play mobilized in rehabilitating Elizabeth's reputation survived for reuse within living memory. A key fragment of one such costume drama returned to celebrate another heir to the English throne and future head of the Anglican Church as recently as the late 1940s, in what now seems a doubly poignant way. The occasion was a Renaissance court entertainment—but a simulated, pastiche one, its incidental feasting inhibited by food rationing: *The Masque of Hope. Presented for the Entertainment of HRH Princess Elizabeth on the occasion of her visit to University College, 25 May 1948 by OXFORD UNIVERSITY DRAMATIC SOCIETY.* The script, written by two academics, Nevill Coghill and Glynne Wickham, is every bit as gleefully allegorical and apocalyptic as Dekker's *The Whore of Babylon.* The masque's action depicts the combat for post-war England's soul between Hope and Fear—the latter appropriately played by the young Kenneth Tynan. Their conflict is settled in Hope's favour by the intervention of Hymen (it was, after all, only six months since Elizabeth's marriage to the naval officer Prince Philip),[51] who after celebrating the topical Spenserian nuptials of Venus and Neptune, calls upon Clio, the Muse of History, to clinch the argument. She does so by invoking that old standby, Elizabethan nostalgia, as she gestures towards an idealized Elizabethan future imagined in terms of an idealized Elizabethan past:

> CLIO. The Future lies before, unknown and vast;
>   I cannot read the Future, but the Past;
>   Be but our Islanders as they have been
>   No FEAR shall triumph over King or Queen!
>   Yet *Poets* can prove Prophets, and their tongue
>   How old soever, rings out fresh and young.
>   SHAKESPEARE, who saw the Future in its forge,
>   Has prophesied; he has a word to say;
>   And who speak better for him than SAINT GEORGE
>   For gentle Shakespeare, born on George's Day?
> *To the sound of trumpets SAINT GEORGE rides forth before the Map-of-England Curtains on a white horse in full armour with sword drawn. At sight of whom,*

*FEAR and his Crew with a howl of baffled rage flee into their Hell-Mouth and
vanish.*

SAINT GEORGE.   Let me speak, sirs,
For Heaven now bids me; and the words I utter
Let none think flattery, for they'll find 'em truth.
This Royal Lady—Heaven still move about her!—
Though in her girlhood, yet now promises
Upon this land a thousand thousand blessings
Which time shall bring to ripeness: she shall be—
But few now living can behold that goodness—
A pattern to all princes living with her,
And all that shall succeed . . .[52]

And so the Saint continued to the end of the speech, at which a flock of
doves were released and all the bells in Oxford rang, and the Royal Lady
herself could get on with the task of making adequately grateful small
talk to the Principal about the entire production. It's a historical moment
which seems nearly as distant now as that dramatized by Shakespeare
and Fletcher in 1613: indeed Past Times has already begun selling video-
tapes of the 1953 coronation alongside such longer-established historical artefacts as the Elizabeth I perfumed lavender drawer sachet. The
Jacobean plays we have described, Shakespeare and Fletcher's among
them, were able to invent Elizabethan nostalgia out of the need to repair
the late queen's image because Elizabeth I had died just as her own royal
iconography was beginning to unravel. Elizabeth II hasn't been so lucky.
It's perhaps a little sobering to be looking back now towards that May
afternoon of costume drama in 1948, just as Shakespeare and Fletcher's
audience in 1613 had been invited to look back towards a christening in
1533, and to be reflecting on all that might be remembered or forgotten of
our own Elizabethan era.

2

The Private Lives
of the Virgin Queen

Scandal

If one thing distinguishes the eighteenth century's many versions of Elizabeth from the uninflected Protestant nostalgia that characterized much of her mythos in the seventeenth, it is a growing consciousness that her status as a national idol might be at variance with her personal identity as a woman—as we have just seen in the instance of Bristol's imaginary statue of her, at once epic heroine and fussily fashion-conscious spinster. It was still possible in 1661 simply to declare Elizabeth an honorary man—according to Edward Leigh she was 'a Prince above her sexe of a manly courage and high conceit,' and 'besides her sexe, there was nothing woman-like or weak.'[1] But by 1738 Henry St John Bolingbroke, though just as keen to hold up Elizabeth's reign as a political ideal, felt obliged to acknowledge that the Queen was definitely female, however triumphantly she overcame this disadvantage:

Tho a woman, she hid all that was womanish about her: and if a few equivocal marks of coquetry appeared on some occasions, they passed like flashes of lightning, vanished as soon as they were discerned, and imprinted no blot on her character.[2]

It is this perceived discrepancy between womanhood and political authority which preoccupies eighteenth-century accounts of Elizabeth, and which would inspire a whole new repertoire of stories about her between the late Restoration and the accession of Victoria. In a period urgently concerned with national identity in the public sphere and with the personal feelings of women in the private—the period during which the 1707 Act of Union invented Britain, and the sentimental novel invented a new kind of vulnerable heroine—Elizabeth remained an irresistible subject for writers of all kinds, but the memory of her queenly power was felt to pose a problem as much as an opportunity for proponents of the new nationhood and the new womanhood alike.[3] While her reign could still be celebrated as a golden age of religious, military, commercial, and civic advancement, as it is in the relevant volume of David Hume's *History of Great Britain* (1759), and she herself could still be officially remembered as a maternal Britannia—'Mother of her country, a nursing mother to religion and all liberal sciences', in the much-cited English translation of her Latin epitaph[4]—such invocations were inclined to avoid looking too closely at Elizabeth herself. Perhaps the one exception to this general rule is the figuration of Elizabeth as learned lady and thus as role model to (some) women—a tradition that animates Bathsua Makin's *An Essay to Revive the Antient Education of Gentlewomen* (1673) and which still informs George Ballard's *Memoirs of Several Ladies of Great Britain* in 1752.[5] But on the whole, throughout this age of naval warfare and repeated invasion scares, it was the heroine of 1588 who remained a dominant figuration—hence, for example, the reprinting of her Tilbury oration in the *Public Advertiser* of 17 September 1779, and Benjamin West's 1794 painting of *Queen Elizabeth going in procession to St. Paul's Cathedral after the destruction of the Spanish Armada.* Yet she herself, rather like the unseen Gloriana who gives her title to Spenser's *The Faerie Queene* without ever appearing in the poem's action, is often pushed to the margins of such texts. When Thomas Arne, the composer who had produced the newly united Britain's *de facto* National Anthem by setting James Thomson's 'Rule, Britannia' to music, set out a patriotic opera in 1754, he naturally chose the defeat of the as his subject, but less predictably his *Eliza* never actually brings

Elizabeth on to the stage (which is instead filled, at the opera's climax, with model ships). This manner of dealing with Elizabeth is both parodied and explicated by Mr Puff's patriotic tragedy 'The Spanish Armada', as hilariously rehearsed in Sheridan's comedy, produced at the height of the fashion for sensibility, *The Critic, or, a Tragedy Rehearsed* (1779). Like Arne, Puff assiduously keeps his queen offstage, though 'she is to be talked of for ever; so that egad you'll think a hundred times that she is on the point of coming in'.[6] Both Arne and Sheridan, like Heywood in *If you know not me, you know nobody*, part 2, before them, tacitly admit that the Armada icon, symbol of the virgin impregnability of the nation, lacks dramatic and narrative interest for contemporaries. No wonder perhaps that, attending the rehearsal together with Mr Sneer, Mr Dangle expresses anxiety as to whether Puff has been able to introduce adequate love interest to enliven his military and nationalist theme. Puff's reply perfectly exemplifies the ways in which romance might in this respect supplement the historical record, while Sneer's response expresses a well-grounded anxiety that this literary strategy might contaminate Elizabeth's reputation as a national icon:

> PUFF. Love!—Oh nothing so easy; for it is a received point among poets, that where history gives you a good heroic out-line for a play, you may fill up with a little love at your own discretion; in doing which, nine times out of ten, you only make up a deficiency in the private history of the times.— Now I rather think I have done this with some success.
>
> SNEER. No scandal about Queen ELIZABETH, I hope?
>
> PUFF. O Lud! no, no.[7]

The writers and artists that we deal with in this chapter are precisely those who fill up the 'heroic outline' of history with 'a little love', so remotivating it. And it would be this potential 'scandal' briefly alluded to by Sheridan, hastily and genteelly dismissed by the ambitious and delicate Puff, that provided the raw materials to make up what the eighteenth century had come to perceive as a 'deficiency in the private history of the times'.

The laugh that Sneer's line certainly got (and was still getting well into the 1840s)[8] was sparked by a constellation of anecdotal materials—

largely apocryphal, and often of thoroughly disreputable provenance—circulating in popular culture, some of them, as we will see, assiduously promoted in much less frivolous specimens of drama about the Virgin Queen. As the anonymous author of *Queen Elizabeths Ghost* (1706) remarked, 'scandal' was always liable to supplement glorious memory in more decadent times: 'Queen *Elizabeth's* Memory would be always Glorious among *Englishmen*: That in Good Reigns Her Majesty's Memory had a more universal Respect, tho' perhaps not altogether so warm as in Bad; for then Scandal Writers, and others in Conversation, were apt to make their court by Traducing Queen *Elizabeth*'.⁹ Most of these 'scandals' speculated upon the Queen's love-life or lack of it, in the tradition of the political pamphlet *Leycesters Commonwealth* (1584). Such scandals included, at one extreme, a story of a child or children, legitimate or illegitimate, usually fathered by the Earl of Leicester (a story which had originally been fostered, in particular, by the Spanish court in the 1580s, which harboured at least two men claiming to be such children), and at the other the story that Elizabeth owed her chastity to being physically 'uncapable of man' (imparted, for example, by a tipsy Ben Jonson to William Drummond of Hawthornden in 1619, as we have already remarked).¹⁰ In between these extremes, most importantly for English drama and fiction, fell a range of different accounts of Elizabeth's relationship with her last favourite, the Earl of Essex. It was from this scanty and conflicting fund of inherited anecdote (often transmitted through seventeenth-century Continental writers, such as Gregorio Leti), grafted on to a body of Elizabethan artistic and literary representations of the Queen that were fast vanishing into the unreadably archaic, that the Enlightenment gradually evolved a repertoire of plots within which to position Elizabeth, incarnated across a range of texts and artefacts from the most intellectually disreputable to those claiming the status of literary classics or even official history. In these plots Elizabeth was newly supplied with appropriate, if frustrated, feminine sentiments to animate the stiff and baffling court dress of official history. Thus Pierre Bayle's *Historical and Critical Dictionary* (1710) supplements a pretty orthodox account of Elizabeth's reign with lengthy ever-encroaching footnotes brimming with speculative and salacious material designed at once to represent Elizabeth as tremblingly susceptible to feminine passion and to explain (what otherwise becomes inexplicable) her games of political *coitus interruptus*:

it is certain, she had no *Vulva*, and the same Reason, which hindered her from marrying, ought also to hinder her loving coition. She might love, and in truth she did passionately love . . . , but such was the make of her body, that she could not be sexually known of any Man without suffering excessive Pains: nor become big with Child, without exposing herself inevitably to lose her life in the birth of the Child.[11]

For the French historians that Bayle is here drawing upon, passion, however thwarted, is what qualifies Elizabeth as a woman, and as a potential heroine, however disappointingly chaste, of the proto-novels known as 'secret histories' produced very successfully by Marie d'Aulnoy and others for Restoration high society. *Leycesters Commonwealth* was itself cannily repackaged in 1706 as *Secret Memoirs of Robert Dudley, earl of Leicester, prime minister and favourite of Queen Elizabeth* to capitalize on this fashion for pastiche court memoirs spiced up with plenty of sexual misdemeanour in high places. As the eighteenth century wore on in Britain, the Queen had increasingly to be made plausible within the contemporary literary genres that above all others constructed the new affective femininity—'she-tragedy', a style of play organized around the sufferings of a female protagonist (most famously exemplified by Thomas Otway's *The Orphan*, 1680, Nicholas Rowe's *The Fair Penitent*, 1703, and *Jane Shore*, 1714), and its prose successor, the sentimental novel, as pioneered by Samuel Richardson.[12] These genres centrally depict the heroine of sensibility—a figure in attractive disarray, victimized by her own emotions and by the heartlessness of the world, and ultimately forced to capitulate to the intransigent plotting of sentimental narrative, whereby she is, in as distressing a fashion as possible, violated.

A Princess in Captivity

The cultural pressure to develop an acceptable and recognizable female interiority for Elizabeth along these lines is demonstrated early in this period by a series of texts which bypass her powerful role in maturity to concentrate exclusively on her youth, representing her as the exemplary victim of her elder sister Mary's hatred. In the same line as Thomas Heywood's *If You Know Not Me, You Know Nobody*, part 1, and *England's Elizabeth*, these later texts are none the less profoundly different in their shift of interest from Elizabeth's destined Protestant sainthood to her personal suffering, restating her religious and political near-martyrdom as sentimental persecution. This change is already visible in Pepys's response to the rewritten version of Heywood's play which he saw in 1667, a show which he seems to have regarded primarily as a weepie with some secondary historical interest, and this assimilation of the Queen to an increasingly dominant view of womanhood as affecting victimhood is further exemplified by *The Ladies Dictionary; being a general entertainment for the fair-sex* (1694), which heads its whole entry on the subject 'Elizabeth, Queen of England, her sufferings'.[13]

Still, even by concentrating on the figure of the captive princess it was undoubtedly difficult to produce Elizabeth as a heroine of sensibility, because as far as the core of her legend went she was embarrassingly—unlike her more suitably unfortunate historical colleagues and relatives (notably Jane Shore, Ann Boleyn, Lady Jane Grey, and Katherine Grey)[14]—not a victim, but a survivor. (The consequent lack of story attaching to Elizabeth is evidenced by the misleadingly entitled *The Novels of Elizabeth Queen of England* (1680) by Marie d'Aulnoy, most of which in fact concentrates on Anne Boleyn's virtuous passion for Henry Percy, thwarted at every turn by evil court machinations, until these at length bring her an innocent victim to the block.) This problem with the Elizabeth-as-vulnerable-princess ploy is neatly illustrated by the performance and publication history of the anonymous play *Courtenay, Earl of Devonshire; or, The Troubles of the Princess Elizabeth. A Tragedy* (London, 1690), which adopts Mr Puff's suggestion of adding romantic interest to received history, dramatizing the young Princess Elizabeth's supposed love affair with a man with whom her name was linked during Wyatt's rebellion. This tale of star-crossed lovers, in which the infatuated Courtenay unwisely turns down a proposal from his old flame Bloody Mary, incurring such jealousy and wrath by his 'rebel passion' for

Elizabeth that his political rebellion is almost irrelevant to his near-execution, was turned down by the playhouses and never performed.[15] The author's aggrieved and indignant preface is remarkably, if inadvertently, illuminating on the problems of producing a national icon and a conventional heroine rolled into one: apparently the play was rejected on two counts, the first because (despite the judicious supplementary inscrtion of the execution of Lady Jane Grey) there was not enough 'Distress' to the story (even this oppressed juvenile Eliza, being the destined Gloriana of England, cannot generate sufficient pathos), the other because the managers, anticipating Mr Sneer's aversion to scandal, 'do not approve that Queen *Elizabeth* is made a young amorous Lady, and that in a time when such warm thoughts were never imputed to her by that Age nor any since'.[16] Even a fledgling Virgin Queen, apparently, could not be comfortably assimilated within a conventional she-tragedy, inescapably invested in her potential penetrability.

Elizabeth does occasionally reappear as a sympathetic captive princess into the eighteenth and nineteenth centuries, though her youthful imprisonments would not reappear as a key motif until the appearance of Margaret Irwin's *Young Bess* (1944). An illustration appended in 1789 to William Shenstone's poem 'The Princess Elizabeth', for example (drafted in 1754, but revised and first published a decade later), represents Elizabeth imprisoned at Woodstock as a distant but recognizable forebear of Richardson's Pamela (Fig. 7). For all her vestigial ruff and Tudor roses, her style of femininity is strikingly modernized; it is secured both by her vaguely gothic imprisonment (mildly reminiscent of Ann Radcliffe's window-gazing Emily St Aubert in *The Mysteries of Udolpho*, 1794) and by her wistful (if fleeting and almost certainly apocryphal) wish to be as free as the milkmaid in the background to love and be loved. (This is the very episode, originally taken from Foxe, which had been developed so congenially into a touching song-and-dance routine in the rewritten 1667 version of Heywood's *If You Know Not Me* seen by Pepys.) For one brief and presumably comforting moment, Queen Elizabeth can be captured 'each ambitious thought resigning' and indulging a charmingly implausible pastoral fantasy:

S. Shelley pinx!   *C. Taylor sculp!*

QUEEN ELIZABETH.

————————— *captive lay.*

Each ambitious thought resigning —

London, Publish'd July 1, 1789 by C. Taylor N.º 10 near Castle Street, Holborn.

FIG. 7. An illustration (by one S. Shelley) to William Shenstone's 'The Princess Elizabeth. A Ballad' (1764), published when the poem appeared (as 'The Complaint of the Princess Elizabeth') in the anthology *The Cabinet of Genius* (1787–90). This pastoralized Princess Elizabeth, imprisoned at Woodstock, envies the passing milkmaid her freedom to love and to be loved: the princess has been transformed from the Protestant near-martyr represented in Foxe's original sixteenth-century version of this apocryphal incident into a victimized eighteenth-century sentimental heroine before her time.

'Would indulgent Heav'n had granted
    Me some rural damsel's part!
All the empire I had wanted
    Then had been my shepherd's heart.

·   ·   ·   ·   ·   ·

Rustics had been more forgiving;
    Partial to my virgin bloom:
None had envy'd me when living;
    None had triumph'd o'er my tomb.'[17]

So powerful was this desire to pastoralize the future queen that it was around this time that an undeniably eighteenth-century straw hat came to be exhibited at Hatfield House as Elizabeth's preferred gardening wear. The manuscript version of the poem, however, betrays what had to be excised to maintain Elizabeth as mere heroine of sensibility under any such attractive 'rushy Bonnet':

Better far the rushy Bonnet
    Than a Crown, well understood;
While perhaps there blushes on it
    Some unhappy Rival's Blood![18]

Only axing this stanza can preserve the princess from the guilt of successfully wielding power—in this case, of course, against the Queen of Scots (of whom more later).

Similarly sentimentalized depictions of a perforce domesticated Elizabeth in captivity turned up as late as the 1830s, as in the curious picture of Elizabeth imprisoned at Woodstock as a fully-fledged Victorian Jane Eyre by J. Graham, and in William Harrison Ainsworth's popular classic *The Tower of London: A Historical Romance* (1840). On the whole the subject of the imprisoned princess proved more congenial to Americans, who regularly chose, in the context of the enormous popularity of pictures of the misfortunes of Lady Jane Grey and Mary, Queen of Scots, to try to make their careers as history-painters with this subject.[19] (Perhaps Elizabeth was more saleable as victim in a country less closely engaged with the deaths of other queens, and less sure at the time of its imperial might, though seeing itself through a lens of Protestant destiny.)[20] Possibly the most mendacious and revealing of these exercises in stripping Elizabeth of power was performed by Tom Taylor's play *'Twixt Axe and Crown* (1870), which, by ingeniously postponing Courtenay's execution to the moment of Mary's death, lets Elizabeth off having to express triumph, and brilliantly argues that the Queen's future success as national monument is to be understood in terms of the purest pathos:

> Dead! he is dead? There is too much death! One death gives me a crown—another robs me of my love! of all that made the crown a treasure! to be shared with him, but nothing, Courtenay being gone! What now remains for me?[21]

This ploy would eventually be revived in the 1940s and 1950s, as we will see, when Irwin's *Young Bess* and its film adaptation would represent the newly crowned Elizabeth as forever grieving for the lost Admiral Seymour, a tragically disappointed would-be wife instead of a triumphantly successful Virgin Queen.

The Queen in Love

Eighteenth-century anxieties about producing Elizabeth as both an eligibly grief-stricken heroine of sensibility and at the same time a more-than-adequate sovereign precipitated a completely new plot-structure which, in various mutations, and in multiple tonal variations, was destined to haunt plays, novels, and history books alike. Within this plot-structure the Queen is consistently represented as being torn by conflicting impulses, caught between her personal feminine sentiments and her role in (or as) the state, divided against herself and therefore not in full possession of, or fully identified with, her public political power. She can thus appear as the victim, for all her historical victories, of the secret and agonizing strife between her passions and her position.[22] This struggle comes to crisis most characteristically at those moments when Elizabeth is represented, as she is here by Henry Jones in 1753, signing death-warrants, an act particularly offensive to contemporary ideas of what constituted proper womanly behaviour:

[ELIZABETH]. Let me all the Monarch reassume!
   Exert my Power, and be myself again!—
   O ill-performing disobedient Heart!—
   Why shrink'st thou fearful from thy own resolve?[23]

There were, in fact, only two death-warrants that counted: that of Elizabeth's last favourite, the vaultingly ambitious Robert Devereux, Earl of Essex, and that of Mary, Queen of Scots, Elizabeth's cousin and rival claimant to the English throne. Both executions form the nucleus for stories that remain potent to this day, stories that derive most of their power from the way that Elizabeth's femininity and her state-sanctioned power mutually compromise each other.[24]

The *locus classicus* for the representation of the self-divided Queen is the persistent and largely apocryphal anecdote appended to the execution of the Earl of Essex on 25 February 1601. The story appears to derive initially from Essex's refusal to sue for pardon after sentence was passed, despite the urgings of his friends, and his hopes of pardon notwithstanding.[25] The apocrypha, however, holds that Essex *did* sue for mercy, but that his message was never received by the Queen due to treachery. This suggestion first appears as an allusion in John Webster's *The Devil's Law-case* (1623),[26] and was then taken up by La Calprenede in his play *Le Comte d'Essex* (1639), the first version to involve the ring which ultimately becomes the central prop in this legend.[27] Although rejected by the historian Clarendon in his *Difference between Buckingham and Essex* (*c.*1641), it featured with variations in a number of seventeenth-century memoirs, notably Francis Osborne's 'Traditional Memoires on the Raigne of Queen Elizabeth' (1658) and Louis Aubery's *Memoires pour servir a l'histoire de Hollande et des autres Provinces Unies* (1680, 1688). It was first worked up as an independent prose narrative in the influential *The Secret History of the most renowned Q. Elizabeth and the E. of Essex* (French version 1678, translated into English in 1680), which was thereafter widely reprinted and rehashed throughout the next century.[28] Constructed as a set of first-person confessions (including one attributed to Elizabeth herself) in which women tell their love-secrets to confidants, and in which the cross-currents, misunderstandings, and intrigues of the court are amply displayed, *The Secret History*'s story and its affect formed the basis for John Banks's immensely successful play *The Unhappy Favourite: or, the Earl of Essex* (1681), the first late Restoration she-tragedy to combine pathos with costume drama. Such was this play's impact, and such the compelling sense made by its plot, that at least three eighteenth-century plays sought to rework and update it, including James Ralph's *The Fall of the Earl of Essex* (1731), Henry Jones's *The Earl of Essex* (1753), and Henry Brooke's *Earl of Essex* (1761). Although this story has some basis in historical fact (it seems to be true, for example, that when Essex did burst into the Queen's bedchamber she did use him 'kindly' at first, before having him put under house-arrest), its flagrant fictionality in other respects—the provision of a secret wife in the person of the Countess of Rutland to replace his real spouse Frances Walsingham, widow of Sidney; the unwarranted claim that the Countess of Nottingham was a spurned ex-mistress; and the frequent strategic 'forgetting' of the Essex Rebellion—solicits attention. What needs within the culture did this 'secret history' meet?

As the frontispiece to *The Secret History* suggests (Fig. 8), the emphasis here is on a private, feeling, and physical Elizabeth divorced from her crown—which instead of being on her head surmounts the title panel above her, without which we would never know this was a likeness of a queen, let alone of Elizabeth, at all. (This is indeed the perfect image of how this genre likes to think history is really lived: as well as being without the crown, Elizabeth has no ruff or breastplate to mark her out as anything other than an emotionally excited woman in tête-à-tête with a generically heroic male, overseen for the benefit of posterity by a shadowy eavesdropper. The attractive suggestion that we as readers occupy the illicit and exciting position of this eavesdropper is underscored by the titillating but fraudulent suggestion that the book itself is contraband, smuggled in from 'Cologne'.) *The Secret History* gives us an Elizabeth who, according to her own account, interspersed with sighs and tears, was secretly in love with Essex, and was only manipulated into having him executed for high treason. As the attractively titled novella 'The Earl of Essex: or, The Amours of Queen Elizabeth' contained in *The Secret History* puts it:

Fig. 8. The frontispiece and title-page to *The Secret History of the most renowned Queen Elizabeth and the Earl of Essex* (1680). This much-reprinted little book saw the salacious and dramatic rumours about Elizabeth's dealings with her last favourite which had been propagated by French *memoirs secretes* throughout the earlier seventeenth century translated into English and imported into England— though not, as the spurious imprint claims, via Cologne. As this aspiration to the status of illicit goods implies, the book offers the underside of triumphal national history, purporting to show the real, female motives of an Elizabeth entirely distinct from her crown (as in the frontispiece, where it surmounts the title panel instead of being on her head).

She was highly Renowned above the Women of her time, for Courage, and Strength of Mind; yet too Weak to be Proof against the Impressions of Love. She had a passionate Tenderness for the unfortunate Criminal, which was his Advocate . . . and was so far from taking pleasure in a publick Revenge of him, that she abhorred in her Heart those cruel Maxims that crost her Inclinations.[29]

This amorous reading of the last phase of Essex's career—presenting his abrupt rises and falls in political favour, box on the ear in the council chamber and all, as the outward symptoms of what was really a volatile secret liaison—would find the historical incident in which Essex hurried back to court from Ireland in order to explain himself personally to the Queen, bursting into her private chamber, especially congenial. This episode becomes a central scene in Banks's *The Unhappy Favourite* and its descendants, and it's easy to see why. Undressed, the Queen turns out to be a woman—in fact, a modern woman. Robert Smirke, for example, illustrated the emblematic scene of Essex's irruption in precisely the manner pioneered on the stage, in an engraving published more than a hundred years later, in 1806 (Fig. 9). Smirke's Elizabeth is recognizable as royal only by the ermine trimming of her negligée: the stress is on representing this voluptuous, flowing-tressed figure as sympathetic, responsive, melting, everything a tender sensibility could wish for in a woman. Secretly nubile and vulnerable, this Elizabeth is suggestively surrounded by a discarded slipper and the framing, parted labile curtains; this image demands an erotic response from the viewer as powerful as the Earl's is presumed to be. It is only later in the public council chamber, when she has reassumed the Queen with her state clothes and her crown, that, under pressure from her ministers (in particular the unscrupulous Robert Cecil), she summons up the full rigours of state power and has Essex arrested. (Different dramatizations are more and less scrupulous about distinguishing this incident from Essex's subsequent full-scale rebellion, which they are usually inclined to suppress.) In the Tower, Essex begs for his life by attempting to send Elizabeth a ring which she had earlier given him, together with a promise that she would grant any request that it should accompany. That earlier apocryphal moment of intimacy, again central to these secret histories and

FIG. 9. Robert Smirke, *Interview between Queen Elizabeth and the Earl of Essex.*
Smirke's eroticized version of Essex's unscheduled irruption into the Queen's private
chamber was originally published as an engraving in 1806. Illustrating the incident as
dramatized by sentimental playwrights such as John Banks and Henry Jones, Smirke
shows Elizabeth, once caught in private without the trappings of monarchy, as the very
image of melting womanhood. When the picture reappeared in an early Victorian
women's magazine, however, Elizabeth's implacable, official authority was partly
restored: this voluptuous vignette is contained within a border, surmounted by the
crown that is so noticeably absent from the picture itself, and two new panels are added
at the lower corners in which the public Elizabeth boxes Essex's ears and signs his
death-warrant.

plays alike, provides the frontispiece to Elizabeth Inchbald's 1807 edition of Henry Jones's *The Earl of Essex* in her *British Theatre* series (Fig. 10), and as this image and its caption make clear it is presented as something very like a clandestine betrothal. But the incarcerated ex-favourite makes the mistake of choosing a cast-off lover, the jealous and vengeful Countess of Nottingham, as his messenger, and she does not deliver it to the Queen, sometimes passing it instead to her jealous husband, sometimes simply concealing it. Meanwhile, Elizabeth is upset by the news that Essex has secretly married the young, lovely, and entirely fictitious Countess of Rutland, which the Countess betrays while pleading rather counter-productively for her husband's life. (In some later treatments of the story Rutland is pregnant for good measure, and runs into eroticized madness on Essex's death.) The confrontation between this tearful subject and the outraged Queen is depicted in Fig. 11, a theatrical print from the 1790s dramatizing the rivalry between Miss Brunton and the greatest of all eighteenth-century tragedy queens, Sarah Siddons:[30] unfortunately for Rutland, during this interview too Elizabeth is wearing the crown and has returned to her role as implacable embodiment of state power. After much unhappy vacillation in soliloquy, Elizabeth signs Essex's death-warrant soon afterwards. It is only after the Earl has been executed that Elizabeth learns, from a repentant Nottingham, that he had tried to send the ring to his queen; on hearing this, she delivers the immortal apocryphal line 'God may pardon thee, but I never can' (reported in Hume's *History of Great Britain* in the 1750s), and is plunged into a remorseful decline, from which, we are assured, she will never recover. So important is this account of the Queen's death in securing her sentimental femininity that throughout the eighteenth century the two years that really elapsed between the execution and her deathbed were usually collapsed, explicitly or implicitly, into a much shorter period; as Nathaniel Crouch put it in 1695: 'To conclude, her happiness and her power both seemed to lie buried in the Tomb of Essex, whose absence with continued sighs and tears she bemoaned for some four months, and then was likewise laid in her grave.'[31] By 1761, Henry Brooke was despatching her even more quickly, his Elizabeth announcing almost immediately after Essex's death:

EARL OF ESSEX

QUEEN ———— TWIXT YOU AND ME
THIS RING SHALL BE A PRIVATE MARK OF FAITH.
ACT IV.   SCENE I.

PAINTED BY HOWARD   PUBLISHED BY LONGMAN & C⁰   ENGRAVED BY J. FYE

FIG. 10. The frontispiece to Elizabeth Inchbald's 1807 edition of Henry Jones's *The Earl of Essex* (1753), depicting the crucial, intimate scene in which the Queen gives Essex the ring which will later be intercepted, fatally, when he tries to send it from the Tower to plead for a reprieve. ''Twixt you and me | This ring shall be a private mark of faith', runs the caption. This is one of the last illustrations to the Elizabeth and Essex plot to treat Elizabeth's imputed secret love sympathetically: later artists (such as David Wilkie Wynfield and Augustus Egg: see Figs. 19 and 20) would emphasize the fact that in real life the Queen was Essex's senior by more than thirty years.

Mrs. SIDDONS & MISS BRUNTON,

as QUEEN ELIZABETH & LADY RUTLAND

Fig. 11. Mrs Siddons and Miss Brunton as Queen Elizabeth and Lady Rutland, imagined in the scene from Jones's *The Earl of Essex* that finds the fictitious Lady Rutland,
whose marriage to Essex has hitherto been a secret, ill-advisedly revealing all as she
pleads for her husband's life. This print of Sarah Siddons as the jealous Elizabeth and
Anne Brunton as the peremptorily dismissed Rutland was not published until 1807,
towards the close of Siddons's career and long after Brunton had actually emigrated
to America, but its design probably dates from 1791, when Brunton chose the role of
Rutland for her Covent Garden benefit. Intriguingly, Siddons never actually played
Elizabeth: the print reflects both her real-life rivalry with Brunton (who was specifically hired by Covent Garden in 1785 to compete with her), and an evident sense that
this was a role Siddons *ought* to have played. Siddons is still best remembered, perhaps
not coincidentally for this piece of fantasy casting, as the greatest Lady Macbeth
of her time.

Cecil—I will no more ascend my throne,
The humble floor shall serve me; here I'll sit
With moping melancholy, my companion,
'Till death unmask'd approach, and steal me to my grave.
Cecil—I never more will close these eyes
In sleep, nor taste of food   And Cecil now,
Mark me—You hear Elizabeth's last words.[32]

In short, this enduringly popular historical fiction, at any rate in its most sympathetic forms, carves out a secret, susceptibly feminine Elizabeth from unpromising historical materials; the suffering heart beneath the apparently invulnerable breastplate is revealed at last, and public triumph merely conceals private tragedy. The Queen's internal split is usefully elaborated by the provision of deputies and proxies: the Queen's inadmissible but womanly desire for Essex is played out in the voluptuous pathos of the Countess of Rutland, her destructive jealousy is scapegoated on to the vindictive blocking figure of the Countess of Nottingham. These characters help Elizabeth voice all sorts of personal and suitably feminine motivations: a tender, jealous, and frustrated passion in place of political expediency; a feeling tendency to relent, which she overcomes only to her own regret and undoing; and, finally, a terminal case of heartbroken melancholy. This plot-structure (adaptable to an astonishing range of casts, as we will see) constellates possible female subject-positions across a spectrum ranging from the illegitimate but virtuous to the illegitimate and wicked, clearing thereby a precariously legitimate position between them for the female sovereign. This accounts for its enduring popularity long after both *The Secret History* and Banks's play had been left to moulder quietly on the shelf.[33] Mrs Ansley's painting *Queen Elizabeth giving a ring to the Earl of Essex*, exhibited at the Royal Academy in 1824, suggests, for example, that this story was well enough entrenched by the early nineteenth century to need only minimal textual gloss. The story persisted long after historians had scrupulously refuted it: the ring supposedly involved, cut with a cameo of Elizabeth, was changing hands under this high-priced provenance in the early twentieth century, and is still on display near

Elizabeth's funeral effigy in the museum at Westminster Abbey, securing romance in the very shadow of official royal history.[34]

But the precariousness of maintaining that sentimental identity could
adequately inhabit triumphal national identity became increasingly evident towards the end of the eighteenth century. The Essex story did not
always entirely do the job of sentimentalizing Elizabeth, especially when
artists took to depicting her encounters with Essex's wife or with
Nottingham. Edward Francis Burney's turn-of-the-century water-
colour *Queen Elizabeth and Lady Essex*, for example, shows Elizabeth
haranguing Lady Essex who reclines, apparently on her deathbed,
bathed in a saintly glow. There does not seem to be enough room in this
picture for *two* sentimental heroines. The repeated eighteenth-century
efforts to make a sentimental heroine out of Elizabeth seemed strained
enough by the end of the century to provoke the young Jane Austen to
parody in her spoof *History of England* (1791). Austen ridicules and triv-
ializes contemporary efforts to give Elizabeth the feelings of a conventional lover by comparing the imbroglio with Essex to the interminable
negotiations between the heroine Emmeline and her suitor Delamere in
Charlotte Smith's popular sentimental novel, *Emmeline* (1788)—a comparison already drawn, in what Austen clearly feels to be an inappropriate, gauche, and damaging manner, by Emmeline herself. In the rest of
Austen's history, Elizabeth is condemned (in a splendidly over-the-top
manner) as a callous monster compared to one contemporary much
better suited to being cast as a heroine of sensibility, Mary Stuart. In this
it is entirely characterisitic of its time: the romancing of the Queen's
femininity as both supplemental to, and suppressed by, history in the
interests of stable nationhood is invariably shown up as almost impossible to sustain when the figure of Elizabeth Tudor is confronted by that
of her cousin, rival, and political victim, Mary, Queen of Scots.[35]

The Rival Queens

The Queen of Scots was perceived by eighteenth-century culture as all
woman. Wife, mother, and lover, in the eighteenth century's many versions of the dealings between Elizabeth and Mary, the Queen of Scots

invariably lays claim to the simultaneously legitimate and illegitimate position of the distressed heroine of sensibility, embodying the fate of Scotland, with Elizabeth demoted to the altogether more equivocally virtuous and altogether less 'interesting' position of the official, if frequently reluctant, instrument of the English state. The fierce controversy that raged throughout the first century of troubled union between Scotland and England over whether the Queen of Scots colluded in the murder of her husband Henry Darnley with her lover the Earl of Bothwell, or whether she was entirely innocent and Bothwell (as was claimed at the time) kidnapped, raped, and married her by force, made Mary, whether in the guise of calumniated innocence or tragic susceptibility, easily assimilable to heroinical and national femininity, and to the genres with which it was associated. Appropriately to the heyday of the epistolary novel of seduction, this historical controversy was even sparked by the publication of a batch of love-letters, the Casket Letters, supposed to have been exchanged between Bothwell and Mary.[36] Thus in 1725, introducing her best-selling translation from the French of Pierre le Pesant, Sieur du Boisguillebert's 'secret history' of the Queen of Scots (originally published in Paris, 1675), that queen of popular romance writers, Eliza Haywood, describes Mary's story as ready-made 'romance':

The Life of this celebrated Princess has something so extraordinary in the whole Course of it, and is so very mournful in the Catastrophe, that, without adding anything to the Truth, it will appear in the recital as surprizing as any Romance whatsoever.[37]

Over the next two hundred years, the genre in which the Queen of Scots seemed most at home shifted from secret history to the sentimental epistolary novel (*vide* W. H. Ireland's extraordinary exercise in forging the fragmentary diary of Mary's infatuated and ill-fated court musician, *Effusions of Love from Chatelar to Mary Queen of Scotland. Translated from a Gothic manuscript. . . . Interspersed with Songs, Sonnets, and notes explanatory*, 1805) to the romantic gothic in the mode of Friedrich Schiller's tragedy *Maria Stuart* (1800) and Sir Walter Scott's novel *The Abbot* (1820), to Victorian history-painting, and so to the Hollywood spectacular. As her home genre shifted, so too subtly did she dislimn, evolving from heroine of sensibility to romantic guilty grande dame. In whatever mode she was displayed, however, Mary Stuart remained a remarkably durable and potent version of femininity, a femininity that a remarkable number of women, and women writers, seemed to want to occupy, although admittedly on their own terms. Something of this is registered in the popularity of masquerade dresses loosely based on contemporary portraits of the Queen of Scots and the surprising frequency with which prominent ladies from the early 1700s to the late nineteenth century chose to have their portraits painted in this particular mode of fancy dress.[38] Whilst in the early period this certainly signalled Jacobite sympathies, by the end of the century it seems to have signalled a British national heritage translated into a deliciously inefficient femininity: hence Jane West, writing her conduct manual for young ladies in 1801 (which was on the whole hostile to women's ambitions to wield power outside the home), chose Mary as her example of truly 'amiable' womanliness, measured by her inability to operate successfully in the public sphere:

The miseries of the unhappy Queen of Scotland, so evidently ascribable to the graces, the virtues, and the failings of her sex, must, while they still draw the tear of pity for her fate, excite our lively sympathy for every woman who is called to the dangerous estate of sovereign power; . . . The symmetry of her person, the susceptibility of her temper, the graces of her manner, the elegance of her accomplishments, the warmth of her attachments, all that made the woman amiable, destroyed the queen.[39]

At once utterly absurd and vividly illuminating, James Hayllar's painting *I'm Mary Tween of Tots* (n.d., c.1870s), which depicts a winsome toddler dressed as Mary, bears witness to the extent to which the royal victim, despite her reputation as adulteress and murderess, could come to represent the ultimate in infantilized and incompetent femininity.

The fates of the two queens were of course historically intertwined; one queen sought to supplant the other, one was responsible for the execution of the other in a satisfyingly dramatic denouement. But more than that calls them into confrontation. Their stories seemed to double and moralize one another's: where Mary had chosen marriage, motherhood, and possibly illicit love with her favourite Bothwell, Elizabeth had chosen the single life and doomed her favourite Leicester to an inter-minable, on-again off-again flirtation. In the history books this might be taken as an example of Elizabeth's political wisdom and even of her heroic self-sacrifice in the interests of keeping her country English and free of foreign interlopers, as opposed to the thoroughly immoral Mary who only got what was coming to her by being insufficiently grateful. But in the dreaming of fiction, the two queens find themselves facing off in a contest of femininities which Elizabeth is always in danger of losing.

The canonical fiction for the period of the two queens' dealings is pro-vided by another immensely popular drama by John Banks, *The Island Queens: or, The Death of Mary, Queen of Scotland* (1684), which, after a twenty-year ban prompted apparently by the succession crisis of the 1680s, remained (revised as the more sentimental *The Albion Queens* in 1704) a staple of the repertory into the 1790s. (It's an index of Banks's sense of his chosen genre of costume-drama she-tragedy that when he wasn't dramatizing Elizabeth and Mary he wrote plays about Anne Boleyn and Jane Grey). The Queen of Scots is here represented enmeshed in a doomed love affair with the Duke of Norfolk—who had indeed cherished thoughts of marrying her which were to bring him to the block in 1572, though in this play their deaths follow hard upon one another. In the play his ambition for a crown is subordinated rather implausibly to a desire for domestic bliss (4). The imprisoned Mary is presented initially through Norfolk's impassioned verbal tableau of her, at which his auditor Elizabeth is 'melted all to pity' (12), an entirely appropriate and indeed virtuous response to the genre which Norfolk both exploits and inhabits, that of affective tragedy. For the first time in history, but by no means the last, the queens meet (perhaps it is needless to say that though the possibility of a rendezvous in York was discussed around 1562 it never took place): in fact in this play they meet twice. Despite Elizabeth's wounded vanity, political and personal, she is won over to demonstrative affection in these meetings by the Queen of Scots's virtuous innocence. Nevertheless, prey to the wicked misrepre-sentations of Mary dripped into her ears by her scheming counsellors,[40] Elizabeth is persuaded to the unfeminine act of signing a death-warrant for her 'sister', suffering as she does so a metaphoric rape:

DAVISON. The Deed is done at last, but forc'd from her
  With greater art than Virgins made to yield,
  Wh'are loth to part with what they long to grant,
  Till ravish'd from them.

Her natural sensibility horribly violated by this deed, Elizabeth looks forward to the end of her life and sees only sleepless remorse. The net result in 1704, on the eve of Union, is a tragedy that does its level euphemistic best to exculpate both women in order to save both as exemplars of the feeling womanhood upon which Britain is founded; it seeks to offer, as the Prologue has it,

  A *Queen* Distress'd, to touch the Ladies Eyes,
  A *Noble Prince*, that for her beauty dies;
  A *British Queen* lamenting their sad Fate,
  And mourning over the Unfortunate.
  Who is here, that cou'd so cruel be,
  As not to mourn at their sad Tragedy?
  To see such Honour and such Beauty fall,
  And *England's Queen* mourn at their Funeral.[41]

The national importance of making sure that both queens 'suffer' equally is illustrated a few years later by the laconic and anonymous *Observations and Remarks upon the Lives and Reigns of King Henry VIII, King Edward VI, Queen Mary I, Queen Elizabeth, and King James I* (1712): 'Nothing ever seem'd to reflect upon her Memory, but the Death of *Mary* Queen of Scots, of which so much has been said *Pro* and *Con*, that I shall add nothing to it; but that they both deserve to be *pitied*, the one for her *sufferings*, and the other for being the cause of them.'[42] However, Lovelace's comparison of his rape of Clarissa to Elizabeth's execution of the Queen of Scots points up the extent to which that death-warrant threatened to cancel Elizabeth's claims to a modern femininity:

But for a more modern instance in my favour—Have I used Miss Harlowe as our famous maiden queen, as she was called, used one of her own blood, a sister-queen; who threw herself into her protection from her rebel subjects; and whom she detained prisoner eighteen years, and at last cut off her head? Yet . . . do not honest Protestants pronounce *her* pious too?—And call her particularly *their* queen?[43]

Because this execution has always seemed particularly compromising to Elizabeth's record, writers regularly tried to exonerate Elizabeth by representing her indecision over executing her rival as emotionally driven rather than politically motivated. For Eliza Haywood in 1725, Elizabeth's irresolution betrays the queen in conflict with the woman: 'Never was Woman in a greater Dilemma than this self-divided Queen.'[44] For good measure, Haywood follows the signing of the warrant with Elizabeth's lurid dream of her own execution, a master-stroke which converts guilt to victimhood by proxy. Only by such a ruse can Haywood rescue Elizabeth's femininity—for, if the Queen of Scots represented everything that was feminine, her executioner must necessarily represent everything inimical to that femininity.

Sixty years later, at the height of the cult of sensibility, Sophia Lee would publish the text which is usually cited as the most important 'missing link' between sentimental fiction and the full-blown historical novel, her best-selling proto-gothic romance *The Recess* (1785). It is striking in this context because, although this labyrinthine and compelling novel ingeniously manages to combine the exciting pathos derived from the story of Mary, Queen of Scots, with that of the Earl of Essex, it conspicuously excludes Elizabeth from any of the available sympathetically conflicted positions, relegating her purely to a blocking function. Where *The Albion Queens* promoted an official British history, *The Recess* is emotionally invested in romance as the residue or supplement to that history, and it suggests that the official pro-Gloriana view of history depends crucially upon the wholesale suppression of female narrative and feminine sensibility, which it understands as both virtuous and profoundly illegitimate.

The Recess draws upon an old tradition of representing Elizabeth as destroyer of court love affairs. In part, this derived from the mores of the Elizabethan court (Elizabeth's consent was required before her maids of honour could marry, and those favourites caught marrying without permission, notably Leicester and Raleigh, found themselves conspicuously and occasionally permanently out of favour), and in part it derived from the vexed politics of the succession (on learning of their marriages, Elizabeth imprisoned the sisters Katherine and Mary Grey, claimants to the throne). At the end of the seventeenth century, Elizabeth's actions in this respect could still be construed as strongly moral (in polemicized contrast to the laxness of the Stuart court); so in 1693, for example, the anonymous author of *The Character of Queen Elizabeth* offered this enthusiastic gloss upon her court's sexual mores:

She alone was able to furnish her whole Sex with the examples of Chastity, Temperance, and all other Vertues: And she was very vigilant to keep her Family and Court in severe Discipline. She persuaded all Married Women to pay a modest Respect to their Husbands, as to their Superiors. She kept a severer Guard upon her own desires, than upon those of others that were about her; so that by degrees she made them seem at least like her self, because she ever laboured so to have them. *She banished from her Court all Drunkenness, Filthiness, Immodesty, and the very fame and suspicion of Wantonness. Whoredoms, Rapes, Adulteries, and Incests, were Crimes she detested*; and if she found any of her Retinue, how great soever they were, guilty of them, they must never more come before her. . . . To conclude, she shewed her self the Irreconcilable Enemy of all that had been found guilty of any base or immodest and unchaste Action.[45]

Equally, however, the Queen's interference could be read in the then hugely successful mode of the French scandal-novel or *roman-à-clef*, in which the anti-heroine is typically motivated by a combination of rebuffed passion and political ambition. Thus *The Secret History of the Duke of Alencon and Q. Elizabeth. A True History* (1691) offers a passionate, tyrannical, duplicitous, and fading queen in competition for the affections of Alençon with the impossibly youthful Marianna, second daughter of Henry VIII by Catherine of Aragon, and thus the true heir to the throne, a conflict which Elizabeth resolves for good and all by sending the lovely unfortunate a pair of efficiently poisoned gloves (upon which Alençon dies of melancholy). This, then, is the beginning of representing Elizabeth as destroyer of a legitimate but powerless femininity, the version of Elizabeth that, elaborated and transmuted in consonance with middle-class sentimental ideology, underlies Sophia Lee's novel.

Capitalizing on the legend that the Queen of Scots miscarried of twins (supposedly by Bothwell), *The Recess* presents us with twin sisters, immured since infancy underground, who, proving to their astonishment to be the illegitimate daughters of Mary, Queen of Scots, by her husband the Duke of Norfolk—unauthorized sequels, in fact, to Banks's *Island Queens*—have a peculiarly convoluted and problematic claim to Elizabeth's throne. The elder, Matilda, accidentally meets and falls in love with Elizabeth's first favourite Leicester, and subsequently marries him in secret, a secrecy that later makes her vulnerable to the unwelcome although irreproachably delicate addresses of Leicester's nephew Sir Philip Sidney, of whose affections Elizabeth is equally jealous. The younger, Ellinor, is on the point of marriage with Essex but as a result of court machinations they are separated and he marries another in the belief that she is dead; they later elope with one another into a brief domestic idyll. The two sisters thus come to occupy the respective positions of the hapless Amy Robsart (Leicester's real-life bride) and the fictional Rutland imagined by *The Secret History*. In addition to these intrigues, Leicester supplies a narrative of his involvement in the Courtenay–Elizabeth affair, his involvement in a triangle with Elizabeth and his future first wife Lettice Knollys, Countess of Essex, and in yet another as Mary, Queen of Scots, and Elizabeth vie for his affections. The stories of Matilda's and Ellinor's lives are of entombment punctuated by brief escapes, followed by further incarceration; their lovers are for the most part presented also as suffering victims of sensibility, whose respective falls from favour are ascribed entirely to Elizabeth's enraged discovery of their clandestine relationships. In keeping with the novel's willingness literally to undermine the official version of history, and consonant with its tragic view of the ways in which the individual is born into and subjected by historical circumstances, the narrative form is classically sentimental, consisting of a series of characteristically fractured, partial (in both senses) first-person narratives 'entombed' one within the other. This foregrounding of interiority is exemplified most notably by Ellinor's own memoir, which, unacknowledgeable within the record of 'History', symptomatically disintegrates into madness and is completed by a stranger because the 'fair unfortunate . . . will never more be her own historian'.[46]

What *The Recess* exhaustively demonstrates is that by 1785 sentimental female identity—private, domestic, and bourgeois—can be construed, perhaps especially by a woman writer, as antithetical both thematically and discursively to official national history, personified here as Elizabeth herself. This antithesis is explicitly staged in one of the most powerful set pieces of the novel, a confrontation after the execution of Essex between the mad Ellinor (who, erupting from her underground existence into the historical space of the court, tellingly parrots lines historically spoken by Mary Stuart at her own execution) and the Queen, who is represented as rightly rebuked by Ellinor's indictment of her as an unwomanly monster, and who is ever after haunted by this spectre at one remove of the Queen of Scots.

The ways this plot-structure is predicated upon a femininity lost to, or indeed constitutively suppressed by, history, embodied in fictional disinherited daughters, are usefully elaborated by another exercise in the gothic underside of history, the sentimental epistolary fiction *The Statue Room* (1790) by the pseudonymous (and evidently Catholic) 'Rosetta Ballin'. Here, once again, Elizabeth appears as vindictive blocking figure, disinheriting, imprisoning, and ultimately poisoning the true heir to the throne, yet another of Catherine of Aragon's second and hitherto unknown daughters, the lovely if improbably named Adelfrida. The murder of Adelfrida at the climax of the first movement of the novel is prompted by Elizabeth's jealous rage at discovering Alençon's secret marriage with her charming prisoner, a marriage consummated while the Duke was nominally courting the Queen. As in *The Recess*, the Queen also interferes with the happiness of the daughter of her favourite and the disinherited heroine, here the beautiful Romelia, who finds herself, like the Countess of Rutland and Ellinor, pleading at court for the release of an imprisoned spouse, and is then herself immured and condemned to death, having unwisely declared her parentage in a fit of temporary madness. In Ballin's story the Queen's many and picturesque crimes (too many to detail here, unfortunately) are, as nearly as the intransigence of the historical record permits, punished by an abortive but entirely justified assassination attempt by the sharp-shooting Romelia at a masquerade—'the ball went through her hair, and took off part of her crown'.[47] *The Statue Room* thus effectively argues in its elaborately plotted three volumes that Elizabeth's power is predicated upon the wholesale destruction of virtuous married happiness; so unfeminine is this Elizabeth that her very claim to queenship must be illegitimate.

Perhaps one more example will drive home the astonishing power of this plot of the disinherited daughter of the Queen of Scots who steals Elizabeth's femininity away—both in the sense that she engrosses the reader's sympathies and in terms of plot. As a more satisfactorily feminine woman, she can steal the Queen's lover too. The full title of this anonymous novel published in 1820 is so comprehensive by way of plot summary that we will quote it in full: *Rose Douglas. or, The Court of Elizabeth. An Interesting Historical Tale Detailing the Life and Singular Adventures of Rose Douglas, the lovely daughter of Mary, Queen of Scots: her Interview with Queen Elizabeth, and residence at Court; the singular events which introduce her to the notice of the Earl of Essex; their attachment and private union; the rage of Elizabeth on discovering their marriage; the treatment of the lovely Rose; the Death of the Earl and sufferings of the ill-fated Countess*. All that remains is to note that Rose is the surviving twin daughter of the Queen of Scots by the Duke of Norfolk, that she is pregnant by her husband Essex, and that she is granted a brief interview with her condemned mother, the anguish of whose execution throws her into premature labour. Essex's rebellion is entirely prompted by Elizabeth's insistence that he should renounce Rose; his execution none the less casts Elizabeth into a delirious melancholic decline in which she returns relics of the Queen of Scots to Rose, who (most unusually for the genre) remarries a nice Englishman called Sir Everard and lives happily ever after. In this novel there is hope for a reconciled sentimental modern British domesticity after all.

At the beginning of the nineteenth century, however, Mary herself began to feature as grandly and generously passionate, diminishing her companion piece the sentimental Elizabeth still further into something half-hearted and even perverse. In 1800 the Queen of Scots gave up suffering in unmerited distress and now embodied powerful, if thwarted, transgression. A proud, guilty, and deadly seductress, she became a card-carrying Romantic with a little help from Friedrich Schiller, amongst others. *Maria Stuart* (1800), the dramatic source for Donizetti's important opera *Maria Stuarda*, confronted the two queens with each other

only to claim paradoxically that the imprisoned Mary achieved romantic grandeur and freedom by deliberately rushing on her fate, leaving
Elizabeth grasping at an empty and meaningless victory (Fig. 12).
Throughout their subsequent lives in the nineteenth century, the two
queens would haunt and double each other, each betrayed, in different
senses, by the death-warrant one or other holds. They appear perched
at opposing ends of the mantelpiece as a match-pair of bronzes by
Mathurin Moreau (1870), and in innumerable Victorian magazine illustrations where the central image of Elizabeth derived from an official
portrait is flanked and qualified by a narrative vignette featuring her
lovely, romantic, congenially disempowered victim, Mary, Queen of
Scots.[48] But the useful national trope of Elizabeth as a queen divided
between state and womanly sentiment had now collapsed in the presence of the Queen of Scots. Mary Stuart engrosses the late eighteenth-
century romance of the feminine in exact ratio to her sexual guilt,
disinheritance, defeat, and death, while the ageless virgin Elizabeth
dwindles into the unattractive and heartless instrument of history, conceived explicitly as that which destroys and excludes the true feminine.
As the author of Merrie England (1851) was to put it:

the memory of [the Queen of Scots's] beauties, her talents, and her sorrows, has
ever since fired young and enthusiastic hearts for her. The Historian has softened the severity of History, and Poets have delighted to linger over her name.
Sir Walter Scott, Schiller, Burns, have deplored and delineated her sufferings;
nothing can be easier than for the intellect to make out a case against her,
but it is wanting in moral consistency and proportion; and Elizabeth, in every
particular, shrinks into the coquette, the schemer, the traitress, almost the
murderess upon the mention of the name of Mary.[49]

Sentiment is firmly identified with the losing side of history. Elizabeth
is what remains. Treacherous, mendacious, duplicitous; conscienceless,
dishonourable, brutally politic; vengeful virago, religious changeling;
vain, ostentatious, insatiate.[50]

If nothing else, then, this conspectus of efforts to incorporate the
figure of Elizabeth within the sentimental plot demonstrates how peculiarly obstructive she was, as a historically powerful woman, to the cul-
ork of persuading gender ideology to underwrite nationalism.

FIG. 12. In reality Elizabeth and Mary, Queen of Scots, never met, but on the stage they have been doing so ever since John Banks composed *The Island Queens* (1684). They have never faced off more influentially than in Friedrich Schiller's *Maria Stuart* (1800), and this early nineteenth-century illustration to Schiller's confrontation scene makes it very clear what is at stake in the queens' rivalry. If Mary is to be all wronged womanhood, the perfect sentimental national heroine, Elizabeth must dwindle into a caricatured, power-hungry usurper, a barren and unfeminine bird of prey.

These efforts none the less register the ways in which, as Benedict Anderson has remarked, the emergence of modern nationalism is inextricably bound up with the emergence of a novelistic version of individual subjectivity.[51] That these attempts rarely succeed underscores, however, the way in which the novelistic, the sentimental, and the feminine were none the less frequently represented as being problematically supplementary, or perhaps even inimical, to the discourse of triumphant nationalism. By so evidently disrupting the otherwise apparently comfortable alignment between sentimentalism and nationalism, the figure of Elizabeth reveals particularly clearly that that which Lynn Hunt has argued for in the French context may well be true also for eighteenth-century Britain; that national identity is classically constructed around a homosocial imperative to rescue a sentimental heroine in distress. The fraternal French revolutionaries, according to Hunt, felt that they were rallying in defence of poor Marianne, the suffering personification of French liberty, but it was very difficult to produce Good Queen Bess as a comparable figure for England. It is instructive in this context to compare the ways in which Scottish nationalism found (and has continued to find) the figure of Mary, Queen of Scots, so congenial (despite her historical position as a Frenchified interloper to whom early nationalists, led by John Knox, were so intransigently opposed); the anonymous author of the historical novel *The Court of Holyrood* (1822), having vehemently disposed of Elizabeth as a worthy focus for English national pride, defines his fellow Scottish patriots as the quintessentially sentimental readership of their national heroine's text:

We are proud of the national sentiment in Scotland which is associated with the name of Mary Queen of Scots. A simple chronicle of her sufferings . . . was the first tale of sorrow over which we wept. . . . In graver manhood . . . we are not ashamed to acknowledge, that we cannot peruse the volumes of her wrongs without emotion. This feeling . . . while it shall endure, and pervade the bulk of our population . . . may be held as a proof that loyalty [*sic*], and the love of justice, and hatred of oppression, are among our permanent national characteristics.[52]

But even had it been possible to dramatize Elizabeth as a sentimental heroine, there remained the distinct problem that this would entail (as it generally did in the case of the Queen of Scots) a recognition of culpable flaws, faults, and failures in the persona of the Virgin Queen. No wonder, then, that Sheridan's Mr Puff is compelled to split his Gloriana into two characters—the heroic and historical armed Queen Elizabeth at Tilbury, of whom 'no scandal' is to be spoken (and who is, as we have already noted, kept in the green room as the ultimate precaution against it), and the altogether more engaging Tilburina. Daughter of the Governor of Tilbury Fort, hopelessly and illicitly in love with the dashing commander of one of the Spanish ships, Don Ferolo Whiskerandos, it is Tilburina who fills up the 'deficiency in the private history of the times' by displaying her susceptibly 'contending passions.' In an explicit parody of Henry Jones's *The Earl of Essex*, she goes conventionally mad in white satin for the pleasure of the likes of Mr Dangle:

> Poor young lady! I feel for her already! for I can conceive how great the conflict must be between her passion and her duty; her love for her country, and her love for DON FEROLO WHISKERANDOS![53]

It is, after all, only her pathetic exit, 'gone to throw herself into the sea to be sure' (384), that clears the way for the great patriotic finale:

> *Scene changes to the sea—the fleets engage—the musick plays 'Britons strike home.'—Spanish fleet destroyed by fire-ships, etc.—English fleet advances—musick plays 'Rule Britannia.'* (385)

Scandal Averted

The eighteenth century saw the figure of the Queen definitively divided into two bodies: one public, the other private; one gendered masculine, the other feminine. The uneasiness of her position within the culture was further compounded by two factors: the newly constitutional monarchy continued to be fundamentally dynastic, which made the Queen seem uncomfortably exceptional as both a woman and as childless; at the same time, in the age of Walpole, state power became increasingly associated with career politicians and male rhetoric, which put Elizabeth in an uneasy slantwise relation to the state power which she originally embodied. The resulting conundrum of the nature of the Queen's power is therefore expressed in fictions about her femininity fulfilled or unfulfilled, and its relation to the newly imagined national. This conundrum will be solved in very varied ways over the next two centuries; at the close of the eighteenth century, though, the only way to preserve Elizabeth unequivocally as a national icon within the novelistic was to dissociate her figure from the plot-structure we have been describing, to follow Sheridan in filling that structure instead with explicitly fictional characters. Elizabeth, for example, serves simply as historical colour in Francis Lathom's *The Mysterious Freebooter; or, The Days of Queen Bess. A Romance* (1806) before reappearing in the denouement as dea ex machina; so far from obstructing the Rutland/Essex-like secret marriage between her godchild Rosalind de Mowbray and Edward, she secures their nuptial bliss as a reward for their services in saving her from assassination. By carefully sidestepping the possibility that Elizabeth's personal passions might actually implicate her within the terms of such a plot, Lathom is able to preserve her as a facilitating rather than a blocking figure, a historical character governing, rather than condemned by, the ideology of sentiment.

This is substantially the strategy followed by Sir Walter Scott in his immensely influential novel *Kenilworth* (1821), which would remain a yardstick for fictive representations of both Elizabeth and the newly christened 'Elizabethan' age in Britain, America, and on the Continent until about 1860.[54] Scott significantly avoids both Essex and Mary, Queen of Scots, choosing instead to deal with Elizabeth's first favourite Robert Dudley, Earl of Leicester, and his unfortunate first wife Amy Robsart, who died in the autumn of 1560. This story he embeds, anachronistically enough, within an account of the 1575 Kenilworth festivities, based upon the recently republished contemporary accounts of George Gascoigne and Robert Laneham, popularized by John Nichols.[55] This anachronism is fundamental to the fiction, since it enables Scott to bring Elizabeth out of the claustrophobic court and those genres associated with it (most especially the secret memoir and the gothic), out into the fertile English countryside, pausing on progress through her nation.

Indeed, reading *Kenilworth* in the context of its precursors, it is hard not to be struck by the way in which Scott sedulously avoids the conventional opportunities that his choice of plot offers. Like previous writers, Scott largely ignores domestic and international politics, despite concentrating upon a portrait of the personal ambitions of the Earl of Leicester within a panorama of the jostle for preferment in the Elizabethan court. Like his precursors too, Scott takes some astonishing liberties with the historical record. But neither the dismissal of politics nor the historical anachronisms are brought into service of a sentimental plot in quite the way that one might expect, given Scott's source material. In fact Scott sets up the plot-structure with which we are already familiar (at the expense of historical accuracy) only to abort it spectacularly. *Kenilworth* effectively conflates two entirely separate episodes in the life of the Earl of Leicester: his first marriage to Amy Robsart, and his second to Lettice Knollys, Countess of Essex (who was, by her first husband, the mother of Elizabeth's last favourite the Earl of Essex). As a matter of historical record, without question known to Scott, Leicester's first and entirely public marriage to Amy Robsart had taken place in 1550, well before Elizabeth came to the throne in 1558; they had been married for ten years when she came by her death on 8 September 1560, at what was an embarrassingly opportune moment for Leicester's long-standing and increasingly scandalous flirtation with the Queen—a flirtation that was thought by many to be tending towards a marriage. (Whatever possibility there might have been of such a match was effectively scotched by the scandal following the Countess's death, which in its most virulent form credited Leicester with murder and the Queen with complicity.)[56] Leicester was involved with the then-married Countess of Essex in 1565, and again from 1573—indeed, she was probably present at the Kenilworth festivities in 1575—and they married secretly in 1578, a marriage that the Queen discovered only in 1579 and which led to the temporary disgrace of the favourite. In the face of these facts, *Kenilworth* offers the reader an Amy only recently and secretly married to Leicester at the time of the Kenilworth festivities. Leicester's ambition as favourite and developing desire to marry Elizabeth prompts him first to conceal his marriage and then, egged on by trumped-up charges of adultery against Amy, to order her murder, an order rescinded too late. The similarity of Amy to a number of tragic figures we have already discussed, notably the Countess of Rutland and Matilda, situates her squarely in the tradition of the sentimental heroine, and so we might expect a variation upon the usual triangle of Queen–favourite–illicit wife.

Instead, however, Scott systematically aborts this plot's conventional possibilities. He makes it clear, for example, that the Queen has already rejected Leicester's suit before she even knows of Amy, removing this as a possible motive for Amy's murder on either of their parts:

'No, Dudley,' said Elizabeth, yet it was with broken accents—'no, I must be the mother of my people. Other ties, that make the lowly maiden happy, are denied to her sovereign. . . . Were it possible—were it *but* possible! But no—no; Elizabeth must be the wife and mother of England alone.'[57]

That the Queen does not know of Amy's existence at the moment of encouraging Leicester's 'language of love' (317) clears her of immorality; that she has already rejected him before the set-piece confrontation with Amy allows her to appear not as illicit rival but as authority figure, even though the discovery of Leicester's clandestine marriage is in fact averted by the insistence of all concerned (from a mixture of motives honourable and dishonourable) that Amy is in fact the wife of Leicester's villainous henchman, Sir Richard Varney. Lifted out of the sentimental structure in this way, the Queen may be made briefly more sympathetic when she does finally find out that Leicester has been making love to her under false pretences: 'a tear actually twinkled in her proud and angry eye' (373). None the less, the sentiment that brings her to tears is not principally love slighted but humiliation at her own weakness. This removal of the Queen from the sentimental plot is made all the more viable by shifting the narrative interest more generally to two alternative triangular relationships: the competition between Varney and Leicester, and between the apocryphal, abandoned, and noble suitor Tressilian and Varney as Leicester's surrogate, for the affections of Amy. The Queen who emerges in this rebuilt plot is by no means as conventionally placed as Scott was to suggest in his later prefatory description—'at once a high-minded sovereign and a female of passionate feelings, hesitating betwixt the sense of her rank and the duty she owed her subjects on the one hand, and on the other her attachment to a nobleman who, in external qualifications at least, amply merited her favour'.[58] *Kenilworth* carefully exculpates the Queen from anything either illicit or consequential in her 'passionate feelings'. In doing so it earns its hard-won epigraph, 'no scandal about Queen Elizabeth, I hope?' No, indeed.

3

Good Queen Bess
and Merrie England

Given the hostility of some of the novelizations of Elizabeth's relations
with Essex and with Mary, Queen of Scots, which we have been discussing, it is perhaps just as well that Scott's *Kenilworth*, together with its
strategy of exempting the Queen from any direct implication in yet
another fatal love-triangle, was also able to invoke another apocryphal
relationship altogether in its bid to preserve Gloriana as the presiding
spirit of Old England's golden age. In an incidental episode in the novel,
Elizabeth receives a petition from bear-baiting entrepreneurs who hope
that she will close down the newly established theatres which are affecting their business, and she takes the occasion to canvass her court's opinions about contemporary drama. She is especially keen to hear their
views about 'one Will Shakespeare (whom I think, my lords, we have
all heard something of),'[1] and she herself voices a prescient certainty
that his history plays in particular will in time be recognized as a permanent part of the national heritage. A flattering recitation by one
of her courtiers of the 'fair vestal thronèd by the West' speech from
A Midsummer Night's Dream only confirms her enthusiasm, and
she crumples up the petition and throws it into the Thames. As the

Queen remarks to Shakespeare in one of many nineteenth-century stage burlesques of *Kenilworth* (confirming as she does so that he is the better poet of the two),

> Something tells me whilst I look at you, through you I shall attain
> Just cause for men and women to ne'er forget my reign.[2]

At the same time as it does its best to exculpate Elizabeth from the logic of the sentimental novel, *Kenilworth* also inserts the Queen, much more successfully and influentially, within the anecdotal. The anecdote—essentially, an emblematic mini-narrative, often designed to crystallize something its audience feels it knows already—is the genre with which we will be dealing most centrally in this chapter, together with its consumer manifestation as the souvenir. Both are used to tie Elizabeth not just to the state and to the official Church, but to the national culture, especially via Shakespeare.

This process had been given a particular impetus down the eighteenth century by the Act of Union, which officially brought Great Britain into being in 1707, and produced a state which functioned even internally as an empire and therefore demanded loyalty to an idea rather than simply to a piece of territory or to the English crown. Both Elizabeth and Shakespeare retrospectively participated in the invention of a British way of life—insular and commercial—and a British literary heritage, the new national formation of the Enlightenment placing ever more emphasis on a distinctive national culture.[3] In the examples we will be discussing, Elizabeth's eternal youth and indeed the persistence of her own fame becomes a figure for the perennial vitality of this national culture, and the anecdotes which detail her ever-more intimate represented relationship with the national poet supply a useful new way of identifying her with the whole nation rather than simply the claustrophobic intrigues of the court.

Elizabeth and the National Diet

Even before the official invention of Britain, it is true, th[e] Elizabeth had gathered associations with particular notions

English virtue, her own virile performance at Tilbury blurring over into a general notion of Elizabethan manliness. The character Manly in Newcastle's *The Variety* (see Chapter 1) provides one example; another such pro-Elizabethan humourist on the seventeenth-century stage is Thomas Shadwell's Sir Edward Hartfort in *The Lancashire Witches* (1682), described on the cast list as 'A worthy Hospitable true English Gentleman, of good Understanding and honest Principles', and carefully identified with a broadly Whig version of a native lifestyle unchanged since Queen Bess's happy reign:

> DOUBTY. You have extreamly delighted us this morning, by your House, Gardens, your Accommodation, and your way of Living, you put me in mind of the renowned *Sidneys* Admirable description of *Kalandar*.
>
> SIR EDW. Sir you Complement me too much.
>
> BELLFORT. Methinks you represent to us the Golden days of Queen *Elizabeth*, such sure were our Gentry then; now they are grown Servile Apes to Foreign customes, they leave off Hospitality, for which we were famous all over *Europe*, and turn Servants to Board-wages . . .
>
> SIR EDW. You are too kind, *I am a true English-man, I love the Princes Rights and Peoples Liberties, and will defend 'em both with the last penny in my purse, and the last drop of blood in my veins, and dare defy the witless Plots of Papists.*
>
> BELLFORT. Spoken like a Noble Patriot.[4]

The process of associating the late queen not just with the nation but with a particular idea of the national culture accelerates after 1707, however, when the knot of ideas deployed in this piece of dialogue— Elizabeth, Elizabethan literature, anti-Catholicism, hospitality, resistance to Continental fashions—begins to find expression not just on the stage but in popular song. The most famous example dates from the frenetically anti-Spanish and pro-Elizabethan decade of the 1730s, when its first stanza appeared in Henry Fielding's play *The Grub-Street Opera:* it would soon enjoy the status of an honorary national anthem. It has so faded from popular memory over the last century, however—and the crises over BSE and foot and mouth disease have made it so profoundly unlikely that it will ever be rehabilitated—that it will be necessary to quote its lyrics at some length:

When Mighty Roast Beef was the Englishman's Food
It ennobl'd our veins and enriched our Blood:
Our Soldiers were Brave and our Courtiers were Good:
Oh! The Roast Beef of old England, and old English Roast Beef.

Our Fathers, of old, were Robust, Stout and Strong,
And kept open House, with good Cheer all day long.
Which made their plump Tenants rejoyce in this Song,
Oh! The Roast Beef of old England, and old English Roast Beef.

When good Queen Elizabeth sate on the throne,
Ere Coffee and Tea and such slip-slops were known,
The world was in terror if e'er she did frown.
Oh! The Roast Beef of old England, and old English Roast Beef.

In those days, if Fleets did presume on the Main,
They seldom, or never, return'd back again,
As witness the Vaunting Armada of Spain.
Oh! The Roast Beef of old England, and old English Roast Beef.[5]

The notion of Elizabeth as plain-speaking English beef-eater is wide-spread down through the Napoleonic wars, and partly through the popularity of this song she would be adopted as one of the heroines of that key personification of Britishness, John Bull. One 1819 political cartoon, *John Bull in Clover. John Bull done Over*, juxtaposing images of national prosperity and national ruin, shows its prosperous incarnation of John Bull reclining at his ease in an armchair, the parlour wall behind him adorned with a framed portrait of 'Good Queen Bess' and a copy of 'The Roast Beef of Old England.'[6] Elsewhere in popular patriotic culture Elizabeth might be presented not just as a consumer of beef but as an active exponent of scientific research on behalf of her armed forces and her meat industry alike. A song in *John Bull; or the True Briton* (1808), for example, 'Royal Reasons for Roast Beef', relates how

> Queen Bess once fed three men for a year
> On different kinds of food,
> To see which might the best appear
> To do a Briton good . . .

The first two men, fed on mutton and veal respectively, are rendered practically effeminate, in fact well-nigh French, by their experimental diets, and are declared fit to serve the Queen only as tailors and milliners. The last, however, has clearly developed into the right national stuff:

> The third he came to be question'd in kind
>   And as loud as he could bawl
> When asked by the usher on what he had din'd,
>   Cried, 'Beef—and be d—n'd to you all'.
> Queen Bess she gave him her fist with a smile,
>   And swore it was her belief,
> The Devil himself couldn't conquer this isle
>   While Britons were fed upon beef.[7]

This popular image of Good Queen Bess as a true daughter of Bluff King Hal and a worthy pin-up for John Bull naturally gave some writers offering a less rosy picture of Elizabeth's reign pause: the 1792 prologue to Mary Deverell's tragedy *Mary, Queen of Scots*, for example, expresses some trepidation at the prospect of trying to persuade a London audience to think ill of a queen who 'gen'rous, open, hearty and sincere, | Eat good old English beef, and drank strong beer.'[8] Both perspectives are acknowledged in Thomas Dibdin's 'Elizabeth' in 1813, a splendidly succinct doggerel account of all that was then felt to be memorable about her reign. Dibdin too juxtaposes Elizabeth the beef-eater with Elizabeth the betrayer of Mary, Queen of Scots, but in this case he is able to find a way of trumping both. The poem appears in Dibdin's *A Metrical History of England*, and appropriately to this educational context it takes the form of a sort of catechism, each stanza summarizing a different aspect of Elizabeth's fame. Glory alternates with infamy throughout: the Queen's joyful coronation and contemporary renown, for example, are followed by a disapproving distillation of the Essex story:

> Who lov'd Lord Essex 'bove his peers,
> And cut his head off, (tho' with tears),
> Of which, alive, she box'd the ears?
>   O fie, sir.

There follows an assertion of her virginity, despite her many suitors, and a wonderful evocation of the rugged, manly Old English diet followed even by her ladies-in-waiting:

> Whose merry maidens fared, with glee,
> On beef and beer, not toast and tea,
> Whenever hungry they might be,
> Or dry, sir?

This leads on naturally enough to the Queen's martial performance at Tilbury—'Who rode on horseback to the coast, | Infusing valour in that host, | Which gave the proud Armada's boast | The lie, sir'—but the triumph of 1588 is then, unusually, counterpoised with two whole stanzas about the disgrace of 1587:

> Who can find language to excuse,
> Or any terms too harsh to use,
> (And here it costs my flippant muse
> A sigh, sir),
>
> While we record her envy mean,
> Whose malice, cruelty, and spleen,
> Doom'd Scotia's dear devoted Queen
> To die, sir?

From here, however, all is an ascending chorus of praise: she was always careful to employ only good advisers; she was prodigiously learned; she rewarded merit; her court was distinguished for its artistic and intellectual talent. But Dibdin saves the best of Elizabeth's redeeming features until last:

> And, climax of a wond'rous age!
> Who first saw Shakespeare's genuine page,
> Give truth and nature to the stage?
> Eliza.[9]

Elizabeth and the National Poet

In treating Elizabeth as someone who can ultimately be redeemed as the soul of Merrie England, despite her faults, by association with Shakespeare, Dibdin is following a tradition which was by now more than a century old, its emergence almost exactly parallel to the eighteenth century's dramatization of Elizabeth as the unwomanly signatory to death-warrants—to which here as elsewhere it is offered as the antidote. The connection between the Queen and the playwright was first revealed in 1702, in connection with *The Merry Wives of Windsor*, a text which (together with *A Midsummer Night's Dream* later on) repeatedly provides templates for this category of national folklore. In his introduction to *The Comical Gallant*, an adaptation of the play, John Dennis explains that his belief that this farce deserved rewriting was based not only, and not even chiefly, on his own reading of it, but on royal authority:

> That this Comedy was not despicable, I guess'd for several reasons: First, I knew very well that it had pleas'd one of the greatest Queens that ever was in the World . . . This Comedy was written at her Command, and by her direction, and she was so eager to see it Acted, that she commanded it to be finished in fourteen days; and was afterwards, as Tradition tells us, very well pleas'd at the Representation.[10]

There are, undeniably, reasons why this play in particular might have attracted such an anecdote, or why lingering hearsay about its real-life première might in time have escalated to include the direct participation of the Queen. The play's last act includes one Fairy Queen already— even if it is only Mistress Quickly in disguise—and alludes to the cere- monies of the Order of the Garter, to which Shakespeare's then patron George Carey, Lord Hunsdon, the Lord Chamberlain, was admitted at Windsor early in 1597. These ceremonies were followed by a Garter Feast at the Palace of Westminster on St George's Day, 23 April, attended by the Queen, and the play's topical references to the Garter suggest that *The Merry Wives of Windsor* may have been composed expressly for per- formances associated with this event. However, the notion of Gloriana not just chatting familiarly with a common player but designing his most Merrie English comedy and personally supervising its composition is far too consonant with the needs and desires of eighteenth-century cul- tural nationalism to be true, and it becomes even less likely (and more useful) when it reappears in more elaborate form seven years later. According to the biographical preface appended to Nicholas Rowe's edition of the Complete Plays in 1709, Elizabeth not only commissioned *Merry Wives* but showed Shakespeare 'many gracious Marks of her

Favour', and the general 'direction' of the play's composition described by Dennis had a very specific bent: Rowe reports that Elizabeth had a particular enthusiasm for Sir John Falstaff, and demanded that *The Merry Wives of Windsor* should 'shew him in love'.[11]

Some of the implications of this anecdote—which has remained a staple of the repertoire of vignettes about Elizabeth and Shakespeare ever since, and is still frequently retold as unquestioned fact—are immediately apparent. From the point of view of the emerging cult of Shakespeare, it helped clear the Bard's name of a good deal of unsavoury later seventeenth-century gossip. In general the Enlightenment had inherited a conception of Shakespeare as an untutored and lawless Warwickshire yokel, his writings full of verbal and dramatic excesses which found their corollary in a biographical tradition dominated by tales of rural petty crime. The Shakespeare of seventeenth-century gossip, for example, seduces Burbage's mistress and Sir William Davenant's mother, writes gratuitous pasquinades against local worthies, pronounces tragic declamations while slaying calves, and, above all, steals deer, allegedly from the Stratford squire Sir Thomas Lucy, whose retaliatory persecution was supposed to have driven Shakespeare to London, where he could find employment only as a holder of horses outside theatres.[12] A story according to which Shakespeare was on familiar terms with Queen Elizabeth, his lowest and most farcical comedy written by royal command, might retrospectively promote him from poacher to Poet Laureate at a single stroke.[13]

Perhaps more significantly in its own time, however, this anecdote marks a convergence on the figure of Elizabeth of political and cultural nostalgia. By the simple expedient of declaring her, the head of the English state, to have been the patroness of Shakespeare, in 1709 fast becoming the figurehead of English literature, his authorship is appropriated as a cultural expression of her authority. The wave of middle-class cultural nationalism on which Shakespeare was rapidly ascending towards near-divine status is thus conveniently subsumed by the older political cult of Queen Elizabeth, or perhaps vice versa: her reign hereby becomes a golden age when royal power and literary excellence were one, when this Britannia ruled not just the waves but the poetic lines.[14] The imputed link between Elizabeth and the hitherto disreputably over-virile Shakespeare confirms Elizabeth's native manliness ('It is a strong mark of Queen Elizabeth's masculine character, that she should fall in love with Falstaff, who since her time has scarce had a female admirer', wrote Francis Gentleman in 1774),[15] and it is only fitting that it should be made via a Shakespearean character, Falstaff, who is himself a romantic supplement to received history, his corpulent body—persistently associated with roast beef—putting some apocryphal flesh on the bare bones of Holinshed's *Chronicles*.

Dennis would compound his initial association of playwright with monarch in 1707, when he had Shakespeare return in person to speak a prologue to *Julius Caesar*, ingeniously claiming that it was his play which inspired Elizabeth's patriotic resistance to the Spanish:

> *The Ghost of Shakespeare rises to trumpets and flutes, playing alternately.*
> Hail, my lov'd Britons! how I'm pleas'd to see
> The great assertors of fair Liberty,
> Assembl'd here upon this solemn day,
> To see this *Roman* and this *English* play!
> This tragedy in great *Eliza*'s reign,
> Was writ, when Philip plagu'd both land and main,
> To subjugate the western world to Spain.
>
> .   .   .   .
>
> My noble scenes Eliza's soul inspir'd,
> And Britain with a just disdain was fir'd,
> That we who scorn'd great Caesar here should reign,
> Should take an universal king from Spain.[16]

Characteristically for its time, this prologue slips quietly from 'English' to 'Britain', backdating the invention of Britain to Elizabeth's time and representing Shakespeare's play as inspiring the nation and the Queen alike. Such connections between Shakespeare, Elizabeth, and British supremacy, indeed, would become commonplace over the ensuing decades. The prologue to Lewis Theobald's *Double Falshood*, 1728 (an adaptation of the otherwise lost Shakespeare-Fletcher collaboration *Cardenio*, 1612–13) equally sees Shakespeare's literary supremacy as a cteristically British expression of 'Eliza's *golden Days*':

Such *SHAKESPEARE*'s Genius was:—Let *Britons* boast
The glorious Birth, and, eager, strive who most
Shall celebrate his Verse; for while we raise
Trophies of Fame to him, ourselves we praise:
Display the Talents of a *British* Mind,
Where All is great, free, open, unconfin'd . . .

The epilogue, though at first it feigns a cynically modish disdain for
Shakespeare as one of the 'Moral Bards of Good Queen *Bess*'s Days',
follows Dennis's lead in equating Shakespeare's literary power with
Elizabethan military force:

In *SHAKESPEARE*'s Age the *English* Youth inspir'd,
Lov'd as they fought, by him and Beauty fir'd.
'Tis yours to crown the Bard, whose Magick Strain
Cou'd charm the Heroes of that glorious Reign,
Which humbled to the Dust the Pride of *Spain*.[17]

Dennis's suggestion of an easy familiarity between poet and
patroness—with Shakespeare taking suggestions as to comic plots from
Elizabeth, and Elizabeth taking suggestions as to foreign policy from
Shakespeare—would be much taken up and elaborated over the course
of the eighteenth century, continuing helpfully to clean up Shakespeare's
image and warm up Elizabeth's in the process. When a monument to
Shakespeare was at last installed in Westminster Abbey in 1741 its
pedestal prominently featured a head of the writer's alleged patroness
Elizabeth,[18] and by 1763 it was already a matter of established fact that
Elizabeth had saved the young Shakespeare's dawning career by personally intervening, for the good of English literature, to rescue him (with a
royal pardon) from Sir Thomas Lucy's prosecution for deer-poaching.
(This story is solemnly recorded in that ancestor of the *Dictionary of
National Biography*, the *Biographica Britannica*.)[19] These unusually close
patron–client relations would be conclusively and dramatically confirmed by a more remarkable, if less authoritative, text laid before the
public in 1794. Addressed to 'Master William Shakespeare atte the
Globe bye Thames', it is no less than a personal letter from Elizabeth,
thanking 'goode Masterre William' for some 'prettye Verses', and

reminding him to bring his best actors for her entertainment when he visits her at Hampton, for 'the lorde Leiscesterre wille bee withe usse.'[20] As its orthography now makes painfully obvious, this letter is a crude forgery—one of the earliest efforts of William-Henry Ireland—and by early 1796 it was being wonderfully ridiculed by the likes of James Boaden, who published a parody in *The Oracle*: 'We give thee nottice thatt wee shalle *drinke Tea* withe thee bye Thames Tomorrowe, thou Monarche offe the *Globe* . . . P.S. More offe oure virgin beautye . . .'[21] But Ireland's success in gaining almost universal credence, if only for two giddy years, shows how well he understood precisely what the late eighteenth-century public wanted to believe about Elizabeth's dealings with Shakespeare. Putting his artistic talents at the service of her desire to impress a preferred suitor, Ireland's Shakespeare provides Eliza's hitherto frustratingly invisible libido with its literary expression. The male National Poet's texts can henceforward be read as records of the female national icon's sensibility.

This may sound like an extremely fanciful interpretation of one of the ideas informing Ireland's forgery, but it is amply confirmed by one of Ireland's contemporary defenders. For George Chalmers, Ireland's hint of an intimate correspondence between the Bard and his monarch might simultaneously nationalize Shakespeare's sexuality and reveal Elizabeth's. Writing after Ireland has been exposed as a fake, Chalmers none the less wonderfully develops his suggestion that Shakespeare sent 'prettye Verses' to Elizabeth, in *An Apology for the Believers in the Shakspeare-Papers* (1797). Refusing to accept that 'Shakspeare, a husband, a father, a moral man, addressed a hundred and twenty, nay, a hundred and twenty-six *Amourous* Sonnets to a *male* object!', Chalmers assures his readers that the Young Man sequence, advocating marriage and procreation, is in fact addressed to a woman—and to who else but Elizabeth I? The poems' masculine pronouns should not mislead us: 'Elizabeth was often considered as a man', he insists.[22] On Shakespeare's side, unofficial homosexual attraction is here neatly converted into public, heterosexual duty, at a single romantic stroke: the Bard, already regarded as Elizabeth's court poet, is here further positioned as her gynaecologist, the apparently unorthodox sexuality expressed in the

Sonnets thereby safely reidentified with the national interest. Elizabeth, by the same ploy, is retrospectively made fertile, albeit as a mother of the national literary canon rather than of a dynasty: the poems which Shakespeare finally declares to be more enduring than mere flesh and blood, outlasting the gilded monuments of princes, become Elizabeth's honorary children, the fruits of her hitherto secret association with the writer. The *Sonnets* thus become fragments of a real-life historical epistolary novel starring the two most important incarnations of England's golden age. Yet another new anecdote from the time of the Ireland forgeries, widely reprinted in the press during 1796, describes how Elizabeth, during one of her frequent visits to the public theatres, walked across the stage of the Globe while Shakespeare was playing a king, and, when the levelling professional obstinately remained in character, dropped a handkerchief in the hope of attracting his attention. 'But, ere this be done,' ad-libbed the 'mimic Monarch', 'Take up our SISTER's handkerchief.' Significantly, when this story is next retold (by Richard Ryan, in 1825) the upwardly mobile punch line is rewritten so as not to preclude a less fraternal role, its language coming instead to resemble that of Henry V's courtship of Catherine of France: 'And though now bent on this high embassy, | Yet *stoop* we to take up our *Cousin's* glove.'[23] In a later variant on the story this hint of potential romance between actor and monarch is intimated by casting: the play in progress is *A Midsummer Night's Dream* and Shakespeare is playing Oberon, so this exchange becomes an encounter between Shakespeare as Fairy King and Elizabeth the Fairy Queen. 'Od's pittikins!', exclaims a delighted Gloriana, 'our Magnifico is cousin-german to all regal minds.'[24]

To place Elizabeth and Shakespeare side by side in the *Sonnets* or at the Globe is to bring them still closer together than they might appear in the making of *The Merry Wives*, and from the 1790s onwards the new stories which proliferate about their relations, equally flattering to Shakespeare's status, underline more and more clearly his progress towards eligibility as a suitor for more than literary patronage. To return once more to Sir Walter Scott, for example, *Kenilworth*, with an anachronistic zeal worthy of Shakespeare himself, teases the maximum significance from the *Biographia Britannica's* version of the deer-stealing: Scott's Elizabeth does not just enjoy Shakespeare's plays and defend his theatre from a bear-baiting consortium (despite the fact that the Kenilworth festivities took place when Shakespeare was only eleven), but insists that Shakespeare never kissed Sir Thomas Lucy's keeper's daughter, in a manner which suggests that she herself is jealously susceptible to his personal charms.[25] Their relationship is far more central, however, in one of many texts Scott's novel influenced, the first English play to feature Shakespeare as protagonist, Charles Somerset's 'Historical and Legendary National Drama', *Shakspeare's Early Days* (1829). *Shakspeare's Early Days*, like *Kenilworth*, expunges all other imputed kissing from the story in order to stress the Bard's status as his queen's special favourite. Fleeing Stratford as usual after poaching venison—this time, ingeniously, in the cause of virtue, for the succour of a starving peasant—Somerset's Shakespeare arrives in London, pursued by Sir Thomas Lucy, where, after calling hastily on Burbage to deliver the manuscript of his first play (*Hamlet*), he is not only pardoned by an enthusiastic Elizabeth but is invested as Poet Laureate, minutes after the defeat of the Armada. Elizabeth is once again Shakespeare's dea ex machina, recognizing and rewarding his literary merit to produce the happy ending in exactly the manner which would be repeated in 1998 by the denouement of *Shakespeare in Love* (where Judi Dench's Oscar-winning Elizabeth endorses not *Hamlet* but *Romeo and Juliet* and goes on to commission *Twelfth Night*). But there is more to it than that: in the climactic tableau with which Somerset concludes his play, Shakespeare kneels centre stage while Elizabeth hangs a miniature of herself, framed with diamonds, around his neck, and the whole supporting cast sing a rousing chorus: 'Shakspeare! Shakspeare! none beside! | Shakspeare is his nation's pride!'[26] Conspicuously absent from this chorus, however, is Anne Hathaway, deleted from the story altogether so as to give Somerset room to celebrate instead the burgeoning national romance between Elizabeth and her pet playwright—which this final tableau comes very close to representing as a betrothal, cemented at the very apogeee of England's Elizabethan self-definition, the vanquishing of the Armada.

The dawning suggestion of an actual romantic attachment between Elizabeth and Shakespeare, hovering so close to the surface here, seems finally to have become inescapable by the mid-nineteenth century. In France, where in 1804 Alexandre Duval had already produced a play called *Shakespeare Amoureux*, the composer Ambroise Thomas dramatized the erotic dimension of the patroness–poet relationship in his delightful opera *Le Songe d'une nuit d'été* (premièred in 1850, though drafted thirty years earlier, to a libretto by Rosier and De Leuven). As its title suggests, this opera does derive vaguely from *A Midsummer Night's Dream*, but only in that it tells a story about Shakespeare and Elizabeth in which the poet plays Bottom to her inspiring Titania. Thomas's Elizabeth sets out to rescue Shakespeare from his corrupting association with the drunken Falstaff (in this rendition a real-life keeper of her Richmond Park deer) by appearing ravishingly to him in disguise as the personification of his Muse, leading him through the park by moonlight with a series of Queen-of-the-Night-style coloratura arias. In response to the yearning amorous raptures she thus inspires, she laments in musical asides that her crown rules out any less creatively sublimated love affair.[27] Even back in Victorian England, the relationship between the Bard and Eliza was by now definitely hotting up. In successive paintings celebrating Elizabeth's alleged commissioning of *The Merry Wives*, for example, the Queen and her poet grow ever closer. In David Scott's *Queen Elizabeth Viewing the Performance of 'The Merry Wives of Windsor' at the Globe Theatre* (1840), now in the Theatre Museum,[28] (Plate 5), the two immortal literary collaborators gaze intently at Falstaff during the most priapic moment at which Shakespeare's play 'shews him in love', the climax of act 5, as he hubristically prepares to enjoy both Mistress Ford and Mistress Page in his guise as Herne the Hunter. Like the Essex plot, this depiction of the Queen as attentive spectator of Falstaff's ruttishness conveniently grants her the susceptible female subjectivity so frustratingly lacking from official history. Conceding the Virgin Queen an enthusiasm for sexual play, albeit in the service of the specifically middle-class morality and culture which Mistresses Page and Ford are actually defending, this painting makes its distinctly youthful-looking Elizabeth into the merry would-be wife of Windsor Castle. It uses the occasion, too, to reinstate this vital, perpetually fresh-looking Elizabeth at the centre of Merrie England's golden age. Not only is the Globe brought under her aegis by the provision of a royal box (her unhistorical presence at a public theatre for a Shakespeare première another striking anticipation of motifs still sufficiently alive to have been redeployed by *Shakespeare in Love*), but the audience for this historic performance includes almost every famous worthy of her entire reign—recognizable around the Queen are Leicester, Essex, and Walsingham, and elsewhere can be seen not just Shakespeare but Raleigh, Spenser, Southampton, Fletcher, Beaumont, Burghley, Cecil, Dr Dee, Drake, and even Sidney, sporting one of his more casual breastplates for the occasion. Shakespeare's Globe here anticipates not just the Royal National Theatre but the National Portrait Gallery.

Back at court, and this time physically much nearer her preferred love poet, an even more nubile Elizabeth gazes raptly towards Shakespeare's hose in John James Chalon's *Shakespeare reading to Queen Elizabeth*, and Elizabeth listens swooningly to her Laureate's voice in a whole line of such compositions: *Shakespeare's Interview with Queen Elizabeth* (James Stothard, 1827, Fig. 13); *Shakespeare reading one of his plays to Queen Elizabeth* (John Wood, 1835); *Shakespeare reading before Queen Elizabeth* (John Laslett Pott, 1875), *Shakespeare reading* Macbeth *before Queen Elizabeth* (Eduard Ender, undated); *Shakespeare reading* A Midsummer Night's Dream *to Queen Elizabeth* (Henry Nelson O'Neil, 1877); *Shakespeare and Queen Elizabeth* (Joseph Haier, 1886); and, outdoing them all in sheer festive merrieness, *A Christmas Play by Shakespeare before Queen Elizabeth* (Sir John Gilbert, undated).[29] The flirtation between Elizabeth and Shakespeare is still heavier in one of the most intriguing of all derivatives from Dennis's *Merry Wives* story, a water-colour by Charles Cattermole, part of a whole sequence depicting incidents from Shakespeare's life, now in the RSC's collection in Stratford. In *Shakespeare Reading the 'Merry Wives of Windsor' to Queen Elizabeth* (*c.*1860: Plate 6), Elizabeth is not only an intimate collaborator with Shakespeare, the co-progenitor of Falstaff's amours, but is identified with another Shakespearean character entirely. Cattermole's painting sets this encounter between the Bard and his patroness neither at the Globe nor the court, but in a more charged venue, at once royally public and amorously clandestine; a state barge on an obscure reach of the

Painted by T. Stothard RA.   Engraved by W. Ensom.

SHAKESPEARE'S INTERVIEW WITH

QUEEN ELIZABETH.

Published by William Pickering, Chancery Lane, Sept. 1824.

FIG. 13. Thomas Stothard (1755–1834), *Shakespeare's Interview with Queen Elizabeth* (1827). The eighteenth and nineteenth centuries' frequent depictions of imaginary meetings between Elizabeth and Shakespeare—whether in novels, plays, operas, forged corespondence, or, as here, engravings—show their relations growing ever cosier and more intimate: here the Bard shares a blushingly amused Elizabeth's leisure moments with a handsome favourite in a private corner of the grounds at Nonesuch Palace.

Thames. By her association with Shakespeare, Elizabeth can be revealed, at last, as a timelessly enchanting Cleopatra—according to this picture too, age cannot wither her. Shakespeare, meanwhile, presenting her with what is at once their shared erotic fantasy and their joint dramatic offspring, is not just a favourite but a secret lover, a potential partner: the painting's setting alludes not just to *Antony and Cleopatra* but to the occasion when Leicester, flirting in a state barge with Elizabeth, is reported to have jokingly told the Spanish ambassador he could see no reason why they should not be married there and then. The hint is made gloriously explicit in a novel, Robert Folkestone Williams's *The Secret Passion* (1844), the finale of a trilogy about Shakespeare's life and times which had begun in 1838 with *Shakespeare and his Friends; or 'The Golden Age' of Merrie England*.[30] According to Williams, the Queen

would have had [Shakespeare] right willingly to have been her husband, had he not had already a wife of his own. Nevertheless, this stood so little in the way of his advancement that his fortune was made presently by her Highness, who would scarce let him out of her sight, and it was with much ado he could escape from her to attend to the wants of his young family . . .[31]

How, indeed, could she have resisted the sincere, bluff, provincial soul of Merrie England, the masculine Bottom to her regal Titania? As John Collis Snaith would later describe their encounter, Shakespeare was the only person ever to appear at Elizabeth's court who was man enough for her:

But there was not a trace of the sycophant about this man who conversed with her as modestly, as readily and as easily as he would have done with a lounger in a tavern. And while the gallants and fine ladies were not a little shocked by the unaffectedness of the man's bearing and marvelled not a little that one so august should bestow so much notice upon a common play-actor, the Queen, on the other hand, seemed almost to forget for the moment the dizzy eminence to which it had pleased Providence to call her.

The truth was she dearly loved what she called 'a man.' And this was a scarce commodity in the exotic atmosphere which surrounded Elizabeth Tudor . . . It was a sad sight for many an astonished and resentful eye to observe the Queen and the man 'Shake-scene' . . . walking quite apart from all the rest, up one alley and down another, talking and laughing heartily on terms which perilously

approached equality . . . And it was not here that the scandal ended. A little
later when the Queen dined a place was set for the man Shakescene at her own
table . . .[32]

Once Shakespeare has risen to the status of Elizabeth's fellow national icon, then, the two find themselves posthumously embarked on a narrative trajectory which, starting by attributing a share in Shakespeare's
literary creativity to his queen so that they may be celebrated together as
figurative mother and father of the national culture, cannot resist pro-
pelling them, despite every historical record to the contrary, towards a
literal coupling. The strategy of conferring an inner self on Elizabeth by
involving her in the comedy of Shakespeare instead of the she-tragedy of
the Countess of Rutland proves simply to condemn her to another
narrative logic equally incompatible with her status as England's
implacably Virgin Queen—this one, however, with an amorous rather
than a tragic conclusion. Over the course of the eighteenth and nineteenth centuries, the official iconic portraits of Gloriana and the literary
texts of Shakespeare were read compulsively together into a historical
novel in which the coincidence or collusion of Tudor absolutism with
Renaissance drama metamorphosed into the clandestine romance of
Elizabeth Tudor with William Shakespeare: the imagined union
between the native genius and his queen becomes another version of the
unity between land and crown elsewhere affirmed by the Tilbury icon or
the Ditchley portrait. That this whole process was informed and driven
by cultural nationalism is made splendidly clear by a pragmatic and self-
consciously tongue-in-cheek contribution to the genre, George Bernard
Shaw's fund-raising playlet *The Dark Lady of the Sonnets* (1910). Here an
incognito Elizabeth is ardently wooed by Shakespeare, who, on learning
her real identity and therefore seeing that any actual liaison is impossible, propositions her instead for a crown subsidy for his playhouse.
Elizabeth of course agrees that this would be a splendid thing, so that the
play leaves them disappointed as lovers but, as in the earlier examples we
have sketched, ratified in their roles as collaborative cultural icons—
parents of the National Theatre, *faute de mieux*.

Since the early twentieth century, this Shakespearean s[
Elizabeth's mythos has converged, sometimes with bizarre resu[

the sentimental love-plot patterns described in Chapter 2. In more recent fictions about Queen Elizabeth and Shakespeare, the apocryphal intimate link between the two is usually established via fictitious characters who are at once sentimental heroines on the Countess of Rutland model *and* embodiments of Shakespearean comedy. Twentieth-century historical fiction specialized in providing Elizabeth with a whole series of cross-dressed confidantes, fatally inclined to steal away from her court disguised as men to flirt (at the very least) with Shakespeare—a crowd of amiable Principal Boys who had already proliferated long before Gwyneth Paltrow had even heard an English accent. H. F. Rubinstein and Clifford Bax's *Shakespeare: A Play in Five Episodes* (1921), in which Shakespeare is as ever Elizabeth's favourite writer, features a Dark Lady who would be a player if only she were male, and within a few years her successors would be managing such personal transformations as they could in this direction. In this descent, for example, is Lord Burghley's hitherto unknown niece Phyllis, heroine of Miriam Michelson's *Petticoat King* (1929), loved by Elizabeth's beloved favourite Hugh Dorsey, and driven to adopt male disguise to elude Eliza's jealous vigilance. In this garb (strategically reciting Shakespeare's amorous sonnets) she herself, Cesario-like, accidentally and embarrassingly becomes Eliza's newest favourite, before the lovers finally escape from Gloriana to Virginia. Just a year earlier had appeared the most thoroughly transsexual of all Elizabeth's fictional Shakespearean protegé[e]s, the protagonist of Virginia Woolf's dazzling meditation on the relations between literature, national identity, and gender from the Renaissance to modernity, *Orlando*, a Ganymede-like male favourite and Shakespeare fan at Elizabeth's court who metamorphoses into a more Rosalind-like woman during the eighteenth century.[33]

From here onwards, the Shakespearean gender-bending around fictionalized Elizabeths never stops, the state and empire now personified by monarch and playwright apparently perceived in ever more perverse terms. In Cunliffe Owen's amazingly earnest novel *The Phoenix and the Dove* (1933)—written in a style somewhere between W. H. Ainsworth and D. H. Lawrence—the young Elizabeth Vernon is erotically admired by a literally hermaphrodite Queen Elizabeth who, doubly jealous over

Miss Vernon's liaison with the Earl of Southampton (whom s/he also fancies), finally achieves some consolation in an intimacy with the bisexual Shakespeare who has already bedded each of them in turn. Toning all this down slightly for wartime, Caryl Brahms and S. J. Simons published their comic novel *No Bed For Bacon* seven years later, in which we meet Viola, a stage-struck lady-in-waiting who moonlights in drag as a boy actor. She has an affair with Shakespeare, who composes sonnets for her, and she of course becomes the inspiration for the role of Viola in *Twelfth Night*.[34] This particular Viola's most recent descendant before her recycling in Tom Stoppard and Marc Norman's screenplay for *Shakespeare in Love* (1998) was the Yentl-like Rebecca Lopez of Faye Kellerman's ghastly so-called thriller *The Quality of Mercy* (1989), another recreational cross-dresser, who gets forced into one bed by a caricatured lesbian Elizabeth and talked into another by Shakespeare. Unable to save her better-known physician father from execution, Shakespeare immortalizes her as Jessica in *The Merchant of Venice*. (Kellerman, incidentally, has sued the producers of *Shakespeare in Love* for plagiarism: their defence would presumably be to point out that they were quite obviously plagiarizing not from her but from *No Bed For Bacon*.)

So it is that the need to produce a British national culture out of the surviving traces of Good Queen Bess's mythologized golden days mandated the rewriting of Elizabeth and Shakespeare as increasingly flirtatious poet and patroness, as potential husband and wife, and finally as sexually ambiguous rivals for the favours of transvestites. Could this long-term compulsion to force Shakespeare and Elizabeth together bring them any closer still? The answer, curiously but with a perverse logic, is yes, at least among certain so-called non-fictional writers who have continued to find the historical traces of Elizabeth's private life and Shakespeare's sadly inadequate to their sense of what England's Eliza and England's Bard ought to have been to one another. As early as the end of the nineteenth century Orville Ward Owen, the industrious author of *Francis Bacon's Cypher Story* (1893–5), was willing to assure the public that concealed in the Shakespeare folio and elsewhere were hitherto undecoded writings by Sir Francis which revealed him to have been not only the real author of the Shakespeare canon but a

legitimate son of Elizabeth by the Earl of Leicester (and as such broth-
er to the Earl of Essex: see *The Tragical Historie of our late brother the Earl
of Essex. By the author of Hamlet, Richard III, Othello, As You Like It, etc
... deciphered from the works of Sir Francis Bacon by Orville Ward
Owen, M.D.*, 1895).[35] This harrowing story returns in C. Y. C. Dawbarn's
*Uncrowned: A Story of Queen Elizabeth and the Early Life of Francis
'Bacon', As Told in his Secret Writings and in Other Contemporary Records of
Her Reign* (London, 1913), and it is developed in full by Alfred Dodd's
*The Marriage of Elizabeth Tudor. Being an exhaustive inquiry into her
alleged Marriage with the Earl of Leicester and the alleged Births of her Two
Sons, Francis Bacon and the Earl of Essex: an historical research based on one
of the themes in 'Shakespeare's Sonnets'. . . by the author of 'Shakespeare,
Creator of Freemasonry', 'Francis Bacon and the Brethren of the Rosicrosse',
and Editor of 'Shakespeare's Sonnet-Diary', etc, etc* (London, 1940).
William R. Leigh produced only a mild variant on this plot in *Clipt
Wings* (New York, 1930, a possible source for Comyns Beaumont's *The
Private Life of the Virgin Queen*, 1946, quoted in our introduction): here it
is Cecil, not Essex, who is Bacon's sibling (a half-brother, being 'the bastard of the base Burleigh', 35), and Bacon writes *Hamlet* deliberately to
expose his own situation as the unacknowledged true heir to Elizabeth's
throne. (He must do so even earlier than the Shakespeare of *Shakspeare's
Early Days*, since his father Leicester, who died in late 1588, is still around
to recognize Claudius as a portrait of himself, 50, but perhaps this is an
inappropriate way of reading a play which elsewhere depicts Elizabeth
in residence at Buckingham Palace, 42.) It all ends in tears: Elizabeth is
once more strangled to death by Cecil (even though in this version he is
her own son), and Ben Jonson and Michael Drayton, determined to
maintain Bacon's alias, murder the Warwickshire actor who has been
employed to claim Bacon's plays as his own, one William Shaxper.[36]

A happier variant on the family romance of Good Queen Bess and
the national poet, however, would be provided in 1952. Identifying
Shakespeare once more as Elizabeth's only rightful mate, the poet of her
secret inner life, Charlton and Dorothy Ogburn argue in *This Star of
England* not only that 'Shakespeare' was really the 17th Earl of Oxford,
but that the Queen was secretly married to him. (Outdoing Chalmers,

FIG. 14. The illogical end-point of the claim that Shakespeare was Elizabeth's protégé was reached by those mid-twentieth-century conspiracy theorists who argued that 'Shakespeare' was in fact just her pseudonym. In the 1990s, experiments with the computerized analysis of Renaissance images led some to compound this allegation with a claim that the portrait on the title-page of the Shakespeare Folio was itself merely a disguised likeness of the Queen. This androgynous image of a composite Elizabethan Shakespeare or Shakespearean Elizabeth appeared in *New Scientist* in November 1991.

the Ogburns are still more ingenious at thereby keeping homosexuality out of the Young Man sonnets: according to their theory, the poems *are* addressed to a male object, the Earl of Southampton, but they express only a filial affection, since he was Oxford's and Elizabeth's son.) It was left to one George Elliott Sweet to go the whole way four years later. Completing the apparently unstoppable convergence of Gloriana and the Bard initiated by Dennis two and a half centuries earlier, *Shakespeare the Mystery* (1956) simply and elegantly claims that Elizabeth herself was the real Shakespeare—or, to put it another way, 'Shakespeare' was the secret, real Elizabeth. In fact Sweet's batty legacy has been taken up more recently by computer graphics experts, some of whom have attempted to demonstrate that the title-page of the First Folio 'really' depicts Elizabeth by matching half of the Droeshout engraving of Shakespeare on to the other half of the Gower portrait of Elizabeth (Fig. 14), occasionally trying out bits of Francis Bacon with it for good measure.[37] A Falstaff who may be either Herne the Hunt

Mother Prat, a Cleopatra wearing Antony's sword or perhaps an Antony dressed in Cleopatra's tires and mantles, this final image gives Elizabeth, however she may have the body of a weak and feeble woman, the heart and stomach of a poet, and a national poet of England too—and at the same time allows Shakespeare to come out as Ganymede, a boy-princess cross-dressed as a man. Here at last is a role fit to be played by Judi Dench, Gwyneth Paltrow, *and* Joseph Fiennes all at once, a Shakespeare and Queen Elizabeth not only equipped to personify an altogether more post-modern Britain, but doubtless quite capable of being in love with him and/or herself.

Queen Elizabeth Slept Here

Or perhaps of just having a nice cup of tea instead, stirred with a pair of matching spoons. Among Elizabeth's more mainstream twentieth-century manifestations, perhaps none is more congenial to the British mind than her appearance in silver plate on the head of a souvenir tea-spoon, paired with another spoon identical save that the image it bears is of Shakespeare. These artefacts, as if belatedly realizing James Boaden's *jeu d'esprit* about Elizabeth inviting the Bard to tea, can now be obtained from the National Portrait Gallery gift shop in London, a retail outlet where most shelves not preoccupied with Elizabeth's father and his various wives are instead dominated by likenesses of the Swan of Avon and the Virgin Queen, from the Shakespeare mouse-mat to the Darnley portrait wristwatch. (The ingenious use made of the characteristic wide shape of the Queen's skirts by the Elizabeth I tea cosy and egg cosy also deserves comment, yet another instance of the perennial desire to warm the national icon up a little below the waist.) This profusion of Elizabeths and Shakespeares among the NPG's merchandise is not altogether surprising: historically, the whole gallery is organized around likenesses of Elizabeth and Shakespeare. Its collection was founded in the 1850s when it acquired the Chandos portrait of Shakespeare, a picture which was soon accompanied by the Ditchley portrait of Elizabeth (Plate 4), which was originally hung directly opposite it.[38] That these two cornerstones of this British pantheon should ultimately have metamorphosed into teaspoons seems in many ways only apt: here are the two greatest celebrities of the golden age simultaneously rendered impeccably national and respectably domestic, joined forever in that key British religious ritual, afternoon tea. As far as the National Portrait Gallery is concerned, whether Britain is to be defined by its heroic ancestors or by its post-modern souvenir kitsch, Queen Elizabeth and Shakespeare are completely inseparable. As this example may suggest, the connections between Elizabeth, Shakespeare, and Britishness drawn so insistently by the texts we have discussed in this chapter are now perhaps most obvious around the tourist industry. It is in the promulgation of a nostalgic, half-timbered idea of Elizabethan England that the vigorous cultural nationalism of the eighteenth and nineteenth centuries finds its faint contemporary echoes: the mock-Tudor gift shops of Warwickshire ('Shakespeare's County', as the signs on the M40 motorway declare it) are still busily perpetuating a set of notions and indeed of commercial practices founded a couple of centuries ago.[39] One of the objects offered for the inspection of early Bardolatrous pilgrims to Stratford-upon-Avon in the early nineteenth century was 'a gold Tissue Toilet or Table Cover' supposedly given to Shakespeare by 'his friend and admirer, Queen Elizabeth' (a spurious souvenir or relic here precipitating this anecdote of gift-exchange),[40] and her patronage of the national poet was again stressed in a local context by Tresham D. Gregg's verse-drama *Queen Elizabeth; or, the origin of Shakespeare* (1872). This play invents an anecdote of its own: the Queen meets Shakespeare during her visit to nearby Kenilworth in 1575, but, unlike Scott, Gregg is prepared to acknowledge their real respective ages at the time—his Shakespeare is still a precocious ten year old. As ever Elizabeth recognizes his burgeoning talents and awards him the literary prize which founds his career, this time for out-composing another promising schoolboy, Francis Bacon. Warwickshire is not only Shakespeare's county but Elizabeth's: as any reader of Scott's *Kenilworth* knows, Queen Elizabeth slept here.

It was from Kenilworth, indeed, that Elizabeth's retrospective reblessing of the English shires began, with the publication of John Nichols's massive three-volume reprint of contemporary accounts of her receptions at Kenilworth and elsewhere, *Progresses and Public Processions*

of Queen Elizabeth, between 1788 and 1805. Arcane and cumbersome as
this publication (by the Society of Antiquaries) might appear at first
sight, it provided one immediate source and stimulus for Scott's best-
selling novel, and its appearance coincided with a general interest—in
popular culture no less than among historians—in linking Elizabeth to
specific English places, connecting her glorious reign not just with the
national culture but with the national landscape and its local communities. The very phrase 'Elizabeth slept here' suggests the revival of an older
conception of monarchy, though now one which has been divorced from
the state, in which royal power is located in a royal body in place (as it is
in the Ditchley portrait); the idea haunts, too, in part because it carries a
hint of the Arthurian mythologization of Elizabeth as the once and
future queen who is *only* asleep, like Arthur under the hill, and who
will rise again in England's hour of need—roused, presumably, by the
beating of Drake's drum.

 This desire to locate Elizabethanness found further expression in the
later nineteenth century via a boom in the facsimile re-enactment of the
Queen's progresses, staged as local pageant-plays, a fad which lasted well
into the Edwardian period. It would find echoes in children's fiction, as,
for example, Monica Edwards's *The Summer of the Great Secret* (1948),
which describes the making of a cinematic re-enactment of Elizabeth's
visit to Dunsford. (Elizabeth is celebrated as a civic patroness in a comparable manner by the statues of her on the Victorian Gothic façades of
Manchester Town Hall and of the Russell Hotel in London, and by John
Hassall's magnificent painting of *The State Entry of Queen Elizabeth into
Bristol, August 14, 1574*, Frontispiece).[41] All this overlaps very readily into
the deliberate promulgation of tourism. Before Scott's novel had even
appeared, Mrs Lewis Bowen had already published 'Lines Written Near
Kenilworth Castle, in the Year 1800' (in *Kenilworth Castle; and other
Poems*, Salop, 1818), a poem which collates themes of sentimental retire-
ment and the chivalry of bygone days with an account of Elizabeth's
visit, and the whole book is supplied with notes about the site itself
which amount to a miniature tourist puff.[42] The success of *Kenilworth*
in its turn did much to popularize existing published accounts of
Elizabeth's progresses and to encourage tourists to retrace her steps:

hence, for example, *Kenilworth Festivities: comprising Laneham's Description of the Pageantry, and Gascoigne's Masques, represented before Queen Elizabeth* . . . (Warwick and Leamington, 1825), which was sold at the castle itself by way of tourist guide. Elizabeth Harcourt Mitchell would repeat this trick for Dover Castle in *Her Majesty's Bear* (London, 1884), which follows an account of Elizabeth's procession into the town on a white horse with a warm recommendation of 'the room still known as Queen Elizabeth's banqueting hall . . . The oak floor still remains, and those who think about it, and care about it, may have the satisfaction of placing their feet where those of glorious Queen Bess once trod' (279).

It is very clear from contemporary reviews of Scott's novel that what its first readers most enjoyed was its evocation of Elizabeth's age as comprehensively jovial, confirming the vision of Merry England which was already luring increasing numbers of tourists to Warwickshire. As *The Port Folio* had it,

[Scott] has manifested a hearty good will towards the velvet meadows of bonny old England and her royal oaks. He has a kindred feeling with those who revelled, in olden time, on Christmas cheer and quaffed October ale. He handles the quarterstaff and the bow with the familiarity of one who practised in those feats from infancy. He presents to our eyes the moated castle, the lofty turrets, and the storied tapestry of English chivalry, until we feel ourselves contemporary with his heroes.[43]

The *Monthly Review* was even more nostalgic, declaring that Scott had done well to choose 'the splendid reign of Elizabeth' as his setting, since all English people instinctively recognize it as closer to the core of their imaginative territory than is the present day.

When the scene is laid in the good old time of Elizabeth, we feel ourselves more at home . . . The . . . truly English characteristics of that time were to be found in their fullest strength and prominence . . . We have therefore great delight in straying back to our ancestors of those days, partaking though in fancy of their honest hospitalities, listening to the smart but somewhat coarse reciprocations of their dialogue, mixing in their merry though sometimes intemperate carousals, and escaping, even in fiction, from a less romantic stage of society, of which the traits are tamely and coldly monotonous.[44]

This dream of coming home to Elizabeth's Merrie England is still very much alive, fuelling a major industry not just around Kenilworth but at Hatfield, the site of Elizabeth's internal exile under Bloody Mary. By the time *Kenilworth* appeared an implausibly modern-looking straw hat was already on display at Hatfield as the very headgear which Elizabeth had worn while engaged in the no less implausibly hyper-English pursuit of tending her garden, and around the same time a particular tree in the park was identified as the very one under which she was sitting when she heard the news of her accession in 1558. It is, needless to say, an oak, and it is a resonant symptom of the way in which such once-potent national symbols have dwindled to adjuncts of a kitsch tourist trade that the tree was moved in 1978 to one corner of the Hatfield souvenir shop, where until a major refurbishment in the 1990s it shaded a waxwork Princess Elizabeth who contemplated her destiny among shelves of heraldic ash trays and china figurines (Fig. 15). Elsewhere at Hatfield, however, the *Monthly Review*'s idea of Good Queen Bess's reign as a lost English idyll of honest hospitality and intemperate carousal is rather more vividly realized. 'My Lords and sweet Ladies, come join us at The Old Palace, Hatfield Park, for an evening of feasting and merrymaking', cries the brochure:

So the invitation goes out today, as it did long ago in 1556 . . . In this historic set-ting, where Queen Elizabeth held her first Council of State, you can sit back and revel in the atmosphere and entertainment of an Elizabethan Banquet every Tuesday, Thursday, Friday and Saturday evening . . . When you first arrive at The Old Palace you may purchase an aperitif in the Lower Solar Room which was once part of the childhood apartments of the young Princess Elizabeth. Then you move into the Great Hall itself to enjoy a magnificent five-course meal of royal proportions including red or white wine and mead. One of a bevy of buxom serving wenches will be in constant attendance to ensure that everything is to your satisfaction and that your glass is constantly replenished. From the moment you take your seat you will be under the spell of a troupe of costumed minstrels and players. Singing songs and sometimes saucy ditties of the period, performing some of the picturesque ceremonies and customs of the Elizabethan era, they move from table to table serenading you as you dine.

Nor are these delights any longer confined to the English: 'A translation of the history of the Old Palace and an explanation of the customs of the

FIG. 15. A waxwork Elizabeth and her oak, posing for the tourists: postcard, Hatfield Old Palace, *c.*1980. According to Robert Naunton's *Fragmenta Regalia* (1641), Elizabeth greeted the tidings of her accession on 17 November 1558 by falling to her knees and quoting from Psalm 118: 'This is the Lord's doing; it is marvellous in our eyes.' In time Accession Day became a national holiday, and years later a particular oak tree in the park at Hatfield was identified as the very one under which the princess had been standing when she received the news. Eventually it died, and from 1978 until a refurbishment in the 1990s its corpse found itself engaged in this perpetual inert re-enactment of its alleged moment of glory, in one corner of the Hatfield gift shop.

"Court" is available free of charge in seven languages for those guests who would like one.'

This blurb is all too easy to laugh at, but the fantasy it offers still has a powerful imaginative hold—after all, the banqueting hall is regularly sold out. But just as this longing to enjoy Old English good cheer chez Gloriana is not new, nor is our tendency to find it at least a fraction comic. The commercial exploitation of the merrie Elizabethan associations of particular English places and buildings was already coming in for its share of ridicule as early as 1889. 'She was nuts on public houses, was England's Virgin Queen,' wrote Jerome K. Jerome in *Three Men in a Boat*. 'There's scarcely a pub of any attractions within ten miles of London that she does not seem to have looked in at, stopped at, or slept at, some time or other.'[45] Jerome's crack nicely recycles in comic mode the earlier idea of Elizabeth as a beer-drinking, beef-eating national termagant—a notion whose survival is demonstrated by the cult popularity of a particular photograph in the National Portrait Gallery's collection: it depicts a grim-looking Glenda Jackson in full Elizabeth I costume clutching not a death-warrant but a pint of Guinness, during a pause between takes on the set of the 1971 film *Mary Queen of Scots* (Fig. 16). A comparable cartoon likeness of a pint-bearing Elizabeth was adorning posters for the Hogshead Ale Houses chain of pubs as recently as 1996: under the slogan 'Discover World Ales at Hogshead' a surprised Queen is offered a packet of potato crisps by a kneeling Sir Walter Raleigh. (Shakespeare, too, has done his posthumous bit for the selling of beer, as any Flowers' Bitter beer-mat can bear witness.) The Elizabeth Slept Here joke is developed most fully as the central running gag of *No Bed For Bacon*, which backdates the added commercial value accruing to places where Elizabeth has slept to her own lifetime—here the parsimonious Queen herself is the founder of this cynical trade, rewarding her servants not with money but by giving them beds in which she has slept on the grounds that these will become valuable heirlooms. Only the one courtier who desperately wants one—Bacon—is perpetually unable to acquire it, and he is further humiliated when the Queen's favoured playwright pillories him as Malvolio in *Twelfth Night*. In the long term, however, he will get his own back: just as Elizabeth here devises the

Fig. 16. Glenda Jackson's seven performances as Elizabeth in 1971—in the film *Mary Queen of Scots* and in the six television plays that make up *Elizabeth R*—established her as one of the definitive incarnations of Gloriana for the later twentieth century. Terry O'Neill's photograph, snapped between takes on the set of *Mary Queen of Scots*, seems to confirm this identification between the actress and the queen, suggesting that even off-camera Jackson was just such a tough, no-nonsense beer-drinker as the Good Queen Bess of national folklore. The fact that this particular pint is of Irish stout adds a further, political irony to the effect of anachronism produced by the juxtaposition of Elizabethan costume and modern tankard.

Elizabeth Slept Here industry, so Bacon personally invents the Authorship Controversy:

Bacon nearly burst into tears. No matter, he promised himself, he would get even with Master Will for this. He would devise some dark revenge, something deep and literary to obscure Will's name to all posterity. Bacon should deface the name of Shakespeare![46]

With this sort of flippancy attaching to the ideas of Merrie Tudor England, the Virgin Queen, and her beloved national poet alike by 1941, the project of inventing the next monarch's reign a decade later as the New Elizabethan Age was never going to be without its discontents and its sceptics, as we will see in Chapter 6. But for the nineteenth century, as our next two chapters will show, the Elizabethan England enshrined in Nichols's republished *Progresses* remained a potent national fantasy—however awkwardly Elizabeth herself might fit the version of queenship promulgated by Victoria.

4

The Faery Queen and Victorian Values

Within two decades of the publication of *Kenilworth*, which had done what it could to rescue Elizabeth from the many charges of unwomanliness laid against her during the first era of sentimental fiction, Gloriana, patron of Shakespeare or not, found herself with a posthumous rival whose image might warp hers even more fatally than had that of Mary Stuart. On 20 June 1837 the young Victoria ascended the British throne. At the time the reputation of the monarchy as an institution was arguably at an all-time low, the princess herself was virtually an unknown, and queens regnant had been few and far between. In this atmosphere it was inevitable that the new queen would be assimilated to her most illustrious predecessor as a Virgin Queen, Gloriana herself, and this despite Victoria's own thoroughly conventional condemnation of that lady as immodest.[1] In 1831, for example, two Members of Parliament were already arguing that on accession the princess should assume the title Queen Elizabeth II, a title altogether more Britishly auspicious than her own promised to be;[2] J. S. Mill, being surly about the newly crowned monarch in his capacity as editor of the *Westminster Review*, growled scathingly that 'unless she has the qualities of Elizabeth she wi be nothing';[3] Lord Holland, writing to the British ambassador in Paris, reported that he had been to court to see 'our Virgin Queen' and returned 'quite a courtier & a bit of a lover';[4] and both Lord John Russell on her accession, and *The Times*, reporting the birth of her eldest son in 1841, compared Victoria 'with the two previous queens regnant, Elizabeth and Anne'.[5] Most strikingly, Victoria was conflated with Elizabeth in an extraordinary painting by Charles Robert Leslie (1794–1859), who had already made something of a reputation by painting *May day Revels in the Time of Queen Elizabeth* (1821) and who had been commissioned by Victoria to paint *The Queen receiving the Sacrament at her Coronation* in 1838. *Lord William Cecil giving the news of her accession to Princess Elizabeth* in the garden of Hatfield House (Fig. 17) depicts an Elizabeth-as-Victoria.[6] The picture mendaciously translates Tudor court politics into the romantically sexy language of the sort of genre painting which took as its subject the courtship of pretty girls in vaguely historical fancy dress in sunny gardens. This image could best be glossed, not by Holinshed's account of Elizabeth's accession, but by the delectable chivalry with which the scene of the young Victoria receiving the news of hers at Kensington Palace three centuries later was regularly invested. Both H. T. Wells's painting *Queen Victoria receiving the news of her accession* and Mary Gow's watercolour *Princess Victoria receiving news of her accession* breathe a sentimental fervency identical in tone to Leslie's painting, precisely the tone of the future premier Disraeli's evocation of the moment in *Sybil* (1845):

In a palace in a garden—not in a haughty keep, proud with the fame but dark with the violence of ages; not in a regal pile, bright with the splendour, but soiled with the intrigues, of courts and factions—in a palace in a garden, meet scene for youth, and innocence, and beauty—came the voice that told the maiden that she 'must ascend her throne'.[7]

The fact that Leslie's painting even exists points to the ways in which a nineteenth-century Elizabeth might be hypothesized as a useful alter ego for the young Victoria; the nagging incredulity that this picture raises in the mind of the viewer, however, points to the ways in which, as a modern monarch, Victoria could not in the end be poured into the

FIG. 17. Charles Robert Leslie (1794–1859), *Lord William Cecil giving the news of her accession to Princess Elizabeth* (c.1840s). Leslie, a passionate admirer of Robert Smirke and Thomas Stothard, specialized in painting illustrations to history (often depicting scenes from Shakespeare and Scott), and he made his name with *May Day Revels in the Reign of Queen Elizabeth*, 1821; but after Victoria's accession in 1837 he was commissioned to paint the new Queen, and his later works include much-acclaimed treatments of Victoria's coronation and of the christening of her first child. In this painting the two sides of his work converge: this is Elizabeth implausibly reimagined as a premonition of Victoria, given dark hair, strangely nineteenth-century looking headgear, and an unlikely maidenly bashfulness—albeit with a hint of slyness—about accepting the crown.

mould of an Elizabeth, or Elizabeth into that of Victoria. In what follows, we shall be describing some of the occasionally contradictory ways in which the myths of these two queens nevertheless mutually constituted each other from Victoria's installation as heir presumptive in 1830 until her posthumous apotheosis in the early years of the twentieth century. Although Elizabeth remained a key figure in accounts of England's Protestant destiny (which in some quarters, as we will see in Chapter 5, were growing ever more grandiose), popular ideas about her personal character would reach an all-time nadir during the reign of her most famous successor as queen regnant.

Two Queens in One Isle

At its most euphoric, the nation over which Victoria ruled continued to venerate Elizabeth as the Good Queen Bess who had ruled over the never-never land of Merrie England conjured by *Kenilworth*. She was still invoked, too, as the ageless Faerie Queene of the golden age of romance and chivalric feeling, and—sometimes in nakedly self-interested ways—as the patroness of Spenser and Shakespeare. David Scott's 1840 painting of her attending a star-studded Globe (Plate 5), for example, was part of a concerted effort early in the new reign to solicit royal patronage for the arts, and when Victoria responded to such pressure by commissioning Charles Kean to supervise theatrical performances before her court at Windsor in 1848 *The Times* duly recognized the precedent for this potentially unrespectable proceeding:

The fact that the sovereign bespoke a series of English theatrical performances as a recreation in her own palace, has at least the charm of novelty to recommend it to the attention of the curious. Fancy has wandered back to the days of Elizabeth and the first James, when such means of amusement were not uncommon; and perhaps, wandering forward, has augured that a new stock of dramatists worthy to compete with those of the Elizabethan era may spring into existence from the effect of the Windsor Theatricals.[8]

As the 'Elizabethan' also became, in the wake of the Catholic Emancipation Act of 1829 and in the context of the Oxford Movement, the crucial founding moment when a divided England rent by religious faction was reunited as one nation (as we will see in the next chapter), Elizabeth was increasingly lauded as a passionately populist and unsectarian queen, one who had ruled through the love of the people rather than primarily through the exercise of divinely sanctioned despotism. Rather oddly, Elizabeth was thought to have sponsored the development of almost any sort of modernity associated with the greatness of Victorian Britain, spanning the emergence of Baconian science and the invention of domestic conveniences, both, of course, major features of the royal-sponsored Great Exhibition of 1851: it cannot have escaped the Victorians' attention that thanks to Sir John Harington Elizabeth was the first English monarch to possess a water closet.[9] 'It is from this period . . . that we can first date the rise of a conception which seems to us now a peculiarly English one—the conception of domestic comfort' wrote F. de Rothschild in 1884.[10] In her foreign policy she was held to have presided over the founding of the British Empire, via her courageous and romantically reckless patronage of that curious species, the sea-dog, exemplified by Drake and the gallant Raleigh (again, the subject of the next chapter). Sir Walter's legendary courtesy to his queen became one of the nineteenth-century's favourite images of the manly and Ruskinesque chivalry Elizabeth is supposed to have promulgated at her court: hence the popularity of such widely reproduced genre paintings as *The gallantry of Sir Walter Raleigh* (Samuel Drummond, 1828), *Sir Walter Raleigh spreading his cloak as a carpet for Queen Elizabeth* (William Theed, 1853), and *Sir Walter Raleigh laying down his cloak for the Queen* (Andrew Sheerboom, 1875: Fig. 18).[11] This heavily modernized notion of the nature of Elizabeth's power was reinforced and perhaps even necessitated by Victoria's presence on the throne, successively imagined as romantic young queen, 'the rose of England', patroness of Charles Kean's Shakespeare and of the Great Exhibition, Disraeli's Fairy Queen and the future Empress of India, for the most part politically powerless but increasingly the repository of a tremendous emotional investment on the part of her subjects. Vice versa, Victoria's queenship could be legitimated and elaborated by this powerful fantasy of Gloriana. In 1843, for example, the Mayor and Aldermen of Southampton threw down their cloaks in the style of Raleigh to cover puddles in the path of

Fig. 18. Andrew Sheerboom (1832–80), *Sir Walter Raleigh laying down his cloak for the Queen* (1875). According to Thomas Fuller's *History of the Worthies of England*, 1662, when Raleigh first arrived at court he 'found the Queen walking, till, meeting with a plashy place, she seemed to scruple going thereon. Presently Raleigh cast and spread his new plush cloak on the ground; whereon the Queen trod gently over, rewarding him after with many suits for his so free and seasonable tender of so fair a foot cloth.' This romantic incident, though much parodied since, was a favourite with Victorian genre painters determined to celebrate Elizabeth's reign as a golden age of manly chivalry despite whatever misgivings they may have entertained about Elizabeth's personal character.

young Queen, an incident considered worthy of illustration in at least one contemporary periodical.[12] It is, therefore, rather startling to discover that, despite Gloriana's usefully inflated iconic status, by mid-century depictions of the private woman behind the national myth were for the most part even more hostile than earlier texts such as *The Recess*, and would remain so until about the 1870s.

The nineteenth century's deepening sense of the split between the national icon and the private woman was perhaps rendered inevitable by the growth of a strain of popular biography of queens and courts, often explicitly stimulated by the presence of Victoria on the throne, together with the huge popularity of this genre's close cousin, history-painting. Both genres were fascinated alike by the feminine, domestic, anecdotal, and biographical as the underside of the more officially historical, and interested in its potential for morally exemplary narrative directed at girls and young women.[13] The effect was to fracture Elizabeth decisively into two opposing incarnations—national and sexual—which became increasingly difficult to fit together. This problem is vividly displayed by William Cooke Taylor's *Romantic Biography of the Age of Elizabeth* (1842), which includes a plate of Elizabeth (based upon an authentic portrait) reverently captioned 'The Founder of our Colonial Empire' opposite a satirically journalistic account of the way 'her passion for flirtations continually interrupted state affairs'.[14]

Cooke's stated ambition was 'to substitute Daguerrotypes for Fancy portraits' (i. 4); in other words, to supersede the sort of portrait favoured by the wealthier (including on more than one occasion Victoria herself) who regularly chose to have themselves painted in romantically historicized fancy dress. Instead, Cooke offered as a mode of history the aggressively modern form of domestic middle-class portraiture which Victoria herself came to favour from about 1847 onwards.[15] Viewed through this lens of modern, middle-class sexual morality, the modern-dress Elizabeth turned out to be anything but the prevailing ideal of Victorian womanhood, and from around the 1820s she elicited a 'singular mixture of admiration and contempt',[16] supposed as she was to unite undoubted political and intellectual abilities with what the *Quarterly Review* termed 'the most craving vanity, the most irritable jealousy, the meanest duplicity, and the most capricious and unrelenting spite, that ever degraded the silliest and most hateful of her sex'.[17]

All too feminine in her vices, Elizabeth was nevertheless culpably unwomanly because, instead of refusing political power in favour of exerting an uplifting, softening influence, she had retained absolute executive authority.[18] Her celebrated chastity, having guaranteed and maintained that authority, thus came to be construed not as virtuous but as aggressive, humiliating, hypocritical, mean, and vicious. Hence Elizabeth might be demoted from the virginal to the merely 'half-chaste'. For the deliberately iconoclastic Byron in 1821, for example, sardonically comparing Gloriana with Catherine the Great, Elizabeth displayed her lack of proper royal womanhood most clearly by a parsimony that was as much sexual as financial, expressed by the unpitied crime of her old age in executing Essex:

> Love had made Catherine make each lover's fortune;
>   Unlike our own half-chaste Elizabeth,
> Whose avarice all disbursement did importune,
>   If History, the grand liar, ever saith
> The truth: and though Grief her old age might shorten
>   Because she put a favourite to death,
> Her vile, ambiguous method of flirtation,
> And Stinginess, disgrace her Sex and Station.[19]

Paradoxically, because Elizabeth's virginity was seen to be illicitly exploitative, it was possible simply to convert it into its equally anti-domestic shadow, a latent, frustrated, or actual promiscuity. So in 1825 Hugh Campbell's immodest, wanton, and licentious Elizabeth is not only denied all moral credit for her actual chastity, but made a monster of perpetual lust by it, suffering from 'some obstructions from nature, which disabled her from the offices of a wife, precluded her from the pleasures of a prostitute, and, contending with her strong desires, raised such a ferment and fire within her, as she was ever endeavouring, and never able, to extinguish'.[20] Nor was Campbell alone in brooding over this imputed aspect of Elizabeth's private character. By 1853, there was a lively public debate in progress over Gloriana's 'morals': *Fraser's Magazine*, for example, ran a lengthy two-part article in October and

November of that year dealing with the suggestions of wantonness put about by, amongst others, John Lingard, Sir James Mackintosh (in the *Cabinet Cyclopedia*), and Lord John Campbell. The historical evidence cited by such figures, decided *Fraser's*, was 'doubtful, at the best', but that might be more than enough to condemn in such a case: 'when the character of a lady is at issue, to doubt is to condemn. No one professes to doubt on such a point, unless he believes that there is no longer any room for doubting.'[21] But nineteenth-century writers on any side of this question, whether they believed Elizabeth promiscuous, chaste, or ambiguously one or the other, emphatically agreed that above all she had wilfully and irresponsibly refused to be domesticated:

> there are very few traits of her character which represent her clothed in any of the gentle proprieties of womanly beauty and grace; the dignity she had was of the throne, not of the sex, and her appearance and demeanour were only not coarse, because she was a queen . . . ; she would not have been a desirable wife for any of us, she would always have made herself felt most emphatically in any scene of life. She carried to the British Throne, it must be admitted, something of the valour and vehemence of those more modern ladies, whose wont it is to preside at the stalls of the great Fish Bazaar of Tower Street, London.[22]

Elizabeth's newly discovered womanly shortcomings were rendered especially spectacular in the context of the successive royal personae constructed around her young successor on the throne of England. At her accession in 1837, for example, Victoria found herself depicted as only incidentally and even reluctantly queen. Elizabeth Barrett's early poem 'Victoria's Tears' (published 8 June 1837), characteristically, constitutes the princess as a victim child-queen, another Jane Grey: 'while the heralds played their part | For million shouts to drown— | "God Save the Queen" from hill to mart— | She heard through all, her beating heart, | And turned and wept! | She wept, to wear a crown.'[23] Between 1840 and 1861, the years of Victoria's marriage to Albert and the births of their nine children, the Queen presented herself and was represented as elaborately wifely, maternal, and domestic, a persona depicted most memorably and enchantingly by Winterhalter in 1846.[24] In May 1842 the *Illustrated London News* was celebrating a spectacle of state power discovered to be the practice of domesticity:

Queen Victoria will never appear more exalted in the world's opinion than when each side of the picture is thus revealed—the great Queen and stateswoman in the gorgeous palace—the young, lovely, and virtuous mother amidst the pure joys of sylvan retreat and domestic relaxation. Our artist has chosen for illustration one of those happy moments of maternal life when the magnificence and etiquette of the Queen are put aside by womanly tenderness for the expression of a mother's love.[25]

This royal domesticity was in fact explicitly premissed upon the monarchy's loss of direct political power—witness the contemporary fascination with the doomed absolutist Charles I as the ideal family man, surrounded by his children.[26] Increasingly a politically impotent institution with only residual constitutional powers, 'inspiring' and 'influencing' the nation as its symbolic wife, the monarchy found its perfect representation in, as Margaret Homans has remarked, 'the spectacle of royal domestic privacy, a privacy that centred on the ever-plumper figure of [the] Queen as wife and mother'.[27] In the 1880s, twenty unpopular years of mourning Albert past, Victoria's renovated persona still relied upon a certain domesticity, though it was finally translated in portraits and in panoramic family photographs alike into an extraordinary amalgamation of her monolithic endured widowhood and her vast grandmotherhood of European monarchies.[28] In this context, John Ruskin's formulation of female influence as a form of private queenship in 'Of Queen's Gardens' (1864) was perhaps neither as mystic nor as grandiose as it now tends to sound:

you must be, in many a heart, enthroned: there is no putting by that crown; queens you must always be; queens to your lovers; queens to your husbands and your sons; queens of higher mystery to the world beyond, which bows itself, and will for ever bow, before the myrtle crown and the stainless sceptre, of womanhood. But alas! you are too often idle and careless queens, grasping at majesty in the least things, while you abdicate it in the greatest . . .[29]

Despite Elizabeth's precedent for a rhetorical self-imaging as wife and mother to her nation—entirely familiar to Victorian historians, and destined to be practically added to Britain's unwritten constitution by Solomon J. Solomon's painting of her dramatic display of her coronation ring in the House of Lords—envisaging her within the terms of this romance of vulnerable, morally influential, and domesticized queenship proved virtually impossible. Married to her country she may have been, but she was by no means a passive and obedient consort to it, preferring to go on grasping at majesty in the least things. To represent Elizabeth as a reluctant queen in the style of Barrett, despite Leslie's valiant attempt, generally seemed implausible. Representing her as morally influential, the guardian of the soul of the nation, was very nearly as difficult: according to the enormously influential historian J. R. Green, tellingly one of the more sympathetic to his subject, all the 'moral aspects' of Elizabeth's England 'were simply dead to her':

It was a time when men were being lifted into nobleness by the new moral energy which seemed suddenly to pulse through the whole people; when honor and enthusiasm took colors of poetic beauty, and chivalry became a religion. But the finer sentiments of the men around her touched Elizabeth simply as the fair tints of a picture would have touched her.[30]

Elizabeth could be seen as a production of men's sentiment rather than the inspiration for it. Even more damningly, her otherwise redeeming role as patroness of the national literary canon was compromised by her scandalous and greedy vanity; Beatrice Marshall argued, for example, that she had enjoyed *The Faerie Queene* solely as a further boost to her egotism: 'it was only herself in the poem, not the poem, that delighted her . . . Elizabeth saw in the great literature springing up, of which she was the supposed inspiration, nothing but a monument of that gross flattery for which her appetite was insatiable, and to which all the men of light and leading in the country shamelessly pandered.'[31] Representing Gloriana as exerting appropriate forms of female power proved similarly impossible; as Anna Jameson would remark in 1834:

It has been said that Elizabeth never forgot the woman in the sovereign: it might be said with much more truth, that she never forgot the sovereign in the woman, and surely this is no praise.—One more destitute of what is called *heart*, that is, of the capacity for all the gentle, generous, and kindly affections proper to her sex, cannot be imagined in the female form.[32]

It was altogether too clear that Elizabeth had not ruled by exerting Victorian forms of womanly power: 'when', asked Jameson indignantly, 'did she comfort or help the weak-hearted? or raise up the fallen? or exalt humble merit? or cherish unobtrusive genius? or spare the offending? or pardon the guilty?'; instead, she had ruled by the obtrusive exercise of 'acts of capricious power'. In short,

On looking nearer, we behold on the throne of England a woman, whose avarice and jealousy, whose envious, relentless, and malignant spirit, whose coarse manners and violent temper, rendered her detestable; whose pedantry and meanness, whose childish vanity and intense selfishness, rendered her contemptible.[33]

Elizabeth's politically obsolete absolutism is diminished in the modern context into a simple rage for engrossing illegitimate personal power— hence her representation as avaricious, jealous, envious, vain, and selfish. If, 'by presenting herself as a wife, Queen Victoria offered the perfect solution to Britain's fears of female rule and of excessive monarchic power',[34] as Homans has argued, her avatar Elizabeth raised these fears in their most virulent form.

During the 1840s and 1850s, years which, suggestively, coincided with Victoria's child-bearing years, this anxiety over Elizabeth's political power—perhaps a surrogate for the cultural anxiety over Victoria's— crystallized into a series of remarkable paintings set in Elizabeth's private apartments in which Elizabeth's ageing body was for the first time revealed. So obsessed did mid-Victorian culture become with the figure of the old Queen, indeed, that Kingsley could observe ruefully in 1859 that 'it is much now-a-days to find any one who believes that Queen Elizabeth was ever young, or who does not talk of her as if she was born about seventy years of age covered with rouge and wrinkles'.[35] For the first time, Queen Elizabeth was regularly pursued into the privacy of her bedchamber, to be triumphantly discovered not as a secretly vulnerable sentimental heroine but merely as a superannuated flirt in unflattering undress, all wrinkles and no rouge.

The Crooked Carcass

> Her conditions are as crooked as her carcass.
>
> (The Earl of Essex on Elizabeth)

> There are few sovereigns that make a more splendid and imposing state-figure in the regal statue-gallery of England than Queen Elizabeth; and as few, in sooth, that can less afford to be faithfully limned and displayed *en déshabille*.
>
> (William Russell, 1857)[36]

Prior to 1848, Gloriana appeared in disarray or *en déshabille* only on one occasion; the unheralded return of the Earl of Essex from Ireland to her very bedchamber in 1599, much dramatized in *The Unhappy Favourite* and its successors, and voluptuously depicted by Robert Smirke, as we have seen, in 1806 (Fig. 9). Smirke's image of a young and pneumatic Elizabeth discovered in charming disarray—one hand protecting her loosely covered breast, the other lifting away her long and luxuriant hair[37]—was republished in the 1830s with a new border, which supplies by contrast two vignettes of the be-ruffed and crowned public monarch in action. One shows Elizabeth administering the notorious box on the ear to Essex, the other depicts her signing his death-warrant: the montage once more underlines the separation encoded by the Essex story between the private, feeling woman and the public monarch who is heartbreakingly obliged to have her favourite killed. In 1875 David Wilkie Wynfield returned to the subject of Essex's return from Ireland in his *Incident in the Life of Elizabeth I* (Fig. 19), which provides a dramatic contrast with the earlier visualization. Gone are the lusciously heaving bosom and the luxuriantly disarranged hair. In their place is a nearly bald and diminutive Queen, shorn of ruff, jewels, farthingale, robe, and, shockingly, wig, all of which are prominently scattered around the focal point of the picture. Essex has caught her in front of the mirror, in the act of reassembling her public, feminine image, her false head of hair suspended in the hands of the more matronly of her attendants (and from this period onwards such representations of the Queen would be frequently haunted by wigs and mirrors, as we will see). Clearly the

Fig. 19. David Wilkie Wynfield (1837–87), *Incident in the Life of Elizabeth I* (1875). Wynfield cruelly transforms earlier depictions of Essex's irruption into the Queen's private chamber (such as Robert Smirke's, Fig. 9). Instead of having the romantic boldness to surprise a nubile, secretly amorous queen without her crown, Wynfield's Essex merely commits the social solecism of catching an old lady without her wig.

meaning of this vignette of Essex's intrusion had changed dramatically over the intervening years.

Why? The historical record, of course, contained a good deal to embarrass a Smirke-style *mise-en-scène* of Elizabeth in her bedroom, not least the hard fact that when Essex went to his death on Tower Green aged thirty-five, Elizabeth was sixty-eight.[38] But despite a thriving industry from the 1790s onwards in depictions of the Queen's death (such as Smirke's own, Fig. 9), it would not be until the second quarter of the nineteenth century that Elizabeth would actually be discovered as a ridiculous, if dangerous, old fraud. In 1822, Mary Roberts's companion poem to her sentimental set piece on the Queen of Scots, 'Elizabeth', contents itself with describing her grandeur, her jewels, her throne, etc., before pointing out gleefully that the 'Dreadful and dreaded Elizabeth' is none the less subject to Time and Death.[39] But by 1824, this conventional suggestion was being amplified by Walter Savage Landor into a commentary fixated on Elizabeth's sexual obsolescence. Imagining the conversation between Elizabeth and her last suitor Alençon, brokered by their respective advisers Cecil and Fénélon, Landor unmasks the courtly language of sentimental passion as used to the Queen by the continual asides of all the players, concentrating particularly on the forty-year-old Queen's unwarranted personal vanity. We are left with Anjou's pen-portrait of a sexually voracious old maid well past her sell-by date as a woman, if not as a political *parti*:

'those long narrow ferret's teeth, intersecting a face of such proportions, that it is like a pared cucumber set on end. And then those foxy eyelashes and eyebrows! And those wildfire eyes, equal in volubility to her tongue and her affections, and leering like a panther's when it yawns. . . . Sacré! the skinny old goshawk, all talon and plumage.'[40]

Landor's satirized Queen is not herself aware of the yawning gulf between her market value as political asset and as woman, but she would not be allowed to preserve this particular vanity very much longer. The most important visual depiction of the old Queen was certainly that of Augustus Leopold Egg, who, in 1848, exhibited his canvas *Queen Elizabeth Discovers She Is No Longer Young* (Fig. 20) at the Royal

FIG. 20. Augustus Leopold Egg (1816–63), *Queen Elizabeth Discovers She Is No Longer Young* (1848). Clearly influenced by Paul Delaroche's hostile depiction of Elizabeth's deathbed (Plate 2), Egg's punitive painting—illustrating a supposed incident after the execution of Essex, when Elizabeth, Richard II-like, called for a looking-glass for the first time in many years—crystallizes the Victorians' unprecedented preoccupation with Elizabeth's old age. In this image the Queen's guilt, senescence, and obsolescence all signify one another.

Academy, a painting which met with such approval that it earned the artist his associateship.

Egg's ambitious painting penetrated the royal bedroom to discover, shockingly, not Gloriana but an old woman amidst her courtiers and ladies, forced into full realization of mortality by the mirror held up by her truly youthful lady-in-waiting, struck into an immobile trance of humiliated vanity. Around her suddenly shrunken and petulant form the gaudily stiff skirts have crumpled and collapsed, and her haggard face stares straight out at the viewer. This complicated picture, heavily influenced by Delaroche's image of the Queen's death (Plate 2), insists not merely (like Landor) that the Virgin Queen is old, but that she herself, caught out, should recognize the fact in full pitiless conclave. This *lèse-majesté* achieves its impact by disestablishing Elizabeth's official portraits' mendacious claims to timelessness; as every Victorian child knew, these had been rigidly controlled by Elizabeth to save her personal vanity. The magazine *Bow Bells*, for example, offered this *aperçu*:

When Queen Elizabeth sat for her picture in her old age, she ordered the artist to paint her portrait without any shadows, for shadows she knew would reveal the marks of age in her queenly countenance; and, with all her courage, 'good Queen Bess' had not strength of mind to look her wrinkles in the face. She could defy the Spanish Armada, but she was afraid of her own infirmities.[41]

Egg's painting itself thus aspired to act as a true looking-glass; its supposed authenticity (lavishly endorsed by the critics) was guaranteed by its bypassing of such 'inauthentic' and fraudulent contemporary portraits as sources in favour of Elizabeth's actual death-mask. Refuting the iconography of Elizabethan absolutism, the canvas unmasks the ageless Gloriana as a uselessly bedecked moribund old harridan.

According to the catalogue's explanatory quotation, this picture too is an illustration to the Essex plot, showing an incident alleged to have occurred during Elizabeth's last illness, which is ascribed here as elsewhere to misery over his death: 'In the melancholy of her sickness she desired to see a true looking glass, into which she had not looked for twenty years.'[42] The Queen's self-discovery in Egg's picture, therefore, is brought on by her grief over Essex's execution; her guilt seems to be realized as a sudden, catastrophic ageing. It is an unprecedentedly aggressive way of representing this previously tear-jerking, tragic end to their story. It is interesting in this context to note that nineteenth-century depictions of the confrontation between Elizabeth and the woman said to have prevented Essex from successfully obtaining a reprieve, such as the American John Gadsby Chapman's *Queen Elizabeth and the Countess of Nottingham* (1843), Thomas Musgrove Joy's *Interview Between Elizabeth I and the Countess of Nottingham* (1855), and Edward Francis Burney's misleadingly titled *Queen Elizabeth and Lady Essex* (n.d.) all similarly portray Elizabeth as a bedizened old hag, berating a sentimentalized, domestic, and youthful Nottingham; contemporary responses to these paintings emphasize horror at the spectacle of the Queen wreaking her fury on a dying woman, and contrast the Countess's genuine remorse with Elizabeth's selfish cruelty in refusing her forgiveness.[43] Like Egg, despite illustrating a plot historically sympathetic to Elizabeth, these artists actually express extreme hostility to the Queen, and seem to encode her heartless execution of Essex within the revelation of her age.

Egg's image might have been related to at least two political arguments by the visitors to the Royal Academy viewing in 1848, that turbulent year of European revolutions and of domestic unrest (including an abortive Chartist riot outside Buckingham Palace itself and a reputed Chartist march on Osborne).[44] The first was to do with whether the monarchy itself, regarded by many as paralysingly expensive, was for all its display of hereditary power actually as obsolete as the post-menopausal woman supposed to have been the most glorious of all English sovereigns. The second was specifically to do with revolution, for by the mid-nineteenth century the death of Essex as popular hero and spirit of chivalric Elizabethanism at the hands of a merciless and despotic old woman could point a moral about arbitrary power both at home and abroad. This is, for example, the burden of the historical novel *The Noble Traytour* (1857) by 'Thomas of Swarraton, Armiger', which casts Essex, friend of Raleigh, Shakespeare, and the virtuous English squire Sir William Cheney, as the true—if spoiled and undisciplined—child of the age, snuffed out by the tyranny of the old Queen. Above all, *Queen Elizabeth Discovers She Is No Longer Young*, by destroying Elizabeth's magical agelessness, a central component of contemporary nationalist Elizabethan nostalgia, lays some claim to being a political essay on the current state of England. It is no wonder that Charles Kingsley's attempt to defend Elizabeth's status as a worthy epicentre for her nation's golden age had to include a vindication of her use of cosmetics:

[her youthful beauty] had been an important element in her great success; men had accepted it as what beauty of form and expression generally is, an outward and visible sign of the inward and spiritual grace; and while the inward was unchanged, what wonder if she tried to preserve the outward? If she was the same, why should she not try to look the same? And what blame to those who worshipped her, if, knowing that she was the same, they too should fancy that she looked the same, the Elizabeth of their youth, and should talk as if the fair flesh, as well as the fair spirit, was immortal? Does not every loving husband do so, when he forgets the grey hair and the sunken cheek and all the wastes of time; and sees the partner of many joys and sorrows not as she has become, but as she was, ay, and is to him, and will be to him, he trusts, through all eternity?[45]

Inverting Egg's proposition—that the national icon merely expressed the Queen's overweening and unfounded personal vanity—Kingsley argues instead that Elizabeth's deeply national femininity (characteristically imagined in marital terms, despite Elizabeth's awkward status as spinster) was best expressed by her painted face. This is precisely the vision rejected by Wynfield's vision of the old Elizabeth stripped of her sexual glamour along with her wig and gorgeous clothes, perhaps another essay on whether Elizabeth's state power—used in its most extreme form against the most manly man of her age—is adequately legitimated by the femininity of her private body, or whether her political conditions are indeed as crooked as her carcass. Comparatively anodyne though it is alongside Egg's much more savage painting, Wynfield's treatment none the less suggests that the disastrously superannuated Queen has, as it were, cheated both the hitherto infatuated Essex and, by extension, those moderns who have bought into the myth of Gloriana.

In 1849, the year after Egg's picture was shown, the Christmas pantomime at Drury Lane was entitled *Harlequin and Good Queen Bess, or, Merrie England in the olden Time. A Grand Historical! Metaphorical!! Allegorical!!! and Diabolical!!!! PANTOMIME*, a text no less illuminating

about the relation between this newly hostile view of Elizabeth and contemporary strategies for celebrating Victoria. Collapsing together Elizabeth's courtships, the Kenilworth festivities, and Walter Scott's story of
Elizabeth's dealings with Leicester and Amy Robsart, the pantomime
sets out to 'make the town confess | The funniest figure of fun was GOOD
QUEEN BESS'.[46] Elizabeth, in keeping with the cross-dressing traditions
of the genre, here becomes Drag Queen Bess, her mockheroic splendour
entirely a matter of intimate items of costume:

> Grand *entrée* of her Majesty, GOOD QUEEN BESS, attended by her Nobles and
> Dames of Honour, bearing the various parts of her Dress. LORD BURLEIGH
> carries the Royal Red Wig and Golden Crown—SIR WALTER RALEIGH the
> Royal Petticoat—the EARL OF ESSEX, attends with Royal Blushes, in the
> shape of a Rouge Pot—LORD BACON carries the Royal Ruff—Good Queen
> Bess is attired in a morning wrapper, and cap . . . (12)

Once the Queen has put on the full royal panoply, the rest of the pantomime gives a lightning tour of the Queen's coquetry with her various
foreign and domestic suitors before exhorting her to abandon this form
of political courtship in favour of an altogether more Victorian version
of affective monarchy: 'Instead of dreaming more of Cupid's darts, |
Dream of a throne built on your people's hearts.' Her implied conversion
is rewarded with 'A Pantomime Vision of the Destruction of the
Spanish Armada', moralized in terms as much to do with Palmerstonian
gun-boat diplomacy as with the days of Drake:

> Henceforth is England mistress of the seas!
> Her flag 'shall brave the battle and the breeze.'
> In triumph now—in ages yet to come,
> And still the sea shall guard each English home.
> While then, as now, with pride 'twill be confess'd,
> A fair hand wields Old England's sceptre best. (20)

Victoria—as implied passenger on a property ship, at least—finally
arrives herself during the show's naval and wholly unElizabethan finale,
in which contemporary events and the 'fair hand' on today's sceptre
supersede the representation of Elizabeth altogether: this takes the form
of a 'GRAND MOVING DIORAMA',

Illustrative of HER MOST GRACIOUS MAJESTY's Visit to Ireland; shewing the
following points of interest;—Departure from OSBORNE—Passing Cowes;
and approaching the NEEDLES—the Royal Yacht passing through the Fleet,
off PORTSMOUTH—The EDYSTONE [*sic*] LIGHTHOUSE—Passing the LAND'S
END at SUNSET—The Royal Squadron, by Moonlight—and Arrival at
QUEENSTOWN. (20)

This pantomime farcically restates Egg's view of the old Elizabeth's
royal authority as a sexiness fraudulently constructed out of paint and
farthingale by showing Elizabeth to be a man under the petticoats: this
is a ploy which would be shared not only by successors in the same frivolous genre, such as *Good Queen Bess: An Extravaganza* in the 1890s, but
even by one historian: 'She was a masculine woman simulating, when it
suited her purpose, a feminine character', claimed Beesly. 'The men
against whom she was matched were never sure whether they were dealing with a crafty and determined politician, or a vain, flighty, amorous
woman.'[47] In *Harlequin and Good Queen Bess*, though, the conversion of
this cross-dressed Elizabeth and her displacement by a Puff-like
pageant of the Armada can clear away Elizabeth's worryingly free-
floating sexuality before summoning up a vision of a more suitable
female embodiment of the nation, Victoria herself. A successor in this
genre, *Kenilworth, or, Ye Queene, Ye Earle, and Ye Maydenne* (1859), which
calls Elizabeth 'A *Virgin* Queen, *verging* on Fifty, the original strong-
minded Woman: quite a *rough* character, or at least a character in a *ruff*—
with a great deal of *hoop*, and a little *doo-den-do*', similarly ends with a
display of the triumphant modern reign which has rendered Elizabeth's,
though officially glorious, so comically obsolete: it finishes with a
'GRAND DENOUEMENT Representing the Three great Eras of Elizabeth,
Anne, and Victoria'.[48] In 1857, making a similar side-slip in conclusion to
the first ever hostile account of Elizabeth's girlhood imbroglio with
Admiral Seymour, William Russell wrote:

A few more chequered years of patient wariness, and the great prize was
gained—Elizabeth was in her true place on the throne, the visible embodiment
and illustration of national independence . . . and therefore clothed with a personal lustre in her people's eyes which the disenchanting breath of Time has

indeed dissipated, but not happily till the crown of these realms had descended upon the brow of a royal lady whose virtues shed a higher, purer lustre upon the imperial diadem than it confers. Mr Macaulay, in one of his public addresses, eulogized Queen Victoria as 'a milder, better Elizabeth;' a compliment which, at all events, will not render the celebrated historian obnoxious to the charge of flattery or servilism.[49]

Both Russell and the anonymous author of *Harlequin and Good Queen Bess* suggest, finally, that the 'answer' to Egg's problem picture might well have been Victoria for many of its viewers.

The Child of Destiny

The portrayal of Elizabeth as old was for the Victorians the clinching statement of her lack of womanliness, and of the consequent fraudulence of her political power. As such, the aged but sexually voracious Elizabeth stands as the surplus to the Victorian concept of queenship, the historical residue of monarchical power.[50] So it was that Elizabeth's post-sentimental, post-menopausal body dominated mid-nineteenth-century narratives of her private life. Some thirty years later, however, with the ageing and increasingly unpopular Queen Victoria still secluded in heavy mourning for an Albert dead since 1861, campaigns for the rehabilitation of both queens were afoot, the first in the shape of efforts to force Victoria into public appearance to stave off calls for her abdication that had started in about 1870, the second, almost directly contemporary, in the shape of a series of representations of the Virgin Queen as a child.[51]

Why did Elizabeth so suddenly appear as a child? Part of the answer must be that portrayals of Elizabeth as an old woman would, increasingly, have had a largely undesirable topical application to Victoria. Part must also be, of course, the rapid development of histories and historical fiction for children, and especially girls, offering usefully English role models plus a dose of English history in palatable form. That said, in order to render Elizabeth a suitable example for Victorian girlhood, e obliged to go in for a good deal of doctoring of the histori-implest and most effective was to rethink the Virgin Queen the new-found interest in painting historical characters as children or of the sort of juvenile historical fiction pioneered by Charlotte M. Yonge, or of that interesting genre characteristic of girls' reading in the later nineteenth century, 'The Girlhood of Exemplary Women'.[52] Such representations abstract historical or fictional characters out of their known and often compromising actual circumstances, projecting them back into infancy and childhood in order at once to engage the sympathetic attention of the child-audience but also, more importantly, to try to convey the essence of the feminine character before it was overtaken by political or historical contingency.

Both the attractiveness and the trickiness of these strategies are demonstrated by the earliest example of this genre as applied to Elizabeth—William Russell's *Extraordinary Women; Their Girlhood and Early Life* (1857). Russell's vignette of young Bess is in fact anything but sympathetic to the teenaged princess—at once over-wanton and over-prudent—although the accompanying illustration shows her, wishfully, as a pretty and domesticated three year old within an idyllic family setting, apparently in happily ecumenical religious harmony with her elder half-sister Bloody Mary (Fig. 21). Later portrayals of Elizabeth-as-child, however, attempt to realize the message of the picture rather than the text, countering hostile representations of Elizabeth as unwomanly—coded as post-menopausally infertile—by showing her as an acceptably infertile and unwomanly pre-adolescent child-princess. This strategy offered the additional advantage of representing Elizabeth as enclosed within the domestic before her dubious entry into public life, as well as presenting her entirely as potential, pre-narrative, pre-history. The pre-sexual childish body, in fact, becomes safely iconic, and can be returned to its function of representing national progress and triumph. Hence the child-princess, the proto-Freudian expression of the private woman, can finally be conflated not only with the Protestant icon but with the Armada icon, as in an 1871 painting by Marcus C. Stone (1840–1921), *The Royal Nursery* (Fig. 22).[53] This painting, which surely owes something to paintings by Winterhalter and Landseer of Victoria and her family, effectively leapfrogs the whole vexed question of Elizabeth's sexed body (though there is a discarded or even beheaded doll apparently standing in for Elizabeth's hapless mother Anne Boleyn)

Elizabeth in the house of Lady Bryan.

FIG. 21. *Elizabeth in the house of Lady Bryan*, an illustration to the rather less sentimental account of the princess's youth supplied in William Russell's *Extraordinary Women; Their Girlhood and Early Life* (1857). The Victorians often preferred to avert their eyes from Elizabeth's politic and flirtatious maturity and old age to contemplate her as a child, still uncorrupted by the harsh and unwomanly realities of absolute power. In the secure, all-female, exclusively domestic realm imagined by this child's-eye-view engraving, Elizabeth can be simply a pious and exemplary pupil to her elder half-sister Mary, the near-mortal religious antagonism which will eventually divide them understood only by the poignantly affected mother-figure of Lady Bryan in the background.

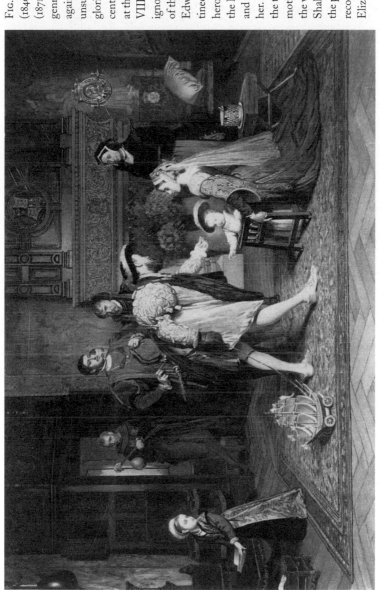

FIG. 22. Marcus C. Stone (1840–1921), *The Royal Nursery* (1871). In this typical Victorian genre painting Elizabeth is again reimagined not as an unsuitably despotic and vainglorious queen but as an innocent child, and a neglected one at that. Stone rebukes Henry VIII's short-sightedness in ignoring Elizabeth in favour of the doomed, sickly Prince Edward by intimating her destined triumph as Protestant heroine of 1588, alluded to by the Bible she has been studying and –he toy galleon in front of her. A discarded doll hints at the tragedy which befell her mother. For the moment, only the wise, compassionate, and Shakespearean court fool—and the picture's implied viewer— recognize the sidelined Elizabeth's importance.

to concentrate prophetically on the disinherited and neglected little girl's future role as the Protestant heroine of Tilbury, flanked by the Bible she has been studying diligently and the toy warship that the doting father has brought for his frail and doomed son Edward, who can't so much as walk. Watched solicitiously by a court Fool, Elizabeth is identified as the deserving Cordelia to her father's Lear. Stone cunningly invests the child-princess with a useful pathos which neither cancels, nor is cancelled by, the intimation of future glory.

A late example of this strain, Harriet Comstock's *The Girlhood of Elizabeth: A Romance of English History* (1914) (probably prompted by the publication of Frank Mumby's compilation of letters under the title *The Girlhood of Elizabeth* in 1909), displays very clearly what was at stake in representing Elizabeth as a child:

> I would have you know and love her, not as the great queen who ruled so mightily—not always wisely or gently—but as the little English maid of royal Tudor stock, who strove to learn that she might overcome error, and who, through much injustice to herself, was ever true and affectionate to those who served her well; and to the end was loyal to her name and country.[54]

Diligent, well-meaning, oppressed, loyal, affectionate, and patriotic, this princess is not yet corrupted by her questionable power. What Comstock offers us is an improbably 'simple maid' (p. v), cloyingly pathetic, depressingly hard-working, who conducts Pollyanna-style government in the bosom of her family. The winsome five year old, for example, scolds her father for his treatment of her elder sister Mary ('had I more like you, little maid, surrounding my throne, I might have been a better king' is the unlikely response, 56), appears 'ever wondrously tender towards children' (153), is best friends with her brother Edward, her cousin Lady Jane Grey, and her projected match Courtenay, and is absolutely nothing more than a favourite niece to her ambitious uncle Seymour. But the familiar difficulty surfaces once again as she is crowned:

> And now?—but now she is the queen! . . . Perchance we might not love her so well as Queen Elizabeth, and so, as the diadem presses her golden curls, let us bid her farewell. (286)

The good-as-gold princess may not translate unscathed into the Queen of the golden age.

One of the effects of restating Elizabeth as child was to bring her back in a controllable form within the sphere of Victoria's monarchy. (It is a curiosity that Victoria herself was to be subjected to metamorphosis into the ideal Victorian girl in Sara Lippincott's probably unauthorized *Queen Victoria. Her girlhood and womanhood*, 1883, and then in the more reputable *The Girlhood of Queen Victoria: a selection from Her Majesty's diaries between the years 1832 and 1840*, c.1900, both of which seem to have been designed to re-domesticate the ever more formidable Empress of India). This reimagining of the Armada icon as exemplary Victorian child perhaps received its definitive incarnation at the Mansion House juvenile fancy-dress ball held in January 1887 expressly to mark the now hugely popular and public old Queen's Golden Jubilee. The occasion began with a procession of 150 children dressed as British sovereigns and their most notable subjects since the Conquest; the star part was Elizabeth I, played by the nine-year-old Lord Mayor's daughter (Fig. 23) in a costume clearly adapted from the Ditchley portrait:

Queen Elizabeth herself could not have wished for a more dignified representative than the great Monarch had in Violet Hanson on her ninth birthday. The costume worn by her small Majesty at the Mansion House was very complete and historically correct. It consisted of a bodice and train of that rich material known as silver brocade—a pattern fully worked in silver thread on a white satin ground—with full sleeves of the same, slashed for plain white satin to be drawn through; a white satin stomacher and petticoat, much adorned with pearls and diamonds; a big and elaborate ruff and a wonderfully curled and twisted head of auburn hair with a Royal diadem set on top, and a 'bob' pearl drooping on to the forehead. The train of the Queen of the evening was carried by a page yet smaller than herself . . . and in her Majesty's train were Shakspeare, Raleigh, Amy Robsart, and two other Maids-of-Honour, and a small edition of the Lord Mayor of London . . .[55]

This diminutive and decorative Elizabeth could pay her court entirely suitably to the Queen of Great Britain and Empress of India because she had been reduced so spectacularly to a mere sign of the Elizabethan. The Virgin Queen's real power and unscrupulous courtships are here

Fig. 23. Violet Hanson, on her ninth birthday, as the Virgin Queen. As well as being frequently reimagined as an exemplary Victorian child, Elizabeth was on this occasion impersonated by one. At the 'juvenile fancy dress ball' held at the Mansion House to celebrate Victoria's Golden Jubilee in January 1887, Miss Violet Hanson, the daughter of the Lord Mayor of London, took the starring role of Elizabeth in a parade of English sovereigns. Her costume, commented the approving *Illustrated London News* (which published this illustration), was 'very complete and historically correct', and she was helped with it by 'a page yet smaller than herself'. Also 'in her Majesty's train' were 'Shakspeare, Raleigh, Amy Robsart, and two other Maids-of-Honour, and a small edition of the Lord Mayor of London'.

remembered only by the ghostly presence in her train of Amy Robsart. Moreover, it seems likely that the reporter's delight in this piquant miniaturization of the Virgin Queen was none the less underpinned by something rather more serious; it was, after all, not unreasonable to suppose that the body within that particular farthingale was indeed virginally domestic, still safely subject to her father, even if he was himself miniaturized in her train. Only infantilized in this way could the Virgin Queen pay decorous homage to Queen Victoria, and the legacy of her unfeminine political acumen be superseded by Victoria's decorative constitutional and domestic virtues:

In her we may see the predecessor of that noble lady who now wields the sceptre of Great Britain, and whose constitutional faith and domestic virtues have as much tended to adorn the throne of England, as the political sagacity of Elizabeth did to secure it.[56]

Postscript

These two Elizabeths, the barren old maid and the virgin child, illustrate in the extreme how hard the Victorians found it to provide Elizabeth with an acceptable feminine private self, let alone one that would seem congruent with her other more public careers as national symbol in the mode of the current queen, raised by her Golden and Diamond Jubilees to equally mythic status. In 1897, at the Devonshire House fancy-dress ball given to celebrate the Diamond Jubilee, the court of Queen Elizabeth was certainly represented, but, pointedly, not by the royal party, who arrived in quasi-Elizabethan costume to be sure, but as the court of Marguerite de Valois. As Edward Spencer Beesly remarked in 1892, reflecting explicitly on Elizabeth's old age and implicitly upon Victoria's:

to a woman who has passed through life without knowing what it is to love or be loved, who has no memory of even an unrequited affection to feed on, who has never shared a husband's joys and sorrows, never borne the sweet burden of maternity, never suckled babe or rocked cradle, who must finish her journey alone . . . without the cheer of children or the varied interests that gather around the family—to such a one, what avails it that she has tasted the excitement of public life, that she has borne a share in politics or business—what even that her aims have been high or that she has done the State some service, if she has renounced the crown of womanhood, and turned from their appointed use those numbered years within which the female heart can find present joy and lay up store of calm satisfaction for declining age?[57]

The same view might even invade historical fiction. H. C. Bailey's *The Lonely Queen*, for example (1911), a fictionalized account of Elizabeth's life that starts with her girlhood, demonstrates how thoroughly Victoria's image had by now conditioned that of Elizabeth, since like Wynfield's version of the Essex bedroom scene it neatly reverses the eighteenth century's strategies for representing Gloriana's personal subjectivity. Whereas for Banks and his imitators the sentimental femininity of the Queen could be anchored in the private, for Bailey Elizabeth's sentimental femininity was essentially a matter of canny personal publicity: 'when she grew sentimental she was always dangerous.'[58] Accordingly, canonical sentimental episodes—her sorrowful entry at Traitors' Gate, her musings upon the distant milkmaid, her inscription of 'pathetic sentiments' on a window at Woodstock—all become moments of successful sentimental posturing, dictated by political cunning and a certain meanness that is the true motive power behind this version of what Bailey calls the 'historic doll'. Bailey's novel makes the sentimental not the private but the public face, and the political not the public but the private face of the Queen: her supposed susceptibility does not hold her hostage but is rather an elaborate performance. What is 'inside' the woman is the queen, rather than the other way about. Even more consonant with the perspectives of Egg or Beesly is this novel's unprecedented choice of endpoint: instead of closing at the close of the Leicester imbroglio, like *Kenilworth*, or with the death-warrants of Mary or of Essex, the end of Elizabeth's story is understood as the moment at which she recognizes her own sterility. Elizabeth's last line in the book is the desolate cry she is supposed to have uttered on learning of the birth of the future James I: 'The Queen of Scots is delivered of a fair son, and I, I am of barren stock!'

However, by the time this novel appeared, the death of Victoria had opened the way towards a new manner of rethinking the female body into royal power, for one exceptional writer at least. Nine years after Victoria's state funeral in 1901, writing a sequel to the nationalistic set of historical mini-romances for children that makes up *Puck of Pook's Hill*, Rudyard Kipling entitled one story 'Gloriana', to which he added a poem called 'The Looking-glass' as a pendant. As we might expect from Kipling, 'Gloriana' is largely concerned with empire and its costs, and we will be looking at it in some detail in our next chapter: but the poem that follows it both recapitulates and transforms some of the motifs that had preoccupied the likes of Egg, and it amply deserves quotation in full:

> *Queen Bess was Harry's daughter!*
> *The Queen was in her chamber, and she was middling old,*
> *Her petticoat was satin and her stomacher was gold.*
> *Backwards and forwards and sideways did she pass,*
> *Making up her mind to face the cruel looking-glass.*
> > *The cruel looking-glass that will never show a lass*
> > *As comely or as kindly or as young as once she was!*

> The Queen was in her chamber, a-combing of her hair.
> There came Queen Mary's spirit and it stood behind her chair,
> Singing, 'Backwards and forwards and sideways may you pass,
> But I will stand behind you till you face the looking-glass.
> > The cruel looking-glass that will never show a lass
> > As lovely or unlucky or as lonely as I was!'

> The Queen was in her chamber, a-weeping very sore,
> There came Lord Leicester's spirit and it scratched upon the door.
> Singing, 'Backwards and forwards and sideways may you pass
> But I will walk beside you till you face the looking-glass.
> > The cruel looking-glass that will never show a lass,
> > As hard and unforgiving or as wicked as you was!'

> The Queen was in her chamber; her sins were on her head;
> She looked the spirits up and down and statelily she said:—
> 'Backwards and forwards and sideways though I've been,
> Yet I am Harry's daughter and I am England's Queen!'
> > And she faced the looking-glass (and whatever else there was)
> > And she saw her day was over and she saw her beauty pass
> > In the cruel looking-glass that can always hurt a lass
> > More hard than any ghost there is or any man there was![59]

Kipling's poem sets up a narrative logic whereby Elizabeth's sins against womanliness—executing the quintessentially feminine Queen of Scots, denying the love of Lord Leicester—are embodied not only as ghosts that rack her old age but are registered, Dorian Gray-like, upon her mirrored face as age. But Kipling goes one step further than, say, Egg some sixty-odd years earlier in showing a queen in part exonerated from these sins by her courage in facing down—literally—the price that queenliness has exacted from the woman. To put it another way, she looks into her glass and doesn't see the accusing ghost of the young Victoria, the domestic womanliness she has rejected. Hence Kipling would go on to celebrate a posthumous truce between an Elizabeth less of Essex than of the Golden Speech, and a Victoria celebrated as inspiring a national sentiment valorized above any dreams of territorial aggrandizement. It is a measure of the extent to which both the power of Elizabeth and the sexuality that figured it had been absorbed within a passionate but entirely respectable relationship between nation and female sovereign that by 1911, in a poem entitled *The Bells and Queen Victoria*, Kipling was explicitly casting the Empress of India as heir to the Faerie Queene—but not so much to Elizabeth's power, domestic or imperial, as simply to the power of Britons' love. Here Victoria's apotheosis as the self-denying darling of a national love affair finally completes, even as its contours are defined by, that of Elizabeth.

> THE BELLS:
>
> Here is more gain than Gloriana guessed—
> Than Gloriana guessed or Indies bring—
> Than golden Indies bring. A Queen confessed—
> A Queen confessed that crowned her people King.
> Her people King, and crowned all Kings above,
> Above all Kings have crowned their Queen their love—
> Have crowned their love their Queen, their Queen their love.[60]

5

*An Empress and
her Adventurers*

The Virgin Queen lived out many, and conflicting, lives in the Victorian imagination, serving for some as a nightmare incarnation of the tyrannically unfeminine; but despite the often phobic representations of her as an anti-Victoria especially in literature for women and girls which we saw in our last chapter, one of the most enduringly powerful of nineteenth-century stories about English history was that, designed for boys and men, which hailed Elizabeth and the Elizabethans as the progenitors of nineteenth-century nation and empire-building. This was institutionalized during Victoria's reign by the establishment of national learned and professional societies named after their Elizabethan avatars and often engaged in republishing their works: the Camden Society in history (1838), the Shakespeare Society in the study of Elizabethan drama (1841), the Spenser Society in the study of Elizabethan poetry (1867), the Selden Society in the study of sixteenth-century legal history (1887).[1] But it is with the intellectual territory of the Parker Society (1840, named after Elizabeth's first Archbishop of Canterbury and involved in the republication of early Protestant theological works), and especially that of the Hakluyt Society (1846) that we engage here. This is the story

Gloriana as Protestant national heroine became embroiled in mid-Victorian religious controversy and its aftermath, and how her role as architect of the national Church and patroness of colonial adventure was related to contemporary narratives about imperial expansion and domestic security. A new set of characters and incidents here leap into prominence to dramatize the Queen's relationship with her country: for the first time since their deaths the figures of Sir Francis Drake and Sir Walter Raleigh come to flank that of the Queen as prominent and integral parts of the national pantheon.[2] The swashbuckling romance of these adventurers, their buccaneering exploits in the New World and their defeat of the Armada in the Old, were now perceived as the first stirrings of an ever-mightier national destiny; they called up a new set of genres to do them justice, informed by a grandiose sense of historical panorama and heroic supermasculinity. First came prose epics in history and the boy's own novel of adventure; then interminable verse epics and epic dramas, mercifully too immense in scale ever to be performed; then the sweeping pomp of civic murals, and, last of all, the crowded bustle of the historical pageants which came into favour in the early 1900s and reached a crescendo of popularity in the 1920s and 1930s. Given the reservations felt by many Victorian commentators about her personal character, it is not surprising that the figure of the Virgin Queen herself flickers disconcertingly in and out of these celebrations of 'the spacious times of great Elizabeth', as Tennyson termed them in 1832.[3] Often not extensively visible in narrative (rather in the manner pioneered by Spenser, Arne, and Mr Puff) she functions all the same as the iconic embodiment of her island empire and as the chivalric inspiration to Victorian and Edwardian generations of manly young empire-builders. By 1907 this version of the Queen is such a staple that it can be conveniently condensed into an agreeable and allegorical flirtation between monarch and patriotic buccaneer Johnnie Morgan in Tom Bevan's rousing boys' novel of adventure *Sea Dogs All! A Tale of Forest and Sea*:

'I am sick of pretty speeches, and thought to find a plain unspoiled Englishman who would speak nought but truth. . . . Dost not find mine eyes *green*?' she asked, and leaned a little forward in her chair.

1. Solomon J. Solomon (1860–1927), *The Commons Petition Elizabeth to Marry*
(1911). This painting, reverently installed in the Palace of Westminster, affirms
a long-established idea of Elizabeth as bride of her country and mother to her
people. It depicts the Queen's reply to Parliament (February 1559), as elaborated by William Camden decades later: "'I am already bound unto an husband,
which is the kingdom of England...' And therwithal, stretching out her hand,
she showed them the ring with which she was given in marriage and inaugurated to her kingdom in express and solemn terms. "And reproach me so no
more," quoth she, "that I have no children: for every one of you, and as many as
are English, are my children and kinsfolks."'

2. Paul Delaroche (1797–1856), *The Death of Queen Elizabeth* (1827). Delaroche's lurid, melodramatic, and hugely influential painting, by contrast with Robert Smirke's earlier, sympathetic account of the same event (*Queen Elizabeth Appointing Her Successor*, Fig. 3), treats Elizabeth as grotesquely obsolete, both personally and politically. Her despairing death, pestered by a courtier who may be either imperiously demanding the coronation ring from her finger or vainly trying to persuade her to take to her bed, is presented not as a solemn moment of constitutional continuity but as an unlamented dead end.

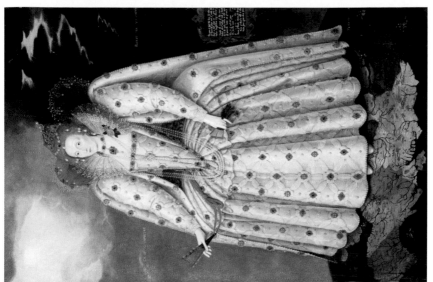

3. Federigo Zuccaro (c.1542–1609), the 'Darnley' portrait (1575). Painted when Elizabeth was 42, this was the first Tudor portrait to separate its royal sitter from the crown and sceptre, visible on a surface behind the standing Queen. Depicting her as a woman alienable from her queenship, this has been one of the modern period's favourite images of Elizabeth.

4. Marcus Gheeraerts the Younger (1562–1635), the immense 'Ditchley' portrait, (c.1592), in which Elizabeth stands on her country. In the "Ditchley" portrait Queen, crown and island become one. Elizabeth is England, woman and kingdom are interchangeable' (Sir Roy Strong).

5. David Scott (1806–49), *Queen Elizabeth viewing the performance of 'The Merry Wives of Windsor' in the Globe Theatre* (1840). Scott uses the rumour that Queen Bess commissioned *The Merry Wives* as the occasion for a knowingly unhistorical image which seeks to sum up the entire English Renaissance, with Elizabeth and Shake-speare as its double centre. The audience includes not only the Bard (in blue sleeves) but many of the period's other celebrities, including Leices-ter, Essex, Walsingham, Burghley, Jonson, Spenser, Sidney, Dr Dee, Beaumont, and Fletcher. On stage Falstaff, disguised as Herne the Hunter, is led gleefully on by Mistresses Page and Ford. England, surely, never got much merrier than this.

6. Charles Cattermole (1832–1900), *Shakespeare Reading 'The Merry Wives of Windsor' to Queen Elizabeth* (*c.*1860)from a whole series depicting the life of Shakespeare. In Cattermole's watercolour Elizabeth and her pet poet, their apocryphal intimacy given an improbable waterborne setting, become not just the co-authors of Falstaff's amours but a latterday Anthony and Cleopatra.

7. Elizabeth and Empire glorified: A. K. Lawrence, *Queen Elizabeth the Faerie Queene of her Knights and Merchant Venturers commissions Sir Walter Raleigh to sail for America and discover new countries* (1927). Lawrence's visionary image was painted as one of a series, 'The Building of Britain, 877–1707', commissioned by Sir Henry Newbolt for St Stephen's Hall in the Palace of Westminster.

BAKER STREET MADAM OFFERS DOMINATION, CORRECTION AND DISCIPLINE.

MADAME TUSSAUDS WHERE THE PEOPLE MEET THE PEOPLE.

8. Elizabeth and Empire disavowed: the Baker Street Madam of this 1996 advertisement for London's famous waxworks, clearly, is not only Madam Tussaud but also a sado-masochist's stepmotherly old Britannia, of whom these three fearsome, gunboat-dispatching women are all offered as personifications.

9. The infantile queen's two bodies: Queenie, Nursie and Melchie, from *Blackadder II*, BBC2, 1985. Miranda Richardson's lethally childish flirt of an Elizabeth—part Mrs Thatcher, part Sarah Ferguson—is seen here with her Nurse (Patsy Byrne) and her burlesqued Burghley, Lord Melchett (Stephen Fry). The show's running gag of the Queen's perpetual juxtaposition with the bovine Nursie consciously or unconsciously parodies the Renaissance doctrine of the monarch's two bodies.

10. The old queen's two bodies: Quentin Crisp as an impressively intense and vulnerable Elizabeth in Sally Potter's film adaptation of Virginia Woolf's *Orlando* (1992). Potter's casting of this self-proclaimed expert in how to become a virgin not only literalizes and outdoes Elizabeth's rhetoric about having the body of a weak and feeble woman but the heart and stomach of a king, but is faithful to her source-novel's origins as a response to Lytton Strachey's *Elizabeth and Essex: A Tragic History* (1928). In Strachey's psychologized biography, written at the same time as *Orlando* and much discussed with Woolf while in progress, Elizabeth is herself represented as an honorary male homosexual, her infatuation with Essex likened to Hercules' desire for the page-boy Hylas.

11. Josephine Barstow as Elizabeth, 1993, in Phyllida Lloyd's Opera North revival of Benjamin Britten's *Gloriana* (1953). With Margaret Thatcher's resignation still a recent memory and with Elizabeth II now in her sixties, Britten's opera about the old queen's tormented self-renunciation in the interests of State—ill-suited for its Coronation Year première—suddenly made sense.

12. Romance about to give place to history. Cate Blanchett's nubile young Tudor in Shekhar Kapur's *Elizabeth* (1998), dancing milkmaid-like on the greensward. Instead of stripping away the queen's robes of state to reveal the desiring woman, Kapur begins with a 'normal' Elizabeth and dramatizes her transformation into the painted sexless icon of historical memory. The underlying point—the presumed incompatibility of womanhood with power—remains much the same.

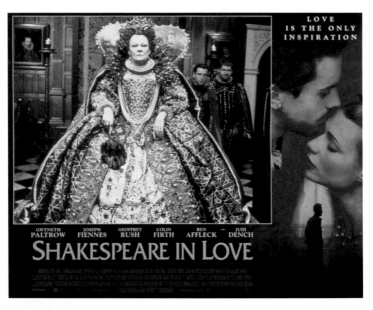

13. History pushing romance into the margins. Judi Dench's Elizabeth dominates this poster for John Madden's *Shakespeare in Love* (1998), forcing the unhistorical love-plot between Lady Viola and Shakespeare off to one side. The old woman of history is perennially opposed to the young woman of romance, though in this film, with the figure of Shakespeare mediating between them, the two turn out to be versions of one another as well.

'There is the ghost of the verdure of England in them, your Majesty, and the sheen of the blue of her skies and her seas.'

'And thou dost consider them, therefore, to be perfect for England's Queen?'

'God made you, your Majesty, and we daily thank him for his abounding goodness and wisdom.'

A faint blush stole into Elizabeth's cheeks, and the blue-green eyes danced.

'Thou dost see merrie England mirrored in these pale orbs?'

'The country lives in your Majesty's heart, and the heart looks out through the eyes.'[4]

It is the inception and development of this powerful story of manliness that this chapter tracks; despite unmistakable signs of disintegration in the 1930s, that ethos of Elizabeth-sponsored manliness was still being invoked—albeit tentatively—at the height of the invasion scare of the Second World War.

A Protestant Heroine, her Sea-Dogs, and her Empire

> The age . . . seemed to breed men of a sterner, tougher fibre than that which forms the staple of modern life. . . . Religious tolera-tion, the child of the nineteenth century, was an unknown quality in the sixteenth. . . . men learned in the profession of the religion in which they believed to suffer and be strong.[5]

The late Victorian period saw the development of a large-scale industry in ripping yarns for boys, in which Elizabeth acquires an astonishing number of aspiring young empire-builders as honorary sons. The genre takes its inception from Charles Kingsley's fiercely Protestant *Westward Ho!* (1855), which we will be examining in detail below, but, extraordinar-ily, a great deal of the output later in the century is ecumenical in intent. The 1890s and early 1900s saw the first ever patriotic literary texts about Elizabeth and her England to boast Catholics as their protagonists, a development which would certainly have baffled and enraged the genre's distant forebears, Thomas Heywood and Thomas Dekker. This was a rash of adventure stories, set in Elizabethan England and mostly aimed at boys, which took as heroes young courtiers who were loyal servants of the crown despite being Papist recusants. Such is Guy Ratcliffe, spy-hero of A. E. Aldington's *The Queen's Preferment* (1896) whose family, as he says, 'belonged to the old Romish faith, in the which I had been brought up, albeit I had latterly conformed for the sake of peace and quietness, and, as I considered, not having given the matter much thought, as a loyal patriotic subject should do.'[6] Ratcliffe will go on to serve Walsingham, and will be imprisoned by the Queen for his obstinate resurgent Catholicism, but ultimately he will prove his loyalty by refusing to be tempted to assassinate the Queen by a disguised (and dissimulating) Leicester. Crying 'I will teach thee what it meaneth to tempt me with thy damnable treasons', he seizes his interlocutor by the throat, 'whereupon, kneeling on his chest, I caught him by the ears, and lifting his head therewith knocked it forcibly against the floor.'[7] More than half-strangled, Leicester is eventually rescued only by the personal intervention of the Queen, who has been concealed behind the arras. Ratcliffe survives to an honoured old age under the patronage of the Queen. Robert Haynes Cave's *In the Days of Good Queen Bess* (1897) also features a loyal Catholic, Sir Adrian Trafford, who saves the Queen's life but is alienated from her when his Jesuit brother is hung, drawn, and quartered for complicity in the Babington Plot. Confronting the Queen with his narrative of the execution, he reduces her to tearful exclamation:

'We might have been friends; but your brother's blood rises up from the ground to forbid it. . . . Now, go; leave me: yet ere you go know this, that I never liked and esteemed you so much as I do today, and I promise you that this barbarous rite of a barbarous age shall have no more place in my realm. . . . Farewell, and believe that Elizabeth would have saved your brother, if she could.'[8]

Another such protagonist, the hero of Beatrice Marshall's *The Queen's Knight-Errant; A Story of the Days of Sir Walter Raleigh* (1905), is knighted for his services to his queen: '"Vidal—Gervase Vidal of Devon," the Queen repeated. "Beshrew me, was he not one of those loyal Catholics who brought a contingent to our forces at Tilbury. Bring him hither to me and he shall receive his reward."'[9] There are others, too: Caroline Holroyd's *Seething Days: A Romance* (1894), for example, demands citation, if only for its evocative title.

Viewed together, the sum total of these turn-of-the-century fictions is to exculpate Elizabeth from personal responsibility for the persecution of Catholics, and to assert the fiction of an Elizabethan patriotism that overrode all sectarian differences. They mark the historical moment when the Protestant heroine definitively mutates into a heroine who presides over a secularized or at least ecumenical nation. The road to this turn-of-the-century more-or-less détente was, however, surprisingly arduous, and this was chiefly as a result of the great mid-Victorian religious revival that reignited the question of the relations between Church and state. The history of the Reformation burst into fiercely renewed controversy, and with it the question of Elizabeth's own relation to the religious controversies of her time.

In 1826, for example, the Eton debating society considered the motion 'Was Queen Elizabeth justified in her persecution of the Roman Catholics?'—the vote was that she had *not* been justified, by a bare majority of one.[10] Despite appearances, the question was of more than schoolboy interest. It had a burning topicality, for, in 1829, largely in response to discontent in Ireland, the Catholic Emancipation Bill became law. Roman Catholics would no longer be barred from holding office in the government or the judiciary. Together with the repeal of the Test and Corporation Acts in 1828, which released dissenters from similar disabilities, the Act supposedly inaugurated a new secularized state of modernity based upon religious toleration. Instead, fanned by the modernizing habits of a Parliament which not only reformed itself with the Reform Act of 1832 but showed signs of turning its reforming zeal on to the Church of England, a new spirit of religious controversy broke out—epitomized by, though not confined to, the so-called Oxford Movement—and would condition the temper of the times across four decades. It would not be until the century was on its deathbed that the heat would finally fizzle out of the long-standing and impassioned debate that electrified the Church of England.

The Oxford clerics who published the series of sermons known as *Tracts for the Times* from 1833 to 1841 were opposed to state intervention in the Church, an opposition which prompted a wholesale review of the Church's relations to both public and private life on the part of John

Keble, John Henry Newman, and others who advocated a revival of much Catholic doctrine and practice, and eventually led to Newman's scandalous high-profile conversion to the Roman Catholic Church in 1845 and the consequent resignation of his Oxford fellowship. The conversion of Newman and others of his scholar-cleric colleagues made astonishing news because Roman Catholicism had hitherto been confined to old Catholic families, the Irish, and other assorted foreigners. Now, it seemed, instead of Roman Catholicism being in the nature of a family heirloom or hereditary disease, it could be a matter of intellectual preference. In sum, the high-church revival, taken together with the contemporaneous low-church revival, made for an explosive ideological cocktail; out of it vapoured at mid-century a particularly virulent anti-Catholic hysteria. This hysteria necessarily had a profound effect upon the historical representation of the Tudors, the dynasty that had initiated, struggled over, and finally established the Protestant Reformation.[11]

One way in which this religious debate would crystallize was in yet another phase of the argument over the relative merits of the 'sister queens' Elizabeth and Mary, Queen of Scots, most recently exemplified in the hostile portraiture of the English queen in the Catholic John Lingard's influential and much-reprinted and adapted *A History of England* (1819–30). As we have seen, Elizabeth had been vilified for her treatment of Mary in sentimental fiction since the time of *The Recess* (1785), but in the nineteenth century a whole line of further novels for girls and women took up Mary's cause in an explicitly pro-Catholic manner, most importantly the Kebleite Charlotte M. Yonge's *Unknown to History; A Story of the Captivity of Mary of Scotland* (1882).[12] In Yonge's fiction and in the many contemporary important history-paintings, Mary appeared not merely as glamorous victim and thus perfect womanly woman but as the inspirer of a proper and feeling manly chivalry, sometimes explicitly compared to the sycophantic facsimile lavished on her elder rival. Mrs Markham's immensely popular *A History of England . . . For the use of young Persons* (*c*.mid-1820s), for example, follows an account of the fate of the Queen of Scots with a 'conversation' between her and her two young boy-scholars which begins with one of them exclaiming, 'I dare say Mary had done a great many wrong things; yet I am sure I should have been like Anthony Babington, and have entered into any plot that could have been thought of to get her out of the power of that deceitful old Queen.'[13] This is, after all, substantially the plot of Yonge's *Unknown to History*.[14] Protestant sympathizers (both English and American) were obliged to retort by once more remembering Elizabeth's oppressed youth, depicting her as equally nubile and dignified under the religious persecution of her sister. This is the point of Daniel Huntington's *A Child Bringing Flowers to the Princess Elizabeth, when a Prisoner, in the reign of Mary* (1848), of Marcus Stone's canvas *The Princess (afterwards Queen) Elizabeth obliged to attend Mass by her sister* (1869), of Emmanuel Leutze's painting of Elizabeth imprisoned in the Tower (the Bible prominently displayed), and of Tennyson's sympathetic depiction of her in his play *Queen Mary* (first performed in 1876). This too, was the burden of William Frederick Yeames's depiction of Elizabeth's court in pointed mourning after the massacre of French Protestants in 1572, *Queen Elizabeth receiving the French Ambassadors after the news of the Massacre of St Bartholomew* (1866).

However, much the most powerful and dominant depiction of the struggles of the Reformation came in the form of a thoroughly controversial history book: James Anthony Froude's gripping twelve-volume *History of England from the Fall of Wolsey to the Death of Elizabeth* (1858–70), which all Victorian considerations of the period took as a reference point. A considered and hostile response to the religious controversies of the Oxford Movement and Tractarianism, Froude's *History* became in extracted and abridged form for schools and the general public the most influential account of Elizabeth and the Reformation. Together with his other writings, it formed the backbone of other central fictions of the 'Elizabethan' purveyed by Froude's friends Charles Kingsley and Alfred, Lord Tennyson, amongst others. Strongly Protestant in its sympathies, Froude's history none the less told the story of how national integrity and autonomy and a nascent empire were forged from the religious compromise of the Elizabethan Settlement. The contemporary legacy of that compromise, according to Froude, was that England had been preserved from the European revolutionary upheavals of 1848, in his view the inevitable, if slow-to-manifest, ef the European counter-reformation. It was a compromise which had to be defended in the religious controversies over the episcopacy that pre-occupied mid-Victorian high churchmen in Oxford, which for Froude were the latter-day continuation of Elizabeth's own troubles with 'Martin Marprelate' and other religious dissidents.

Froude took on Thomas Babington Macaulay's fundamentally Whig thesis that the modern nation-state was founded by the Glorious Revolution of 1688, by arguing that the roots of Victorian modernity were to be found instead in Elizabeth's reign. Elizabeth herself, he con-tended, was all but Catholic in her personal convictions, disliked Puritanism, and, secular in her temperament, was anxious to promote a spirit of religious toleration. She 'desired only a general peace, outward order and uniformity, with liberty to everyone to think in private as he pleased.' [15] As he formulates it, Elizabeth's 'theory was two centuries before its time.'[16] Her religious moderation found its corollary in a 'free proud spirit' which 'would permit no clergy to fetter the thoughts and paralyse the energies of England.'[17] Protestant free-thinking or 'pro-gressive intelligence' compels mutual toleration of individualistic belief; its intellectual energy makes empire-building possible, and the Elizabethan age accordingly sees the decline of imperial Spain (ossified by the Inquisition) and 'the first beginnings of that proud power which, rising out of the heart of the people, has planted the saplings of the English race in every quarter of the globe, has covered the ocean with its merchant fleets; and flaunts its flag in easy supremacy among the nations of the earth.'[18] This argument that the broad toleration of the Elizabethan Settlement, embodied by Elizabeth herself, was the foun-dation of the modern nation-state, came to fruition rather later in that series of turn-of-the-century boys' own adventure stories, at which we have already glanced. However, Froude's other important contribution to mid-century culture was to be his celebration of the Elizabethan seamen as the flowering of national Protestant masculinity in opposition to Catholic effeminacy and degeneracy.

Froude's early essays concentrated upon the Elizabethan seamen, inspired by the scholarly reprinting of Elizabethan accounts of explo-ration carried out by the Hakluyt Society.[19] Although the founders of the Society seem to have intended to celebrate Hakluyt as a merchant adventurer and early advocate of Free Trade, this commercial reading was largely set aside in favour of Froude's nobler vision, first expressed in his highly critical review essay of the Society's edition of Hakluyt's *Voyages*, 'England's Forgotten Worthies,' published in 1852. According to Froude, Hakluyt was no mere publicizer of ways of making money out of unfamiliar travel destinations, but had compiled 'the Prose Epic of the modern English nation' and of the nascent British empire. He celebrated 'the seamen who in the days of our own Elizabeth . . . went out across the unknown seas, fighting, discovering, colonizing, and graved out the channels, paving them at last with their bones, through which the commerce and enterprise of England has flowed out over all the world.'[20] This view became dominant for the rest of the century, with the added flourish that the Elizabethan seamen had established not just England's status as a global trading nation but its naval supremacy and thus British international power: as de Rothschild was to put it in 1884: 'the Freebooters were the first pioneers of English trade and commerce; they dealt the first and severest blows at the naval enemies of England. By their daring acts and successes they broke the power and prestige of the naval supremacy of Spain and transferred the sceptre of the Ocean to the hands of the sovereigns of England . . .'[21]. Froude's essay inspired, amongst many others, his friend and admirer Charles Kingsley, who set out to write his own modern prose epic of Protestant nation and empire, a major and unprecedented fictional formulation of the Elizabethan, *Westward Ho!* (1855).[22]

It would be hard to overstate the impact of *Westward Ho!*, so embedded does its particular brand of ripping yarn still seem to be in the English psyche, thanks to its long afterlife as a children's classic alongside *Treasure Island*, *Robinson Crusoe*, and *The Coral Island*. Back in the mid-1820s, in Mrs Markham's virtual schoolroom, her two boy-scholars complain that their teacher hasn't told them anything about Raleigh, Drake, Frobisher 'and all those fine old fellows.' Mrs Markham replies that there isn't time to cover them as the tea-tray is coming in, and that, if they really must, they can read about the seamen in 'the Biographical Dictionary.'[23] All that would change after Kingsley's panoramic celebration of epic meritocratic masculinity, which was to set the agenda for boys' history and boys' adventure stories over the remainder of the century and into the next. Here is a taste of this new mode, designed to interpellate the young and impressionable; we are on board the *Golden Hind* in dry dock in Deptford, dining with anyone who is anyone—Humphrey Gilbert, Frobisher, John Winter, and Philip Sidney amongst them:

> Look at the men all around; a nobler company you will seldom see. . . . At the head of the table sits the Lord Mayor . . . none other than that famous Sir Edward Osborne, clothworker, and ancestor of the Dukes of Leeds. . . . The chivalry and promptitude of the 'prentice boy have grown and hardened into the thoughtful daring of the wealthy merchant adventurer. There he sits, a right kingly man, with my lord Earl of Cumberland on his right hand, and Walter Raleigh on his left. The three talk together in low voices on the chance of there being vast and rich countries still undiscovered between Florida and the River of Canada. . . . Raleigh is fain to call to his help the quiet student who sits on his left hand, Richard Hakluyt of Oxford . . .[24]

And so on, for another couple of pages.

Perhaps one of the most striking features of *Westward Ho!* is Kingsley's decision not to portray the Queen. Over the course of this expansive fictionalization of most of the major adventures and expeditions of the Elizabethan sea-dogs, from Drake's circumnavigation to the settlement of Virginia and the defeat of the Armada, she appears only a few times, and then, markedly, only by way of second-hand accounts: a picture on a pageant banner, reported conversations, a letter, and, at the climactic moment of the celebration of the victory in 1588, within a contemporary account of her visit to St Paul's Cathedral which is transcribed word for word. In this way, the Queen herself is safely cleared away into the realm of official myth even for her Elizabethan contemporaries.

And yet, this conspicuous absence of the Queen is, perversely, a sort of representation of her. It is usefully illuminated by Kingsley's treatment of her in his essay 'Sir Walter Raleigh and His Time' (1859) in which, despite the Victorian vogue for dismissing Elizabeth as both personally and politically superannuated exemplified by the likes of Augustus Egg, she appears as the Faerie Queene in an unusual state of agelessness. Kingsley's Elizabeth is preserved not so much by cosmetics (though, as

we've seen, he defended her right to use them), but by an entirely appropriate chivalric adoration on the part of her courtiers and adventurers,
explicable because 'the whole nation is in a mood of exaltation':

There was, in plain palpable fact, something about the Queen, her history, her
policy, the times, the glorious part which England, and she as the incarnation of
the then English spirit, were playing upon earth, which raised imaginative and
heroical souls into a permanent exaltation—a 'fairyland' as they called it themselves, which seems to us fantastic. . . . There can be no doubt that a number of
as noble men as ever stood together on the earth did worship that woman, fight
for her, toil for her, risk all for her, with a pure chivalrous affection which has fur-
nished one of the most beautiful pages in all the book of history.[25]

Noticeably disembodied as an individual woman, this queen is instead a
focal point, a rallying point for young masculinity. Her agelessness is
really conferred by the men who forget that she grows old:

And what blame to those who worshipped her, if, knowing that she was the
same, they too should fancy that she looked the same, the Elizabeth of their
youth, and should talk as if the fair flesh, as well as the fair spirit, was immortal?
. . . There is no feeling in these Elizabethan worshippers which we have not
seen, potential and crude, again and again in the best and noblest of young men
whom we have met, till it was crushed in them by the luxury, effeminacy and
unbelief in chivalry, which are the sure accompaniment of a long peace . . .[26]

The Queen's absence in *Westward Ho!* is thus apparent rather than real.
As Protestant heroine, and as inspirational 'incarnation of the spirit of
those times', she is interfused through the narrative in the shape of that
national spirit which inspires the Protestant, chivalric, and warlike masculinity of the adventurer hero, Amyas Leigh, whose destiny it is to help
defeat Spanish-sponsored Catholicism in both the New and the Old
Worlds. Nor is the woman herself entirely absent, for the fate of the
nation and the empire is played out across the bodies of two women,
both of them surrogates for the Queen, Rose Salterne and Ayacanora.

The narrative drive of the novel is supplied initially by the love of a
number of young Devonshire gentlemen for Rose Salterne. Her lovers
include the Euphuistic poet and courtier Frank Leigh, the low-born
parson John Brimblecombe, and our hero, Amyas Leigh, 'a s

though he knows it not, of brave young England longing to wing its way out of its island prison, to discover and to traffic, to colonize and to civilize, until no wind can sweep the earth which does not bear the echoes of an English voice' (12). Their rivalry is defused within a hundred pages by the formation of 'the Brotherhood of the Rose', sworn both to love her and to serve her by leaving the country for three years and serving their queen. This English Rose thus doubles the Queen as incarnation of the country. Her cavaliers' chivalric masculinity finds expression in exploration, commerce, and war, the assertion of 'free seas and free trade.'

Rose's subsequent history functions as an eloquent allegory of the danger of flirting with fanatical Catholicism: she elopes to South America with the prisoner of war Don Guzman de Soto (a revision in tragic mode of Tilburina's beloved Don Ferolo Whiskerandos) and is betrayed at the hands of the jealous Jesuit-educated traitor Eustace Leigh to a martyr's death at the hands of the Inquisition. Our hero Amyas Leigh, heartbroken, abandons his quest for the lost Rose and instead goes in search of El Dorado, finding a Virgin Queen in the virgin forest, Ayacanora, subsequently revealed to be the lost daughter of an English gentleman and a Spanish Catholic mother, who replaces Rose as the novel's love interest. Amyas imports her back to England, but is unable to return her love because of her Spanish blood. This impasse is only resolved by the defeat of the Armada itself, under English forces, commanded pointedly enough by a loyal Catholic, Howard of Effingham, English first and Catholic second. Pursuing the fleeing galleon commanded by De Soto until it wrecks on Lundy, Amyas is blinded by a bolt of lightning at the very moment of his triumph. Punished thus by God for his unChristian vindictiveness, he reconciles himself in a dream-vision with the dead de Soto, and so (to a very limited extent!) with Spanish Catholicism in general, and on the strength of this gentleman's agreement he marries Ayacanora, now English partly by an act of will and self-education, and partly by marriage. The defeat of the Armada is thus imagined in terms of an (unequal) domestic union of blood and religion, and as an act of colonization of the New World; and it is also formulated explicitly as the birth of the free English-speaking colonial world:

From that hour Ayacanora's power of song returned to her; and day by day, year after year, her voice rose up within that happy home, and soared, as on a skylark's wings, into the highest heaven, bearing with it the peaceful thoughts of the blind giant back to the Paradises of the West, in the wake of the heroes who from that time forth sailed out to colonize another and a vaster England, to the heaven-prospered cry of Westward Ho![27]

Froude's and Kingsley's combined formulation of imperial entrepre-neurship under the sponsorship of Gloriana helped inspire, among many imitations, a spate of racy abridgements of Hakluyt's *Voyages*, ideally meeting the demand which Kingsley fostered for more details about 'Raleigh, Drake, Frobisher, and all those fine old fellows': hence Richard Lovett's *Drake and the Dons, or Stirring Tales of Armada Times* (1888), E. E. Speight's *The Romance of the Merchant Venturers* (1906), *The Spanish Armada, the Last Fight of the Revenge, and other Adventures of the Reign of Queen Elizabeth* (1908), and Albert Montefiore Hyamson's *Elizabethan adventurers upon the Spanish main* (1912). It was to find a congenial home in another genre besides the adventure story, civic art; indeed, without Froude and his popularization by Kingsley the implied narratives of much Victorian and turn-of-the-century large-scale civic art, with its increasingly epic pretensions, would have been incomprehensible to the public.[28] The romance of exploration underpins Sir Edgar Boehm's statue of Drake for Tavistock in 1882, copied for Plymouth, which bears on its pedestal a relief showing Elizabeth knighting Drake at Deptford, and Sir Frank Brangwyn's large-scale mural of 1903 for Lloyd's Register of Shipping, *Queen Elizabeth going aboard the Golden Hind* to meet Drake after his circumnavigation. As late as 1927, A. K. Lawrence painted the Queen and her courtier Raleigh together in his inspirational *Queen Elizabeth the Faerie Queene of her Knights and Merchant Venturers com-missions Sir Walter Raleigh to sail for America and discover new countries* (plate 7), one of a series of eight paintings called 'The Building of Britain, 877–1707' commissioned by Sir Henry Newbolt to adorn the grand stage-set Gothic corridors of Charles Barry's Westminster Palace. ('It is not easy to account, in a sober history, for the fascination which a hard masculine old maid exerted for so long over the young and brilliant men about her,' comments Newbolt's explanatory booklet *The Building of Britain*, before justifying the painting's visionary quality in terms drawn straight from Kingsley, '[b]ut in this picture the feat has been easily achieved. It presents to the eye a spiritual not a material fact. We view a historic scene with the inward vision of the actors in it . . . We see that, which inspired a great generation—we see the Elizabeth they saw, their Gloriana, their Semper Eadem, their Faerie Queen . . .'). Lawrence's painting had a predecessor in stained-glass, the new west window put into St Margaret's Church, Westminster in 1882, which shows Raleigh, Spenser, and Humphrey Gilbert flanking the Queen, with scenes from Raleigh's life depicted below. (Funded by American money, this window points towards another tradition of depicting the Queen and her adventurers, one that, again after Kingsley, placed the inception of America with Elizabethan exploration and settlement insti-gated by Raleigh—and hence the most notable descendant of Lawrence's epic painting is Dean Cornwell's mural on the same subject, commis-sioned by William Randolph Hearst for his anglophile Warwick Hotel in New York. But more of that in our afterword).

This Elizabethan grandiosity, played out in the adventure novel but also across the ambitious genres of history-painting, epic verse and verse drama, and, latterly, full-scale pageant, was increasingly dominant as the century wore on, but not entirely unchallenged. The principal exception is the other most celebrated depiction of the Elizabethan seamen that a Victorian ever produced. In 1870, John Millais exhibited his pain-ting *The Boyhood of Raleigh* at the Royal Academy, said to be inspired by the passage in Froude's essay 'England's Forgotten Worthies' which describes Raleigh and his half-brothers Humphrey and Adrian Gilbert playing 'at sailors in the reaches of the Long Stream; in the summer evenings doubtless rowing down with the tide to the port, and wonder-ing at the quaint figureheads and carved prows of the ships which thronged it; or climbing on board, and listening, with hearts beating, to the mariners' tales of the new earth beyond the sunset.'[29] It simply shows two boys on a foreshore, listening to an older seaman. The colouring is startlingly bold, as befits a depiction of a period supposed to be the youth of England. The sheer emptiness of the picture is disconcerting too; as

Leonée Ormond has pointed out, 'in comparison with other Victorian paintings of historical scenes, *The Boyhood of Raleigh* is imaginative and economic, rather than anecdotal.'[30] The ships in the harbour which Froude evokes dwindle to the toy lying in the foreground, and the painting is dominated by the emptiness of sea and sky stretching away to the West. Emblematic of the unknown which Raleigh and his half-brother Humphrey Gilbert are to explore and of, as J. W. Burrows puts it, 'the prospect of an illimitable national destiny,' that emptiness is also eloquent testimony to Millais's ability to take it for granted that his Victorian viewer would be saturated in the romance of exploration and plunder exemplified by *Westward Ho!*[31] The picture insists upon the constitutive power of narrative passed from men to boys in the development of Raleigh from boy to man—he is romanced into a hero, much as Kingsley's hero Amyas Leigh is by listening to the stories of John Oxenham and others. It describes exactly the effect which Kingsley and the many, many writers of boys' fiction who follow his basic schema insist that their books will have on their readers, inspiring them with virile emulation: such is the central drive, for example, of G. A. Henty in *Under Drake's Flag* (1883), J. S. Fletcher, *In the Days of Drake* (1896), Henry St John, author of *The Voyage of the 'Avenger' in the Days of Dashing Drake* (1898), and Ralph Durand, author of *Spacious Days* (1914), to name only four of some twenty-three such titles published from the late 1880s until the end of the First World War. *The Voyage of the 'Avenger'*, indeed, closes with sentiments which might have been taken directly from a Royal Navy recruiting campaign:

A new era has sprung up, an era of metal. The wooden walls of Old England are no more; they are steel and iron walls now. But the hearts of oak that man them are still as fearless, brave, and true as they were long ago; and the spirit of valour animates them today as it did in the brave old days of Dashing Drake.[32]

Just as the mariner who holds the young Raleigh spellbound is telling his own story, so one of the features of this early adventure writing for boys ('healthy and exciting reading' designed to maintain the empire by 'keeping alive the spirit of the Elizabethan heroes'[33]) is that it is often told in the first person: such is Julian Corbett's *For God and Gold* (1887),

Mr Jasper Festing's fictional memoir of his voyage to Nombre de Dios with Drake, or Verney Lovett Cameron's *The History of Arthur Penreath* (1888), and Percy F. Westerman's *'Gainst the Might of Spain* (1915). The desired effect is neatly summed up by the popular historian of 1884, who concluded his biography of Elizabeth with this exhortation:

By studying the reign of Elizabeth, every man's pulse will beat more quickly, and he himself will feel called upon, should the emergency arise, to emulate the noble example set in a distant past.[34]

Yet there seems more than a touch of anxiety in Millais's painting: to rewind Raleigh into a young boy undoes the grand certainties of history just as much as it celebrates individual destiny. J. W. Burrows has remarked of Millais's Raleigh that 'his pinched anxious face and foetal pose unfortunately suggest a rather recalcitrant attitude to the age of expansion, giving an air of expostulation to the seaman who . . . points an imperious finger seaward.'[35] This anxiety—perhaps that boys might not turn into manly colonists, or perhaps that they will—sounds what is to become a recurrent, if muted, note across the century—and it seems to be concerned with the costs that empire-building exacted of men. James Rennell Rodd's episodic poem 'Greenaway' of 1897, for example, redoes the Millais celebration of the romancing of the 'sea-child', but in noticeably elegaic mode, ending from the mother's point of view:

The mother looked out as the westering sun went under the steep moor-side,
And 'Where are those three bonny boys of mine? They are long from their
    home,' she sighed.
But deeper yet had the mother sighed, could she know what the end would be,
For to all save one in the after years their doom came out of the sea![36]

Although Elizabeth is invisible in Millais's essay on manliness, later treatments of Elizabeth and her adventurers often explicitly locate blame with the imperial Queen herself, depicting her as a glamorous, but deadly double to the mother. The fiction of fulfilled femininity embedded in Elizabeth's spiritual motherhood of her sea-dogs might all too easily transform nightmarishly into a vision of a devouring mother, as it threatens to do in Rudyard Kipling's story 'Gloriana' in his collection of historical short stories for children, *Rewards and Fairies* (1910).

The conceit of this collection is that Puck magics up a series of figures from English history to talk with two children, Dan and his sister Una. In this story, on their way to roast, emblematically, potatoes in their 'Kingdom', they meet a mysterious masked woman who half tells them, half acts out the story of how Gloriana, breaking her progress to Rye, banqueted at Brickwall House, received a letter from Philip of Spain, half threats and half love-making, 'and danced him out of a brand new kingdom'.[37] In the course of the entertainment, two young men come to blows, and find themselves explaining themselves to their sovereign:

They confess their fault. It appears that midway in the banquet the elder—they were cousins—conceived that the Queen looked upon him with special favour. The younger, taking the look to himself, after some words gives the elder the lie; hence, as she guessed, the duel.[38]

Both the young men turn out already to have been on expeditions to the Spanish main, and Elizabeth, threatened by Philip with some sort of attack from the Americas, incites them to further unauthorized raids out in Virginia, despite being tempted to keep them at her side at court. The masked woman is haunted by remorse over their subsequent deaths, and is so self-divided that her attempts at self-exculpation slide between first and third person:

'*I* was not to blame . . . She showed 'em again that there could be only one end to it—quick death on the sea, or slow death in Philip's prisons. They asked no more than to embrace death for my sake . . . when my men, my tall, fantastical young men beseech me on their knees for leave to die for me, it shakes me—ah, it shakes me to the marrow of my old bones.'[39]

This older woman of ghostly flickering identities—Queen, Gloriana, Belphoebe, Elizabeth of England, Queen Bess—is wrenched apart with guilt, anxiety, and habitual deception and self-deception.[40] This is the Faerie Queene from a new reverse angle shot, the object of adoration watching her adorers at the very moment of eliciting and manipulating that adoration. It is a remarkable moment in the mythos of Elizabeth, for it is only the second time that Elizabeth narrates herself—though, as we shall see in the next chapter, not the last. Like his ancestors, Dan is seduced by the Queen's apologia: '"Would you have blamed Gloriana for wasting those lads' lives?" "Of course not. She was bound to try to stop him."' Una, Spenserian 'Queen' of her Kingdom, however, says aggressively, 'We don't play that game.'[41]

Una's evocation of the idea of a 'game', at which the lady laughs incredulously before she vanishes from sight and from the children's conscious memory, is unpleasantly pertinent in 1910. Eliciting and manipulating Kingsleyesque chivalric adoration in her romantic adventurers, this queen is none the less pursuing a strikingly inexpansive foreign policy—even the colonization of Virginia is only a backhanded by-product of her anxiety about national security. The whole story is ruled by a sense of the local, domestic present, rather than by the greedy and gorgeous romance of 'that strange and romantic Western fairyland' as Cave's *In the Days of Good Queen Bess* had lusciously described it only thirteen years earlier.[42] It is ruled too by a sense of foreboding and anxiety; the story presages the coming of the Armada, though it doesn't recount it. The 'games' that Elizabeth played with Philip of Spain, also represented by Sir William Reynolds-Stephens's important sculpture of Elizabeth and Philip II playing chess entitled *A Royal Game* (1906–11, Fig. 24), resonated in the early years of the century with 'the great game' played out over Europe, a game which would culminate in the First World War.

The delicately poised guilt and foreboding incarnated by Kipling's story has vanished on the eve of war into the more unabashedly patriotic and swashing mood of Louis Napoleon Parker's *Drake: A Pageant Play* first staged in 1912 in London under Herbert Beerbohm Tree, and revived in 1914 just after the outbreak of war. Fully two-thirds of the piece deals with the romance of the Americas, taking again as one of its main narrative spines the mutiny led by the malcontent Thomas Doughty which was scotched by Drake's expeditious execution of his friend. Unlike a thoroughly plaintive version of this episode produced only ten years before by Alfred Noyes in his huge poem *Drake: An Epic* (1905), Drake suffers no guilt, partly because Doughty

FIG. 24. Sir William Reynolds-Stephens (1862–1943), *A Royal Game* (1906–11). Reynolds-Stephens's straight-backed Elizabeth, affronted by the approach of the Armada, owes something to Stothard's mounted Amazon (Fig. 25), but this grim, pre-First World War depiction of two Great Powers engaged in the Great Game—playing chess with tiny galleons, like Homeric gods contending over the lives of mere mortals—is much less euphoric in tone than Stothard's earlier evocation of the Tilbury rally. The whole composition, in sombre bronze, is tomb-like, as if the effigies of a married couple (which at one time Elizabeth and Philip might have become) have sat up from their unquiet repose in order to continue their bickering forever.

seems to agree it would be only gentlemanly in him to submit to imme-diate execution. On the brink of war, you are for the national enterprise, or against it, there are no half-measures. As this suggests, for the next few years the nagging question of the cost of empire was shelved while the nation dealt with more pressing matters.

After the First World War, the explorers and empire-builders and their Faerie Queene are never again depicted with quite the same sense of conviction in 'high' adult genres. That is not to say, of course, that it wasn't a mainstream fiction by now very deeply entrenched in popular, and especially children's, culture. Still infused with imperial conviction in the 1930s, however, Kitty Barne's charming pageant-play *Adventurers* (1931)—designed to be performed on Empire Day (24 May) by an amateur company of children—illustrates how commonplace certain tropes had become. Written explicitly to inspire within its child-audience 'something of the urge that drove their forebears to this great business of Empire building' so that they can go on to 'the still higher vision, that of the federation of the world', the play opens when three children, dressed for the Empire Day parade in which they are to take part, are lured into a mysterious cave by the 'Urchin', the spirit of imperial adventure.[43] There they are shown a series of visionary episodes conjured up by Hakluyt himself, no fewer than two of which depict Raleigh. The first is a scene in the tradition of Millais, Raleigh as a boy on a Devon beach, badgering an old Spaniard and an old mariner for tales of the New World, and poring over a home-made map; the second shows him in audience with a stingy Queen, whose gold-hunger is contrasted unfavourably with Raleigh's great dreams of Empire and Colonies. The whole concludes with a great procession of historical adventurers, led by Drake and brought up at the rear by a girl in flying-kit as the Urchin yearns onwards towards the future. Nor was Kitty Barne alone in regarding the Elizabethans as appropriate material for the school half-holiday on Empire Day: *The Book of Patriotism for Empire Day* (1919) recommends the earnest reading of sea-dog adventure stories including many of those listed above.

Perhaps it was the very commonplace of this popular fiction, especially as incarnated in the local pageant and amateur play, that brought about its decay—something irresistibly comic, or pathetic, in the too close juxtaposition of heroic Elizabethanism and modern middle-class gentility. In the same year that Kitty Barne produced her *Adventurers*, the great scene of the knighting of Drake was metamorphosed into the centrepiece for a village fete by E. F. Benson's middle-aged mock-Tudor heroine, the chastely inspiriting Queen of Riseholme and cultivator of

'Perdita's Garden', Mrs Emmeline Lucas, or, as she prefers more romantically to be known, Lucia:

The idea of it had been entirely Lucia's . . . She had planned the great scene in it: this was to be Queen Elizabeth's visit to the *Golden Hind*, when, on the completion of Francis Drake's circumnavigation of the world, her Majesty went to dine with him on board his ship at Deptford and knighted him. The *Golden Hind* was to be moored in the pond on the village green. . . . The Queen's procession with trumpeters and men-at-arms and ladies of the Court was planned to start from The Hurst, which was Lucia's house, and make its glittering and melodious way across the green to Deptford to the sound of madrigals and medieval marches. Lucia would impersonate the Queen, Peppino following her as Raleigh, and Georgie would be Francis Drake.[44]

Lucia has certainly internalized the Kingsleyesque notion of the romance of the Elizabethan: 'It's one of the most important moments, this Queen's entry onto the *Golden Hind*. We must make it rich in romance, in majesty, in spaciousness.' Raleigh is in the event written out of the pageant, and the cream of the joke is that, however convincing the awful Lucia is in the star part ('now full of fire, now tender and motherly'), the rough tough Drake is played by the man with whom she will ultimately contract a strictly sexless second marriage, the impossibly camp Georgie, in 'a white satin tunic, with puffed sleeves slashed with crimson, and cloak of rose-coloured silk', not to mention white satin shoes that hurt. On the day, the *Golden Hind* collapses into the village pond.[45]

This threatened emasculation of the Victorian vision is echoed ten years later in Virginia Woolf's last novel, *Between the Acts*, published posthumously in 1941. The novel is structured around the staging of another pageant-play, already by this time a slightly passé genre. Miss La Trobe's attempted sweep through English history from prehistory to the present, however, comes across only as conspicuously fragmented, a scatter of distorted and mutilated clichés. When Elizabeth appears as the presiding genius of her age, the double vision of the local audience produces her as at once grand and absurd, up to the part as patron of tobacco and trade, but a bathetically domesticated end result of Raleigh's adventures:

From behind the bushes issues Queen Elizabeth—Eliza Clark, licensed to sell tobacco. Could she be Mrs Clark of the village shop? She was splendidly made up. Her head, pearl-hung, rose from a vast ruff. Shiny satins draped her. Sixpenny brooches glared down like cats' eyes and tigers' eyes; pearls looked down; her cape was made of cloth of silver—in fact swabs to scour saucepans. She looked the age in person. And when she mounted the soap box in the centre, representing perhaps a rock in the ocean, her size made her appear gigantic.[46]

Domestic, declassée, and dominant, this Elizabeth proceeds to invoke her seamen and adventurers, declaiming

> Mistress of ships and bearded men (she bawled)
> Hawkins, Frobisher, Drake,
> Tumbling their oranges, ingots of silver,
> Cargoes of diamonds, ducats of gold,
> Down on the jetty, there in the west land . . .[47]

The Elizabethan romance becomes in its 1939 setting an act of all-too-consciously willed suspension of disbelief. The text plays out the urgent precariousness in 1939 of 'our island story' and the threatening mismatch between an inherited rhetoric and the actuality—'the ruff had become unpinned and great Eliza had forgotten her lines. But the audience laughed so loud that it did not matter.'[48] Drake and the others—and the genres that typically characterize them—are noticeable by their absence in the play that she then watches, a Beaumont and Fletcheresque confection of lost heirs and lovers, and the most dramatic moment in Woolf's entire novel comes not from Miss la Trobe's play itself but from the ominous passage overhead of an aeroplane. War undoes national heritage whether conceived as epic or as romance, and the effect is melancholic and foreboding in the extreme.

A Protestant Heroine and the Invincible Armada

As well as underpinning the ultimately doomed and recurrently anxious genre of the boys' imperial adventure story, the Victorian reprints of Hakluyt's accounts of the Elizabethan seamen also provided the detailed material for the other major plot in which Drake, Raleigh, and the other seamen starred over the course of the nineteenth and early twentieth centuries, the defeat of the Spanish Armada in 1588. In Victorian and Edwardian culture, the defeat of the Armada came to be seen as the necessary sequel to the New World ventures, as not only the final triumph of the beleagured Protestant nation but as the decisive victory that made possible the rise of a new British empire from the ashes of imperial, Catholic Spain. In these fictions, Elizabeth almost vanishes in all but name, left behind, where the women should be, at home, allowed out on the occasional day-trip to Tilbury.

As we have made plain in Chapter 1, the story of the defeat of the Armada had, since the day that the Queen went to St Paul's Cathedral to give thanks to God for the deliverance of the nation, been an integral part of the mythos of the Queen. The story was, from its inception, broadly a Protestant fiction of justification—divine Providence had intervened to give the English the victory. By the end of the eighteenth century the emphasis had changed slightly: God had intervened not so much on the side of Protestantism, but on the side of a nation's 'Liberty'—an idea that can certainly be traced back as far as James Thomson's poem *Liberty* (1735–6) but which gained the status of cliché rather later. Indeed, God was fast being edged out from the story altogether. In 1798, at the beginning of renewed war with France, Robert Southey, taking his cue from Shakespeare's John of Gaunt, is suggesting an essentially geographical explanation for the Spanish defeat:

> And now the Spaniards see the silvery cliffs,
> Behold the sea-girt land!
>
> O fools! To think that ever foe
> Should triumph o'er that sea girt land!
> O fools! To think that ever Britain's sons
> Should wear the stranger's yoke!
>
> For not in vain hath Nature rear'd
> Around her coast those silvery cliffs;
> For not in vain old Ocean spreads his waves
> To guard his favourite isle![49]

Southey links geography with a suggestion of national destiny. Henry James Pye similarly underlines the uprush of national loyalty that the coming of the Armada supposedly elicited in his wartime *Naucratia; or, Naval Dominion* (1798). By 1805, at the height of the Napoleonic invasion scare, the defeat of the Armada could be again embedded in a story of national solidarity—Robert Anderson's poem 'Britons, United, the World May Defy. Written during a Threatened Invasion' invokes the Armada defeat in its exhortations to the fight, but seems to suggest that the Armada was repulsed by national solidarity: 'Remember proud Spain, and her long-wept Armada, | Then prove to the world, Britons still are the same!'[50] This poem is perfectly glossed by Stothard's 1805 print of Elizabeth at Tilbury, implausibly straight-backed and invincibly armoured, itself a *de facto* propaganda poster to inspire a proper resistance to Napoleon's threatened assault (Fig. 25). Alternatively, a narrative emerged in the time of Nelson which linked national 'liberty' to the powers of the Royal Navy and its captains and commanders: John Thelwall noticeably enthuses over Drake's prowess rather than God's mercy in his panorama of naval victories from Carausius to Trafalgar, *The Trident of Albion: An Epic Effusion; . . . sacred to the Glorious Cause of National Independence* (1805):

> Yet can my Tongue forego thy patriot praise,
> Immortal DRAKE? Can the big heart, that heaves
> With proud impatience, at the galling thought
> Of foreign domination, e'er resign
> The grateful theme?
>
>   Lo! From those cells, abhor'd,
> Where Papal Superstition, midst the groans
> Of tortur'd victims, mutters o'er her spells,
> Blasting the germs of Reason,—issues forth
> The fierce Inquisitor. Him Philip hails,—
> Him and his councils; and, with Bigot Pride,
> Prepares the vast Armada. O'er the Sea
> It spreads—a floating Nation; and foredooms
> The approaching fall of Albion. Racks and Chains
> And ignominious Fetters, ballast deep
> Each threatening bark, scarce buoyant with the threat
> Of meditated Vengeance!

FIG. 25. Thomas Stothard (1755–1834), *Queen Elizabeth at Tilbury* (1805). The Elizabethans, or so this print's emphatically vertical composition seems to suggest, were able to resist the Spanish in 1588 because they were so relentlessly upright. Produced as propaganda during the Napoleonic invasion scares of the early nineteenth century, this image—one of many secularized descendants of Thomas Cecil's *Truth Presents the Queen with a Lance* (Fig. 5)—uses its invulnerably armed Elizabeth to ratify the idea of Britain as an exceptional island kingdom defined in perpetual opposition to the rest of Europe.

> But, behold!—
> Albion, again, the Naval Sceptre shakes,
> And speaks in all his Thunders![51]

The Armada is 'deep-ingulph'd, | In Air exploded, or o'er Ocean strew'd' (32, ll. 126–7) and the victory goes to the weather and to Drake, but not, apparently, to God, despite the poem's stylistic debts to *Paradise Lost*: 'Albion', the nation, takes His place. The notion that the Armada was defeated by national unity reaches its most powerful statement in Thomas Babington Macaulay's poem 'The Armada. July 19th, 1588' written in the year of the Reform Act, and induced perhaps by equal parts of anxiety and euphoria over the future of the nation. Conspicuously and consciously democratic in its semi-ballad mode of rhyming couplets in fourteeners ('Attend, all ye who list to hear our noble England's praise'), this is a fantasy which again links national identity with the land rather than with religion, a virtuoso exercise in romantic topography. The poem does not even tell the whole story of the Armada, but merely strings together evocative British place-names in tracing the chain of beacons lit across the land ('For swift to east, and swift to west, the ghastly war-flame spread'), running from Cornwall up to London, and thence to Wales and the north, rousing fishers, miners, shepherds, rangers, soldiers, squires, and all. With this island mobilized as one, this perennial party-piece implies, the Armada's defeat is inevitable, and need not be described.[52]

The religious revival at mid-century was to transform this largely secularized version of the defeat of the Spanish. In polishing off the harrying of the Armada with God's punishment of Amyas Leigh, Kingsley was neither the first nor the last to reimport God into the narrative. By the 1850s the fiction of national unity and a strong navy had married with the notion of Protestant-favouring divine providence once more. Thomas Hornblower Gill celebrates the harrying of Drake and other 'fearless nurselings of the sea', but then goes on to credit God's organization of the weather. The strained note is most evident in his account of the nation's thanksgiving—'With bowed knees thyself confess | But glorious in the Lord's own glory; | Ring forth with gladsome humbleness | The full divineness of the story!' The moral is drawn at length:

Now Antichrist hath reached his arm in vain
[Truth's] glorious presence from thy soul to tear!
Yes, glow they not with augmented shine,
Those blest leaves of that open Word Divine
So grandly guarded for these eyes of thine!
O rolling ages! ne'er, ne'er forget the grace!
   Still, England, let the peril make
More bright, more blest thy golden while;
   Still sweet let the salvation break
   From thy glad lips, high throned Isle!
Yes, wear this splendour of imperial power,
Gleam glorious in these robes of liberty,
With deeper joy in thy diviner dower,
The Truth that made thee great and kept thee free![53]

Truly execrable as this verse is, it does usefully constellate anti-Catholic hysteria with the notion of a Protestant nation and empire dowered with a 'liberty' underwritten by God. The same religious fervour breathes through the ever-patriotic William Cox Bennett's poem 'The Armada' (c.1868) in *Songs for Sailors* (1872), a collection designed for the consumption of 'our bluejackets': 'Each towering galleon is filled with hate that never tires | To wake the shrieks of tortured saints, to light the martyr's fires.'[54]

This sort of fervour was still available in 1888 when the nation celebrated the tercentenary of the rout of the Spanish. No less a poet than Algernon Swinburne rushed into print with 'The Armada in 1588: 1888', which argues that the Spanish were backing a false, blood-thirsty God:

With God for their comfort only, the God whom they serve; and here
  Their Lord, of his great loving-kindness, may revel and make good cheer;
Though ever his lips wax thirstier with drinking, and hotter the lusts in
             him swell;
For he feels the thirst that consumes him with blood, and his winepress
             fumes with the reek of hell.[55]

The Religious Tract Society published a shilling-book for adults by Crona Temple, *Knighted by the Admiral; or, The Days of the Great Armada* in 1890, half-history, half-novella, which is still interfused with the excitement of the tercentenary celebrations and claims in its peroration that the legacy of the fight off Plymouth Hoe is religious and national freedom:

> Once and for all the bonds that would fain have enthralled men's consciences were shattered and cast to the winds. There are open Bibles in every home—the pure simple English worship of God in every village in the land. It was not only Queen Elizabeth and her people, not only such as Doris Clatworthy and Sir Robert Bulteel that had cause for rejoicing. . . we ourselves, in this free England of ours, have now, at this very day, cause to thank our God for the victory which He helped British hearts and hands to win three hundred years ago.[56]

By the 1880s, however, this sort of rhetoric did not go uncontested by a re-emergent secular ideology of nation. A sonnet, 'The Spanish Armada and the English Catholics' (*c*.1884) written by Aubrey de Vere, Earl of Oxford, a prominent Catholic, claims that national interest comes above religious partisanship:

> A Spanish fleet affront our English shores!
> It must not be; it shall not! Sink or swim
> Our Cause, our lamp of Hope burn bright or dim,
> Long as o'er English cliffs the osprey soars,
> Long as on English coasts the breaker roars,
> No alien flag shall scale our blue sea-rim . . .[57]

What, then, did the events of 1588 say about the nation and its inception? Were they to be understood as a triumph for English Protestantism, or for a state independent of any single church? The argument is epitomized in the story of the Plymouth celebration of the tercentenary. The anniversary was commemorated locally by an exhibition of pictures (by local amateurs as well as London professionals) and relics (including Drake's walking-stick, sword, and astrolabe), an 'official souvenir' which reprinted a selection of poems new and old, a historical lecture, a monument to Drake, a bowls game in honour of Drake's famous sang-froid, and a pageant depicting the English monarchs. There was enough interest in the event for the exhibition to transfer to the foyer of the Theatre Royal, Drury Lane, to accompany a 'great Spectacular Drama' entitled *The Armada*, scripted by Henry Hamilton and Augustus Harris, which culminates in Elizabeth's appearance at St Paul's. The monument itself was organized by a committee headed up by the Catholic Duke of Norfolk, a descendant of Howard of Effingham, the Admiral of the English fleet that sailed against the Spanish. Although Norfolk had been chosen especially to disarm any suggestions that the memorial was anti-Catholic or anti-Spanish, as Leonée Ormond relates,

> The appointment of the Duke of Norfolk may have blunted Catholic anxiety, but it was a red rag to extreme protestant groups. A rival committee was formed to remind the public that the Armada's purpose had been the forcible re-conversion of England to Roman Catholicism.[58]

This rival, Whiggish committee proposed to celebrate the anniversary of 1688 instead, as the real moment when the nation came of age.

The official choice of Norfolk as president of the Plymouth festival suggests that, if politico-religious controversy was by no means dead, it was none the less thought in many quarters that it either was or ought to be moribund. More characteristic of the rhetoric of the time seems to be Emily Henrietta Hickey's rollicking 'A Ballad of the Great Armada' which, despite her own Catholic sympathies, celebrates the victory of Britain's 'sons':

> Full strong in the strength of their life-blood which beat in their every vein,
> They had girt her around with their manhood, and kept her from slavedom and Spain:
> They had fought for their God-given birthright, their country to have and to hold,
> And not for the lust of conquest, and not for the hunger of gold.[59]

This is muscular and manly Christianity in its full flowering. Similarly, Robert Anslow's *The Defeat of the Spanish Armada. A Tercentenary Ballad* (1888), is at pains to stress ecumenical national unity: ''Tis true that in her subjects' love the Virgin Queen stood high, | And Protestant and Papist laid for her some quarrels by.'[60]

The subject elicited a welter of poetry, mostly in the conspicuously manly and democratic ballad form—which had been pioneered as early as the 1790s by W. H. Ireland's 'A Ballad. On the Gallant Defeat of the

Armada', but reached its apogee in Sir Henry Newbolt's famous ballad 'Drake's Drum' (1896): 'Drake he's in his hammock, and a thousand mile awa' | (Capten, art tha sleepin' there below?')', so influential that it haunts the next fifty years of boys' adventure titles before collapsing ingloriously under schoolboy spoof.[61] This profusion of verse was matched by the prominence of the Armada as a subject for painters. In 1864, John Evan Hodgson had painted *Queen Elizabeth at Purfleet. The squadron under Lord Howard is sailing down the Thames to attack the Armada: and she bids God-speed to her sailors.* But the new, apparently evergreen, applicability of the subject in the 1880s and early 1900s is suggested by the career of Seymour Lucas, an Elizabethan genre specialist, who produced no fewer than five treatments over thirty-odd years: *The Armada in Sight. 1588* (1880) (the bowls game), *The Surrender: An Incident of the Spanish Armada* (1889) (Don Pedro de Valdes gives up his sword to Drake), *News of the Spanish Armada* (1893) (Philip Receiving the News in the Escorial), *The Call to Arms, Plymouth Quay* (1894) (inspired by Macaulay's poem), and *The King of Spain's Navy is Abroad* (1912).

As anxieties about German armament grew and war came closer, epic versions of Englishness culminating in the defeat of the Armada became ever more prominent. By 1901 James Rennell Rodd was revising his earlier poem 'The Elizabethans' (1897) which dealt mostly with dreams of empire, and was inspired by Julian Corbett's Drake novel *For God and Gold*, into a whopping epic poem, 'The Story of Sir Francis Drake', which carried the story forward from the knighting of Drake to the Armada and his subsequent death.[62] 1905 saw the serialization of Alfred Noyes's vast epic drama entitled *Drake; An English Epic* in *Blackwood's Magazine*, which, despite its melancholic, meditative tone, culminates in the defeat of the Armada, albeit curiously eviscerated. In 1912 the current big name in pageants, Louis Napoleon Parker, wrote *Drake*, produced by Beerbohm Tree at His Majesty's Theatre (with costumes by our friend the painter Seymour Lucas), revived and indeed published in 1914 just after the outbreak of the First World War. This show culminated in a splendid and aggressively expensive trio of set pieces: the bowls game (essentially a staging of Lucas's painting), the surrender of Don Pedro de ... to Drake (a scene almost entirely composed of naval spectacle rather than dialogue, and which again almost certainly did another of Lucas's paintings as a tableau vivant), and finally, the scene of patriotic fervour and thanksgiving at St Paul's, in which Drake conspicuously threatens to upstage the Queen. The final stage direction offers a perfect anticipation of the sort of effects cherished by cinematic swashbucklers two decades later (and appropriately, this play eventually was filmed as the patriotic *Drake of England*, 1935, Fig. 26):[63]

> At the end of the Psalm the PEOPLE all turn towards the QUEEN and DRAKE with outstretched arms. CRIES: 'God Save the Queen!'—'God Save Drake!'—'God Save England!'—Flags are waved. Roses are tossed on high, trumpets blare, bells clash, and the sun quivers on the QUEEN and DRAKE.[64]

Kipling's poem of 1911, '"Together" (England At War)', which was originally designed as part of a children's history of England, puts the main—democratic—burden of these epics much more tersely:

> This wisdom had Elizabeth and all her subjects too,
> For she was theirs and they were hers, as well the Spaniard knew;
> For when his grim Armada came to conquer the Nation and Throne,
> Why, back to back they met an attack that neither could face alone![65]

Unconsciously comic though this impractical-sounding plan of military defence may seem, Kipling, as usual, is bang on the nail with the national mood.

Like the fiction that cast the Elizabethan seamen as the great empire-builders, the fiction of the great seamen as defenders of the realm and the associated notions of national masculinity finally fizzle out some time in the 1930s, and the best-selling *Fire Over England* (1936) by A. E. W. Mason seems to mark that moment decisively. At first glance, this novel's hero Robin Aubrey belongs to the long line of West Country gentlemen adventurers dazzled, patronized, and sponsored by the Queen: the novel begins as ever with its young protagonist star-struck by Gloriana ('A boy of fourteen years, he was made up of one clear purpose and great dreams, and at the heart of those dreams the great Queen was enshrined').[66] He even meets the Queen when she comes to visit his school (Eton), and we may be inclined to suppose that he will grow up

FIG. 26. A loyal sea-dog receives his reward: Athene Seyler's satin-clad Fairy Queen knighting Matheson Lang's Sir Francis in *Drake of England* (1935), adapted from Louis Napoleon Parker's *Drake: A Pageant Play* (1912). By the time this film appeared, such treatments of the episode had already been superbly burlesqued in E. F. Benson's *Mapp and Lucia* (1931), but the depiction of Drake as patriotic swashbuckler would enjoy a brief revival in the post-war 'New Elizabethan' age, when Irene Worth's Elizabeth knighted Rod Taylor's suitably colonial Drake in *Seven Seas to Calais* (1962), and Terence Morgan's Sir Francis undertook a weekly series of apocryphal missions for Elizabeth in the ATV children's television series *Sir Francis Drake* (1962–3).

into yet another sincere, musclebound warrior in the mould of John Ridd in *Lorna Doone*, destined to fit out ships and harry the Spanish treasure fleets. However, even during this opening set piece of the impressionable and aspiring youth's first encounter with Elizabeth we are already not quite in Kingsley's mode: the book's attitude to open warfare is every bit as ambivalent as the time of its composition—on the eve of the Munich agreement—might suggest. Though as ageless and personally glorious as ever, completely at home with her femininity and completely in control of it, this Elizabeth inhabits a divided country rife with traitors (among them one of Aubrey's schoolmasters): 'Enemies enough she had, even amongst those who most pretended their loyalty.'[67] She is admirable, moreover, not as the personification of a united and unthinkingly valiant sixteenth-century Albion but as a modern before her time, pluralist, peace-loving, and humanitarian. Remarkably, Mason thinks her nation was *less* English than that of the 1930s:

Elizabeth was forty-seven years old in this year of 1581, and though she had lived through perils and anxieties intricate enough to age an archangel, she had retained a superb look of youth and strength. She had run neither to angles nor to fat. She was majestical and homely; a great Prince with her sex at her finger's ends; she was more English than she knew. For she was English of our day— English in her distaste for cruelty, English in her inability to nourish rancour against old enemies, English in her creed that poverty needed more than the empty help of kindly words.[68]

As Robin Aubrey matures, he is less and less fired by his admiration for the Queen and more by a questionable desire for revenge on the Spanish, whom he believes tortured and burnt his father alive in the Inquisition. In the event, surrounded by betrayals and conspiracies, he is obliged to put away all boyish romantic dreams of open chivalric warfare and become a conspirator himself: when he embarks for Spain he is dressed not as a soldier but as an Italian valet, sent by Walsingham to infiltrate Santa Cruz's household and spy out the Armada preparations. He participates in the Armada's defeat not as a sea-dog but as a hitch-hiking saboteur, who joins the fleet in disguise and dives into the sea off Chesil Beach after firing one of the galleons. Thus does he wind up swimming back to his true love, the usual nubile surrogate for Elizabeth, here pointedly called Cynthia. The defeat of the Armada is neither down to divine intervention, the weather, nor national manliness, but is the outcome of an intelligence coup. This novel not only marks the coming of age of a strain of historical spy fiction, it also marks the end of a particular version of the Elizabethan. It is only appropriate that Alexander Korda's film version, made within a year of the book's appearance (with Laurence Olivier and Vivien Leigh as the juvenile leads and Flora Robson as Elizabeth), was not released in the USA until 1941, when it was deliberately used to drum up support for invasion-threatened England's struggle against Nazi Germany. Hitler couldn't be defeated by divine intervention and English valour alone, either.[69]

Perhaps, then, it is no coincidence that it was also in the 1930s and even into the war years that the whole story of Tilbury and the Armada threatened to become entirely absurd, as W. C. Sellar and R. J. Yeatman's treatment of the episode in their spoof schoolboy history *1066 And All That* suggests:

THE GREAT ARMADILLO

The Spaniards complained that Captain F. Drake, the memorable bowlsman, had singed the King of Spain's beard (or Spanish Mane, as it was called) one day when it was in Cadiz Harbour. Drake replied that he was in his hammock at the time and a thousand miles away. The King of Spain, however, insisted that the beard had been spoilt and sent the Great Spanish Armadillo to ravish the shores of England.

The crisis was boldly faced in England, especially by Big Bess herself, who instantly put on an enormous quantity of clothing and rode to and fro on a white horse at Tilbury—a courageous act which was warmly applauded by the English sailors.

In this striking and romantic manner the English were once more victorious.[70]

Both the lingering importance of this fiction and its increasing instability are neatly illustrated in the very successful wartime comic novel by Brahms and Simon, *No Bed for Bacon* (1941), heir to the tradition of Victorian burlesque. Written in London at the height of the Blitz, it is, like *Between the Acts*, a markedly uneasy concoction—a burlesque which still more than half-believes the story it is burlesquing, even as it buries it in a pot-pourri of clichés—potatoes, cloaks, Shakespeare, beds, 'Elizabeth Slept Here', and tobacco.

In many ways, *No Bed for Bacon* represents an uncomfortable collision, brought on by war, between one construction of the Queen inherited from the Victorians—post-menopausal, tyrannical, capriciously spiteful, foul-mouthed, and absurdly vain, ale-drinking, given to public schoolboy practical jokes, and 'haunted by the shadows of her own misdoing'—and her Victorian alter ego, Elizabeth of England, presiding over national security and imperial expansion.[71] Set in 1594, six long years after the defeat of the Armada, with its Essex already prematurely plotting his rebellion, the central episode shows Elizabeth on progress to St Paul's for the annual thanksgiving, surrounded by her court, with her sea-dogs—just as Froude would have wished—closest to her: 'a rigid precedence had somehow got itself observed. Nearest Elizabeth lay her beloved pirates—Drake, Hawkins, Seymour, Frobisher, Howard, and Raleigh, with Burghley and Kit Hatton inserted among them.' They reminisce about the coming of the Armada:

'There, there, my pirate,' she said. 'It was your Armada.'
'Ah,' said Drake wistfully.
'A man was alive then,' said Howard.
'You are right,' said old man Hawkins. 'Those were the days.'
'Those were not the days,' said Elizabeth sharply. . . .'They were the good old days for you, my pirate,' she said. 'But these are the good days for England.'
'Haven't had a fight in years,' said Drake sulking.[72]

This is a curiously melancholic scene to be writing at the height of the Blitz. The defeat of the Armada is attributed to Spanish incompetence, delay, and inexperience, which only just outweighed the unreadiness of the English fleet, thereby narrowly enabled to 'out-sail', 'out-cannon', and 'out-manoeuvre' them.[73] The official description of the war as a 'high epic encounter' 'between freedom and authority', as Elizabeth puts it, muddles her lady-in-waiting Lady Meanwell—it doesn't quite make sense to her. Although the Queen re-recites the Tilbury speech in a moment of excitement, the mood remains uncertain. Burlesque is certainly applied to debunk the baddies: woven in and out of this set piece is a miniaturization of the Blitz itself—the farcical fire-raising activities of the Hitlerian 'Born Leader', treasonously attacking not the nation but the national poet, as he tries to raise a mob to destroy Shakespeare's playhouse. The English mob, however, refuse his leadership, and in the end he burns down the wrong theatre. For the same reason, Essex is equally unsuccessful in rousing treason and trouble. But burlesque equally attacks, like a corrosive acid, those who would normally be the goodies; after all, it is impossible to take the camp Raleigh with his succession of ill-fated cloaks or the acquisitive toady Bacon and his quest for a bed in which 'Elizabeth has slept' in any way seriously.

If *No Bed for Bacon* is strikingly retrospective in its setting, sliding away from the muscular certainties of the early years of the century, three years later Margaret Irwin's important novel *Young Bess* (1944) would construct the Armada as personal destiny, but a rather remote and mildly burdensome one. The novel opens with the twelve-year-old princess on the deck of the *Great Harry* with her father and his last queen: at a moment of crisis, when Henry is about to make irrevocable accusations of religious heresy against the puritanically minded Catherine Parr, Elizabeth screams to create a diversion, and, hard put to it to find an excuse for the scream, invents a sighting of the French fleet. She is saved by a sort of miracle, for the French fleet does indeed appear over the horizon, and lands briefly on the Isle of Wight, before turning tail. Yet they are only the precursor to the real threat, the Armada:

The fortune-tellers were now saying that they had known all along that this was not the invasion England had to fear; her real danger . . . would not come for more than forty years. . . . 'anyway it's naught to me,' [Bess] said, for who cared what would happen more than forty years hence, when she would be an old, old woman, if indeed she could bear to live as long as then?[74]

In the year of D-Day, the Armada is shuffled away as something the reader already knows is won by 'an old, old, woman', in favour of a different story, a fiction of a young England embodied by a young woman. Looking forward now, the unconquered but exhausted nation saw with new hope the young Princess Elizabeth, who would become Elizabeth

II in 1952, bringing in her train the short-lived but entrancing fantasy of New Elizabethanism. It is that fantasy, its effect on the depiction of Elizabeth herself, and its place in the twentieth century's longer line of intimate glimpses of Eliza, which will occupy our next chapter.

6

Elizabeth Modernized

Perhaps it goes almost without saying at this stage that the warrior queen who ambivalently championed Little England against the threat of invasion in *No Bed for Bacon* and *Fire Over England* in 1941 was, as usual, leading a double life. Early twentieth-century culture still needed, apparently, to make up a convincing inner self for the enigmatic woman who embodied such an important part of the national mythos. Official historians' biographies, the most important of which was J. E. Neale's definitive *Queen Elizabeth I* (1934), tended to discard any notion of a sentimental or sexual private self in favour of providing their subject with strictly political motives, or, increasingly, with a simple political ineptitude or indifference circumvented by the tactful and tireless Cecils. But this was more than compensated for in other genres by a spate of experimental biographies, historical novels, opera, and costume drama which produced a new set of private, affective lives for the Queen. If the Victorians burst into the Queen's bedroom and discovered the real Queen by finding her undressed, the nascent twentieth century would force its way still further; prying with equal gusto into her fantasies and her orifices. Yet curiously enough, what these modern investigations reveal is that what exerts real fascination by the end of the century is not the Queen's body, but her extravagant carapace.

What most bothered twentieth-century culture throughout was that old conundrum—Elizabeth's compromised femininity, expressed in her virgin status. If for her own later reign her virginity had encoded a useful exceptionality, for the eighteenth century sentimental sacrifice, and for the Victorians a sort of mean-minded welshing on the sexual contract, for the twentieth century the Queen's virginity connoted not so much celibacy as non-reproductive sexuality. Over the course of sixty years or so two main ways of thinking about that sexuality strive for pre-eminence. On the one hand, it was possible to understand the queen's flirtatious virginity as a form of perversity, a sexuality excessive in self-display which yet never delivered what it seemed to promise. The flauntingly childless Queen might begin to look like a drag queen, embodying an excitingly fraudulent or at any rate fluid sexual ambiguity; this, broadly speaking, is the way that high modernist texts reschedule hostile Victorian portrayals of the Queen, and, accordingly, they tend to pick up the Essex plot once again. On the other hand, more normative versions of the Queen, mandated especially by the accession of the young wife and mother Elizabeth II at mid-century, deal with Elizabeth's unmarried childlessness by asserting that despite her public chastity, necessitated by now incomprehensible and obsolete political imperatives, she had been quiveringly alive with bona-fide reproductive heterosexuality, even if such instincts were usually frustrated, hushed up, or consciously renounced. Hence in the 1940s and 1950s she makes her debut as a thoroughly normal would-be (and on occasion actual) wife and mother, a doubling prefiguration (albeit in more interesting clothes) of Elizabeth II. This, the purview of the woman's novel and the woman's film, was sometimes achieved by picking up the story of the princess's adolescent relations with her uncle Thomas Seymour, or, more often, by elaborating the story of Elizabeth's life-long relationship with the Earl of Leicester, who at mid-century becomes central to popular ideas about Elizabeth for the first time since *Kenilworth*.

These two mutually cancelling versions of Gloriana's private self—one associated with genres predominantly coded masculine, one with women's genres—were entwined together like a double helix throughout the bulk of the century, making up the genetic resources for modernist, post-modernist, and popular versions of Britain's inner self. By the 1970s, however, in the context of feminism, permissiveness, the now widely available Pill, and a steeply rising divorce-rate, the issue of Elizabeth's failure to marry and reproduce all but vanishes. In a cultural environment in which sexuality was now severed from marriage and reproduction, and in which women increasingly were expecting to wield equal power in the public sphere, the Virgin Queen was magically trans-formed into a role model for career women, eventually coming to double the career-politician-cum-dominatrix, Mrs Thatcher, who in the 1980s reunited femininity and the realities of state power. This coincidence opened the way to new satiric portrayals of the Queen as outside the proper reproductive cycle. Finally, the figure of this flirtatious but non-reproductive Queen became peculiarly charged for the 1990s, the decade of spin—all promise and no delivery. At the end of the century we find ourselves looking at a post-modern Elizabeth whose status far out-weighs any real power, an Elizabeth for a culture which has successively come to disbelieve in the power of the established Church, the viability of a dynastic monarchy, the coherence of the island-nation, the nobility of a long-dead imperial project, the necessity of heterosexual reproduc-tion (let alone within the nuclear family), and perhaps even in the power or appropriateness of the cultural transmission of a national heritage.

In what follows, then, we shall be looking firstly at the way in which the Bloomsbury coterie sought to write Elizabeth as a source for a post-Victorian, post-imperial modernity; then at the New Elizabethanism and its aftermath, a period when Elizabeth became a home-subject for women's fiction and a potential role model for modern women as never before; then at the way in which Gloriana was repeatedly invoked in the 1980s both for and against Thatcherism; and, by way of conclusion, we will be taking a look at the ways in which the 1990s invented an Elizabeth for a media-driven age supposedly evacuated of historical signifiers and historical significance alike. Perhaps paradoxically, it was none the less this very climate of *fin-de-siècle* uncertainty which gave rise to one of the most successful of all redeployments of the Virgin Queen, Dame Judi Dench's immortal Oscar-winning eight minutes in John Madden's *Shakespeare in Love*, and it is with that film's elegant condensation of so much of Elizabeth's accumulated mythology that we will draw this account of her multiple afterlives to a close.

Elizabeth in Bloomsbury

> No one has intrigued the modernist more than the 'Virgin Queen.' There are the most contradictory estimates regarding her personality, her character, her womanhood . . . Queen Elizabeth remains a baffling enigma—the Sphinx Feminine of the English race . . . Even the fictionists have never interpreted, by creative insight, the mysterious workings of her soul. None of her biographers has been skilful enough or great enough to unveil the English 'She-Who-Must-Be-Obeyed' . . . our modernists have created by turn the fond Myths of a sexless Queen, an abnormal hermaphrodite, even a male Pope Joan, incapable of real affection, untouched by sex impulse. At one moment she is placed on a pedestal of ice as a frozen statue disdainfully scorning the touch of physical passion, and at another she is represented as craving and striving after the excitement of many lovers in impotent desire.
>
> (Alfred Dodd, 1940)[1]

Like their eighteenth- and nineteenth-century forerunners, early twentieth-century exponents of what is still dimly recognizable as secret history try to pin down Elizabeth's elusive and unsuitable sexuality, at once embarrassingly celibate and greedily flirtatious, 'scorning' and 'craving' simultaneously. The bulk of high modernist texts about Gloriana, whether biographies, novels, or operas, owe their existence to a feeling that the Queen's chastity was odd, if not downright warped, a feeling which would be explored ever more fully as the theories of Freud gained wider acceptance over the course of the century. T. S. Eliot accuses the Queen of sterility by association in *The Waste Land* (1922), invoking her fruitless water-borne flirtation with Leicester as one more of the poem's instances of sexual-dysfunction-on-Thames,[2] but many writers had already gone further. What binds such texts together is a sense of the Queen's sexuality as somehow asymmetrical; her desire is not congruent with her body. At the simplest, this results in the elaboration of the old charges that the Queen was malformed and/or infertile (revived by

Frederick Chamberlin's *The Private Character of Queen Elizabeth* in 1921); in its more fantastical forms, it extends to the claim that she was not female at all. In 1910, for example, Bram Stoker, author of *Dracula*, published what he claimed was a local legend from Bisley in Gloucestershire, where Elizabeth had been kept for a while in infancy when still a disinherited princess. According to the legend, the young Elizabeth had in fact died in an accident just before a visit from her father Henry VIII, and in terror her governess Kat Ashley, at the last minute, dressed a substitute in the princess's clothes—her own seven-year-old son. Luckily the boy was such a naturally gifted female impersonator that the substitution was never detected. All is therefore explained: Elizabeth's persistent refusal of marriage, her supposedly unfeminine intellectual gifts, and her manly defiance of the Spanish Armada. The national heroine was a Renaissance boy-player all along. This take on Elizabeth as what Dodd would call 'a male Pope Joan' became sufficiently mainstream to be taken up (and taken off) in W. C. Sellar and R. J. Yeatman's parodic *1066 And All That* (1930), which begins its section on Elizabeth with the matter-of-fact declaration that 'Although this memorable Queen was a man, she was constantly addressed by her courtiers by various affectionate female nicknames, such as Aurora-borealis, Ruritania, Black Beauty (or Bete Noire) and Brown Bess . . . and was in every respect a good and romantic Queen': in this reading, as we have seen, the English achieved their victory in 1588 because Elizabeth 'put on an enormous quantity of clothing and rode to and fro on a white horse at Tilbury—a courageous act which was warmly applauded by the English sailors.'[3] This passage's ambivalent sense of Elizabeth as an instance of gender transgression—a self-made national art object of magnificent and enabling over-the-topness with a special appeal for sailors, at once potentially ludicrous or pathetic but also 'romantic' and as such definitely positive—informs more highbrow modernist representations of the Queen too, such as Cunliffe Owen's solemn bodice-ripper *The Phoenix and the Dove* (1930). Here, elegantly if implausibly, the Queen turns out to be literally and medically a hermaphrodite, a discovery that drives the appalled Earl of Essex to the last extremity of rebellion, but tamps her as the bisexual Shakespeare's soulmate.[4]

Such literal-mindedness, though, was largely replaced as the century progressed by accounts of Elizabeth which provide her with excitingly modern (for which read also deliciously ambiguous) sexual motivations rather than a new sex. The most influential writing about the inner Elizabeth published between the wars, Lytton Strachey's ground-breaking and controversial 'tragic history', *Elizabeth and Essex* (1928), preferred psychobiography to medical detective work, transmuting the Victorian trope of the Queen undressed into something new:

It was the age of *baroque*; and perhaps it is the incongruity between their struc-ture and their ornament that best accounts for the mystery of the Elizabethans. It is so hard to gauge, from the exuberance of their decoration, the subtle, secret lines of their inner nature. Certainly this was so in one crowning example . . . the supreme phenomenon of Elizabethanism—Elizabeth herself. From her visible aspect to the profundities of her being, every part of her was permeated by the bewildering discordances of the real and the apparent. Under the serried com-plexities of her raiment—the huge hoop, the stiff ruff, the swollen sleeves, the powdered pearls, the spreading, gilded gauzes—the form of the woman van-ished, and men saw instead . . . an image of regality, which yet, by a miracle, was actually alive . . . The great Queen of [posterity's] imagination . . . the lion-hearted heroine . . . no more resembles the Queen of fact than the clothed Elizabeth the naked one . . . Let us draw nearer; we shall do no wrong now to the Majesty, if we look below the robes. (10–11)

Strachey's sense of the Queen is as a sexual body that is concealed by the very dress that claims so excessively and aggressively to display it—the aesthetic of high camp. Conventionally enough, Strachey's peek under Elizabeth's dresses is carried out through yet another intimate retelling of the tale of her revealing involvement with the Earl of Essex.[5] What Strachey sees, however, is not what the Victorians saw, a disgusting and self-deluded old woman at her toilet (the mandatory scene of Essex's incursion into the bedchamber is duly played out, but with a singular lack of gusto), not a body but a private history, a damaged childhood, and a compromised heterosexuality. This manner of psychoanalysing Gloriana, crude and even clichéd as it may seem now, would be enor-mously influential: it animates Hilaire Belloc's *Elizabeth: Creature of Circumstance* in 1942, for example, and it is demonstrably still alive today, standing, for example, behind the surprising claim made by child psychologist Elinor Kapp (reported in *The Times* in 1996) that the mere expression in the eyes of the portrait of Elizabeth as a thirteen year old, now at Windsor Castle, 'reveals a childhood of abuse'.[6]

Strachey goes beyond Victorian and Edwardian portrayals of the Queen as innocent child and devouring old woman by neatly conflating the two. His study reinvents Elizabeth as a post-Freudian textbook hysteric, the guilty sexual obsessions and incapabilities of the old woman traced to childhood and adolescence. *Elizabeth and Essex* diagnoses the Queen as a sufferer from deep-seated trauma over the successive deaths of her mother Anne Boleyn and her subsequent stepmothers, a condition complicated by the indelible neurosis induced by the execution of her uncle and reputed lover, Admiral Thomas Seymour, which renders her hysterically incapable of intercourse. Nevertheless, 'though, at the centre of her being, desire had turned to repulsion, it had not vanished altogether'; on the contrary, her natural amorousness plays itself out in interminable flirtations, ever more voraciously as she grew to old age. Not quite fully heterosexual, as queen she is liable to experience her unconsummated desire for male courtiers as in fact homoerotic, akin to Strachey's own difficult love for Roger Senhouse (amongst others). Here she is, having summoned 'some strong-limbed youth to talk with her in an embrasure', her sexuality cognate not with that of a frustrated Victorian spinster but with that of the male bisexuals she has learned about through studying classical mythology:

Her heart melted with his flatteries, and, as she struck him lightly on the neck with her long fingers, her whole being was suffused with a lasciviousness that could hardly be defined. She was a woman—ah, yes! a fascinating woman!—but then, was she not a virgin, and old? But immediately another flood of feeling swept upwards and engulfed her; she towered; she was something more—she knew it; what was it? Was she a man? She gazed at the little beings around her, and smiled to think that, though she might be their Mistress in one sense, in another it could never be so—that the very reverse might almost be said to be the case. She had read of Hercules and Hylas, and she might have fancied herself, in some half-conscious day-dream, possessed of something of that pagan masculinity. Hylas was a page—he was before her . . . but her reflections were disturbed by a sudden hush. Looking round, she saw that Essex had come in. He went swiftly towards her; and the Queen had forgotten everything, as he knelt at her feet. (28–9)

It was predictable that Strachey's story of deep-seated psychological abnormality should be piggybacked on to the nineteenth century's vision of the sexually indecorous relations between the old Queen and her last favourite. What is new is both the weight Strachey places on the Essex episode and the attitude he adopts towards the earlier views which had condemned it as altogether too unlike the home life of our own dear queen Victoria. To Strachey, it is the Essex imbroglio which makes retrospective sense of Elizabeth's 'mysterious organism', illuminating much of her past career (both public and private) even as it brings that career to a culminating crisis. It is not political expediency but depth psychology which explains Elizabeth's conduct throughout, and Essex's death is dictated by a passion of outraged vanity and a sense of agonized betrayal which stirs up the darkest recesses of her childhood self:

She felt her father's spirit within her; and an extraordinary passion moved the obscure profundities of her being, as she condemned her lover to her mother's death . . . but in a still remoter depth there were still stranger stirrings . . . was this, perhaps, not a repetition but a revenge? . . . Manhood—the fascinating, detestable entity, which had first come upon her concealed in yellow magnificence in her father's lap—manhood was overthrown at last, and in the person of that traitor it should be rooted out. (263–4)

Like the Victorians, Strachey had seen something in the Essex affair that could not be assimilated to the nineteenth century's preferred notions of the manly Elizabethan age: his castrating mother of an Elizabeth is completely at odds with, or in excess of, the needs of the state and the needs of national triumphal history. For Strachey, though, Elizabeth's perverse non-utilitarian individuality, all that had made her a potential object of horror to the nineteenth-century imagination, is something to be celebrated. Along with many of his Bloomsbury colleagues, he elevates a peculiarly indecorous sexuality into the very essence of the Elizabethan, finding in Gloriana's unreproductive self-aestheticizing and sexually ambiguous excess the very spirit of the modern. But if Strachey's view was widely welcomed among the intelligentsia, the Middle England which still loved *Westward Ho!* and Froude was horrified: according to Mrs Wilfrid Ward, writing in 1932, a new society was advertising in the quality newspapers for patriotic members disgusted with 'the manner in which Her Majesty [Elizabeth I] is invariably held up to obloquy and ridicule'.[7]

Strachey's hugely successful evocation of Elizabeth and the Elizabethans as brilliant, vital, urgent, innovative, sexy, bewilderingly contradictory, profoundly dangerous, and perplexingly, alluringly bisexual ('the flaunting man of fashion, whose codpiece proclaimed an astonishing virility, was he not also, with his flowing hair and his jewelled ears, effeminate?', 9) found an echo in an experiment in pseudo-biography published a couple of months earlier by Strachey's friend Virginia Woolf, *Orlando* (1928). In the event Woolf greatly disliked Strachey's portrayal of Elizabeth, perhaps finding it tawdry and salacious (as did many reviewers), or perhaps subscribing—like many other modern women writers, as we will see—to a rather different sense of the Queen as empowering. Her own experimental novel, however, is in some respects very similar to Strachey's—unsurprisingly, since Strachey and Woolf were closely associated and certainly discussed *Elizabeth and Essex* while it was still in draft.[8] Like Strachey, Woolf had a major interest in the Elizabethan as a model for anti-Victorian modernity, a time of vitality, innovation, brilliance, young imagination, vehemence, violence, and amorousness.[9] Like Strachey, too, she had a long-standing investment in Elizabeth, having first written on her in 1909, then again in 1919 and in 1920; just before the publication of *Elizabeth and Essex* she had published an essay on the wax effigy of the Queen in Westminster Abbey.[10] (As we have seen, her last novel *Between the Acts* would also include a glimpse of Eliza.) Woolf's fantastical fiction, a tribute to her then lover Vita Sackville-West, is the mock-biography of a double-sexed protagonist who survives throughout a pageant-like history of Britain from the end of Elizabeth's reign to the 1920s, spontaneously changing sex early in the eighteenth century. It elaborates what Strachey on the whole only implies—the founding place of Elizabethan ambiguous and transgressive sexuality within the modern self and the modern nation.

Orlando opens by establishing the inception of modern national sub-jectivity—personified in Woolf's hero/ine—within the Elizabethan. In a scene which looks like a version of Elizabeth receiving the news of her accession in the park at Hatfield, Orlando is called away from dreaming under a great oak tree and into national history 'somewhere about the year 1588' by the great Queen herself when she comes to visit his father's house.[11] Late and flustered, throwing himself upon his knees, he offers the Queen a bowl of rosewater, and tumbles into a euphoric variant on, and sequel to, the Essex plot. This young cousin of the Queen will be the old Queen's very last favourite, and yet will survive the experience, which will serve merely as the gateway to the rest of his/her history. As such, Orlando stands within a well-established tradition of apocryphal fav-ourites of Elizabeth, who in less intellectual specimens of the contempo-rary historical novel often function as more fortunate doubles for Essex; see, for example, the irrepressible Jack Montagu in Isabel Pateson's *The Fourth Queen* (1926), who gets caught up in the Essex rebellion but is spared on the strength of a posthumously delivered letter from the Earl; Hugh Dorsey, hero of Miriam Michelson's *Petticoat King* (1929); or the Oliver who turns up in C. E. Lawrence's *Gloriana: A Romance of the Later Days of Queen Elizabeth* (1939) as a substitute junior Essex who maintains, unlike the Earl, a proper recognition of Eliza's greatness until the last. Like Strachey's Essex, Orlando is vouchsafed an apprehension of the old body beneath the stiff fabrics, albeit discreetly metonymic:

Such was his shyness that he saw no more of her than her ringed hand in water; but it was enough. It was a memorable hand; a thin hand with long fingers always curling as if round orb or sceptre; a nervous, crabbed, sickly hand; a com-manding hand too; a hand that had only to raise itself for a head to fall; a hand, he guessed, attached to an old body that smelt like a cupboard in which furs are kept in camphor; which body was yet caparisoned in all sorts of brocades and gems; and held itself very upright though perhaps in pain from sciatica; and never flinched though strung together by a thousand fears; and the Queen's eyes were light yellow. (9)

Called to court, given a ring from off the Queen's finger, invested with an office and the Order of the Garter, granted houses and estates, sent on missions and recalled from them, subjected to quasi-maternal suffocating embraces and to 'promises and strange domineering tendernesses' (11), Orlando follows the career of Essex in a more euphoric and casual vein. The final crisis of his relationship with Elizabeth is narrated in an outrageous and brilliant collapsing welter of most of the anecdotes the Victorians had cherished about the old Queen: her vengeful antipathy to the marriage of her favourites and her ladies, her fear of mirrors, her status as an honorary armed warrior, her paranoid fear of assassination, and her perishing of grief over Essex:

One day when the snow was on the ground and the dark panelled rooms were full of shadows and the stags were barking in the Park, she saw in the mirror, which she kept for fear of spies always by her, through the door, which she kept for fear of murderers always open, a boy—could it be Orlando?—kissing a girl— who in the Devil's name was the brazen hussy? Snatching at her golden-hilted sword she struck violently at the mirror. The glass crashed; people came running; she was lifted and set in her chair again; but she was stricken after that and groaned much, as her days wore to an end, of man's treachery. (11–12)

As always in this plot, young love is the real high treason, the successful assassination attempt. Orlando escapes Essex's fate by suffering it only as a reflection; it is in fact the Queen who, breaking Gloriana's glass, dies of the experience, and who is transformed into mere historical residue. Woolf's hero/ine survives to carry the spirit of the Elizabethan into the present—and thus this Elizabeth, unlike Strachey's, is essentially generative rather than destructive. This point is nicely taken up in Sally Potter's 1992 film adaptation, where it is explicitly Elizabeth who confers Orlando's magic agelessness, granting him the house on the condition that he should not decay. ('For you. And for your heirs, Orlando. The house . . . But on one condition. Do not fade. Do not wither. Do not *grow old*.')[12] At the penultimate moment of the novel, when the clock is about to strike for midnight, Thursday, the eleventh of October, Nineteen Hundred and Twenty-Eight, the dead Queen arrives once again at the great house, now visionary, and Orlando welcomes her with the cry, 'Nothing has been changed' (232). Beginning and ending this 'biography' of the nation, Elizabeth and all that she stands for governs past and present—subject, house, nation, empire. *Orlando* brilliantly transposes the Victorian epic of the manly empire into the modernist genre of psychobiography, with all its baggage of decentred sexuality. But, of course, in the years after the First World War, it was wishful thinking to insist that 'Nothing has been changed'. (215)

The New Elizabethans

> England has been happy in her Queens. For which reason we count ourselves fortunate to have a Queen upon the throne once more . . . As we look forward to the years that form the closing half of this Twentieth century, we find ourselves kindling the hope that they will prove to be a new Elizabethan age, renewing the glories of the Tudor Queen.
>
> (Lewis Broad, 1952)[13]

In the years after the Second World War, by contrast, something definitely had changed. The last important statement of Strachey's story of the old Queen and Essex came in the shape of Benjamin Britten's opera *Gloriana* (1953), commissioned to mark the coronation of the young Queen Elizabeth II, and the frosty reception it met on its first night vividly marks a sea change in the dominant representation of Elizabeth I at mid-century. Performed six days after the coronation to an audience which included the new Queen, her husband Prince Philip, diplomats and dignitaries in full court dress, *Gloriana* had been conceived (at least by those who had commissioned it) as a national opera to express the buoyant spirit of the new reign. It must have been expected that it would participate in contemporary efforts to renationalize the Tudor queen as a glorious exemplary forbear of the woman who had also acceded to the crown, to much bright if rather willed hope, at the age of twenty-five. Given Britten's bias towards a homoerotic subtext it was perhaps inevitable, however unwise, that he should take up Lord Harewood's suggestion that the basis of William Plomer's libretto should be Strachey's *Elizabeth and Essex*, just as it was inevitable that Britten's long-time lover Peter Pears should be cast as Essex. The opera's them is the clash between public responsibility and private desires, resolved finally by Elizabeth's vindictive and yet agonized renunciation and execution of Essex. The generic mix of the opera reflects this thematic preoccupation, alternating between public scenes of stirring Elizabethan pageantry and masque, set to pastiched Elizabethan music, and scenes designed to reveal the private life behind the public façade, written in a spare modern style. The love that Elizabeth bears Essex, however, is here reimagined as an impossible romance: it is only possible if the two lovers succeed in privately realizing the official fantasy of Gloriana's eternal perpetually rejuvenating youth. But if Essex as a dreamer can make that willed suspension of disbelief, even, momentarily, when faced with the ghastly and desperately sad figure of mortality in the dressing-room scene, it is not plausible to the Queen herself; as Elizabeth sadly sings, 'the time and the day are past, and the echoes are mute'. The perpetually renewed romance between Gloriana and the young men of England is, post-war, shown to be impossible; in place of a romance with the 'red rose of England', they are confronted with a frightful *memento mori*. Britten's opera was out of date; in portraying a queen of England winning power at such disastrous cost to her lover and herself, he was harking back to post-war exhaustion. The epilogue, Elizabeth's death scene and apotheosis, makes it plain that renouncing even the fiction of passion in favour of history has cost Elizabeth her singing voice and all that it represents, her proper (female and modern) subjectivity. The trappings and conventions of realism—both visual and narrative—vanish, and the Queen begins to utter herself solely in famous prose quotations from the end of her life, interrupting herself only once with one last elegaic and epitaphic phrase that reprises her love duet with Essex which fleetingly imagined a place beyond historical contingency: 'In some unhaunted desert there might he sleep secure.' As she renounces all love other than that of her people, all desire outside history, she turns and sees 'a death-like phantom of herself. It approaches and fades.' It is the ghost of dead romance vanishing before the history book. As a whole, the piece is decidedly melancholy, not to say grotesque, in its unreconciled juxtaposition of the public persona of the Queen with the intermittently foolish, selfish, absurd, vindictive, and appallingly tragic old woman, and in its assessment of the cost of history to the woman, and, by extension, to England.[14]

The first audience of this opera were variously bored, embarrassed, and downright shocked by it. Particular exception was taken to Britten's rendering of the dressing-room scene. In the words of a defender of the piece:

Gloriana was quite long, the evening was warm, the intervals seemed endless, stick-up collars grew limp, and well before the end a restlessness set in. 'Boriana' was on everyone's lips. Most distressing was that in one scene the elderly Queen Elizabeth I removed her wig from her head and was revealed as almost bald: and this was taken, for no good reason at all, as being in bad taste.[15]

Undressing the elderly Queen was now in bad taste. The reason that it was so, however, was as good as it gets, and it was sitting there in the audience. There sat the newly crowned young Queen in the royal box, hung about with all the hopes of a 'new Elizabethan age'. The *London Express*'s coronation souvenir *Coronation Glory: A Pageant of Queens, 1559–1953* (1953) compared her 'golden reign of promise' to the first Elizabeth's 'golden reign of discovery' and went on to affirm that 'womanly, beautiful, gay and richly accomplished, she has brought to a sorely tried world a vision of abundant youth, with its ideals and faith in the future'.[16] It was surely hardly surprising that this audience was restive before an opera which by presenting an aged and weary embodiment of England, fatal to the hopes of her young men, was so evidently at odds with the entire contemporary project of reinventing austere post-war England as sexy, vital, and young. Nor that a piece so evidently sceptical about the happily transparent relation between lovely public pageantry and private body, which the court had been at such pains to hammer home since the day of the new Queen's birth, should be unwelcome. Britten's tactlessness extended even to his construction of Elizabeth as above all English at a time when the reigning monarch was foregrounding her functional political importance as a figurehead for the Commonwealth. Far more in tune with the mood of the times was the take on the wig motif provided by Myrtle Jackson's *The Queen and Tansy Taniard* (1949), the central conceit of which was the rustic Tar

Taniard's gift of her magnificent red hair to make Elizabeth I's new wig, in exchange for which the Queen promotes her marriage, with woman-to-woman advice and a gift of land. If for Britten and his many predecessors the detachability of the Queen's wig meant denuding, demystification, and renunciation, here the wig is magically transformed into a conceit of a nationalized female body sponsoring national domesticity for an Elizabethan ex-land-girl.[17]

In 1936, with the abdication of Edward VIII in favour of his younger brother George VI (and the decision not to alter the Act of Settlement, which some had thought to amend to permit a joint future queenship of both his daughters together), it had become clear that the heir to the throne would be a young woman called Elizabeth. Even before that time, the future Elizabeth II had been publicized as the ideal ordinary extraordinary Baby: when she was only two, Anne Ring's charming and saccharine *The Story of Princess Elizabeth* (1930) burbled that 'she is the World's best known Baby, and what a delightful thought it is that the Baby herself is unconscious of it!'.[18] Strikingly, although Ring opens her little book with a parallel between the little princess and her namesake, this comparison proves to be unfavourable to Gloriana, who turns up here straight out of the pages of Strachey:

Royal Elizabeth, her young limbs hampered by hooped petticoats, her hair pressed close under a tight cap, played at battledore between the yew hedges, or peeped at the reflection of her small determined face in the surface of poor Rosamund's pool.

And the servants watching her were unaware that as long as England lives she will be reverenced, and her glorious reign, set with the jewels of gallant names, will shine for ever as 'the spacious days of great Elizabeth.'

And now this England has in her keeping another precious Princess Elizabeth, whose future holds possibilities as richly romantic as those of the first of her name, but whose bright babyhood is in strange contrast with the warped childhood of the little girl of Woodstock.[19]

Similar anxieties informed *The Princess Elizabeth Gift Book* (c.1935), which carried a portrait of the then nine-year-old princess as a frontispiece to a collection of stories and poems by the famous which included 'A Sixteenth Century Princess Elizabeth at Hatfield, A Poem by Lord David Cecil'. In this poem the 'warped' young Elizabeth Tudor is glimpsed as a ghost:

> Square rings flashed from her narrow hands,
> In stiff brocade she rustled by
> From sharp and waxen countenance
> Her glances darted restlessly.

> She paused, she sighed, she clenched her hands,
> The knuckles through her rings showed white,
> Then turning as in stately dance
> Moved sad and splendid out of sight.[20]

This melancholy anti-Windsor is just one of the princesses in danger that this anthology dreams up, and a very dubious alter ego she makes for a modern princess who was otherwise appearing in company with her sister as an ideally happy child in such pieces as Marion 'Crawfie' Crawford's *The Little Princesses* (1950).

However, at Elizabeth II's accession in 1952, a year after the Festival of Britain, the media managed to invent a 'New Elizabethanism' out of the war's resurgent cultural nationalism, a short-lived euphoria that provided both a welcome escape from the miseries of post-war austerity and a displacement of national anxieties over Britain's future relations with the Empire (the dwindling remains of which had just been renamed the Commonwealth), the Common Market, and the United States. The first stirrings of the trend made their appearance around the young princess around 1948, as we have seen, when the newly-wed princess visited Oxford and attended Neville Coghill's ambitious *Masque of Hope*, which adapts Cranmer's prophecy speech from the end of Shakespeare and Fletcher's *Henry VIII* as a vision of the new Elizabeth's glorious future.[21] As the coronation approached, the term 'New Elizabethans' became a stock-in-trade of contemporary journalists. A classy children's magazine and a rhapsodic survey of British youth both took it as a title, and the *Daily Express* published a cartoon 'Who Will Be THE NEW ELIZABETHANS?' (Fig. 27), quoting a phrase which Woolf's *Orlando* had used to describe the old Elizabethans as they did so:

FIG. 27. 'Who will be THE NEW ELIZABETHANS?' asked the *Daily Express* headline above Michael Cummings's cartoon on 11 February 1952. 'As a stimulant to your understanding of history, the Daily Express recreates an Elizabethan scene—but peopled by the Men of Fame we know today . . . and LEAVING FIVE FACES MISSING.' The copy underneath the image provided further explanation and exhortation, culminating in an unexpected quotation from Virginia Woolf's *Orlando*: WHAT NAMES WOULD YOU ADD TO THOSE WHO INHERIT THE NATION'S HIGH HONOURS? There is an allure about the word Elizabethan which lights up an excitement in the mind of even those who do not usually take an interest in the past. For this reason—to prompt you to seek inspiration from England's Golden Time—the Daily Express presents a tableau which mixes the Sixteenth Century with the Twentieth, presents the People of Fame we know today in the setting of that age of "strength, grace, romance, folly, poetry, youth." Cummings seems to have imagined a rather more intellectual court than Elizabeth II would in the event assemble: among 1952's 'People of Fame' (on either side of the central Sir Winston Churchill, presumably imagined as the modern counterpart to Lord Burghley) are Ralph Vaughan Williams, Benjamin Britten (whose opera *Gloriana*, composed to mark her coronation, the new Queen apparently loathed), T. S. Eliot, Christopher Fry, Graham Sutherland, Alexander Fleming, Frank Whittle, Margot Fonteyn, Henry Moore, Edith Evans, Laurence Olivier, and John Gielgud.

to prompt you to seek inspiration from England's Golden Time—the Daily Express presents a tableau which mixes the Sixteenth Century with the Twentieth, presents the People of Fame we know today in the setting of that age of ... 'strength, grace, romance, folly, poetry, youth'.[22]

To aspire to New Elizabethanism was broadly to hope for a new era of adventure, exploration, and expansion (hence the superb timing of Sir Edmund Hillary and Sherpa Tensing's conquest of Everest, the news breaking on Coronation Day itself, 1953), coupled with brilliant intellectual achievement, and, above all, with modernity nurtured by a long-lasting peace. England would be as it had been under the first Elizabeth, 'tranquil, united, independent and free'.[23] The new Queen, would, like her predecessor, inspire national prosperity as a result of a heady mix of thrifty housewifery and chivalric aspiration. As Richard Dimbleby was to remark: 'There is no doubt that a woman on the throne brings out the innate chivalry in man and fires him with a more adventurous spirit, and to greater achievement.'[24] In time the point was taken even by Richmal Crompton's scapegrace schoolboy, William, who in the story 'William the New Elizabethan' sees the coronation on television and is fired, along with his usual gang, by just such chivalric and adventurous aspirations. However, as elsewhere, it was translating these impulses into the contemporary world that proved tricky, as William's colleague Henry finds:

'Well, you see,' said Henry, trying to elucidate the theme, 'they had a Queen Elizabeth then an' they did things for her in a sort of historical way an' we've got a Queen Elizabeth now so we've got to do things for her in a sort of modern way.'

In the event, their newly inspired longing for Drake-style adventure finds expression only as an attempt to reach new territories by digging, together with a xenophobic campaign of petty theft which serves as a perfect satire on the entire imperial project: 'We'll take treasures off foreigners an' bring 'em back for the Queen.'[25] By 1956, the idea would be even more tarnished, as the sardonic comments of another notable 1950s schoolboy, Molesworth, suggest (in 'How to be a Young Elizabethan'):

No one kno wot to do about anything at the moment so they sa the future is in the hands of YOUTH i.e. some of the weeds you hav just seen. As if they kno what to do about it at their age. All the same we are young elizabethans and it can't be altered—i expect drake felt the same way . . . Fie fie—the grown ups canot kno what a privilege it is to be YOUTH in this splendid age of Queen Bess—when all are brave proud fearless etc and looking with clear eyes at the future . . .[26]

But in the heady atmosphere surrounding the coronation itself, the assimilation of the two Elizabeths seemed an ideal method of restating British identity, rhetorically at the very least. A good deal of real and mock-Tudor started to appear in print, including *The Queen's Garland: Verses Made by her Subjects for Elizabeth I, Queen of England Now Collected in Honour of Her Majesty Queen Elizabeth II* (1953). As this little poem by a Devon amateur published to celebrate the approaching coronation suggests, island culture, merriness, and peace were all delightfully transferable between the two queens:

> Elizabeth of England
> You set our hearts aglow!
> You throw a bridge across the years
> To Drake and Plymouth Hoe.
>
> Elizabeth of England,
> Shall you be any less
> Than she who rings through history
> As 'England's Good Queen Bess?'
>
> .   .   .   .
>
> Elizabeth of England,
> May strife and discord cease,
> God pour on you His blessing
> In a reign of Love and Peace.[27]

Similarly, the many coronation guides and souvenir programmes usually make a little bow to the accounts of Elizabeth I's coronation.[28] While eulogists stuck to the triumphal, imperial Gloriana or Good Queen Bess or even the woman solemnly vowed to her country, all was well; the rot set in, as usual, when the Virgin Queen's private life obtruded.

The young Queen, her dashing seafaring husband, and her growing family epitomized not simply hope for the future but a new, if short-lived, post-war celebration of romantic love, together with a return to homemaking and child-rearing as a noble ideal. The accession of Elizabeth II marked a new and, by and large, very successful era for the monarchy, in which Britain and the Commonwealth were presided over, as in their Victorian heyday, by a wife and mother and her Royal Family. Marion Crawford's best-selling sequels to *The Little Princesses*, *Elizabeth the Queen* (1952), and *Mother and Queen* (1953), set out to describe the young Queen as 'an excellent housewife and mother'—for 'what', the author asks archly, 'can more reveal the woman than—motherhood?'[29] Domestic, romantic, responsible, modern, lovable, informal, according to 'Crawfie', 'in every way Queen Elizabeth's nature proves her to be a Woman of Her Time'.[30] This description, however, suggests a woman less of her time than of the previous century, her monarchy consciously modelled on Victoria's wifely fecundity. Indeed it is a matter of record that Elizabeth II admired Queen Victoria; she was set at an early age to read her great-great-grandmother's journal.[31] How suitable, then, that Richard Dimbleby should appropriate Tennyson's lines to Queen Victoria to conclude his book of the moment, *Elizabeth our Queen*: 'A thousand claims to reverence close | In her as Mother, Wife and Queen' (181).

In this atmosphere, even though a queen seemed at this juncture in history so much more suitable as a figure to embody the nation, the barren virgin Elizabeth I became a positive liability. The new Queen herself did not care for the comparison, remarking in her Christmas broadcast to the Commonwealth for 1953:

Some people have expressed the hope that my reign may mark a new Elizabethan age. Frankly I do not myself feel at all like my great Tudor forbear, who was blessed with neither husband nor children, who ruled as a despot and was never able to leave her native shores.[32]

The aggressively promoted 'normality' of the new Queen, like Victoria's, reinscribed her predecessor once again as thoroughly abnormal; *Country Life's* coronation number, for example, described the new Queen as having been 'uniquely fortunate among English Queens, because of the unremarkable background of her youth, which allowed her to grow up as a normal girl of her time' and continued,

With this serene, clear-eyed young wife and mother one may contrast . . .
Elizabeth I, grown watchful, wary and hard by walking in danger of her life amid
the savage intrigues of Tudor religion and politics . . .[33]

This description of Elizabeth I is recognizably derived from Margaret
Irwin's wartime classic, *Young Bess* (1944), and makes it plain that nine
years later Irwin's frankly sexy, vain, power-hungry, and viciously flippant daughter of a desperately dysfunctional family was in urgent need
of a make-over into something a little more in harmony with the group
portrait of the present Royal Family peacefully drinking tea in the break-
fast room of Buckingham Palace. Indeed, the extent to which the 1950s
needed to normalize the Virgin Queen as romantic heterosexual may
be accurately measured by the difference between Irwin's wartime
best-seller and the film made of it nine years later in 1953, starring Jean
Simmonds as the princess.

Both Irwin's trilogy and Edith Sitwell's best-selling poetic history
Fanfare for Elizabeth (published in extracts in 1945 and in its entirety the
following year) deal with the princess's career from childhood to accession. As this description suggests, one young princess heir apparent
begets another; but the immediate post-war mood is quite different
from that of the coronation. Sitwell and Irwin tell the story of a girl who
survives to become queen only at great personal cost, and with this story
they tell, effectively, the story of a nation which won the war and lost the
world. Both pick up the story of Elizabeth's perilous adolescent tangle
with Admiral Seymour, which in their hands becomes the story of the
nation's coming of age.

Unlike Strachey, the more patriotic and pro-Elizabethan exponents
of historical fiction in the twentieth century had preferred not to dwell
on the Seymour scandal. In 1904, for example, Edward Parry's novel
England's Elizabeth simply skipped the whole episode, affecting to consider it a fabricated slander,[34] and in 1909 Woolf had remarked temper-
ately that the young princess had been ripe for a flirtation, but on the
whole this heavy flirtation between a fourteen year old and a thirty-eight
year old had not been regarded as appropriate. Elswyth Thane's *The
Tudor Wench* (1932) and Amanda Ellis's *Elizabeth the Woman* (1951) both
provided substitute teenage romantic interest, in Thane's words 'dim,

honest dreams of youth', to replace Seymour's dubious sexual entrepreneurship on the one hand and Elizabeth's dangerous experimentation on the other.[35] In these novels, Elizabeth is unconsciously and innocently attracted to page-boys instead: Elswyth Thane produces Fernando—half-Irish, half-Spanish—who is in love with his young mistress, and of whom the ambitious and unscrupulous Seymour is so jealous that he ends up disgracing himself in a sword scuffle with our young gallant; *Elizabeth the Woman* provides the equally novel theory that Elizabeth was not in love with Seymour because she was actually in love with the fifteen-year-old Irish page, Barnaby, her brother's ex-whipping-boy. Both writers insist that the rumours of the princess's attachment to her stepmother's husband had been sponsored by him for his own advantage. Growing up and calf-love replaces sex and scandal and pays dividends of romantic pathos: 'At fourteen, shadowed by vague, impending storms, her sky already overcast by the still dim disasters of her royal future, her early-blooming Tudor passion stirred by the knowing Latin in [Fernando]—Elizabeth was in love.'[36]

By contrast, both Sitwell and Irwin take the Seymour affair seriously for pretty much the first time. Sitwell's remarkably dark portrayal of Elizabeth's childhood builds a picture of the child as both haunted by death and as Death herself: 'from her first cry, Death followed her everywhere.'[37] Fearing the fates of her mother, of Jane Seymour, and of Katherine Howard, the young girl represses her own sexuality, with such success that she survives the Seymour affair by a whisker: 'Looking at her now, sleeping so quietly, you can hear no sound from that peaceful heart, of the drums and tramplings of a hundred conquests—nor could you foretell that terrible end.'[38] The price of national victory will be fearful to the eighteen-month-old baby who is 'doomed to a . . . life of grandeur and loneliness and all-seeing wisdom'.[39] This princess, like her counterpart in Jeanette Dowling's (later Letton's) derivative play *The Young Elizabeth* (1948), takes warning forever from Seymour's fate; Robin Dudley's idllyic courtship of Elizabeth in the Tower, for example, is baffled of its consummation at the very last moment by a vision of her dead first lover the Admiral. Irwin's heroine similarly survives the Seymour affair at the cost of self-repression. 'Young Bess' is a girl in part seduced by Seymour's glamour and his strong attraction towards her as a 'child-woman', in part simply experimenting with the mechanisms of sexual attraction, and in part compromised by the sentimental folly and venal ambition of her governess Kat Ashley and her cofferer Thomas Parry, who do everything they can to further Seymour's interest with her. And Elizabeth experiments on others besides Seymour, too, including the ever-convenient page-boy Barnaby. She manages eventually to transmute the fatal sexiness inherited from her mother into a national sexiness—her twelve-year-old ambition despite her flirtatiousness is to have 'everyone' love her, and to remain untrapped by marriage.[40] But her survival comes at a price; after Seymour's execution, she is shown suffering a nervous breakdown and then taking refuge in her studies to fit herself for the throne, presciently composing poetry that won't appear for another thirty years as she does so:

She worked,—or someone else did, whom she had ceased to recognize as herself.

She saw this other self sit at her books and write, heard it give the right answers, a shadow moved by some strange mechanism, while all the time she stood apart. Very rarely her own self stirred; once it took up her jewelled pen and wrote words that had nothing to do with her lessons:

> I love and yet am forced to seem to hate,
> I seem stark mute, yet inwardly do prate;
> I am, and am not—freeze and yet I burn,
> Since from myself my other self I turn.
>
> .   .   .   .   .   .
>
> My care is like my shadow in the sun—
> Follows me flying—flies when I pursue it;
> Stands and lives by me, does what I have done.
>
> .   .   .   .   .   .
>
> Or let me live with some more sweet content
> Or die and so forget what love e'er meant.

She stared astonished at the lines. Why had she written them?[41]

In Irwin's third novel in the series, *Elizabeth and the Prince of Spain*, Irwin's princess is nearly on the throne, a consummate political survivor of the attentions of Seymour, Courtenay, Philip of Spain, and Robert Dudley. 'Raw, new, showy', Irwin's Elizabeth personifies the England of the post-war years; modern, young, and vulnerable, she survives her own sexuality through courage, wit, and her unfaltering determination to ascend the throne.[42] As Alison Light points out, 'the making of a national identity is implicit in the strengthening of Elizabeth's ego'.[43] From the opening scene of *Young Bess*, which shows the child Elizabeth aboard the royal flagship the *Great Harry* spotting the would-be French invaders, to the finale of *Elizabeth and the Prince of Spain*, which foreshadows the Armada as the realization of Philip's implacable hatred of Elizabeth for her youthful humiliation of his sexual pride, the story describes how a girl and a nation are made fit to repel invasion and to achieve indestructible autonomy.

Yet, come coronation year, for a Britain weary of counting the post-war cost in fictions of repression and renunciation, Irwin's ruthless, damaged heroine had to be remade by Hollywood in the saccharine image of the new Queen. The film of *Young Bess* (1953) is explicitly interested in assimilating its heroine to the new Queen. The opening credits leave little doubt of the identification, producing a big royal coat of arms and a thoroughly modern coronation fanfare. As the news of Mary's death and Elizabeth's accession arrives at Hatfield, Kat Ashley and Parry reminisce and then dissolve into a flashback dramatization of the Seymour episode. Politics are sidelined in favour of love in the minds of both Admiral Seymour (Stewart Granger) and Elizabeth (usefully played by Granger's real-life wife Jean Simmonds): the age gap is discreetly reduced from the scandalous to the merely sexy, and the princess is gratifyingly normal both in her inability to resist the matinée idol and in her explicitly voiced desire to become not an absolute monarch but a sailor's supportive wife. So strong is the film's desire to heterosexualize the future queen that it recklessly provides an apocryphal idyll; dashing naval Seymour escapes prison at the last moment before execution and comes to say goodbye to Elizabeth, a goodbye that ends up in bed, or so the conventional cutting technique suggests. This climax is followed by a flash-forward back to the triumphant but forever lonely Elizabeth being newly acclaimed as queen on a balcony reminiscent of

Buckingham Palace, and the final credits roll anachronistically over a nice close-up of the current crown jewels. Any anxiety the Victorians might have felt about such a wanton queen here magically changes into the assurance that the Queen is truly feminine after all—before suggesting that, having loved, consummated, and lost, she might as well get on with ruling England as a poor second to blissful domesticity with her handsome naval officer, a sentiment of the sort regularly attributed to Elizabeth II.

The new atmosphere of romantic and reproductive domesticity, conceived of as a national duty in the aftermath of war, thus changed the Virgin Queen into a sexual romantic, at once yearning for ordinariness in the shape of husband and children, and remaining a notable, perhaps secretly envied, escapee from family life—the Other Woman. The story of the Tudor queen in the woman's historical novel from the 1950s onwards is a story of the struggle to represent Elizabeth in relation to romantic and reproductive domesticity. In undertaking this feat the genre revives two strategies already familar to us from the eighteenth century: either the Queen proves to have a secret romantic history, or she blocks the secret romances enjoyed on her behalf by proxies. What is new, however, is that such novels almost invariably take as their central action Elizabeth's relations with her long-standing favourite, Robert Dudley, Earl of Leicester, for, although the film of *Young Bess* achieved a striking success in normalizing the Seymour episode, it was much easier to assimilate a post-coronation love affair with Dudley to romantic domesticity, despite the impediments presented by Amy Robsart. Now at mid-century, for the first time, the affair was used centrally to establish the Queen's relation to love, marriage, and procreation, drawing her into a much-elaborated intimacy with her favourite to emphasize her heterosexual 'normality'. Sydney Carroll published the first dramatic treatment of this plot, *The Imperial Votaress*, in 1947—in which Elizabeth and Leicester secretly marry and have a son (who conveniently dies young)—but Carroll had no expectation that it would ever be produced, his anxious preface anticipating vilification for suggesting that the national heroine was anything but a virgin.[44] But attitudes changed:

after the 1950s, it was virginity that was all but a disgrace—better to be carried away with passion than to refuse the invitation.[45]

Kenilworth's sense of Leicester as a political schemer for the political and amorous favour of the Queen generally gives place in the post-war years to an emphasis on young love, the relationship between Elizabeth and Leicester traced to an apocryphal meeting of princess and courtier when both were imprisoned in the Tower during the reign of Mary. Irwin uses their mutual attraction in *Elizabeth, Captive Princess* (1948) and *Elizabeth and the Prince of Spain* (1953) to certify Elizabeth's heterosexuality, bringing them to the brink of bed no fewer than three times while carefully making sure that circumstances intervene to make consummation impossible. Josephine Delves-Broughton's successful *Crown Imperial* (1949, revealingly retitled in its American edition the following year as *The Heart of a Queen*) is one of the first, though by no means the last, to go further; the story of Elizabeth's career is framed in large part by Dudley's endlessly frustrated efforts to 'subdue and possess that wayward but enchanting creature'.[46] What is unprecedented is that he is in part successful—she comes to his bed, disguised as Lettice Essex, she insists that she loves him as much as he could desire, and they increasingly live in a sort of secret domesticity. What she will not yield to is marriage, which would necessitate giving over the throne—and since Delves Broughton's queen is conveniently aware that she is barren, marriage would be dynastically futile as well as politically dangerous. With this brilliant twist, therefore, Elizabeth is both normalized—she surrenders all to Dudley without risking impregnation, she is credited with a passionate and frustrated longing for children—and yet she remains 'virgin', outside or beyond marriage:

('But,' she thought, 'sometimes it's intolerable when Robin and I are together with the boy and I think he might be ours . . . Or remembering the stolen hours in that poor garden of the Tower, and Robin tossing that other child up in play, or when it rode upon his back and he held its little legs with his strong brown hands. I used to comfort myself with fantasies—of a better garden with my own children beside me and my husband . . .')

'Robin,' she said aloud. 'There are two things I have always wanted. The

Crown of England. Yes! Even from childhood. That I have. And I wanted my love to love me, as I, him. To give him a son. To give a son to England. A son who would bridge my two worlds of desire. And that I cannot have! How long will you love me, Rob?'[47]

Despite Leicester's subsequent marriage to Lettice Essex (née Knollys), the Queen remains the most important woman in his life. Their final conversation is just after Tilbury, when to his astonishment she agrees, in a thoroughly womanly fashion, to take off her armour and return to London for her safety:

'It was a relief, Rob, you can't understand. To yield. To your strength.'
He said: 'I think of that night in Windsor when you first came to me with your green cloak around you—'
'I could—and did—give you the woman, but never the crown.'
'It took me long years,' he said with a crooked smile, 'to learn that the crown is virgin.'[48]

Under the kingly armour, she is all wife. She dies remembering the gardens at Hatfield and Robert's kiss, and after her death her successor James finds her most prized possession, Leicester's last letter, annotated in her own hand.

In this novel, Delves-Broughton opportunistically updates a long-standing fiction about Elizabeth—her affection and desire for children, for which, needless to say, there are only the very thinnest shreds of historical evidence. Bids to launder Elizabeth for the consumption of young Victorians had often taken up a story that we have already encountered, that of the five year old who visits the imprisoned princess bringing flowers as a cover for a secret message of some sort: this child even turns up in the frontispiece of Agnes Strickland's *History of England*, and its fictional descendants include John Bennett's *Master Skylark* (1865),[49] little Sunbeam the gaoler's daugher in Beatrice Harraden's *Untold Tales of the Past* (1927), and the captivating Perdita of Rosemary Sutcliff's *The Queen Elizabeth Story* (1950).[50] The logical, or illogical, end point to this line of fictions about an Elizabeth who loves children is provided by a novel itself written by a twelve-year-old child, Alexandra Sheedy's immortal *She Was Nice to Mice: The Other Side of Elizabeth I's Character*

Never Before Revealed by Previous Historians (1975). This vision of an Elizabeth so covertly domestic that she make pets of her palace's rodents ends by making the connection implicitly drawn by Delves-Broughton and Sutcliff. The modern mouse who has been reading the first-person Elizabethan mouse-memoir which makes up the bulk of the book, Esther, moves into Buckingham Palace: '*And then she made a lovely discovery. The queen occupying the Palace was Elizabeth II. How fitting!*'[51] What Delves-Broughton brings to the fore, however, is the first Elizabeth's imputed desire for children of her own, and the question of her fertility and its relation to her virginity, or the lack of it, is central to the many such novels which followed during the 1950s and early 1960s.

Broadly speaking, and ruthlessly glossing over many differences of emphasis, the burden of these many romances is either that she would have if she could have but she couldn't because she might have become pregnant; or, that she did, and that she either didn't have children, or even that she did. So Delves-Broughton's queen is sexually active because she is infertile, but Evelyn Anthony's Elizabeth in *All the Queen's Men* (1960) despite her cautious refusal to go beyond heavy petting, is just as red-blooded—'The danger of pregnancy was too obvious to need stressing. Elizabeth refused to contemplate such a risk, but with Dudley at least she was too honest to pretend that her technical chastity was due to moral scruples. If she could take a lover, she would take him.'[52] The protagonists of novels such as Jeannette and Francis Letton's *The Young Elizabeth* (1954), Jean Plaidy's *Gay Lord Robert* (1955), and the same author's *The Young Elizabeth* (1961) fully inhabit the genre of heterosexual romance in its most Mills and Boon or Harlequin strain, fictions which present Leicester as the stock romance hero—handsome, quick-tempered, masterful, proud, exuberantly virile, an irresistible, dangerous, unscrupulous scoundrel. Elizabeth is, of course, spirited and wilful. The long struggle between them is the very stuff of the bodice-ripper, the Queen generally finding some excuse for eventually submitting in one fashion or another—even if this full submission is only posthumous, as we saw in the instance of a late survival of this strain, Kay's *Legacy* (1985). Nor is this portrayal of Elizabeth and Leicester as the Virgin Queen and the Gipsy simply a case of the bodice-ripper reformatting history in its own image for a niche market: this narrative governed popular history just as surely as it governed historical romance, both upmarket and downmarket. The jacket blurb to the respected Elizabeth Jenkins's *Elizabeth and Leicester: A Biography* (1961) says it all. Puffing the Leicester intrigue as 'one of history's fascinating and enigmatic romances', the blurb continues:

> Leicester's bold masculinity, his savoir vivre, and the self-confidence of a man who is tall, powerful, and active—all fitted him exactly for the post of companion and mentor to the remarkable Elizabeth. . . . A woman of infinite complexity, she savored with equal delight the comfort, security, and admiration Leicester gave her and the excitement sparked by the suspicion that he was a predatory animal who would do anything—even betray her—for the power and prestige he craved.
>
> Against a background of magical brilliancy we see the exquisite red-haired sovereign and her dashing suitor in their moments of gaiety and glory. . . . We also see Leicester's fantastic defiance and Elizabeth's blazing anger clash in spectacular quarrels that invariably subside in loving reconciliations.[53]

Something of the strain that this process of normalizing Elizabeth's sexuality involved during the 1950s, though, is registered in another strategy historical romances developed for dealing with the Queen, in which she appears instead in her familiar post-*Recess* guise as a blocking figure. For some writers it was still altogether more plausible to see Gloriana as a jealous and thwarted home-breaker, precisely the enemy of post-war domestic bliss, bent on destroying other women's familial happiness for reasons more personal than political. Hence, for example, Alice Harwood's novel, *So Merciful a Queen, So Cruel a Woman* (1958), in which Elizabeth is 'a sinister hypocrite, giving rein to love herself but allowing no other woman to love',[54] and a series of depictions of Elizabeth's relations with Lettice Knollys, Leicester's second wife, from *All the Queen's Men* (1960)[55] to Constance Heaven's *The Queen and the Gypsy* (1977). In such romances as these Elizabeth may be construed as so warped by her forced renunciation of her sexuality that she cannot occupy the centre of the narrative, but has to be narrated by an alternative, powerful, spirited, and sexual woman, such as Knollys herself in Victoria Holt's *My Enemy the Queen* (1978).[56]

But in any case by the 1970s things had changed almost out of recognition: for one thing the phrase 'New Elizabethans' had scarcely been heard in years, perhaps not since the suitably youthful Peter Hall had founded the Royal Shakespeare Company in 1960–1 and the Beatles had been dragged into the celebrations of Shakespeare's 400th birthday in 1964 (with Ringo obliged on a TV special to play a cloak-laying Walter Raleigh in a comedy sketch, and the whole Fab 4 obliged to act out 'Pyramus and Thisbe' from *A Midsummer Night's Dream* as another). Whereas for the 1950s Elizabeth by and large desired domesticity, whether she actually achieved it or not, the decade that saw the publication of Shirley Conran's *Superwoman* had rather different feelings about that particular role. In a Britain post-Baby Boom, post-permissiveness, post-Pill, on the eve of the Equal Pay Act and the selection of a woman as leader of the Conservative Party, and headed by a newly menopausal Queen, women's historical fiction begins to suspect that Elizabeth may in fact have had it made, that she had managed to conduct a sex life on her own terms without marriage, domesticity, or children, and that she had managed to have a career and power in the public sphere into the bargain. What Elizabeth now meant to women readers was something other than just failure or success as either lover, wife, or mother. When she had been depicted as a career woman before, her public work had normally been presented as at best a pitiful consolation prize—as in the Hollywood film *The Virgin Queen* (1955), which closes as Bette Davis ruefully gives up her dream of romance and settles, sighing, to a desk laden with official papers. Historical novels of the early 1970s, however, while still interested in Elizabeth's relations with Leicester, change emphasis and scope—they typically cast an eye right across the Queen's reign up to the Armada and Leicester's death, and narrate Elizabeth's life as something not entirely shaped by her relationships to particular potential partners. These 'career' novels include Julia Hamilton's *The Last of the Tudors* (1971) Jaclyn Hope-Simpson's *Elizabeth I* (1971), Helen Thorpe's *Elizabeth, Queen and Woman* (1971), Freda M. Long's *The Queen's Progress* (1971), Maureen Peters's *The Peacock Queen* (1972), and Pamela Bennett's *My Dear Lover England* (1975). The queen tha writers construct begins to look like a woman who has managed t it all'—her political successes as a career superwoman are not founded on a hysterical (or even, latterly, a sadistic) celibacy, but are enabled by the careful and prudent management of her heterosexuality. This account of Elizabeth I could still be made congruent with contemporary accounts of Elizabeth II, however, if Gloriana's refusal of domesticity was represented as a noble renunciation in the national interest: at the time, especially in the wake of an unprecedentedly intimate television documentary about the Royal Family's leisure hours (1969), the present Queen was regularly being depicted as heroically giving up her own domestic privacy. This careful and glamorous tinting of Elizabeth II with duty and romantic renunciation sometimes makes her 1970s biographies sound very much like the more stern and patriotic of con-temporary Elizabeth-and-Leicester novels. Graham and Heather Fisher's *The Crown and the Ring: The Story of the Queen's Years of Marriage and Monarchy* (1971), for example, gives off a concentrated whiff of pre-cisely the emotive high-minded tosh formula shared by the two forms:

As the princess grew from girlhood to womanhood, a young man named Philip and an age-old institution called monarchy were alike to woo her. Time and again highlights of her courtship by Philip were to be matched, and sometimes surpassed, by similar highlights in her apprenticeship to monarchy. . . . The crown and the ring . . . and over the years since the Queen and her husband have had to learn to live with both; to adjust not only to each other as husband and wife but also to a third partner called monarchy. It has perhaps not always been an easy task.[57]

The tension between the period's excited sense of Elizabeth I as inde-pendent, self-willed career woman and its equal desire to assimilate her to the stories about the heroic sacrifices of queenship circulated on behalf of her latter-day namesake is nowhere more apparent than in one of the most successful of all dramatizations of Elizabeth's life, *Elizabeth R* (1971). This important series of television plays—a landmark in the coming of age of colour television and of BBC2, among much else—instantly constituted Glenda Jackson as the canonical face of Elizabeth for the last quarter of the twentieth century (Fig. 16). The series is espe-cially important in the history of representations of Elizabeth because of its quasi-official character as a BBC production (produced at a time when the BBC were responsible for two of only three television channels), and because of its consciously official tone and large scale:[58] it is hard to imagine any television programme now achieving anything like the same level of national attention and national consensus, ambivalent and fractured as the project remains. Made up of six plays by different playwrights, *Elizabeth R* constituted itself as a popular pageant history, running through all the essential famous episodes—Seymour and Bloody Mary; the Leicester courtship; the Alençon suit; the problem of Mary, Queen of Scots; the crisis of 1588; the Essex rebellion and the Queen's subsequent death. Its aim was not to shock by any new insights or angles, but to induce a comfortable national glow, appealing across class and gender—hence, for example, its indulgently post-1940 treatment of Tilbury, in which the Queen's oration, delivered in a rousingly straight history-book manner, is provided with an approving commentary from two red-faced private soldiers in its audience, their vernacular assent to her rhetoric reminiscent of the lines given to NCOs in wartime propaganda films or to Corporal Jones in *Dad's Army*. (Hence, too, the series' very pro-Elizabeth and pre-devolution view of Mary, Queen of Scots, who surprisingly and unconventionally produces the most lacklustre episode of the series.) However, its studio-bound preference for close-ups, and its writers' focus on and disagreements over the one character all its episodes share, make it slightly less bland and univocal than its producers may have intended.

The series' mainstream ambition makes these plays invaluable as a description of which stories were constituting the myth of Elizabeth in 1971. It is noticeable, for example, that the only two completely new apocryphal scenes which *Elizabeth R* adds to the received tradition of historical romance are both designed to reinforce Elizabeth's sexual normality. The second play in the sequence, *The Marriage Game* by Rosemary Anne Sisson, concerns itself with Elizabeth's relationship with Leicester, which finally reaches a crisis in a private scene where he overcomes her fear of marrying and suffering her mother's fate and she agrees to a secret marriage. On time at the rendezvous, he eventually gives her up; she appears later, when he has gone. '*Leicester*: You came but too late. *Elizabeth*: You waited but not long enough.' The failure of their loves is explained as a fortuitous failure to synchronize. The second such episode appears in the third play of the cycle. Julian Mitchell's *Shadow in the Sun* shows the Queen undergoing a full gynaecological examination to demonstrate that she is perfectly capable of bearing Alençon's children should they marry: historically, this indeed happened, but what the documentary record does not reveal is that Elizabeth was induced to take Alençon's courtship seriously by a last-minute desire for children before it is too late: '*Elizabeth*: I want to be young again. . . . And I want not to feel Time like a dead child in my womb.'

The heroine of *Elizabeth R* thus functions within well-defined conventionalities—heterosexual normality, self-control, love of the people, religious tolerance, political moderation. However, there is nothing conventional about the way in which she transcends these six disparate stories: this is an Elizabeth, unlike that of most historical romances or single plays, who cannot be dismissed as having declined into nostalgic self-repetition, or suffered some kind of inner death, once she has inherited the crown, or chosen not to marry Leicester, or given up Alençon, or killed Mary Stuart. What holds this series together is not its sense of public duty but Glenda Jackson, whose Elizabeth survives six different plots and remains in excess of all of them.[59] The effect produced, by sheer accident, is very like the cumulative effect of Elizabeth's disparate real-life portraits—an effect of multiple and contradictory subjectivities rolled up in one enigmatic body which overspills the historical record in all directions. The overall impact of the series, moreover, is much more in favour of a distinctly 1970s view of Elizabeth-as-sexy-career-woman than the scripts alone would suggest. *Elizabeth R* may have made Glenda Jackson look like Elizabeth I for an enormous public (however she may regret the extent to which it has overshadowed her later work in the theatre and on film, her identification with the role has done her subsequent political career no harm at all), but it also made Elizabeth look like Glenda Jackson, a visibly tough-minded, supremely professional performer making a very exciting career for herself, demanding her courtiers' and her nation's attention and loving every minute of it.

Despite Jackson's bravura, however, the official, pageant-procession tone of *Elizabeth R* still marks it out as an establishment piece, its scripts designed to underline the public-spirited personal sacrifices made by all good English monarchs. But within seven years two striking portrayals of the Virgin Queen would actually invoke her as an anti-establishment figure—and, very specifically, as a figure opposed to all that Elizabeth II was by now felt to embody. In 1977, the year of the Silver Jubilee celebrations (which included the nostalgic but unconvincing relighting of the Armada Beacons in homage to the second Elizabeth), the young Queen had become an old Queen, and Britain's power and influence had unarguably declined: as the Sex Pistols memorably pointed out in 'God Save the Queen', best-selling record of Jubilee week, 'there's no future | In England's dreaming'.

Celebrated in a distinctly lukewarm manner, the Silver Jubilee prompted some sad retrospection about 'New Elizabethanism'. This looking back more in sorrow than in anger is at the heart of A. S. Byatt's novel *The Virgin in the Garden* (1978), an essay on the state of England which takes the representation of Elizabeth I as one of its central conceits. The preface is set in 1968, in the National Portrait Gallery at a performance of (an old) Elizabeth I by Flora Robson before an audience that includes such distinguished academic specialists in Tudor iconography as Roy Strong, Frances Yates, Antonia Fraser, and Helen Gardner, to be followed by a dinner-party given by the heroine Frederica for old friends, including the bisexual writer Alexander Wedderburn. Unable to find the Darnley portrait of the younger Queen, he contemplates, by way of definite second best, the Ditchley portrait of the old Queen: 'an alternative Gloriana, raddled, white-leaded, bestriding the counties of England in thunderstorm and sun, painted an inch thick, horse-hair topped and hennaed, heavy with quilted silk, propped and constricted by whalebone.'[60] The gap between the Darnley and the Ditchley defines one of the principal preoccupations of the novel as a whole. Set in the 1950s, 'a kind of no-time, an unreal time', the core narrative describes the rehearsal and performance of a Coghillesque verse drama by Alexander about the teenaged Elizabeth's sex-games with Seymour, to be performed as part of the coronation festivities.[61] Like Irwin, Byatt selects the Seymour affair as her central episode for her exploration of the coming of age of post-war England and the conscientiously willed, visibly doomed Elizabethan nostalgia at its heart. The play occasions plenty of sexual intrigue, experimentation, substitution, and transgression, not least on the part of the teenage Frederica who plays the gauche princess trying out her sexual power for the first time with her uncle Seymour. By and large the novel endorses an undomesticated, sexually liberated princess and her alter ego, the ambiguously double-sexed Alexander, at the expense of the Dimblebyesque romantic domesticities of the era, exemplified by the fate of Frederica's older sister, Stephanie.

Derek Jarman's film *Jubilee*, released in the same year, makes the connection between the new valorization of the anti-domestic Queen and the repudiation of the values expressed by the present monarchy violently clear. Also an essay on the state of the nation, the film opens with a frame-fiction, the Virgin Queen consulting Doctor Dee, who conjures up a dystopian vision of her country's future through the interposition of his Shakespearean familiar, Ariel. What she sees is a dark, desolate, and violent shadow of her own golden age, the Armada beacons transformed within a present-day England into punk pyromania. The actress who plays Elizabeth I in the frame doubles as the punk girl Bod, responsible for beating up the present Queen, complete with handbag, on a deserted wasteground and stealing her crown. The double-casting identifies Gloriana as the sexy, entrepreneurial, violent, and frankly polymorphously perverse polar opposite to the stuffy suburban reproductive respectability embodied by Elizabeth II. For the gay Jarman, what is valuable about the Virgin Queen is precisely that, in terms of the family or dynastic romance, she hadn't in fact founded anything. In this punk anti-masque to the Jubilee celebrations, she can be presented as the still-venerated personification of a mystical, pre-British England—hence her depiction in a garden, and on the clifftops of the south Dorset coast—the willingly perverse incarnation of a homeland fit for homosexuality.[62]

Jarman's pulling apart of correspondences between Elizabeths I and II points to the general collapse, among the intellectual classes at least, of royalism, visibly crisis ridden in 1977. The Virgin Queen is promoted to become sponsor of the uncertain, dangerous future rather than the patron of a complacent and bankrupt past, an unpredictable, raw, self-aggrandizing entrepreneur rather than a cautious and responsible con-server of peace and social stability. It was indeed a prophetic vision. Within a year of *Jubilee*'s release Mrs Thatcher would come to power, a leader who, by virtue of her sex, would inevitably come to embody the British state and so to double the Queen. Thatcher, moreover, stood for much that Elizabeth II did not—meritocracy, overweening ambition, power, commercialism, entrepreneurship, greed, new money, power-dressing, militarism, a sadistic sexiness. A man's woman, with an all-male Cabinet as her court. In its own way, it looked like another new Elizabethan era.

Elizabeth I: The Downing Street Years

In 1979, Margaret Thatcher came to the throne—or rather, was elected to 10 Downing Street, and certainly by the end of her eleven-year reign, Thatcher had come to occupy a position of rival or alternative to the Queen, perhaps in her own mind (as was indicated by her growing habit of using the royal 'we', most famously in her announcement to the press that 'we are a grandmother'), and certainly in the minds of others.[63] At the same time, despite the rather threadbare efforts to promote her as a wife and mother of super-respectability in the mode of the Queen, Thatcher pinched the big role going begging in the national psyche, aggressively personifying the discredited armoured Britannia, and earning herself over the Falklands War of 1982 the soubriquet of the Iron Lady, and a torrent of misogynistic satire directed at her as an ambiguously manly woman.[64] Dominating, aggressive, confrontational, buccaneering, she was 'masculine'; post-menopausal, post-sexual, post-romantic, she called up the figures of the nanny, the matron, and the governess—in Marina Warner's words she 'tapped an enormous source of feminine power; the right of prohibition'.[65]

It was therefore not surprising that a small but significant strand in her mythos also began to assimilate bits and bobs of the story of the origi-nal armoured and sexually ambiguous Queen, the Queen, moreover, who had wielded real power rather than merely an empty handbag. Not only did she update the warrior queen of the Armada into the heroine of the Falklands and the determined Eurosceptic, she also bore comparison with the politic Queen ruling over her Cabinet by a heady mix of untrustworthiness and sexual favouritism (think of Cecil Parkinson and Jeffrey Archer), to such an extent that during the second Thatcher government a copy of J. E. Neale's classic biography circulated surreptitiously among Tory MPs with certain passages felt to be especially applicable to the Leaderine heavily underlined.[66] The perfectly presented public mask, the crafted voice and immaculately fixed hairstyle, the encasing suits, spoke of an attention to self-iconizing PR that the (beleaguered and hostile) academy was starting to attend to in the iconography of the Virgin Queen. In 1988 Thatcher was caricatured as Gloriana in *The Washington Monthly*: apparently internalizing the parallel in 1990, just hours before her fall, she even wore an Elizabethan costume to the Lord Mayor's banquet.[67] The point sank in, as is witnessed by a 1996 poster for Madame Tussaud's waxworks, which recognizes Mrs Thatcher as only the most recent incarnation of Britannia the dominatrix: it shows her flanked by the implicitly prototypical Elizabeth and Victoria, under the slogan 'Baker Street Madam Offers Domination, Correction and Discipline' (Plate 8).

The mingled fascination and hatred that Thatcher undoubtedly generated as she came to embody the nation both at home and abroad surely precipitated the return of the drag and drag-haunted old Elizabeth I of perversity into mainstream culture. In 1979, Constance Pratt's novel *Bess* revived Bram Stoker's substitution story after eighty-odd years, with alterations. This time, the illegitimate infant daughter of Henry VIII and Mary Howard is substituted for Anne Boleyn's daughter, a substitution, since the new infant is a pseudo-hermaphrodite, which in the days before 'surgery and hormonal treatments', not to mention therapy, amply accounts for the Queen's sexual repression. More explicit is one of John Cleese's management-training videos of the time, in which the textbook example of how not to chair a meeting is supplied by a sketch in which Cleese himself plays a distinctly Thatcherian Elizabeth hectoring a restive Privy Council. Dario Fo's Genetesque play *Elizabeth: Almost by Chance a Woman* (first performed in 1984), explicitly satirizing Thatcher and Reagan amongst other targets, supplies the ageing monarch with a grotesque variant on her usual doubles and proxies, Dame Grosslady, played by a male actor. In 1992, Sally Potter's adaptation of Virginia Woolf's *Orlando* compounded its source's interest in the transsexual by punningly casting the late Quentin Crisp as Elizabeth, old queen (and self-proclaimed expert on 'how to become a virgin', the title of his second volume of autobiography) as the old Queen (Plate 10).[68]

While Potter's use of Crisp is very much in keeping with *Orlando*'s Stracheyan origins—and indeed Crisp delivers a suitably tender, dignified, and effective performance without a hint of mockery—most of these evocations of Elizabeth in the 1980s and early 1990s are remarkable for their unprecedented quality of ferocious farce, a quality most powerfully expressed in the BBC2 television series *Blackadder II* (1985). In this travesty of post-war British Elizabethanism, scripted by Ben Elton and Richard Curtis, Miranda Richardson plays a Queen (usually called 'Queenie') who is described by her inseparable companion Nursie, in a succinct burlesque of the Elizabeth-as-manly trope, as 'a boy without a winkle' (Plate 9).[69] In this series Merrie England, the Empire, and the Mystique of the Monarchy are definitively dead, though that doesn't prevent the unpleasant and unscrupulous apocryphal favourite Sir Edmund Blackadder (Rowan Atkinson) being obliged to play out a series of courtly farces in the forever-doomed hope of achieving his yuppie-like ambitions. The series works its way through a variety of familiar motifs and narrative patterns, but one of its most remarkable features is its proliferation of cross-dressing plots: its first episode 'Bells' (a conscious travesty of *As You Like It*) deals with Blackadder's love for his servant 'Bob', a woman in drag, and its last closes with Prince Ludwig, master of disguise, killing Elizabeth's entire court and passing himself off as Queen. Elizabeth herself is split yet again into two bodies, the gross and nannyish Nursie and her own more youthful persona (part Thatcher, part Sarah Ferguson) as infantile flirt-cum-tyrannically whimsical axe-woman ('Sometimes I think about having you executed just to see the expression on your face', she tells Blackadder, and claims that Essex didn't mind having his head cut off because 'he knew it was only little me', 151). Greedy and stingy by turns, both bodies are outside the properly sexual, just like Thatcher's —and Richardson's triumphally iconic Queen, trailing shades of Tilbury and Glenda Jackson, may perform as a sort of stripper for her courtiers at a suitably beery party, but explictly has no private parts they might like to see:

> QUEEN. I may have the body of a weak and feeble woman, but I have the heart and stomach of a concrete elephant. . . . First I'm going to have a little drinkie, and then I'm going to execute the whole bally lot of you. (210)

It is very telling that the alter ego Curtis and Elton provide for this at once inadequately and excessively feminine queen should be in the shape of the gross figure of her wet-nurse. The maternal, super-female body which Elizabeth has renounced, Nursie is abjected by the state but integral to it; she serves both as the indelible trace of Elizabeth's infantilism which founds her virginity, and as a last travestied echo of the real Elizabeth's claim to be 'a nursing mother' to her country.

The edge of excitement and disgust to these travesties derives from the way in which Elizabeth could not only be identified as a precursor of the blessed Margaret, but might still represent a moribund monarchy and a disgraced but imperfectly renounced imperial project. Indeed, in the 1990s there was, briefly, a possible reidentification of the two Elizabeths, grown old, like Britain, in disenchantment and endurance. In 1992, for example, the BBC rescreened *Elizabeth R* towards the end of what Elizabeth II called her 'annus horribilis', apparently in an effort to repair some of the damage caused to the Royal Family's image by a string of divorces by reminding viewers of the monarchy's glamour and its penchant for self-sacrifice. A year later Britten's *Gloriana* was at last belatedly recognized as a masterpiece for our times, in a stunning revival with Josephine Barstow as an at once grotesque, terrifying, and pathetic Queen (Plate 11), and it was accordingly reviewed in *The Times* in terms that irresistibly call up the images both of nanny Thatcher in power and of her vilified and tearful exit from Downing Street:

Gloriana . . . is highly relevant today, of course— . . . She signs her beloved Essex's death-warrant, because she knows she must either administer what we would call the 'smack of firm government', or be toppled herself. Politics has

Elizabeth Modernized

changed very little. But the final sight of Barstow's dying Elizabeth—decrepit, loveless and alone—is surely enough to cure anybody of political ambition.[70]

Elizabeth's Last Stand

The years since this revisited, post-Thatcher end of the Essex affair have brought still further pressures to bear on the national identity which Gloriana once underwrote—the constitutional break-up of Britain, the increasing encroachment of the European Union on domestic policy and America on foreign, the further collapse of Anglican worship, the problematic imperatives of multiculturalism—and with them has come a definite sense of the vanishing of England's Elizabeth into Past Times.[71] Elizabeth, however, seems as gamely willing to dramatize even this troubled state of the national psyche as ever, as three very successful recent reworkings of her figure will show. The dream of identifying a real subjectivity within the icon understood through the tropes of the Queen undressed and unmasked is as strong as ever: as Alison Weir conventionally remarked in 1998, 'Today, . . . with our passion for uncovering the most private secrets of our national figures, we are determined to discover the reality that lay behind Elizabeth's carefully contrived public image.'[72] However, the undressing and re-dressing of Elizabeth, one of the longest serving tropes in the repertoire of her representations, has acquired a new valence over the *fin de siècle*, as is unconsciously demonstrated by the relevant programme in Simon Schama's television series *The History of Britain* (2000). The metaphor that governs his peroration is that with the accession of James, Mary, Queen of Scots and Elizabeth I became the *de facto* lesbian parents of a united Britain. The traditionally upbeat flavour of such a happy moment in 'our island story', however, is (unsurprisingly) absent in an era of devolution; the viewer is uncomfortably conscious of looking at a long, long series of shots of the tomb of Elizabeth. This moribund effect is underscored unintentionally by the disintegration of the very trope used in the eighteenth century to naturalize and locate the vitality of the nation, the undressed body of the Queen. Although the programme begins with a shot of the Queen's underclothes, they are mounted on a headless dummy. This rather unsettling effect is only amplified if you know that these are *not* actually the Queen's underclothes, but a 'body' or bodice purchased after her death to serve as the basis for the funeral effigy carried on top of her coffin. They point not towards the living body, but the uninhabited posthumous icon.

With the idea of a United Kingdom under such emphatic devolutionary question marks, the Elizabeth of the 1990s is visibly post-imperial, her former Arthurian claims to being the once and future queen of a united Britain, and even her claims to a unified inner self, in jeopardy. It is fitting in this respect that three of the decade's most striking chroniclers of a newly evacuated Gloriana are all from former imperial territories, namely the Anglo-Irish Catholic novelist Patricia Finney, the Indian film-maker Shekhar Kapur, and the Australian mime artist Nola Rae.[73] Finney, for instance, takes the same old interest in the 'real' Queen beneath the robes to unprecedented demystifying lengths in her Elizabethan spy fiction *Unicorn's Blood* (1998, the sequel to her earlier *Firedrake's Eye*, 1992) which not only opens with the middle-aged de-wigged unmade-up Queen asleep in bed, but undoes her first into a child (her face is relaxed so that 'the guile and statecraft melt away until it is as if a child peeks from behind a crumpled mask'),[74] and then penetrates into her unconscious through her dream of a unicorn, which will provide one of the central conceits of the fiction. A chapter or so later, we are even treated to the unprecedented spectacle of the Queen on 'the Stool'. What Finney does with this bravura piece of *lèse-majesté*, however, is more unexpected, and very 1990s:

The Queen . . . stood and Parry came immediately to drop the lid and assess the results.
'You may tell them that I am utterly constipated,' the Queen told her tartly.
'Again, your Majesty?' Parry asked, amused.
'Aye, again. Tell them I am stopped up with bile and may well take purge. . . . By God, if they will not heed me, let them fear me.' The Queen's bowels were as healthy as ever, but only she, Parry and the chamberer who did the emptying knew that. Meanwhile Parry would pass the word of an unsuccessful Stool and the councillors would tremble, the Gentlemen of the Privy Chamber walk softly and the cooks in the Privy Kitchen prepare further messes of prunes and

dried rhubarb, which she would send back untouched. It cheered her to think of the ripples of consternation spreading from her humble (though velvet-covered) Stool throughout the Court and thence perhaps even into London.[75]

Although this episode clearly plays on the disjunction between the body natural of the Queen and her incarnation as the state, it insists that the real body is just as contingently political as the state body. The most private function of the Queen turns out to be within the purview of politics and PR, and the Queen is shown in the act of manipulating her own publicity even at this level.

This change of emphasis is entirely characteristic of the 1990s. Although part of the buzz of Finney's fiction derives from excavating the secret Queen from her self-mystifications—her secret is that she is no longer a virgin, having been made pregnant by Seymour and forced to procure an abortion—much of it derives not from the thrill of having made the Queen confess (here, actually in writing) but from the necessity of fabricating a cover-up so that national security is guaranteed. The important thing in this book is not so much that the Queen is not a virgin, but that if she is *known* not to be a virgin her government will fall: 'The Virgin Queen. And if she was no virgin . . . The people of Scotland had risen against their queen and thrown her out when she proved to be ruled by her quim; the same might yet happen to the Queen of England.'[76] As she punningly says to her abortionist—'Give me back my virginity. . . . Sew me up again. The seeming is all that matters.' [77]

This self-propagandizing queen for the decade of spin, less Protestant Blessed Virgin than mere Madonna, appears again in the same year at the climax of Shekhar Kapur's award-winning film *Elizabeth*, which caps its cocktail of inherited commonplaces with a belatedly cogent last ten minutes. The film culminates with a vision of the young and sexually active Elizabeth (Cate Blanchett, Plate 12) turning herself into Elizabeth I as a career decision, alluding to her predecessor in the role, Mr Crisp, as she does so. ("Look", she says to Kat Ashley. "I have become a virgin."")[78] Sexual renunciation is here conceived as women's magazine makeover; and the dressing-room scene is reprised not so much so that we can see the Queen without her clothes on, but so that we can see her put them on. Yet this is none the less a death scene, accompanied by the mournful strains of the requiem mass's 'requiem aeternam', dramatizing the heroine's willed transformation of herself into 'stone', at once a simulacrum of a statue of the Virgin and a prophecy of the marble effigy on her own tomb. Renouncing her unfaithful and treacherous favourite Leicester (with whom she has earlier engaged in as passionate an affair as any 1950s novelist could have devised, unfortunately without checking whether he was already married), she shears her hair and replaces it with a wig, covers her face and hands with white lead in a parody of the ceremony of anointing, and constricts herself within the whalebone of the Ditchley portrait white dress, which here becomes a wedding-dress, signifying that she is, as she says, 'married to England'. With this makeover she ceases to be normal and modern and becomes 'Elizabeth', setting herself up as a citation within the dictionary of visual quotations that make up popular history. The film rewinds feminine subjectivity back into history; as Elizabeth moves from her dressing-table mirror out into the throne-room, she definitively exits from the private. Indeed, the novelization marketed at the time of the film's release, closing with an account of what happens there when she meets Leicester again for the first time, understands this transformation as essentially that of becoming the Madame Tussaud's waxwork of Elizabeth in advance:

Then she stopped beside the man standing apart from the rest of her courtiers. 'Lord Robert.'

Robert had been rigid with shock from the moment Elizabeth had entered the room. Now, obeying the command, implicit in her voice, he bent to kiss her hand. He was shaking all over, but Elizabeth's hand was quite still. And deathly cold.

As was the frozen mask when he steeled himself to look up at her. There was nothing there. And nor was there anything in the hidden depths of Elizabeth's soul. For she had been true to her resolution. She had cut out her heart.[79]

In the film the effect is more ambiguously optimistic, of self-making, even self-citation, but what is striking is the way that the film requires the woman to occupy the historical fantasy body, 'the hyper-sign' (to borrow Barbara Hodgdon's term) that is the Queen by the end of the action.[80] In keeping with this transformation, *Elizabeth* ends with a rolling summary of subsequent history, reminiscent of Britten's Queen vanishing into legend: 'Elizabeth reigned for another forty years . . . | By the time of her death England was the richest and most powerful country in Europe | Her reign has been called the Golden Age | Elizabeth | The Virgin Queen.'

Although Kapur is a good deal more sentimental about the 'sacrifice' of the young woman's sexuality than Finney, neither seems very invested in either heterosexual normalization or in homoerotic perversity, despite bedroom scenes ranging from the torridly heterosexual (Kapur) to the routinely lesbian (Finney). Distinctively, the 1990s Queen is depicted as sensibly non-reproductive and narcissistic by rational choice, and what is typically underscored by the fates of the supporting cast of proxies is the unwisdom of choosing love when you inhabit a sexual and reproductive body—Kapur's lady-in-waiting dies in Leicester's arms through wearing a poisoned dress sent to the Queen so as to satisfy his sexual fantasy, Finney's lady-in-waiting dies of a botched abortion. Hence Elizabeth's counterparts and proxies in Finney's novel—the dwarf Thomasina and the child Pentecost—embody a femininity that is only ambiguously or hypothetically involved in the reproductive cycle. Self-pleasuring, self-narrating, self-iconizing, a one-woman limited liability company, this newly virginized Elizabeth decisively exits the heterosexual romance to become a triumphant icon, and nothing but a triumphant icon.[81]

But triumphant icon of what? An Elizabeth as utterly self-fashioned as this is barely the emblem or trace of a self, never mind a nation, and, as far as Kapur and Finney are concerned, the national and especially imperial history for which Elizabeth once stood appears in any case all but over. The ultimate successes of Elizabeth's realm recorded by *Elizabeth*'s closing titles are in the past tense: Kapur's shorthand for English nationalism is the use of Edward Elgar's 'Nimrod' variation on the soundtrack, music which associates that nationalism with the long-dead Edwardian era of empire. His film thus gives the impression, rather like Shakespeare and Fletcher's *Henry VIII* nearly four centuries earlier, of being nostalgic, if nostalgic it is, not just for Elizabeth but for what at the close of this story was still her country's future, though it is now definitively the past.

The questionable political viability of this makeover of Elizabeth is amplified by perhaps the most haunting and haunted depiction of Elizabeth of its time (though much less widely known than Kapur's globally distributed film or Finney's best-selling novel), Nola Rae's one-woman mime *Elizabeth's Last Stand*, scripted in collaboration with Simon McBurney of the Theatre de Complicité in 1990 and still on the road, playing venues as humble as the tiny Theatre in Chipping Norton, as recently as 2000. In *Elizabeth's Last Stand*, the history of the English golden age is not just a construction but a delusion. As the audience wait for the show to begin, an elderly and eccentric pensioner climbs on to the stage, and after a long and inane pause she starts to beguile the penury and isolation of her life by acting out the standard National Curriculum primary school textbook scenes from Elizabethan history, casting her-self as the Queen. In the dingy privacy of her bedsit, this 'Betty' does what she can to perform her own Cate Blanchett-style makeover into Gloriana: a stiff white apron supplies the silhouette of the Ditchley por-trait, a tea-towel becomes a ruff, and a tea cosy a crown. Thus accoutred, she plays out a series of fantasy scenarios: Raleigh, the cloak, and the potato (persuading in sign-language a willing but comically bewildered member of the audience to play Raleigh—so much for modern man inhabiting Victorian fictions of manliness); the execution of Mary Stuart; and even the defeat of the Armada—represented, in a sort of minimalist rendering of Mr Puff's special effects, by old shoes on a sheet. What this show offers is the spectacle of a ruinous personal iden-tity being romantically shored up out of the recycled rubbish of received history. But this romance is clearly the maundering of a batty and inter-mittently vicious old bag ('Something very strange is happening to Betty', as the publicity hand-out has it. 'Maybe she has been living alone for too long.') Rather than giving life to history by inhabiting and ani-mating it, her body discredits and destroys it altogether. ('She thinks she is being stalked by an imperial ghost! Who does she think she is . . . a queen or something?') Superficially funny as this piece is, and squarely based as it is on Elizabeth's enduring appeal as a fantasy figure for women, it is tragic in structure—originally inspired by Rae's reading of a Delaroche-like account of Elizabeth's end, it ends with Betty's death and ambiguous transfiguration, as a stiff angelic white cardboard simulation of the Ditchley portrait seems to carry her dead body into the dry-ice mists of the beyond. It is impossible not to read it as yet another state-of-England play—and, as its title intimates, perhaps the last possible. According to Rae, post-modern Britain is still in the grip of an increasingly implausible self-consoling fantasy of its own history, its national royal mythos here mercilessly exposed as threadbare, amateurish, solipsistic, teetering on the edge of a ridiculous senility.[82] At the end of the twentieth century, then, Elizabeth was liable to look unconvincing in many of her previous incarnations and roles. She had all but grown out of being absolute monarch, British national heroine, muse, imperial inspiration, eternal feminine; as any of these, she threatened to become downright embarrassing.

And yet, much more than the mere dregs of old emotional investments remained, as suggested by the explosion of interest in Tudor history in general and Elizabeth in particular that characterized the late 1990s (and helped launch one of the more unlikely media stars of our time, Dr David Starkey, to national prominence). For one thing, even if Elizabeth no longer had a British state or British empire to found and patronize, there was still England (and indeed Wales). Here Elizabeth might be celebrated not as the first proto-British monarch but as the last Anglo-Welsh one, the last Queen to have been properly identified, thanks to all those progresses, with the soil of the realm itself, before the throne was taken over by the Scottish Stuarts and thence the German Hanoverians and Saxe-Coburgs. If England was now being obliged to rediscover itself as Little England, then Elizabethan nostalgia might be rewritten as a process of going back to the future, a development adumbrated as early as 1978 by Derek Jarman (who would go on to make *The Last of England*, 1987), when *Jubilee* counterpoised a mystically English Elizabeth I against her latter-day British namesake by counterpoising a ruined and corrupted Buckingham Palace against a Virgin Queen seen on the green sea cliffs of Dorset. Furthermore, even Elizabeth's post-imperial critics haven't exactly given up on the Queen as a centrally important and emotionally engaging player in the public sphere. Both

Kapur and Rae pay tribute, although with clearly differing sentiments, to what is left of Elizabeth four hundred years after her death, and what they have in common is a sense of Elizabeth's power as the power of celebrity to rule by way of collective fantasy. This celebrity is defined in part by the vast jewelled carapace that now, it seems, delineates rather than hides the real Queen; for in these post-modern representations we are perhaps interested less in the Queen herself than in our own desire for her. This is acknowledged by the new prominence in popular culture of her dresses, sometimes occupied by a glassy-eyed expressionless figure (as in the candle-lit tableaux of the Queen that punctuated Starkey's television series), or sometimes empty and free-standing on stage, with the Queen's body ranging uncertainly around them (as in Robert North's 1997 ballet of *Orlando*).[83] Part of our interest is in how any body comes to occupy that locus of popular desire and adoration.

The continuing vitality of Queen Elizabeth I as *the* English celebrity, rivalled as such only by the national poet himself, is of course most sig-nally demonstrated by the famous success of *Shakespeare in Love* (1998), in which our continuing collective desire for the Queen is beautifully foregrounded, aroused, and registered by the script's Mr Puff-like insist-ence on keeping us waiting for her throughout most of the film. If his-tory is only what you can remember, it is still what can be re-enacted as fantasy in front of an audience who have come together in part to iden-tify themselves as its legatees. Judi Dench's commanding eight-minute impersonation of Shakespeare's most judicious critic (Plate 13) has been perhaps the most conspicuously successful of all screen Elizabeths, and it manages to combine and reinflect so many of the possible roles and positions by which the last four centuries of English culture have made meaning for Elizabeth that even the most cursory attention to her part in the film might sum up a good deal of our study.

In *Shakespeare in Love* as elsewhere—as David Scott's 1840 painting of Elizabeth watching *The Merry Wives of Windsor* at the Globe suggests— the Queen is herself a site of the national drama, and she steps dramati-cally forward at the close of the première of *Romeo and Juliet* which es this film's climax to take the stage as the film's dea ex machina. nce more construed, Bernhardt-like, as herself a star theatrical performer (with all the potential for camp, for pathos, and for glory that this implies), with her court and her nation as captivated audience to her celebrity. *Shakespeare in Love* furthermore manages cannily to underline and reuse other earlier understandings of Elizabeth's roles, as multiply gendered personification of state power, and as focus and sponsor of the national culture. At one level Dench's queen is the official enforcer of sexual normality: she is the only character who immediately sees through Shakespeare's impersonation of his beloved Lady Viola's aunt when he accompanies Viola to the palace at Greenwich, for example, and the only spectator to recognize that the role of Juliet is being created not by a boy but by an actress. With the authority of the state, Elizabeth insists at the film's close that Viola must return to her proper role as Lord Wessex's new wife and that Shakespeare should refrain from wearing drag next time he visits her court. But the Queen is also the sponsor of cross-dressing: the play she commissions at the end of the film is for once not *The Merry Wives of Windsor* but *Twelfth Night*, the most sexually ambivalent of all Shakespeare's comedies, and even in the act of recognizing Lady Viola's disguise she ruefully perceives this boy-Juliet as her double and proxy: 'I know something of a woman in a man's profession, yes, by God, I do know about that' (148).[84]

While Dame Judi Dench is only the latest of a long series of major actresses to lend the role of Elizabeth glamour and to borrow more from it, her particular casting, however, brings far more to the role than a mere mutually reinforcing celebrity. As a formidably intelligent actress with a very distinguished career, Dench's presence in the role affirms Elizabeth's continuing identification as a model of female achievement, familiar since contemporaries first praised her as 'learned and wise above her sex': but by allusion to this actress's earlier signature successes *Shakespeare in Love* underscores Elizabeth's multiply gendered state power and national body. For viewers of the film familiar with Dench's career on the stages of London and Stratford, her casting as Lady Viola's severe but ultimately benign honorary parent—Fairy Queen as Fairy Godmother—is redoubled by memories of earlier Dench performances, as Juliet and as Viola, and as a series of legitimately and illegitimately powerful older women: Titania, Volumnia, Cleopatra, and another queen who trespasses upon what is construed as a man's profession, Lady Macbeth. For the wider audience of popular film, though, Dench is more closely associated with two other powerful women. Dench had narrowly missed an Oscar a year earlier for her equally definitive performance in John Madden's previous film *Mrs Brown* (a piece of work which had none the less stamped her as the screen's preferred Victoria for our time), so in Dench's person in *Shakespeare in Love*, the old Elizabeth and the old Victoria are reconciled at last. And then, of course, she had also played that other lady M, 007's superior in Her Majesty's secret service: she made her debut in the role (in *Goldeneye*, 1997) by assuring Bond, with a line that might ideally have rehearsed her for one long-running take on Elizabeth, that she isn't the sort of sentimental feminine type who would vacillate over signing death warrants: 'If you think I don't have the balls to send a man out to die, you're mistaken.' But Dench's M is an enabler as well as a prohibiting governess—she may complain about some of his conduct, but she goes on sending Mr Bond off on his romantic adventures—and so is her Elizabeth, saving the players from the officious Master of the Revels, guaranteeing Shakespeare's subsequent career, and choosing not to betray the soi-disant boy-player 'Thomas Kent''s secret identity as Viola. Despite personifying the nanny state, Dench's Elizabeth hereby manages to be the soul of a Merrie England licensed sexually to thrill, and the Queen's national jollity is affirmed, too, during her first sequence in the film, when she laughs uproariously at Lance the clown in *The Two Gentlemen of Verona* and, more English still, throws a sweet to his dog Crab.

Crucially, though, Dench's Elizabeth exceeds even her own Englishness. Norman and Stoppard's script not only celebrates the London theatre business of the 1590s as a founding instrument of English national self-definition, but depicts it as Hollywood *avant la lettre*, supplementing its *No Bed for Bacon* or *1066 And All That* jokes about English schoolboy history with gags about scriptwriters' analysts and venal backers. Although the film is in its own cheerful way just as post-imperial as are the desolating meditations of Nola Rae—in that the colonial enterprise, exemplified here by Lord Wessex's project for establishing a tobacco plantation in North America, is represented as morally dubious, associated not with gallant sea-dogs but with sordid commerce—*Shakespeare in Love* keeps open the possibility of a transatlantic escape, since this queen's protegée and double Lady Viola will eventually be shipwrecked off America and reborn there, alone, 'a new life beginning on a stranger shore' (154). While Dench's old queen, like the Elizabeth played by Bette Davis in *The Private Lives of Elizabeth and Essex* (1939) and *The Virgin Queen* (1955), might be construed as the repressive Old World incarnate (as we will see in our afterword), she also enjoys in Viola a vicarious rejuvenated rebirth in the New World. In this film Merrie England and Virginia coexist.

As the Public Orator put it in 2000, capping Dench's Oscar with an honorary degree from Oxford, he felt that he was presenting 'two Queens at once. We have seen Dame Judi Dench as Queen Elizabeth and as Queen Victoria, both of whom she portrayed with such skill that we thought we were seeing those monarchs themselves, familiar as they are to us all from our earliest childhood.'[85] We thought we were seeing those monarchs themselves, familiar as they are to us all from our earliest childhood: however knowingly *Shakespeare in Love* sets out to pander to a transatlantic collective fantasy of celebrity, however remote its playful, mass-media version of English history may be from the schoolbook solemnities of Froude and Neale, this, surely, is precisely the praise to which costume drama, historical fiction, and historical biography alike still aspire. Elizabeth is familiar because she was long ago adopted as part of a constitutive myth, and one which is more than ever the founding story of the origin of modern Englishness now that the National Curriculum mandates the study of no history before the Tudors. Yet she is also very strange to us, and so we go on wanting a closer look. Like the audiences for Thomas Heywood's chronicle plays soon after Elizabeth's death, we want another chance to gaze at the royal icon, miraculously restored by drama to the present tense of performance; like the readers of *The Secret History* or *Young Bess*, we want to look into history and find it peopled with recognizable selves acting out the nation as a story. Nations constitute themselves by stories: so long as we can find ourselves in the national past and that past in ourselves, it belongs to us. Hence the woman who embodied the English nation at such a crucial point development—and whose posthumous profile has consequently been under special pressure at moments like the eighteenth century, when that nation was being remade as part of Britain, or the end of the twentieth, when that British identity was being partially unmade once again—has been placed time and time again in works which provide us with imaginary roles in or around her story, vantage points from which to feel and to bear witness. The success with which a line of different genres of imaginative writing has brought the past variously alive through the affective mechanisms of romance—making Elizabeth a princess to be rescued, a lover to be wooed by proxy, a parent to forbid and to authorize—has made those sentiments available in modified forms even outside her own nation, as Dench's pan-global triumph itself demonstrates. But it is within her erstwhile realm that her mythos is most various, most rich, and most needed: as a readership or as an audience, we still identify ourselves around this enigmatic and ever-alluring figure. In Heywood we are bystanders at the opening of the Royal Exchange and fellow soldiers ready to resist the invading Armada; in sentimental fiction, eavesdroppers on the privacy of the real woman partly concealed by her robes or the voyeuristic readers of love-letters and confessions, privy to the heartbreakings that underlie official history; in Victorian and modern biography, we are detectives pursuing the Queen's real motives; in boys' adventure fiction, youth to be inspired to serve the national destiny by our chivalric devotion to her virgin image; in *Shakespeare in Love*, voyeurs of a romance plot and spectators of historical drama alike. From historical icon, Elizabeth is made into narrative in the great age of historical fiction, and in recent film (and mime) she has been returning towards iconic celebrity once more.

The desire to revivify the past that continues to animate the successive representations of Elizabeth is nicely dramatized by our Frontispiece, John Hassall's *The State Entry of Queen Elizabeth into Bristol* (*c.*1910). If charmingly old-fashioned in its collective optimism, this painting none the less exemplifies and explicates an affective investment in the living spectacle of Gloriana that has outlived the many political formations it has underwritten over the last four centuries. Here is the icon in movement, set within a busy, animated street scene: the Virgin Queen is just coming into view. She is in white, the bride of her country: she is flanked by soldiers and preceded by a marshal's drawn and upright sword, a symbol of the state's power. Immediately to our right, two small children are entranced, as we are meant to be, and our excitement is mirrored in the faces in the theatre-like gallery on the far side of the street. We have pressed ourselves into the front rank of the crowd, only just clear of the path of the oncoming soldiers (one is looking sternly at us to check we won't be in the way) and of the smooth-skinned flower-strewing pages. Radiant in the centre of the composition, crowned and gauzily beruffed, the Queen looks like her official portraits—kept a distance from us by her attendants, but not entirely remote, now that she has drawn so close. Except that in one respect she doesn't look like those portraits at all. Her eyes do not look unseeingly straight out at us: they are glancing downwards. The key impression the picture strives to give us is that the icon is inhabited, England's Elizabeth is a living woman yet once more: the pageant of history is alive, this perpetual secret at its centre, and as the procession draws level with us we are part of it. We go on hoping that the Virgin Queen will look up and meet our gaze. We are of her own country, and we adore her by the name of Eliza.

AFTERWORD

Virginia in the New World

'Nostalgia' literally means 'homesickness', and this book about nostalgia for Elizabeth had its beginnings in our own experience of life as expatriates, during a decade spent living and working in the United States. Here we were often surrounded by evidence of familiar-looking claims to Elizabethan cultural roots, and by artefacts suggesting an equally familiar investment in the idea of the Queen herself: maps bearing place-names such as Raleigh and Elizabeth City, North Carolina, not to mention Virginia; the Ditchley portrait, reproduced on the cover of the *Norton Anthology of English Literature, Volume 1* (the preferred pre-packaging of America's English literary heritage that is a set text on most American degree courses in English); a poster using a retouched version of the Darnley portrait as an advertisement for British designer fashion at Neiman Marcus in Beverly Hills; the luxurious premises and impressive sixteenth-century book collection of the Elizabethan Club at Yale; an early likeness of Elizabeth much reproduced on greetings cards, fridge magnets, and other souvenirs at the Folger Shakespeare Library in Washington DC; recordings of Hollywood costume films such as *The Private Lives of Elizabeth and Essex* and *The Virgin Queen* proudly displayed under the heading 'Classics' at video rental outlets right across the country. If at home the sign of Elizabeth seemed to be losing some of its cultural resonance along with that of the monarchy itself, then here was a country which had been managing to retain an interest in Elizabeth for years despite having long ago rid itself of its allegiance to the British crown. Our thinking about what Elizabeth had come to mean (and why) in her own realm thus began from our thinking about what she had come to mean in America—something recognizable but in practice utterly different—and so this afterword about transatlantic views and uses of Gloriana should perhaps really have been a preface. We append it here as a test-case in what Elizabeth I and Elizabethan nostalgia might look like under a republic—albeit one in which a quasi-Victorian version of Protestant commercial imperialism survives far more vigorously than it does in present-day Britain. Our subject here might perhaps be summarized as all that lies between Good Queen Bess and Good Queen Bette Davis.

However 'English' representations of Elizabeth may look in the United States, they are necessarily understood in profoundly un-English ways (as anyone comparing British and American discussions of *Shakespeare in Love* can see), thanks in large part to a completely different history not only of political institutions but of the wider relations between women and the public sphere. Even when her image is disseminated through the same texts, Gloriana means inescapably different things to the subjects of hereditary monarch Queen Elizabeth II and to the fellow citizens of hereditary President George Bush Jr.: in particular, the hostile construction of Elizabeth as one of an unbroken line of female personifications of state authority exemplified by the Madame Tussaud's poster of Elizabeth, Thatcher, and Victoria that we looked at in our last chapter (Plate 8) could not possibly carry the same resonance in the USA. This is not because the misogyny, ageism, and sado-masochism on which this poster plays are confined to the Old World, but because in the homosocial political culture bequeathed by the Founding Fathers, women never have embodied state power. (Miss Liberty and Miss America are all very well, but nobody pays taxes to them, and woe betide the First Lady who actually tries to participate in the executive.) What happened, then, when the royal victrix of Tilbury, life and soul of the state, emigrated to the States? Seventeenth-century nostalgia for that image of an androgynous Elizabeth in armour may have done wonders for Heywood and Dekker in London, but how did it play in the Massachusetts Bay Colony?

From the 1600s onwards, the triumphant Anglican warrior queen of Tilbury has enjoyed only a comparatively low profile on the western side of the Atlantic. This is hardly surprising given the Puritan leanings of the early colonists. In her own lifetime English Puritans had by and large recognized Elizabeth as an obvious enemy (a vainglorious woman who hadn't pressed the Reformation nearly far enough, leaving the English Church hopelessly burdened with bishops and popish rituals, as Milton pointed out). Some later English Puritans, however, did buy into the altogether more favourable view that emerged as her history was retrospectively rewritten, seizing on Elizabethan nostalgia as a convenient stick with which to beat Archbishop Laud and the Stuarts from the 1620s onwards: Cromwell, as we noted in Chapter 1, advanced the restoration of a mythical balance of legislature and executive said to have flourished in her reign as one of the chief objectives of the Great Rebellion. So too did at least some of those Puritans who went into exile in New England, albeit in an altogether less urgently pragmatic register.

The Elizabeth of seventeenth-century nostalgia is visibly an apocalyptic figure, a once and future queen whose 1588 is a type of the last battle between good and evil: and it is this translation of Elizabethan history into the terms of the Book of Revelation with which the early Puritan emigrants to the New World were most comfortable. Although such depictions as Cecil's engraving (Fig. 5) were designed to encourage a certain practical and immediate political course—a return from temporizing Stuart pacificism to the supposedly militant foreign policy of Elizabeth—they could instead be read as deferring their proposed quasi-Elizabethan utopia until the Last Judgement. The ballad elegy quoted in Chapter 1 provides a characteristic example, imagining Elizabeth returning on Doomsday to piss on a hitherto still-undefeated Pope. It is exactly this wistfully apocalyptic view of Elizabeth that the early American colonists shared, despite having substantially given up all hope of reforming the English monarchy of both the present and the foreseeable future. Writing in the Massachusetts of the 1640s, Anne Bradstreet composed her poem 'In Honour of that High and Mighty

Princess Queen ELIZABETH of Most Happy Memory' very much in this vein. Bradstreet celebrates Elizabeth as the perfect English monarch, while conceding that perfect English monarchy is in fact past hoping for until, just maybe, the sounding of the last trumpet.

> But happy *England*, which had such a Queen;
> O happy, happy, had those dayes still been:
> But happinesse lies in a higher sphere,
> Then wonder not, *Eliza* moves not here.
>
> .   .   .   .
>
> No more shall rise or set such glorious Sun
> Until the heavens great revolution:
> If then new things, their old form must retain,
> *Eliza* shall rule Albian once again.[1]

It is only in this qualified form, then, that the 1588 strain of nostalgia for Elizabeth could be entertained in pre-Revolutionary America, and of course even this level of approval for a woman perceived as indivisible from the English crown would become difficult, if not impossible, to sustain after 1776. When Elizabeth is remembered by later American Protestants, it is usually as a fellow victim of persecution, the near-martyred princess of Foxe (for artistic examples, see Chapter 2, above). Hence the aptness of the English children's author Cynthia Harnett's bid to break into the American market, *Stars of Fortune* (1956), in which the prisoner of Woodstock is saved from Queen Mary's ire by the children of Sulgrave Manor, the Washingtons, ancestors of another political outlaw, George.[2]

But if the story of Tilbury camp provides one key element of Elizabeth's posthumous mythology, the one which unites her as Englishwoman and monarch, the seventeenth century also produced its counter-story, the story of Elizabeth and Essex, a narrative which functions above all to split Elizabeth from her power. It is the Victorian treatments of that story that we looked at in Chapter 3 which provide the most important foundations for what would emerge around the turn of the twentieth century as the distinctively transatlantic take on Gloriana.

For many nostalgic English patriots, Elizabeth had herself been the most Elizabethan of the Elizabethans, the guiding spirit and inspiration of her age: dashing off a great speech and winning a great military victory in the same breath at Tilbury, she had been regarded as the colleague as much as the patroness of her great artists and adventurers, not just Shakespeare's patroness but well-nigh his co-writer. In the Victorian era, though, Elizabeth and the greatness of her age were regularly (though not invariably) separated, as we saw in Chapter 4: according to some, the late sixteenth century had been a period of spectacular achievement despite, rather than because of, the woman on the English throne, whose last decisive act, as lamented by the anonymous author of the novel *The Noble Traytour* (1855), had been to behead the most heroic, the most *Elizabethan*, Englishman of his epoch. Significantly, the writer who makes this point most explicitly is an American, John S. Jenkins, in his *Heroines of History* (1851). Jenkins's account of Elizabeth's reign concludes, inevitably, with a retelling of the Essex ring plot, in which Elizabeth features as a quasi-incestuous honorary mother: Essex, we are told, 'was a fiery, generous young man, just of age when Elizabeth [was] . . . nearly sixty. Her regard for [him] appeared to be a mixture of motherly fondness and maidenly romance.' But less interesting than this psychological diagnosis is Jenkins's perspective on an explicitly elderly Elizabeth's relation to her culture as a whole:

She was fortunate in ascending the throne when the invention of Printing, the discovery of America, and the Reformation, had just aroused human intellect to new life, and produced great men in every department of human enterprise. Bacon, Shakspeare, Spenser, Raleigh, Sydney and Drake, and other names of like lustre, made the Elizabethan age glorious, not the selfish woman from whom it borrows its title . . . She was an eagle, as one who most visibly hovered over the sunrise of modern intelligence; but in remorseless spirit, as in lean-necked ugliness, she was a vulture; and in absurd vanity, as in the full-sailed finery of her ludicrous dress, she was a peacock.[3]

Mark Twain's obscene squib, '1601' (written in 1876 and published as a pamphlet in 1880), displaying the sixty-eight-year-old Elizabeth in conversation with her court, is equally ruthless about her personal follies and foul-mouthedness.[4] Twain provides the obverse to a significant number of American epic verse dramas which concentrate on portraying an Elizabethanism from which the personal life of the Queen (in the shape of her ageing body and her consequently indecorous love-life) has been expelled altogether, so as to make it more recognizable and appropriable as the origin of both the manly British Empire and the even more manly United States. Jenkins again neatly articulates this split:

[Elizabeth's] life was a long progress from all that is promising and romantic to all that is pitiful and detestable; and her last years were a notable comment on the emptiness of pomp and power. In her reign, the great stars of literature shone, and England, from a second-rate kingdom, began the splendid career by which, at this hour, she boasts an eighth of the habitable globe, forty colonies, and a seventh of the world's population, or one hundred and eighty million subjects. (322)

Writing fifty years later, Nathaniel S. Shaler, Professor of Geology at Harvard, heals this split between Elizabeth and the Elizabethan nation, but only by effectively remarrying her to an entirely different nation and an entirely different genre in his five-volume set of verse dramas *Elizabeth of England* (5 vols., Boston, 1903), a grandiose extension of his earlier, more tentative effort, *Armada Days* (1898), neither of which have, mercifully, ever been performed. Despite his scientific vocation, Shaler asserts, he is qualified to write pseudo-Shakespearean blank verse because he spent his youth 'among people in Kentucky and Virginia who retain much of the spirit and language of the Tudor period' (p. xii). As this may suggest, *Elizabeth of England* rather belies its title, since Shaler's Elizabeth is devoted less to her present-day subjects than to her vision of a future which scarcely involves England at all. At her coronation she speaks of leading her people to 'our promised land' (i. 156), and at Tilbury she is granted a vision of the future, dominated by 'great empires, where our folk had reared | A life like to our own.' 'Make it the guide of this young nation's life,' she prays, 'As that which Israel led from Egypt forth | To the blest lands beyond their slavery' (iii. 112). This is a Tilbury with as much to do with America's wars against Spain in the nineteenth century as with England's in the sixteenth. By the time the old Elizabeth has finally died—haunted by Essex's ghost, and sighing 'My people, O my people' (v. 137)—and by the time the epilogue to this entire interminable epic has described her as 'mother . . . | Unto a land of men' (v. 143), it is pretty clear which people and which land Shaler has in mind.

America thus claimed to possess the real spiritual heritage of Elizabethan England, and many Americans aspired to possess plenty of the real material heritage too. Within a decade of Shaler's epic verse drama one scion of his university, Harry Elkins Widener, began to make visits to the ancestral country in order to buy up Elizabethan books in bulk and bring them home to Harvard (sadly, he went down with the *Titanic* on his way back from one such journey, and the magnificent temple that now houses his collection and many millions of other books besides, the Widener Library, was built only posthumously). Henry Clay Folger, the President of Standard Oil, was involved even more heavily in this large-scale extraction of English cultural capital, obtaining between 1893 and 1928 a third of all known copies of the Shakespeare first folio and an early seventeenth-century portrait of Elizabeth (among much else), all to be housed in a building in Washington DC, the Folger Shakespeare Library, deliberately sited on the same line that links the Capitol, the Supreme Court, and the Washington Monument.[5] (That's about as close as Folger could get to writing the idea of America's Elizabethan legacy into the Constitution itself.) New Haven, meanwhile, got spectacularly in on the act when a bibliophile alumnus, Alexander Smith Cochran, donated the core of another priceless collection, to be housed in a companionable pro-Tudor mansion of its very own, the Yale Elizabethan Club (founded in 1911).[6] One of many remarkable poems given as addresses at this Club's formal occasions makes Shaler's central point rather more succinctly. Charles Seymour's *An Ode in Commemoration of the Four Hundredth Anniversary of the Birth of Queen Elizabeth*, recited on the eve of Accession Day in 1933, invokes 'The Queen of Fairyland, of spacious days | The shepherdess and potentate' as America's Queen more than England's:

> Virginia's Queen,
> You are the West, and we are yours though skies
> And ages and the ocean intervene.
> Our life is but a legacy of ships
> And planted seed, memorial of thought,
> Adventure's residue, engendered of taut
> Rope, tough plank triumphant over sea.

Drake, Raleigh, Smith were but the hands and lips
Of Empire; what they spoke in deeds they caught
From overtones of a far-thundering polity.
Inspired by you they found before they sought.

. . . .

　　　　　　　　Yet remains the link
Of daring, searching toward the blank unknown,
And even as we speak, all but alone
A true Virginian sails toward the Pole.[7]

With the soul of her age fleeing Westwards, that 'selfish old vulture' Elizabeth might none the less embody both the glamour and the pathos of an *ancien régime*, and appropriately the American actress who impersonated her most influentially was a specialist in both glamour and pathos—Bette Davis. Davis achieved her canonical stature as Hollywood's own Gloriana partly by playing the Queen twice, first in *The Private Lives of Elizabeth and Essex* (1939) and then again in *The Virgin Queen* (1955). She earned her 'authenticity', however, by famously flouting the canons of Hollywood beauty, especially as applied to the heroines of costume drama. This was not achieved by her costumes or gestures—which, as Anne Hollander has pointed out, are in reality heavily influenced by fashionable shapes of the 1930s and 1950s[8]—so much as by her insistence on shaving her forehead to get the high, protruding effect supposedly beloved by the Elizabethans. In the later film, a similar effect of dismaying historical authenticity was achieved partly by her increased age at the time of performance.

The Private Lives of Elizabeth and Essex takes the Essex plot and runs many of the manœuvres that we have seen in its many English variants. As the unconventional relative positioning of the stars Davis and Errol Flynn in a still from the ring-giving scene suggests (Fig. 28), this film regards Elizabeth's reign as a time when a woman was, improperly but excitingly, in a superior position to a man: tellingly, the studio, Warner Brothers, vetoed the use of this shot as a publicity still and instead chose another picture in which the composition is inverted, with Flynn cradling Davis on his manly breast. The problematic relation between public and private, between the historical and the sentimental,

FIG. 28. Bette Davis and Errol Flynn in *The Private Lives of Elizabeth and Essex* (1939). With Flynn's manly, enterprising Essex represented as an independent-minded American before his time, Davis's Elizabeth comes to embody a stiflingly maternal Old World. This shot comes from their most intimate scene, in which Elizabeth gives Essex the ring: as ever her tragedy is precisely that she has been placed above him, just as in the corresponding moment in Henry Jones's *The Earl of Essex* nearly two centuries earlier (Fig. 11).

is encoded in another publicity still, this one disseminated among schools and colleges as part of a whole dossier touting the film's educational value (Fig. 29). This is in fact our first tentative admission into the Queen's presence, and it takes place in her bedchamber rather than her throne room. The composition is quite startlingly akin to that of Wynfield's depiction of the wigless Queen, and Egg's painting of her discovery that she is no longer young, in its interest in an elaborate historical setting for a Queen who is, by implication at least, *en déshabille*. (Note, for example, the recurrent features of the wig and the mirror.) Here, however, the folding screen hides the real woman, for whom a shadow, bedizened with wig, ruff, and farthingale, deputizes. It is this old enigmatic doubling of appearance and reality that the film sets out to unravel, but the answer to the riddle is a new one.

In this version the conflict between modern subjectivity and a historically accurate but essentially improper female power is resolved in an entirely unprecedented and intensely American fashion. Maxwell Anderson's script returns to the ring plot's earliest traces, though this is not to say that his own twist on it is any less unhistorical than the *Secret History*. In this film the tragedy of the story is less that the Queen cannot have her favourite as that he cannot emigrate from her: as our initial glimpse into her dressing-room suggests, she is glamorously but archaically stagey, but he turns out to be altogether sincere, as plain-speaking and unmannered as any cowboy despite his doublet and hose. As such he is far too virile to beg. Flynn's Essex, imprisoned after a rebellion which looks like a premature and abortive War of Independence, refuses to send the ring, it being incompatible with his manly dignity to plead for his life to a female sovereign. Anderson thus has to resort to even more apocryphal means than usual to bring the story to its crisis. Elizabeth sets up a secret meeting in the Tower on the eve of Essex's execution, in which *she* pleads with *him* to plead with her for his life. He refuses, sternly renouncing life rather than masculine honour, and departs for the scaffold profile first, leaving her guilty and blighted for life. Despite the historical Essex's lack of involvement in the colonial enterprise, virtually the last lines the film gives Flynn point towards a visionary future in a New World, where a proper manliness will be

FIG. 29. Our first, mediated glimpse of Bette Davis's Elizabeth, anxiously preparing herself to receive Errol Flynn's Essex, in Michael Curtiz's film *The Private Lives of Elizabeth and Essex* (1939), here reproduced as part of a contemporary publicity hand-out designed to convince American schools and colleges of the film's educational value. Presented, in this distinctively American take on the Essex plot, as the personification of a glamorous but doomed *ancien régime*, Davis's queen has her royal, feminine mystique deconstructed from the first into shadows, cosmetics, mirrors, costumes, and wigs: the kinship between this shot and Victorian paintings of the ageing Elizabeth (such as Figs. 19 and 20) is very striking. Mirrors, as so often in Elizabeth's posthumous career, remain of key importance: in one of the film's central sequences, the Queen, convinced that Essex is being lured away by a pretty young lady-in-waiting, smashes the mirrors in which she has been studying her fading beauty, but still sees herself reflected in the fragments.

rewarded and women will know their place: though the Queen offers him unlimited power as her chief minister and consort, none of the scenarios she offers are sufficient for him. He appears to dream instead of somewhere that might offer them the roles not of Prime Minister and monarch, but of President and First Lady: 'If things had been different—you simply a woman, not a queen, and I a man, with no Crown between us . . .' His democratic sense of free manhood is necessarily at odds with her regime: if he did accept her offer, he says, he would be her death. Instead he chooses to end their interview by embracing a fate that is deliberately cast as a departure, turning his back on Davis's cries of 'Stay!' and setting off for the block, out of history, down a staircase into invisibility. (His attitude seems to be, essentially, that if perpetual subjection even to his beloved is all the Old World can offer, then frankly, your Majesty, he doesn't give a damn.) 'I'm old, I'm old!', cries the Queen, abandoned to obsolescence. 'With you I could have been young again! Take my throne! Take England! It's yours!' But as far as this film is concerned, its new glowing Technicolor tones flaunting its commitment to a Hollywood modernity, he is already in a better place. Warners' 1939 publicity materials somehow construed this ending as Essex's self-sacrifice for the good of England—'And so the story ends! A romance dies that an Empire might live! Another photoplay is born!'—but they were nearer to the mark when they described the film as an account of 'The Queen who could be everything but a woman; the man who could be everything but a King', and further labelled Flynn's Essex a hero 'in whom the dream of empire burned more fiercely than the flame of passion.' Whose empire, though, Britain's or America's? The publicists did what they could to make the film, shot before the outbreak of the Second World War but released after it, appear topical—'The international struggle in which Britain is now engaged was in the making four hundred years ago; a world empire was being born'[9]—but if *The Private Lives of Elizabeth and Essex* does dramatize an international struggle, it is not that between Britain and the Axis powers but that between the motherland and its erstwhile colony. The film's director Michael Curtiz felt obliged to remake this film in a different key the following year producing another Errol Flynn Elizabethan costume drama but on would instead urge America to support the British war effort. In *The Sea Hawk* (1940) Flynn plays another favourite, who again has to rush into Elizabeth's palace in quest of a private interview (just like his Essex on his return from Ireland), but rather than an aspiring would-be presidential Essex he is an apocryphal sea-dog along Charles Kingsley lines, one Geoffrey Thorpe, more interested in wooing the Spanish ambassador's niece than in romancing the Queen. Once he has killed the wicked Lord Wolfingham in a duel (a scapegoated wicked aristocrat-courtier in the pay of globally power-hungry Spain) and has successfully reached Elizabeth to deliver the evidence of Wolfingham's guilt and the impending Spanish invasion, he can be knighted instead of executed in the film's last scene, and he is sent not to the block but against the Armada at the film's close, when Flora Robson's Elizabeth delivers an approximation of the Tilbury speech. It is a piece of rhetoric composed with American sensibilities very much in mind:

But when the ruthless ambition of a man threatens to engulf the world, it becomes the solemn obligation of all free men to affirm that the earth belongs not to one man but to all men, and that freedom is the deed and title to the soil on which we exist.

After the war, with the Old World largely conquered in the name of defending this common English-speaking libertarian heritage, and the British Empire available to the USA at bargain prices, the Elizabeth and Essex story could be retold again, but with a difference. The second of Bette Davis's Elizabethan costume dramas *The Virgin Queen* (1955) took up *The Private Lives*' concluding suggestion of American triumphalism by rewriting the Essex plot around the usefully quasi-American citizen Sir Walter Raleigh. In the later years of the nineteenth century, as we have seen, Raleigh had already built up a distinguished curriculum vitae in Britain as an honorary founder of the Victorian British Empire, a fiction which expanded around the turn of the century into a version of Raleigh as responsible for the inception of the 'virile' English-speaking free world, and which would, later still, precipitate a Raleigh imagined as principal sponsor of the 'special relationship'. Martin Hume's contribution to the 'Builders of a Greater Britain' series, *Sir Walter Ralegh: the*

British Dominion of the West (1897), succinctly wraps up much of this, and effectively previews the rest:

It is fitting that a series relating the lives of those who have reared the stately fabric of our Colonial Empire should begin with the story of the man who laid the foundation stone of it. The prescient genius of Sir Walter Ralegh first conceived the project of a Greater England across the seas, which should welcome the surplus population of the mother country to industry and plenty, and make of England the great mart for the products of its virgin soil. . . . [He was driven by the noble ideal of] the planting in savage lands of English-speaking nations, ruled by English laws, enjoying English liberties, and united by links of kinship, and allegiance to the English crown. To them, more than to any other men, is it due that for all time to come the mightly continent of North America will share with England the cherished traditions and the virile speech of the race to which Ralegh belonged.[10]

The American angle on this was to construct a story by which America, via Raleigh, inherited the Elizabethan adventuring spirit. As Frederick Koch, Professor of Drama at North Carolina put it in the preface to his 'pageant-drama' *Raleigh: The Shepherd of the Ocean* (1920), commissioned and performed to celebrate the tercentenary of Raleigh's execution:

It is in the sense of adventure in modern life, . . . that we find our thought of America today. And the first beginnings of this multifarious life we find in the adventure, the romance, the daring accomplishment, the colour and the youth of Elizabethan England . . . the sources of that which now seems most truly American [are to be found in] Shakespeare's England, and in the England of Drake and Gilbert and Walter Raleigh.[11]

This account of American Elizabethanism conspicuously excludes Elizabeth herself. The enterprise of *The Virgin Queen* is, as it were, to tell the story of how this exclusion happened.

This later film reprises many of the structures and scenes of the earlier screenplay. The love-triangle between Essex, a younger woman, and the Queen is replaced by the triangle of Raleigh (a dashing Richard Todd), his young mistress and later bride Elizabeth Throckmorton (Joan Collins), and the Queen, who thus veers between two of her usual positions, as would-be sentimental heroine and as blocking figure (Fig. 30). Many scenes familiar from the Essex plot are replayed—notably,

FIG. 30. Bette Davis as Elizabeth, with Richard Todd as Raleigh and Joan Collins as Bess Throckmorton, in the film *The Virgin Queen* (1955). Dramatized through the usual triangular plot in which she had been regularly embroiled since the days of *The Secret History*, this Elizabeth is once more jealous of a younger woman who has engrossed her favourite's attention (cf. the Queen's rage at the lovely Lady Rutland in Fig. 11). In this 1950s film, however, unlike the earlier *The Private Lives of Elizabeth and Essex*, not only does the favourite genuinely prefer Elizabeth's rival, but Elizabeth is at last able to renounce her own feelings for him. Raleigh's appropriation as an honorary founder of the USA here guarantees him a Hollywood happy ending: Bette Davis's rueful Queen finally sends Todd and Collins off to people Virginia, while she settles down to being a career-woman as a poor substitute for romantic love.

once again, the bursting-in of the favourite upon the undressed Queen. The crucial invented conversation in the Tower between the betrayed Queen and the sexy adventurer imprisoned for capital treason is also reprised. But since this time the central figure is Raleigh, the resolution is different. Gloriana this time succeeds in pardoning her favourite, heroically renouncing love to become more truly the servant of historical progress: and in the last shot of the film Raleigh (and his pregnant wife) sail for the Brave New World, their ship watched by a wistful Queen from her council chamber window. (Perhaps it is worth pointing out here that Raleigh, let alone his wife, never set foot in Roanoke, the colony which he supported and which disappeared without trace.)

Elizabeth's ageing body thus becomes at once the source and the residue of the founding of America; struggling for funding with the Queen, Raleigh can represent the acceptable American face of Elizabeth, that which supersedes the obsolete Old World and exports all that is most important, enduring, and potent of Elizabethanism to become Americanness. This is essentially the burden of Lawrence Schoonover's opening remarks in his popular history *To Love a Queen: Walter Raleigh and Elizabeth R* (1973), published when England had declined (at any rate in the minds of some Americans) to a convenient theme-park-cum-aircraft-carrier in the front-line of the Cold War:

It was a wonderful age, a breathless age, an age of ferment, when everything was new; a youthful age, sure of itself and its future . . .

It was an age when it was equally good to live or die. Manly, fast, flamboyantly they lived, and fearlessly they died . . .

It was the youth of the English language . . . [The Elizabethans] were the first to fix that vigor and manliness that has lasted for four hundred years. Little did they suspect how soundly they wrought; but their lives live today in the genius of the English language . . .

It was also the beginning of youth's end. With the death of the Virgin Queen came a decline of England's preeminence, the twilight of a dazzling age, the *Gotterdamerung* of Elizabethan glory.

Raleigh was the last Elizabethan. (3–4)

The tracing of the Victorian British Empire back to the Tudors is here written out entirely: once England had produced the first honor-

American, its subsequent history could be wholly ignored. Elizabeth's senility is the state in which England has remained since her death, its youth—and its genes —carried off to the West.

This is equally the argument of the longest-running play in American history, Paul Green's 'symphonic drama' *The Lost Colony*, produced on Roanoke Island every summer by the Roanoke Historical Association since the 1920s.[12] In this piece the coming of the Armada is explicitly the reason for the failure of the American enterprise—Elizabeth wavers over the choice between defending her nation or succouring Raleigh's colony. In the event the colonists are abandoned without supplies despite Raleigh's pleas, since the Queen requisitions all ships for the impending confrontation with Spain:

> QUEEN *(to Raleigh)*. It seems that destiny doth make the choice. Between my England and your Virginia, it favors me. Would God it did not in such a tragic way as this. In this hour no ships shall leave England, large or small. For by the sea we live. To lose it is to perish. Gentlemen, a Spanish Armada is set to sail against us. And now, to arms. God save us.[13]

Elizabeth sacrifices the most truly Elizabethan of all the Elizabethans, the brave Virginian adventurers John Borden, Eleanor Dare, and their baby born on American soil, Virginia Dare, to the survival of England, and in so doing irrevocably commits herself to the past—to being Gloriana—rather than to the future—to Virginia. (This is a reading of Elizabeth's relations with America which *Shakespeare in Love* cannily leaves open for its American audience—who can feel pathos at the end of the film not that Lady Viola gets transported to Virginia but that Shakespeare has to stay behind and write plays instead—and it may be worth mentioning here that in one early episode of *The Lost Colony*, long deleted from its current script, Elizabeth had to intervene personally to prevent the young Shakespeare, adoptive honorary American, from volunteering to join Raleigh's colonists.)

This regretfully and regrettably insular Elizabeth, however, has none the less been saved for the American version of what was most acceptable about her reign. The actress Barbara Hird, who currently plays the

Queen in *The Lost Colony*, also stars in an especially written one-woman show about Gloriana by lebame houston, entitled—in a calculated affront to Glenda Jackson—*Elizabeth R* (first performed in 1993). Extensively performed in the USA (at Roanoke, at the Fort Raleigh National Historic Site, and on board a replica of an Elizabethan galleon, among many other venues), it has also toured Britain, playing at venues as diverse as the Edinburgh Festival, the Heraldry Society, and even Elizabeth's own Old Palace, Hatfield. In this play the middle-aged Queen of the Armada victory, who has the body of a weak and feeble woman but the heart and stomach of a king, is neatly reclaimed for America. Elizabeth is found once more in her private dressing-room, this time in 1588—where she confides in the audience for fifty minutes or so about her life and times, particularly about her beloved adventurer Raleigh:

> WALTER RALEGH advises me to acquire a 'New' World . . . My knight in shining armour . . . England's future lies in the 'New' World, he insisted . . . he is so charming. I granted him permission to seek out and colonize territory in this 'New World.'[14]

Raleigh's provoking activities in the Spanish Main are here cited as one of the chief reasons for Philip's impending invasion attempt, and the Queen closes her monologue by rehearsing the big speech she is planning to give to her troops, wielding an impressive property sword as she does so. But this is a warrior queen with a difference (Fig. 31). 'Not what you expected, is it?,' she asks smugly, on her entrance. She has just returned, she explains, from one of her habitual incognito fact-finding pub crawls around London—for which she always disguises herself as a man.[15] This is presented as wholly consonant with her main personal characteristic, the love of freedom ('How does a queen do anything? Any way she chooses', 15). A transvestite without a hint of perversity— emigrated from all those big dresses and heavy crowns, the encumbering Old World paraphernalia of Gloriana—this is an Elizabeth who herself proves to be a swashbuckling Errol Flynn or Richard Todd. At last, here is a Virgin Queen man enough to have founded Virginia. (Or even to

FIG. 31. Barbara Hird as Elizabeth in the American playwright lebame houston's dramatic monologue *Elizabeth R* (1993), performed in tandem with the longest-running play in American history, the Elizabeth-and-Raleigh spectacular *The Lost Colony*, at Roanoke, North Carolina. Taken out of her official dress and crown once more (the dress adorns a dummy behind her, in front of her official coronation portrait), this Elizabeth proves at heart to be all man, or at least all Principal Boy, clad in green doublet and hose and green boots. Accustomed to visiting taverns in male disguise, she seems swashbucklingly manly enough to have founded Virginia herself had she not been otherwise occupied in the Old World.

serve as a role model for the globalizing buccaneers of present-day Wall Street, as she does in one of the latest expressions of America's distinctive special relationship with Gloriana, Alan Axelrod's *Elizabeth I CEO: Strategic Lessons From the Leader Who Built An Empire*, 2001.) It's Queen Elizabeth, sure, but not as we know her.

❧ Notes ❧

INTRODUCTION

1. Thomas Dekker, *Old Fortunatus* (1599), in *The Dramatic Works of Thomas Dekker*, ed. Fredson Bowers (4 vols., Cambridge, 1953–61), i. 113. 'Blest name, happie countrie': comes the reply, 'Your *Eliza* makes your land *Elizium*.'

2. Sidney Carroll, *The Imperial Votaress* (London, 1947), p. v.

3. Edmund Spenser, *The Faerie Queene* (1596), book III, stanza 5. On the multiplication and contestation of Elizabeth's image in her own time, see especially Marie Axton, *The Queen's Two Bodies: Drama and the Elizabethan Succession* (London, 1977); Frances Yates, *Astraea: The Imperial Theme in the Sixteenth Century* (London, 1975); Sir Roy Strong, *The Cult of Elizabeth: Elizabethan Portraiture and Pageantry* (London, 1977) and *Gloriana: The Portraits of Queen Elizabeth I* (London, 1987); Susan Frye, *Elizabeth I: The Competition for Representation* (Oxford, 1993); Helen Hackett, *Virgin Mother, Maiden Queen: Elizabeth I and the cult of the Virgin Mary* (Basingstoke, 1995); Winifried Schleiner, '*Divina Virago*: Queen Elizabeth as an Amazon', *Studies in Philology*, 75 (1978), 163–80. On both this process and its post-modern legatees, see Richard Burt, 'Doing the Queen: Gender, Sexuality, and the Censorship of Elizabeth I's Royal Image from Renaissance Portraiture to Twentieth-Century Mass Media', in Andrew Hadfield (ed.), *Literature and Censorship in Renaissance England* (London, 2001), 207–28.

4. Cf. Dekker, *Old Fortunatus*: 'Some call her *Pandora*: some *Gloriana*, some *Cynthia*: some *Belphoebe*, some *Astraea*: all by seuerall names to expresse seuerall loues.'

5. Her remark about the ring, as recorded by the Scots ambassador Maitland in 1561, ran 'I am married already to the realm of England when I was crowned with this ring, which I bear continually in token thereof.' Elizabeth I, *Collected Works*, ed. Leah Marcus, Janel Mueller, and Mary Beth Rose (Chicago, 2000), 65. For her Feb. 1559 speech to Parliament, in MS versions and in that reported by Camden, see 56–60.

6. Philippa Berry, *Of Chastity and Power: Elizabethan Literature and the Unmarried Queen* (London, 1989), 72–3; David Starkey, *Elizabeth: Apprenticeship* (London, 2000), 23.

7. On 'romance' and the historical novel in particular, see Diane Elam, *Romancing the Post-Modern* (London, 1992).
8. Cf. Starkey's introduction to *Elizabeth: Apprenticeship*, p. xi: 'If [this book] reads like a historical thriller, I shall be well pleased.'
9. Caryl Brahms and S. J. Simon, *No Bed For Bacon* (1941; London, 1999), 19.
10. William Sellar and Robert Yeatman, *1066 And All That* (London, 1930), p. vii.
11. Starkey, *Elizabeth: Apprenticeship*, 143–4.
12. The chief source for this apocryphal exclamation is Sir Robert Naunton's *Fragmenta Regalia: or Observations on Queen Elizabeth, Her Times & Favourites* (1641; ed. John Cerovski, Washington, 1985), 40. On the oak tree, see Chapter 3.
13. See Susan Frye, 'The Myth of Elizabeth I at Tilbury', *Sixteenth Century Journal*, 23 (1992), 95–114; Alison Plowden, *Elizabeth Regina: An Age of Triumph, 1588–1603* (London, 1980), 10–12. Frye may exaggerate the dubiety of the canonical version of the speech (see Elizabeth I, *Collected Works*, 325–6), but the armour is almost certainly a romantic accretion: see Chapter 1.
14. See e.g. Elizabeth I, *Collected Works*, 66.
15. See, for example, *The death of Queene Elizabeth with her declaration of her successor*, fos. 1r–2v, in 'Historical and Political Tracts: Reign of James I', Gordonston Papers (Box V), Beinecke Library, Yale; also Bodleian MS Tanner 85 (60).
16. See Robert Carey, *Memoirs* (London, 1759), 138.
17. Hence a Jacobean allegorical painting of Elizabeth flanked by Time and Death and being crowned by putti—in fact a 'Triumph of Eternity' in which Time has fallen asleep, celebrating the immortality of Elizabeth's fame—attracted a folkloric story that Elizabeth herself had commissioned it after Essex's condemnation, her grief for her favourite at last convincing her of her impending mortality. See Strong, *Gloriana: The Portraits of Queen Elizabeth I*, 163–5.
18. See Robert Person, *A Discussion of the Answere of M. William Barlow* ([St Omer], 1612); Catherine Loomis, 'Elizabeth Southwell: Manuscript Account of the Death of Queen Elizabeth', *ELR* 26: 3 (1996), 482–509.
19. Ben Jonson, *Conversations with Drummond of Hawthornden 1619*, ed. G. B. Harrison (New York, 1966), 15. Jonson seeks to back up this story—which simultaneously affirms Elizabeth's status as Virgin Queen and denies her any credit for it—with further circumstantial detail: 'at the comming over of Monsieur [the Duke of Alençon] ther was a French Chirurgion who hand to cutt it, yett fear stayed her & his death.'

20. See Catherine Loomis, '"Publish their bowels to the vulgar eye": Royal Autopsies in Early Modern England', unpublished paper, Shakespeare Association of America conference, 1997. Loomis's unpublished Ph.D. thesis, '"And All the World Shall Mourn Her": The Literary Response to the Death of Queen Elizabeth I' (University of Rochester, New York, 1996) remains the best single account of the immediate literary aftermath of Elizabeth's death. On contemporary slanders about Elizabeth, see Robert Shephard, 'Sexual Rumours in English Politics: The Cases of Elizabeth I and James I', in Jacqueline Murray (ed.), *Desire and Discipline: Sex and Sexuality in the Premodern West* (Toronto, 1996).

21. Sir Roy Strong, *The Cult of Elizabeth: Elizabethan Portraiture and Pageantry* (1977; London, 1999), 15.

22. 'A deprecation of our usuall lapse in speech bred by the long fruition of our blessed late Soveraigne', in *Sorrowes Joy* (Cambridge, 1603); H.S., *Queen Elizabeths Losse* (London, 1603); *A mourneful Dittie, entituled Elizabeths losse* (London, 1603). We are grateful to Catherine Loomis for writing to us about these poems.

23. Henry Chettle, *Englandes Mourning Garment* (London, 1603), D3.

24. Thomas Newton, *Atropoion Delia* (London, 1603), B4r.

25. The passage is from *Aeneid*, I. 322–5: 'And her son started to answer her: "No, I have neither seen nor heard any sister of yours . . . young lady . . . only, how am I to speak of you? You have not the countenance of human kind and your voice has no tones of mortality . . . Goddess! For a goddess surely you must be."' Virgil, *The Aeneid*, trans. W. F. Jackson Knight (London, 1956), 37.

26. J. E. Neale, *Queen Elizabeth* (1934; 1952; Harmondsworth, 1967), 396–7.

27. Anna Jameson, *Memoirs of Celebrated Female Sovereigns* (1831; 2 vols., London, 1834), ii. 326; *Memoirs of the Loves of the Poets. Biographical Sketches of Women celebrated in Ancient and Modern Poetry* (1829; Boston, 1857), 209. Cf. Jameson's successor in this genre, Lydia Hoyt Farmer, in *The Girls' Book of Famous Queens* (1887; New York, 1927), 172: 'Far differently did Elizabeth meet her doom from the heroic Queen of Scots . . . writhing in agony of body and terror of mind she spent her last hours.'

28. Agnes Strickland, *Lives of the Queens of England* (London, 1851), 772–3, 776–7.

29. On this film, see Barbara Hodgdon, *The Shakespeare Trade: Performances and Appropriations* (Philadelphia, 1998), 110–16, in the introductory section to her valuable, largely psychoanalytic chapter on some of Elizabeth's posthumous manifestations, 'Romancing the Queen' (110–70).

30. Francis Osborne, 'Traditional Memoires on the Raigne of Queen

Elizabeth', originally published as part of his *Historical Memoires on the Reigns of Queen Elizabeth and King James* (London, 1658), 61.

31. Lytton Strachey, *Elizabeth and Essex: A Tragic History* (London, 1928), 286.

32. Comyns Beaumont, *The Private Life of the Virgin Queen* (London, 1946), 298. For the earliest instance of this particular conspiracy theory, provided by Orville Ward Owen in 1895, see Chapter 3. Cf. Anne Meeker, *The Queen's Rings* (Chicago, 1936), 269:

> In the moonlight, streaming through the parted curtains, something like an animal, with wild, green eyes was beside her. She could feel its hot breath. In the weird blue light, she could see its form on her bed! With a superhuman effort, she strained to see—Cecil! Cecil! Cecil! Like a terrible beast, he had her by the throat—pushing—pounding— It was dark.
>
> With a faint gurgle in her throat she lay still.

33. Sidney Carroll, *The Imperial Votaress* (London, 1947), 186–8.

34. Susan Kay, *Legacy* (London, 1985), 647.

35. Benjamin Britten, *Gloriana*: libretto by William Plomer, supplied with the Welsh National Opera CD (Argo/Decca, 1993), 216–22.

I. GLORIANA REVIVES

1. This couplet epitaph is quoted in a number of early lives of Elizabeth and appears in numerous seventeenth-century commonplace books and other manuscript anthologies: see, for example, Bodleian Library: MS Rawl poet 153 fo. 8v.

2. On the renewal of misogynistic criticisms of Elizabeth at the end of her reign, see also Christopher Haigh, *Elizabeth I* (London, 1988), 166.

3. See Leah Marcus, 'Elizabeth', in *Puzzling Shakespeare: Local Reading and its Discontents* (Berkeley, 1988), 51–105.

4. See Louis Montrose, '"Shaping Fantasies": Figurations of Gender and Power in Elizabethan Culture', in Stephen Greenblatt (ed.), *Representing the English Renaissance* (Berkeley, 1988), 31–64.

5. 'Gertrude represents the convergence of three issues—sexuality, ageing . . . and succession—that produced a sense of contradiction, even breakdown, in the cult of Elizabeth in the final years of her reign. . . . The latent cultural fantasy in *Hamlet* is that Queen Gertrude functions as a degraded figure of Queen Elizabeth.' Peter Erickson, *Rewriting Shakespeare, Rewriting Ourselves* (Berkeley, 1991), 83, 86. This argument has been expanded by

Steven Mullaney, in an article called 'Mourning and Misogyny', which sees *Hamlet* as at once lamenting and reviling the old queen before she has even died, a process consummated four years after her death by Thomas Middleton's *Revenger's Tragedy* (1607). In Middleton's play Yorick's skull (the occasion for Hamlet's at once irrelevant and all too topical lecture against female cosmetics) has metamorphosed into the venomously made-up skull of Vindice's dead virgin fiancée, whose name, strikingly, was Gloriana: for Mullaney, the moral of both plays appears to be that the only good Gloriana is a dead Gloriana. Stephen Mullaney, 'Mourning and Misogyny: *Hamlet, The Revenger's Tragedy*, and the Final Progress of Elizabeth I, 1600–1607', *Shakespeare Quarterly*, 45: 2 (Summer 1994), 139–63. For further elaborations, see Lisa Hopkins, '"Ripeness is all": The Death of Elizabeth in Drama', *Renaissance Forum*, 4: 2 (2000).

6. As he had perhaps anticipated, Shakespeare was a direct beneficiary of James's succession—the acting company to which he belonged became the King's Men, his patron Southampton was freed from the Tower—and so too was most of the theatrical profession, since as the first royal family to occupy the royal palaces of England since the successive dysfunctional menages of Henry VIII sixty and more years earlier, the Stuarts had many more occasions on which to hire players for lucrative court performances.

7. 'Regno consortes et una, hic obdormimus Elizabetha et Maria sorores, in spe resurrectiones': partners of the throne and of the grave, here rest we sisters Elizabeth and Mary in the hope of the same resurrection. This epitaph's hint that the Reformation which divided the two in life wasn't in the long term that important cannot have escaped contemporaries.

8. See Julia M. Walker, 'Reading the Tombs of Elizabeth I', *ELR* 26: 3 (Autumn 1996), 510–30; 'Bones of Contention: Posthumous Images of Elizabeth and Stuart Politics', in Julia M. Walker (ed.), *Dissing Elizabeth: Negative Representations of Gloriana* (Durham, NC, 1998).

9. On the immense influence of Camden's anti-Jacobean history on sub-sequent perceptions of Elizabeth, see John King, 'Queen Elizabeth I: Representations of the Virgin Queen', *Renaissance Quarterly*, 43: 1 (Spring 1990), 30–74. For a dissenting view, see D. R. Woolf, 'Two Elizabeths? James I and the Late Queen's Famous Memory', *Canadian Journal of History*, 209: 2 (1985), 167–91.

10. See Anne Barton, 'Harking Back to Elizabeth: Ben Jonson and Caroline Nostalgia', *ELH* 48 (Winter 1981), 706–31, esp. 714–17. For such chroniclers as Greville, the sense of where and how time was moving had definitively changed: as Roy Strong has remarked, 'For the Elizabethans all history led

up to them. For the Stuarts all roads finally led back to Elizabeth.' Quoted in Philip Corrigan and Derek Sayer, *The Great Arch: English State Formation as Cultural Revolution* (Oxford, 1985), 55.

11. On the emergence of Spenserianism as an oppositional discourse for poets under the Stuarts, see David Norbrook, *Poetry and Politics in the English Renaissance* (London, 1984). On Elizabeth's Arthurian mythology, see also the pedigree drawn up for her, now displayed at Hatfield, which in between identifying many other desirable ancestors traces the Tudors' alleged direct descent from King Arthur.

12. 'Upon the Death of Queen Elizabeth', Bodleian MS Ashmole 38, 296–7. This poem does not appear to have been written in the immediate aftermath of the Queen's death.

13. Godfrey Goodman, *The Court of King James the First*, ed. John S. Brewer (2 vols., London, 1839), i. 97–8. Goodman was a bishop: his interest during the Commonwealth in the posthumous vindication of Elizabeth is connected with his sense of the Queen as an opponent of Puritanism and defender of ecclesiastical privilege. On the revival of the Accession Day celebrations, see also Francis Osborne, 'Traditional Memoires on the Raigne of Queen Elizabeth' (1658), 107–8.

14. On the importance of the theatre in articulating a nascent politics of Elizabethan nostalgia, see Curtis Perry, 'The Citizen Politics of Nostalgia: Queen Elizabeth in Early Jacobean London', *Journal of Mediaeval and Renaissance Studies*, 23: 1 (Winter 1993), 89–111.

15. See 'The miraculous preservation of Lady Elizabeth, now Queene of England, from extreme calamitie and danger of life, in the tyme of Queene Mary her sister', in John Foxe, *Actes and Monuments of the English Martyrs* (1563; London, 1570), 2288–96.

16. Samuel Rowley, *When You See Me, You Know Me* (London, 1605), H4v–Ir.

17. Heywood's play may also have been influenced by Thomas Dekker and John Webster's *Sir Thomas Wyatt*, printed in 1607 but written earlier.

18. See Thomas Heywood, *If you know not me, You know no bodie: or, The troubles of Queene Elizabeth* (1605; London, 1606), F2v. On these ceremonies themselves, see *The Queenes Maiesties Passage through the Citie of London to Westminster the Day before her Coronacion* (London, 1559); on Heywood's Elizabeth, see also Georgianna Ziegler, 'England's Savior: Elizabeth I in the Writings of Thomas Heywood', *Renaissance Papers* (1980), 29–37; Kathleen McLuskie, *Dekker and Heywood, Professional Dramatists* (Basingstoke, 1994); F. S. Boas, *Queen Elizabeth in Drama and Related Studies* (London, 1950).

19. Christopher Lever, *Queene Elizabeths Teares* (London, 1607), ar.
20. Thomas Heywood, *England's Elizabeth* (1631; ed. Philip Rider, New York, 1982), 7.

21.   Bones a me Queen, I am *Hobson*, and old Hobson
       By the Stockes, I am sure you know me.
       QUEEN. VVhat is he *Lecester*, doost thou know this fellow?
       Gresham or you?
       GRESH. May it please your Maiestie,
       He is a rich substantiall Citizen.

    Thomas Heywood, *The Second Part of, If you know not me, you know no bodie. With the building of the Royall Exchange: And the famous Victorie of Queene Elizabeth, in the Yeare 1588* (London, 1606), Hv.
22. See Perry, 'The Citizen Politics of Nostalgia', 97.
23. See R. A. Foakes, *Illustrations of the English Stage 1580–1642* (London, 1985), 91–3.
24. See Peter Stallybrass, 'Worn Worlds: Clothes and Identity on the Renaissance Stage', in Margreta de Grazia, Nancy Quilligan, and Peter Stallybrass (eds), *Subject and Object in Renaissance Culture* (Cambridge, 1996), 289–320.
25. Heywood, *The Second Part of, If you know not me*, I3v, Kr.
26. Thomas Heywood, *If you know not me, You know no body. The second part* (London, 1632), Kv. On these revisions, see Madeleine Doran's edition of the play (Oxford, 1935), pp. xii–xix. On this and other recapitulations of the militant Elizabeth see Simon Shepherd, *Amazons and Warrior Women: Varieties of Feminism in Seventeenth-Century Drama* (New York, 1981).
27. See Susan Frye, 'The Myth of Elizabeth I at Tilbury', *Sixteenth Century Journal*, 23 (1992), 95–114.
28. Thomas Dekker, *The Whore of Babylon* (1607; ed. Marianne Gateson Riely, New York, 1980), 96. It may be going too far to suggest that Dekker's choice of name for his idealized Elizabeth deliberately revalues Shakespeare's degraded Fairy Queen—the name Titania itself was perfectly available independently of *A Midsummer Night's Dream*, appearing as one variant for Diana in Ovid's *Metamorphoses*. But Ben Jonson was surely thinking both of *A Midsummer Night's Dream* and *The Whore of Babylon* in 1610 when he set about praising James's doomed, militant heir Prince Henry as Elizabeth's latter-day better half under the name of Oberon; so whether or not Dekker consciously intended it, his cast list did effectively participate in the rescue of the name Titania from mockery and into Elizabethan panegyric.

29. For a slightly different reading of this play's ecclesiastical politics, see Julia Gasper, *The Dragon and the Dove: The Plays of Thomas Dekker* (Oxford, 1990).

30. There are disagreements about the dating of this image, executed by Thomas Cecil and variously known as 'Truth Presenting the Queen with a Lance' or 'Elizabeth I in Armour', but it probably first appeared around 1625, not long before the Hakluyt title-page reproduced as Fig. 1. In historical fact, Elizabeth probably merely carried a baton at Tilbury, if that: her full military costume is a posthumous gift to her legend, here superbly and influentially perpetuated, from the likes of Dekker and Heywood. See also Susan Frye, 'The Myth of Elizabeth I at Tilbury.' A comparable nostalgic image of Elizabeth surveying the destruction of the Armada—this one a large oil painting on wood—was bequeathed to St Faith's Church, Gaywood, by its rector Thomas Hares in 1634: see *The Armada* (exhibition catalogue, National Maritime Museum, Greenwich, 1988), 16.31.

31. In fact this play may have provided an even more detailed anticipation of the post-modern theme park and *son et lumière* than its lavishly detailed and spectacular stage directions alone suggest, since (although we know it enjoyed a few performances at the Globe) its composition may have been prompted by the King's Men's acquisition of the Blackfriars theatre in 1608, the very hall in which the play's central event—the papal inquest into the validity of Henry's marriage to Catherine of Aragon—had taken place.

32. William Shakespeare and John Fletcher, *Henry VIII (All Is True)*, 5.4.17–23. All citations to Shakespeare are to the Oxford modern-spelling edition, edited by Stanley Wells and Gary Taylor (Oxford, 1986).

33. Cf. the links between the trial of Henry and Catherine's marriage in *Henry VIII*, Hermione's trial for adultery in *The Winter's Tale*, and the real-life trial of Anne Boleyn for incestuous adultery in 1536, which *Henry VIII* just stops short of dramatizing. For an alternative but related reading of some connections between these two plays, see Ruth Vanita, '"A woman more worth than any man": Mariological Memory in *The Winter's Tale* and *Henry VIII*' (unpublished paper, World Shakespeare Congress, Los Angeles, Apr. 1996).

34. For a much fuller reading of this play's representation of Elizabeth in its historical and literary context, see Gordon McMullan's introduction to the play in the Arden 3 edition (London, 2000).

35. Haigh, *Elizabeth I*, 167.

36. Wallace T. MacCaffrey, *Elizabeth I: War and Politics, 1588–1603* (Princeton, 1992), 540–1.

37. David Starkey, *Elizabeth: Apprenticeship* (London, 2000), p. x.
38. See Thomas L. Berger, 'Looking for Shakespeare in Caroline England', *Viator: Medieval and Renaissance Studies*, 27 (1996), 323–59.
39. Although her good sense is ultimately vindicated, Lady Beaufield is in some respects a mildly satirical figure for Elizabeth too: a bluestocking, she has an 'Academy', where Mrs Voluble gives a lecture on 'the female sciences', starting with advice on cosmetics for 'old Ladies, that will cozen Nature, and Time, and abuse the men they love best.' *The Varietie, a Comoedy, lately presented by His Majesties Servants at the Black-Friers* (London, 1649), 12–13. On both of these plays, see Barton, 'Harking Back to Elizabeth'.
40. See, for example, C. V. Wedgwood, *Oliver Cromwell and the Elizabethan Inheritance* (Neale Lectures in History, 1970). When Jonathan Swift wrote in *A Discourse of the Contests and Dissentions between the Nobles and the Commons in Athens and Rome* (1701) that 'About the middle of Queen Elizabeth's Reign, I take the Power between the Nobles and Commons to have been in more equal Balance, than it was ever before or since', he was expressing a view that had been widely accepted across the political spectrum for more than half a century. *The Prose Works of Jonathan Swift*, ed. Herbert Davis (14 vols., Oxford, 1939), ii. 63.
41. John Milton, *The Readie and Easie Way* . . . (2nd edn., London, 1660), 88–9. On Milton and Elizabeth, see also Albert C. Labriola, 'Milton's Eve and the Cult of Elizabeth I', *Journal of English and Germanic Philology*, 95: 1 (Jan. 1996), 38–51.
42. Samuel Pepys, *The Diary of Samuel Pepys*, ed. Robert Latham and William Matthews (11 vols., London, 1970–83), viii. 388–9.
43. *The Poems and Letters of Andrew Marvell*, ed. H. H. Margoliouth (3rd edn., 2 vols., Oxford, 1971), i. 212.
44. When Temple Bar was removed this statue, one of very few three-dimensional representations of Elizabeth to survive from her own lifetime, was transferred to a niche in the south wall of St Dunstan's in the West, looking on to Fleet Street.
45. See [Elkanah Settle], *The Solemn Mock-Procession of the Pope Cardinalls Jesuits Fryars &c: through the Citty of London November the 17th, 1680* (London, 1680). See also *The Solemn Mock: Procession: or the Tryal & Execution of the Pope and his Ministers, on the 17. Of Nov. at Temple-Bar; where, being brought before the Figure of Q. ELIZABETH . . . he receives his Final Doom and Downfal, viz. to be burnt with all his FRY into Ashes . . .* (London, 1680). On these demonstrations see Tim Harris, *London Crowds in the Reign of Charles II: Propaganda and Politics from the Restoration until the Exclusion*

Crisis (Cambridge, 1987); John Miller, *Popery and Politics in England, 1660–1688* (Cambridge, 1973).

46. See Edward Gregg, *Queen Anne* (London, 1970), 96, 152. This attempted identification with Elizabeth could be turned against Anne when, during the Sacheverell affair, she banned some of the anti-Catholic demonstrations planned for Queen Bess's Day 1711: see, for example, the satirical poem *Queen Elizabeth's Day* (London, 1711).

47. Cf. Defoe's parallel between Anne's victory celebrations after the victory at Vigo and Elizabeth's after the defeat of the Armada at the end of his poem 'The Spanish Descent', 1702: 'The crowding millions hearty blessings pour: | Saint Paul ne'er saw but one such day before.' Even the Catholic Alexander Pope was prepared to praise Anne by indentifying her with Elizabeth, in *Windsor Forest* (1713): see Vincent Carretta, 'Anne and Elizabeth: The Poet as Historian', *Studies in English Literature*, 21: 3 (Summer 1981), 425–37.

48. Rysbrack also completed a terracotta portrait bust of Elizabeth for Queen Caroline, now at Windsor Castle; see the catalogue to the 1982 Rysbrack exhibition at Bristol Art Gallery, item 51. On Elizabeth's profile in this whole period, see Christine Gerrard, *The Patriot Opposition to Walpole: Politics, Poetry and National Myth, 1725–1742* (Oxford, 1994), ch. 6, 'Political Elizabethanism and the Spenser Revival', 150–84, esp. 150–3, 169–74. The canonical example of Elizabethan nostalgia in the 1730s is provided by Samuel Johnson's *London* (1738), which begins with a tableau of the speaker and his friend paying homage to the soil of Greenwich: 'Struck with the Seat which gave Eliza birth | We kneel, and kiss the consecrated Earth.' Samuel Johnson, *Complete English Poems*, ed. David Fleeman (Harmondsworth, 1971), 61. Johnson's poem is anticipated by, for example, Samuel Wesley's *Spanish Insults, 1729*: 'Nor less illustrious was our realm confess'd | In that bright period which Eliza bless'd . . . | In vain conspired the powers of Rome and Spain; | The deep beneath th'Armada groan'd in vain . . .' In Samuel Wesley, *Poems on several occasions*, ed. James Nichols (London, 1862).

49. *The Merchant's Complaint against Spain* (London, 1738), 44–58. The dialogue between these royal ghosts is imagined as taking place towards the end of James's reign. 'What (Sister and Brother)', cries Elizabeth, 'my Royal Navy lie rotting, who made the Bulwarks and Walls of England, and when I left them were capable to beat the Power and Pride of Spain to Shivers; O this grieves me!' (55). Only Mary is pleased with the posture of affairs.

50. See George Steevens's note to *2 Henry VI*, 3.3.232, in *The plays of William Shakespeare in 10 volumes . . . to which are added notes by Samuel Johnson and*

George Steevens. The second edition, revised and augmented (10 vols., 1778–80), vi. 511.

51. On the 'New Elizabethans', see Chapter 6.

52. Nevill Coghill, *The Masque of Hope. Presented for the Entertainment of HRH Princess Elizabeth on the occasion of her visit to University College, 25 May 1948 by* OXFORD UNIVERSITY DRAMATIC SOCIETY (Oxford, 1948), 18–20. This move of appropriating *Henry VIII* as a tribute to Elizabeth II would be repeated in coronation year, 1953, when Tyrone Guthrie's production, revived in London to packed houses, would topically supply the gentlemen waiting to see Anne Boleyn's coronation procession with anachronistic newspapers to keep the rain off.

2. THE PRIVATE LIVES OF THE VIRGIN QUEEN

1. Edward Leigh, *Choice Observations of all the Kings of England from the Saxons to the death of King Charles the First collected out of the best Latine and English Writers, who have treated of that argument* (London, 1661), 186.

2. Henry St John Bolingbroke, *Letters on the Spirit of Patriotism: on the Idea of a Patriot King: and on the State of Parties, at the Accession of King George the First* (London, 1749), 213–14.

3. On the eighteenth-century development of British nationalism, see especially Linda Colley, *Britons: Forging the Nation, 1707–1837* (New Haven, Conn., 1992).

4. See e.g. John Dart's *Westmonasterium: or, The History and Antiquities of the Abbey Church of St Peters Westminster* (2 vols., London, 1823), i. 170: George Ballard, *Memoirs of Several Ladies of Great Britain who have been celebrated for their writings or skill in the learned languages, arts, and sciences* (Oxford, 1752), 240.

5. See Clare Brant, 'Armchair Politicians: Elections and Representations, 1774', *Tulsa Studies in Women's Literature*, 17: 2 (Fall 1998), 269–82, esp. 276–7 for speculations on the ways Elizabeth as a figure may have enabled feminine participation in eighteenth-century political discourse.

6. Richard Brinsley Sheridan, *Plays*, ed. Cecil Price (Oxford, 1975), 373.

7. Ibid. 358–9.

8. See J. R. Planché, *The Drama at Home: or, an Evening with Puff* (London, 1844), 6:

> DRAMA. But even you can't help me now-a-days.
> Puff's put his hand to bills for me so oft

That in the market they are worthless.

PUFF.   Soft!

No scandal against Queen Elizabeth, pray;
I've come to show you there is still a way
To make your fortune—sink the stage!

We are grateful to Tracy Davis for drawing our attention to this example (drawn from a time at which Sheridan was otherwise completely out of fashion). The line 'No scandal about Queen Elizabeth, I hope!' has remained sufficiently familiar to be included in all editions of the *Oxford Dictionary of Quotations.*

9. *Queen Elizabeth's Ghost: or, A Dream* (London, 1706), n.p.

10. See Introduction, above. This story was variously available to subsequent generations through Horace Walpole's *A Catalogue of royal and noble Authors of England* (1758), the appendix to David Hume's *History of Britain* (1759), William Seward's *Anecdotes of Some Distinguished Persons* (1795–6), and *Notes of Ben Jonson's Conversations with William Drummond of Hawthornden. January MDCXIX* (London, 1842).

11. *Mr Bayle's Historical and Critical Dictionary* (1710; 2nd edn., 2 vols., 1735), i. 760 n. x.

12. For an influential, if problematic, statement of the linkage between the rise of the novel and new ideas of womanhood, see Nancy Armstrong, *Desire and Domestic Fiction: A Political History of the Novel* (New York, Oxford, 1987), *passim*. A very substantial proportion of those writings produced between 1680 and 1840 which seek to narrate Elizabeth as both queen and proper lady may be broadly described as essentially novelistic (a category that includes for our purposes here sentimental or she-tragedy, a genre which the emerging historical novel would ultimately subsume), in that they strive to supply political history with a cast of fully realized inner selves.

13. N.H., *The Ladies Dictionary, being a general entertainment for the fair-sex* (London, 1694), 177.

14. Cf. Anna Jameson's remark that the history of Katherine Grey formed 'a complete romance, and a very tragical one'. *Memoirs of Celebrated Female Sovereigns* (1831; 2nd edn., 2 vols., London, 1834), i. 299.

15. *Courtenay, Earl of Devonshire; or, The Troubles of the Princess Elizabeth. A Tragedy* (London, 1690), 31.

16. Ibid., Preface.

17. 'The Princess Elizabeth: A Ballad alluding to a story recorded of her, when she was prisoner at Woodstock, 1554' (1764), *The Works in Verse and Prose of*

William Shenstone, Esq. (5th edn., 3 vols., London, 1777), i. 124–6. Reprinted as 'The Complaint of the Princess Elizabeth' in *The Cabinet of Genius* (London, 1787–90), with illustration.

18. Manuscript version reprinted in Alice Hazeltine, *A Study of William Shenstone and of His Critics*, MA thesis, Wellesley, 1913 (Menarha, Wis., 1918), 80–1.

19. Notably John Wood's *Elizabeth in the Tower* (unloc., 1836); Daniel Huntington's *A Child Bringing Flowers to princess Elizabeth, when a Prisoner, in the reign of Mary* (New York Historical Society, 1848); Emanuel Leutze's *Princess Elizabeth in the Tower* (New York Historical Society, 1860); Thomas Falcon Marshall's *Queen Elizabeth in the Tower* (n.d.); and Dean Wilstenhome's *In April 1556 Princess Elizabeth was escorted from Hatfield House* (n.d.) There is also the odd early study by the American Mather Brown. Although it is annotated on the back 'Queen Elizabeth Appointing Howard, Duke of Norfolk, Her Lieutenant in the Northern Counties, 1559', this seems a wildly improbable identification, since the sketch actually appears to show Elizabeth with a child, with what look like Beefeaters in the background, and what appears to be a bishop. The only anecdote extant in 1797 when this study was executed about Elizabeth, a child, and a bishop was the episode of Bishop Gardiner's interrogation of Elizabeth in the Tower and his banning of the visits of the child who came to her under suspicion of passing notes to her in bunches of flowers. It is therefore conceivable that the annotation refers to another project altogether. For this picture under its usual title see Dorinda Evans, *Mather Brown, Early American Artist in England* (Connecticut, 1982), 133.

20. On America's Elizabeth, see Afterword, below.

21. *'Twixt Axe and Crown* [New York, 1870], 40.

22. See, for instance, Lucy Aikin's remark that 'She was never able to forget the woman in the sovereign; and in spite of that preponderating love of sway which all her life forbade her to admit a partner of her bed and throne, her heart was to the last deeply sensible to the want, or her imagination to the charm, of loving and being beloved.' *Memoirs of the Court of Elizabeth* (2 vols., London, 1818), ii. 239. See also John Bayley, *The History and Antiquities of the Tower of London* (2 pts., London, 1821), i. 93. A play by Thomas Francklin makes it clear that, once successfully imagined as all woman, Elizabeth can then be presented as standing in need of masculine guidance: by 1837, Francklin is penning the following dialogue between Cecil and Davison on the nature of the Queen's power and how it is regulated.

Davison's suggestion that Elizabeth 'is no stranger to her sex's weakness, /
And condescends sometimes to be a woman' is countered by Cecil:

> There is a female frailty in her nature,
> That sometimes takes the rein; but, thanks to heaven,
> . . . her prudence and her pride
> Have saved her oft; and when deluding love,
> With wily softness, steals into her heart,
> She calls the ruling passion to her aid,
> And bids ambition check the bold intruder.

However, Davison circumvents this description by suggesting that what
checks 'the bold intruder' is actually Cecil's 'paternal care.' *Mary Queen of
Scots, An Historical Play* (London, 1837), 4–6.

23. Henry Jones, *The Earl of Essex. A Tragedy* (London, 1753), 28. See also
Elizabeth's exclamation 'hence with Pity and the Woman's Pangs; /
Resentment governs, and the Queen shall punish' (ibid. 38). This version of
the divided Queen proved enduringly popular; Mary Hays, as late as 1803,
remarks that Essex 'forced her, in the dignity of the sovereign, to stifle the
tenderness and the sentiments of her sex'. *Female Biography; or, Memoirs of
Illustrious and Celebrated Women . . .* (6 vols., London, 1803), iv. 273.

24. In this connection it is interesting to note that Jacqueline Rose has argued,
albeit in the problematic terms of Lacanian psychoanalysis, that the defining limit cases for the power of the modern state are the woman as victim of
execution and the woman as authority for execution. Jacqueline Rose,
'Margaret Thatcher and Ruth Ellis', in *Why War?—Psychoanalysis, Politics
and the Return to Melanie Klein* (Oxford, 1993), 41–87. Rose drafted her essay
in 1987, when a revival of interest in the figure of the last woman to be hanged
in England coincided with moves by the country's first female Prime
Minister towards the reintroduction of the death penalty, but its thesis might
perhaps be as convincingly exemplified by the more enduring national
obsession with the relations between Elizabeth and Mary, Queen of Scots.

25. Elizabeth was supposed to have told Admiral Biron, French ambassador to
England in Sept. 1601, that she would have pardoned Essex had he sued for
mercy, a saying that was printed in French at the Hague in 1607, was repeated in Grimeston's translation of de Serres's *Inventory of the History of France*
(1607), and retailed again in George Chapman's *The Tragedy of Byron* (1608),
5.3.139 ff.

26. 3.3.303–8.

27. John Banks, *The Unhappy Favourite*, ed. Thomas Marshall Howe Blair (New York, 1939), 53.

28. See, for example, 'The Earl of Essex, and Queen Elizabeth', in *Modern Novels in XII Volumes* (only one volume published, London, 1692); *The Secret History of the Most Renowned Q. Elizabeth, and the E. of Essex* ('Cologne' [London], 1695); further editions in various forms and under varied titles in 1705, 1708, 1712, 1720, 1725, 1730, 1740, 1761, 1767, 1775, 1785, 1790, 1799, 1800. Variants on the story appear in [Nathaniel Crouch], *The Unfortunate Court-Favourites of England* (London, 1695); John Seller, *The History of England* (London, 1696); [John Oldmixon], *Amores Britannici. Epistles Historical and Gallant*, in *English Heroic Verse: From several of the most Illustrious Personages of their Times. In Imitation of the Heroidum Epistolae of Ovid. With Notes explaining the most Material Passages in every History* (London, 1703); *A Compendious History of the Monarchs of England* (London, 1712); 'Memoirs of the Unhappy Favourite: Or, The Fall of Robert, Earl of Essex', in *Select Novels and Histories* (London, 1729); Thomas Birch, *An Historical View of the Negotiations between the courts of England, France, and Brussels, from the year 1592 to 1617* (London, 1749); J. P. Hurstone, *Royal Intrigues: or, Secret Memoirs of Four Princesses* (London, [1808]). G. P. R. James was still retailing it as late as 1837 in his *Memoirs of Celebrated Women*. For a reading of *The Secret History* as initiating proto-psychoanalytic readings of Elizabeth, see Barbara Hodgdon, *The Shakespeare Trade* (Philadelphia, 1998), 120–2.

29. *The Secret History of the Most Renowned Q. Elizabeth, and the E. of Essex* ('Cologne' [London], 1680), 2–3.

30. This print of Sarah Siddons as Elizabeth and Anne Brunton as Rutland was not published until 1807, towards the close of Siddons's career and long after Brunton had actually emigrated to America, but its design probably dates from 1791, when Brunton chose the role of Rutland for her Covent Garden benefit. Intriguingly, Siddons, the definitive tragedy queen, in fact never played Elizabeth: the print reflects both her real-life rivalry with Brunton (who was specifically hired by Covent Garden in 1785 to compete with her), and an evident sense that this was the role Siddons *ought* to have played. Siddons is still best remembered, perhaps not coincidentally, as the definitive Lady Macbeth.

31. [Nathaniel Crouch], *The Unfortunate Court-Favourites of England* (London, 1695), 166–7. See also Edward Leigh's *Choice Observations of all the Kings of England* (London, 1661), 187.

32. Henry Brooke, *The Earl of Essex. A Tragedy* (1761; Dublin, 1761), 60.

33. See, for example, Thomas Lookup's *Queen Elizabeth: or, Love and Majesty* (New York, 1876) in which it is the Duke of Nottingham who intercepts the ring, mistaking it for a love-token sent to his wife from Essex. Natalie Hays Hammond's drama, *Elizabeth of England* (New York, 1936) casts Cecil as the villain. Other versions redo the plot with a proud Essex who refuses to send the ring, e.g. N. S. Shaler, *Elizabeth of England: A Dramatic Romance in Five Parts* (5 vols., Boston, 1903), iv. 192–6. See also the film *The Private Lives of Elizabeth and Essex* (1939); see Afterword, below.

34. According to Beatrice Marshall, the ring fetched 3,250 guineas at auction in 1905 on the rumour that it was Essex's ring; it had been expected to fetch only 100 guineas. Beatrice Marshall, *Queen Elizabeth* (London, 1916), 180.

35. For the definitive account of the literary representation of Mary, Queen of Scots, especially in the eighteenth century, see Jayne Elizabeth Lewis, *Mary Queen of Scots: Romance and Nation* (London and New York, 1998). On Lewis's argument, see Michael Dobson, 'Lost Mother', *London Review of Books*, 22: 4 (17 Feb. 2000).

36. The controversy over Mary, Queen of Scots's guilt was active in her own life-time, and was indeed one of the principal causes of her fall from power. Sixteenth- and seventeenth-century defenders of her innocence tended to be Catholic and based in France; detractors tended to be Protestant, as witness the most influential of these, George Buchanan's *A Detection of the Actions of Mary, Queen of Scots, concening the murder of her husband, and her conspiracie, adulterie, and pretended marriage with the earl Bothwel* (1689). The controversy was naturally reactivated by Union and Jacobite agitation. A representative selection of eighteenth-century works that participate in the controversy, expending much effort on weighing the exact admixture of innocence with guilt, might include: the anonymous *The Fate of Majesty, exemplified, in the Barbarous and Disloyal Treatment (by Traiterous and Undutiful Subjects) of the Kings and Queens of the Royal House of the Stuarts* (1720); James Freebairn's *Life of Mary Stewart* (1725), [Samuel Jebb's] *The History of the Life and reign of Mary Queen of Scots, and Dowager of France* (London, 1725); the wonderfully spurious *The Genuine Letters of Mary Queen of Scots, to James Earl of Bothwell: Found in his Secretary's Closet after his Decease; and now in the Possession of a Gentleman of Oxford. Discovering the greatest and most secret Transactions of Her Time. Translated from the French Originals by Edward Simmonds. Never before made Publick. To which is added, Remarks on each Letter, with an Abstract of her Life. In a Letter to the Bookseller, from an unknown Hand* (London, 1726), *Prejudice detected by facts, or, a candid and impartial enquiry into the reign of Queen Elizabeth, so far as*

relates to Mary, Queen of Scots (London, *c*.1750); William Goodall, *An Exam-ination of the Letters said to be written by Mary, Queen of Scots* (1754); John Whitaker, *Mary Queen of Scots Vindicated* (1788); William Tytler, *An Inquiry, Historical and Critical, into the Evidence against Mary Queen of Scots* (1790); William Robertson, *The History of Scotland* (1759); and George Chalmers, *The Life of Mary, Queen of Scots* (1822).

37. *Mary Stuart, Queen of the Scots: being the Secret History of Her Life, and the Real Causes of all Her Misfortunes . . . translated from the French by Mrs. Eliza Haywood* (London, 1725), 1. This was clearly a very marketable commodity, as it also came out in the same year in Edinburgh, translated, abridged, and lavishly annotated by one James Freebairn under the title of *The Life of Mary Stewart, Queen of Scotland and France. Written Originally in French, and Now done into English. With Notes illustrating and confirming the most material Passages of this History, collected from Cotemporary [sic], and other Authors of the Greatest Character and Reputation* (Edinburgh, 1725). What Freebairn's ver-sion makes clear is the relevance of the controversy over the Queen of Scots's innocence to national feeling.

38. For example: Charles Jervais, *Mary Bellende, as Mary Queen of Scots* (early eighteenth century); William Hogarth, *Peg Woffington as Mary, Queen of Scots* (1759); Sir John Watson Gordon, *Madelina, Baroness Gray, as Mary Queen of Scots* (1826); Julius Jacob, *Mary Lowther Ferguson as Mary Queen of Scots for Lady Londonderry's Ball* (1844) (all reproduced in the Mellon Center for British Art Photograph Archive, Yale); *Alexandra, Princess of Wales as Mary, Queen of Scots for the Waverley Ball* (1871). These portraits, of course, serve differing ends, from displaying Scottish nationalism to asserting pro-Catholic sympathies—but all, despite Hogarth's surely sardonic twist in his depiction of Garrick's ex-mistress in one of her more celebrated roles in *The Rival Queens* (1756), are meant to adumbrate a sympathetic and dramatic femininity. For more on this subject see Sara Stevenson and Helen Bennett, *Van Dyck in Check Trousers: Fancy Dress in Art and Life, 1700–1900* (Edinburgh, 1978), 4–8, and Lewis, *Mary Queen of Scots*, 124–5.

39. Jane West, *Letters to a Young Lady* (1801; New York, 1806), 44–5.

40. Increasingly, this is the only excuse that can be found for Elizabeth—see Elizabeth Benger's remark that her actions in the case of Mary of Scotland were 'no less cruel than pusillanimous, as unwise as unjust' and cannot be excused 'unless we suppose that the strong-minded Elizabeth, like the unhappy Mary, was sometimes made the dupe of crafty colluding heads, who sacrificed her fame and her peace to partial policy and sinister counsels.' *Memoirs of the Life of Mary Queen of Scots* (2 vols., London, 1823), ii. 470.

41. Prologue to Banks's play, reprinted as *The Albion Queens . . . As It is Acted at the Theatre Royal* (London, 1704).

42. *Observations and Remarks upon the Lives and Reigns of King Henry VIII, King Edward VI, Queen Mary I, Queen Elizabeth, and King James I* (1712; 3rd edn., London, 1712), 218.

43. Samuel Richardson, *Clarissa, or the History of a Young Lady* (1748; ed. Angus Ross, Harmondsworth, 1985), 1142 (Letter 370).

44. *Mary Stuart, Queen of the Scots: Being the Secret History of Her Life, and the Real Causes of all Her Misfortunes . . . translated from the French by Mrs. Eliza Haywood* (London, 1725), 207.

45. *The Character of Queen Elizabeth: or, A Full and Clear Account of her Policies, and the Methods of Her Government both in Church and State. Her Virtues and Defects. Together with the Characters of Her Principal Ministers of State* (London, 1693), 340–1.

46. Sophia Lee, *The Recess* (3 vols., London, 1785), iii. 152. For influential readings of *The Recess* that foreground the play in the novel between history and romance see Jane Spencer, *The Rise of the Woman Novelist from Aphra Behn to Jane Austen* (Oxford, 1986), 195–201; Lewis, *Mary Queen of Scots*, 136–146.

47. Rosetta Ballin, *The Statue Room* (3 vols., London, 1790), ii. 135.

48. See, for example, the pair of bronze figures by Mathurin Moreau, *c.*1870, each with face turned to the other, Elizabeth's hand resting on a crown, Mary in an attitude of fear apparently holding pen and ink—Sotheby's catalogue May–June 1989. It was common to depict Elizabeth holding the Queen of Scots's death-warrant—see Sotheby's catalogues, Feb. 1989, Apr. 1989, and July 1976. We are grateful to Derek Dobson for the gift of a ceramic statuette of just such a warrant-clutching Elizabeth, made *c.*1900.

49. *Merrie England* (London, 1851), 108.

50. The Elizabeth who destroys sentimental womanhood is still available in 1846, when the pro-Catholic *The Tudor Sisters: A Story of National Sacrilege* (3 vols., London, 1846) was published. This three-decker novel offers a bold new footnote to official history in the shape of Lady Jane Grey's escape from captivity, connived at by an unusually sentimentalized Mary and contrived by the Catholic Alice Jerningham, maid of honour. Once recaptured in deference to the necessities of history, and in the wake of Wyatt's rebellion (villainously plotted by Elizabeth to cause Jane Grey's downfall because of her better claim to the throne), Mary is obliged to sign Jane Grey's death-warrant despite familiar if relocated repinings: 'the tears of the woman almost blotted out the name as the royal fingers traced it' (iii. 198). Its hostile portrait of Elizabeth culminates in 'a virgin's soliloquy' in which she objects

to wedlock on the grounds that it would deprive her of 'the unfettered joys of a virgin queen' suitable to a 'free-born monarch . . . lusty, fair, and love-begot' (ii. 201, 203–4).

51. See Benedict Anderson, *Imagined Communities: Reflections on the Origins and Spread of Nationalism* (London, 1984), esp. 70 ff.

52. *The Court of Holyrood: fragments of an old story* (2nd edn., Edinburgh, 1822), 192–3. This positioning of Mary as a guarantor of a new, literature-based Scottish national identity had earlier been suggested by her casting as judge of a bardic contest in James Hogg's *The Queen's Wake: A legendary Poem* (Edinburgh, 1813), although her choice of her supposed lover, the foreign Rizzio, for first prize is overruled by the vote of the people.

53. Sheridan, *Plays*, 359.

54. For 'Elizabethan', see the *Oxford English Dictionary* for the first instance in 1817 (in Coleridge's *Biographia Literaria*). *Kenilworth* lived on in a range of genres: see, for example, the popular abridgement *Kenilworth Castle; or, Strange things in the reign of Elizabeth. A romance of the sixteenth century* (London, n.d.); stage versions ranging from mainstream drama *Kenilworth, an historical drama* (*c.*1857) to opera in the shape of Donizetti's *Elisabetta al castello di Kenilworth* (*c.*1854); even as one of a set of dioramas for home consumption, *Kenilworth Castle restored. Changing to Queen Elizabeth's . . .* ('Spooner's protean views', London, n.d. [*c.*1830s]).

55. See John Nichols, *The Progresses and Public Processions of Queen Elizabeth . . .* (3 vols.; vols. i and ii pub. 1788, vol. iii pub. 1807, reprinted in 3 vols. in 1823), which draws on the contemporary account by Francis Laneham and the script for the masque by George Gascoigne, *Princely Pleasures*.

56. For a conspectus of Victorian views of the death of Robsart, see 'The Death of Amy Robsart', *Macmillan's Magazine*, 53 (Dec. 1885), 131–40.

57. Walter Scott, *Kenilworth: A Romance*, ed. J. H. Alexander (Edinburgh, 1993), 317.

58. Scott, first paragraph of the 'Introduction' to *Kenilworth* supplied in the authoritative 'Magnum Opus' edition of his complete novels (Edinburgh, 1829–33). The current Edinburgh edition of the novel excludes this material.

3. GOOD QUEEN BESS AND MERRIE ENGLAND

1. Walter Scott, *Kenilworth*, ed. J. H. Alexander (Edinburgh, 1993), 174.

2. *Good Queen Bess: An Extravaganza* (London, n.d. [*c.*1893]), 37.

3. On this process see also Michael Dobson, 'Falstaff after John Bull: Shakespearean History, Britishness and the Former United Kingdom',

Shakespeare Jahrbuch, 136 (2000), 40–55. On the making of a canon of national culture, especially literary culture, see especially John Brewer, *The Pleasures of the Imagination: English Culture in the Eighteenth Century* (London, 1997), 125–200.

4. Thomas Shadwell, *The Lancashire-Witches, and Teague o Divelly the Irish Priest* (London, 1682), 29–30. On this instance see also Jessica Munns, ' "The Golden Days of Queen Elizabeth": Thomas Shadwell's *The Lancashire Witches* and the Politics of Nostalgia', *Restoration*, 20: 2 (Autumn 1996), 195–216.

5. The music, and possibly the verses added after Fielding's first two, were composed by Richard Leveridge in 1735: see Jeremy Barlow (ed.), *English National Songs* (Broadside Band CD, Saydisc, 1993 CD-SDL 400); Henry Fielding, *The Works of Henry Fielding, Esq; with the life of the author* (2nd edn., 8 vols., London, 1762), i. 520.

6. See M. Dorothy George, *Catalogue of Personal and Political Satires in the British Museum*, vol. ix, BM 13192. We are very grateful to Cindy McCreery for alerting us to the existence of this image.

7. *John Bull; or the True Briton* (London, 1808), 19–20.

8. Mary Deverell, *Mary Queen of Scots; An Historical Tragedy* (London, 1792), 'Prologue'.

9. Thomas Dibdin, *A Metrical History of England; Or, Recollections, in Rhyme, of some of the most prominent Features in our National Chronology, from the Landing of Julius Caesar to the Commencement of the Regency, in 1812* (2 vols., London, 1813).

10. John Dennis, 'To the Honourable George Granville, Esq.', in *The Comical Gallant: or the Amours of Sir John Falstaffe* (London, 1702), Act 2.

11. Nicholas Rowe, 'Some Account of the Life, &c. of Mr. William Shakespear', in Shakespeare, *Works*, ed. Rowe (6 vols., London, 1709), i, pp. viii–ix.

12. We are indebted throughout this discussion to Samuel Schoenbaum: see his *Shakespeare's Lives* (Oxford, 1970: also the revised edition, Oxford, 1991). On the seventeenth-century tradition, see *Shakespeare's Lives* (1970), 75–147, esp. 108–14. On Shakespeare and his queen in anecdote and fiction see also Paul Franssen and Ton Hoenselaars (eds.), *The Author as Character* (Utrecht, 1999), and Maurice O'Sullivan Jr. (ed.), *Shakespeare's Other Lives: Fictional Depictions of the Bard* (Jefferson, NC, 1997).

13. On related uses of Elizabeth in this tradition as guarantor of both Shakespeare's national status and his sexual respectability, see Michael Dobson, 'Bowdler and Britannia: Shakespeare and the National Libido', *Shakespeare Survey 46* (1993), 137–44.

14. See Michael Dobson, *The Making of the National Poet: Shakespeare, Adaptation and Authorship, 1660–1769* (Oxford, 1992), 134–64, esp. 136, 146–7, 154–5.

15. John Bell (publ.), *Bell's edition of Shakespeare's Plays . . .* (9 vols., London, 1774), ix. 6. Less sympathetically, Thomas Davies, seeking to excuse the indelicacy of the brothel scenes in *Pericles* by reference to the court for which he believed they had been written, described Elizabeth as 'a masculine and swearing queen.' Thomas Davies, introduction to *Marina* in *The plays of George Lillo* (*c.*1760; facsimile reprint, ed. Trudy Drucker, 2 vols., New York, 1979).

16. John Dennis, 'Prologue to the Subscribers for *Julius Caesar*,' in *A Collection and Selection of English Prologues and Epilogues* (4 vols., London, 1779), iii. 1–2.

17. Lewis Theobald's *Double Falshood* (London, 1728), 'Prologue, written by Philip Frowde, Esq.' and 'Epilogue, Written by a Friend'.

18. See Dobson, *The Making of the National Poet*, 134–64, esp. 140–4.

19. *Biographica Britannica* (London, 1763), 'Shakespeare'.

20. See Schoenbaum, *Shakespeare's Lives* (1970 edn.), 207–9.

21. *The Oracle*, 23 Jan. 1796: see Schoenbaum, *Shakespeare's Lives* (1991 edn.), 159.

22. Schoenbaum, *Shakespeare's Lives* (1970), 235; George Chalmers, *An Apology for the Believers in the Shakspeare-Papers* (London, 1797), 51–2, 55.

23. Schoenbaum, *Shakespeare's Lives* (1970), 308–9; Richard Ryan, *Dramatic Table Talk: or Scenes, Situations, & Adventures, Serious & Comic, in Theatrical History & Biography* (2 vols., London, 1825), ii. 157.

24. Alfred Edward Carey, *The Dark Lady* (1919; London, 1929), 90.

25. Scott, *Kenilworth*, 173–7.

26. Charles A. Somerset, *Shakspeare's Early Days* (London, 1829), 48.

27. On this opera, see especially Gary Schmidgall, *Shakespeare and Opera* (Oxford, 1990), 331–4.

28. On this painting, see James Fowler, 'David Scott's Queen Elizabeth Viewing the Performance of the "Merry Wives of Windsor" in the Globe Theatre (1840)', in Richard Foulkes (ed.), *Shakespeare and the Victorian Stage* (Cambridge, 1986), 23–38; Geoffrey Ashton, *Catalogue of Paintings at the Theatre Museum, London* (London, 1992), 49–51. On its context among other implicit Victorian pleas for royal patronage of the arts, see Chapter 4.

29. These Victorian genre paintings are very difficult to trace: Haier's painting, for example, is in the keeping of Hartlepool Borough Council, and we are very grateful to their Museums Officer, Frank Savage Caldwell, for sending us a polaroid photograph of it. See the list in Roy Strong, *And When Did You*

Last See Your Father? The Victorian Painter and British History (London, 1978), 161–2.

30. On this novel as a source for Scott's painting see Ashton, *Catalogue*, 50. The book was translated into German by Willibald Alexis: on the German tradition of nineteenth-century historical romances about Shakespeare, in which Elizabeth is equally prominent, see Werner Habicht, 'The Making of the Poet: Fictional Explanations of Shakespeare's Artistic Breakthrough' (unpublished lecture, Shakespeare in Love and the Author as Character conference, University of Utrecht, 1999).

31. Quoted in Schoenbaum, *Shakespeare's Lives* (1970), 380. A compilation of Williams's complete set of three novels about Shakespeare's life appeared in an undated New York edition as *Shakspeare Novels*. Cf. *In Burleigh's Days* (London, 1916), 227: '"I must behold this player who can write sonnets such as you have shown me; he cannot be any ordinary man", added the Queen.' She is later reported to have opined that 'Master Spenser would have to look to the laurels he had so lately won in the "Fairy Queen"' (231).

32. John Collis Snaith, *Anne Feversham* (London, 1914), 246–7. The way in which such imagined private encounters between Elizabeth and Shakespeare have become well-nigh mandatory in historical fiction set in the later sixteenth century is burlesqued in Patrick Barlow's *Shakespeare: The Truth* (London, 1993): see 'Chapter XXI: Did the Queen Meet Shakespeare?' (73–80), which supplies an imaginary dialogue not far removed from the spirit of *Anne Feversham*:

> QUEEN. Who art thou? O saucy fellow?
> SHAKESPEARE. A yeoman bold, my virgin Queen.
> QUEEN. So where art thou from, oh yeoman bold?
> SHAKESPEARE. From leafy Warwickshire, my lovelorn Liege.
> QUEEN. Historic Warwick?
> SHAKESPEARE. No, from Stratford.
> QUEEN. Stratford? . . . Dine with me tonight!

We are grateful to Susannah Herbert for sending us this book.

33. This sudden discovery of unorthodox or plural sexuality as the meeting-ground of Elizabeth and Shakespeare is in part fuelled by an anachronistically psychoanalytic reading of Elizabeth's sometimes androgynous iconography, and in part by the effective 'outing' of Shakespeare produced by Oscar Wilde, both by the publication of *The Portrait of Mr W.H.* and by the ramifications of his own trial. On Elizabeth and perversity in the twentieth century, see Chapter 6.

34. This is the novel, incidentally, which Tom Stoppard claims to have read only superficially so as *not* to plagiarize anything from it while writing his share of *Shakespeare in Love*: as a result of its being mentioned in English reviews of the film it was reissued in 1999 in a new paperback edition, billing it as the story of 'Shakespeare and Lady Viola in love'.

35. A recent advertisement for *Baconiana*, the journal of the Bacon Society, is still urging readers to subscribe so that they can learn the answers to such questions as 'Was Bacon the "one and true inventor" of the Shakespeare *Plays*? Was he the bastard son of Queen Elizabeth?'

36. Most of this story is retold in Anne Meeker's novel *The Queen's Rings* (Chicago, 1936). Shakespeare is an intimate chronicler of Elizabeth's secret life in another sense in *The Queens* by 'Aldemah' (Chicago, 1892), a long, blank verse tragedy, supposedly dictated by Shakespeare's ghost, all about Elizabeth's remorse over the execution of Mary, Queen of Scots. Orville Ward Owen followed suit with *The Historical Tragedy of Mary Queen of Scots. By the author of Hamlet, Richard III, Othello, As You Like It, Etc. Deciphered from the works of Sir Francis Bacon by Orville W. Owen, M.D.* (Detroit, 1894).

37. See, for example, *New Scientist*, 132: 1795 (16 Nov. 1991), 15; Lillian F. Schwartz, 'The Mask of Shakespeare', *Pixel* (Mar./Apr. 1992).

38. See Marcia Pointon, *Hanging the Head: Portraiture and Social Formation in Eighteenth-Century England* (New Haven, 1993), 238–43.

39. On Shakespeare, Elizabeth, and the selling of history, see Barbara Hodgdon, *The Shakespeare Trade* (Philadelphia, 1998), *passim*.

40. Schoenbaum, *Shakespeare's Lives* (1970), 158–9. Cf. Virna Sheard's *A Maid of Many Moods* (1902), in which Shakespeare wears 'a mighty ruff fastened with a great pearl, which, I heard whispered, was one the Queen herself had sent him' (115).

41. The painting was commissioned for the Council House. We are very grateful to Sheena Stoddard, Bristol City Council's Curator of Fine Art, for alerting us to the existence of this splendid picture.

42. This recipe would still be fresh enough to be used as material for a prize poem in 1854 by one Alexander M. Bonar, *Kenilworth. A Prize Poem, Recited at Leamington Speeches, Easter, 1854* (Leamington, 1854).

43. *The Port Folio*, II (Mar. 1821), 162.

44. *The Monthly Review*, 94 (Feb. 1821), 147–9. It is probably no accident that the same year which saw Scott publish *Kenilworth* saw Charles Robert Leslie paint his *May Day Revels in the Reign of Queen Elizabeth*. A late survival of the notion of Elizabeth as the soul of her country's jolliest period is provided by Storm Jameson's *The Decline of Merry England* (Indianapolis, 1930),

which describes Elizabeth's nation as 'a happier England than ever before or since' (68) and declares that on 24 Mar. 1603, as Elizabeth's spirit 'flickered up and died', 'The youth of England was over' (73).

45. Jerome K. Jerome, *Three Men in a Boat* (1889; Harmondsworth, 1957), 49. Cf. the burlesqued Elizabethan pageant-play in E. F. Benson's *Mapp and Lucia* (1931), discussed in Chapter 5, below.

46. Caryl Brahms and S. J. Simon, *No Bed for Bacon* (1941; London, 1999), 252.

4. THE FAERY QUEEN AND VICTORIAN VALUES

1. Elizabeth Longford, *Victoria R.I.* (London, 1964), 31.

2. Helmut and Alison Gernsheim, *Victoria R.: A Biography with Four Hundred Illustrations based on her Personal Photograph Albums* (New York, 1959), 2.

3. Quoted in Richard L. Stein, *Victoria's Year: English Literature and Culture, 1837–1838* (New York and Oxford, 1987), 62.

4. Quoted in Cecil Woodham-Smith, *Queen Victoria: Her Life and Times, 1819–1861* (2 vols., London, 1972), i. 140.

5. However—characteristically, as we shall explain—'the former [was] rated tyrannical and unwomanly, the latter a weak character, deficient in regal dignity'. Leonée Ormond, 'The Spacious Times of Great Elizabeth', *Victorian Poetry*, 25: 3–4 (Autumn/Winter 1987), 29–46: 30.

6. This painting does not seem to have been exhibited at the Royal Academy, and is not dated on the canvas. (We have been unable to trace any mention of it in any of the many contemporary biographical notices: it last surfaced when sold at auction by Phillips of London in 1978). It seems likely, however, that it dates from the early 1840s.

7. Benjamin Disraeli, *Sybil* (1845; London, 1895), 47. Wells's painting may be found reproduced in Gernsheim, *Victoria R.*, 28; a version of Gow's water-colour may be found in Longford, *Victoria R.I.*, facing 160. Gow's picture clearly derives directly from Wells's depiction in its portrayal of Lord Conyngham and the Archbishop of Canterbury who announced the news to the young Queen, but the background has been much abstracted, and Victoria herself idealized even more thoroughly as a young and vulnerable girl.

8. *The Times*, 26 Jan. 1849. Quoted in John William Cole, *The Life and Theatrical Times of Charles Kean, F.S.A.* . . . (2 vols., London, 1859), i. 348–9.

9. See, for example, the remarkable Victorian print of Elizabeth supervising Royal Society-style scientific experiments, reproduced in Catherine Bush, *Elizabeth I* (New York, 1985; rev. edn., London, 1988), 103.

10. F. de Rothschild, *Queen Elizabeth* (London, 1884), 35.

11. This tableau is still one of popular culture's favourite (albeit much-burlesqued) emblems of Elizabeth's reign (see, for example, its use as a running gag in *No Bed For Bacon*, 1941, and its appearance at Elizabeth's exit from *Shakespeare in Love*). It enjoyed something of a revival in the 'New Elizabethan' 1950s: see the film *The Virgin Queen* (1955), in which Richard Todd sacrifices his cloak for Bette Davis (on whom more in our Afterword), and even a straightforward genre painting, Thomas Heath Robinson's *Queen Elizabeth I and Sir Walter Raleigh* (1952).

12. See Gernsheim, *Victoria R.*, 82.

13. Lucy Aikin published her *Memoirs of the Court of Queen Elizabeth* in 1818; Anna Jameson her *Memoirs of Celebrated Female Sovereigns* in 1831; Hannah Lawrence her *Historical Memoirs of the Queens of England* in 1839; Agnes Strickland her hugely popular *Lives of the Queens of England* 1840–9 (and in many editions thereafter, including an abridgement for schools in 1867) and her *Tudor Princesses* in 1868; Mrs Matthew Hall her twelve-volume *History of the Queens of England* 1854–9; Mary Cowden Clarke her *World-Noted Women* in 1858. Of these the most important was certainly Agnes Strickland. Friend of both Sir Walter Scott and Jane Porter, guest at Victoria's coronation in 1838, presented at court in 1840, author of *Queen Victoria from Birth to Bridal* (1840), and dedicating *The Lives of the Queens of England* to Victoria, Strickland's life and work persistently join Victoria with her female predecessors, most especially Elizabeth. Under the conjoined influence of these women's histories and the vast success of the new historical fiction sponsored by Scott, Porter, and others, the new generation of future Academicians (Augustus Leopold Egg, E. M. Ward, William Powell Frith, Goodall, C. Landseer) similarly turned from grand historical panorama to, in Carlyle's words, 'a history composed of small dramatic incidents of the everyday lives of England's great men'. Hilarie Faberman, 'Augustus Leopold Egg, RA (1816–1863)', Ph.D. thesis, Yale, 4 vols., 1983, i. 142.

14. *Romantic Biography of the Age of Elizabeth; or, Sketches of Life from the Bye-Ways of History. By the Benedictine Brethren of Glendalough*, ed. William Cooke Taylor (2 vols., London, 1842), i, facing 90.

15. On 'Fancy portraits' see Sara Stevenson and Helen Bennett, *Van Dyck in Check Trousers: Fancy Dress in Art and Life 1700–1900* (Edinburgh, 1978), 1–3. For photography and Victoria, see Gernsheim, *Victoria R.*, 257–8, 261.

16. Jacob Abbott, *History of Queen Elizabeth* (New York, 1849), 207.

17. Review of Sir Walter Scott's *Kenilworth*, *Quarterly Review*, 26 (Oct. 1822), 143.

18. Attempts were made to assimilate the captive Princess Elizabeth to such Victorian favourites as the victim queens Lady Jane Grey or Mary, Queen of Scots, who inspired sympathetic interest in inverse proportion to their success as monarchs, but in general the future hope of the nation was embarrassed as a woman by the sheer scale of her success.

19. Lord George Gordon Byron, *Lord Byron: The Complete Poetical Works*, ed. Jerome J. McGann (6 vols., Oxford, 1986), vol. v, canto IX, stanza 131.

20. Hugh Campbell, *The Case of Mary Queen of Scots and of Elizabeth Queen of England . . .* (London, 1825), 289.

21. See, respectively, John Lingard, *History of the Reformation* (London, 1819–30); James Mackintosh in *Cabinet Cyclopedia*; Lord James Campbell, *The Lives of the Chief Justices of England* (London, 1849). *Fraser's Magazine for Town and Country*, 48 (Oct. 1853), 376.

22. Jacob Abbott, *History of Queen Elizabeth* (New York, 1849), 69.

23. Quoted in Richard L. Stein, *Victoria's Year: English Literature and Culture, 1837–1838* (New York, 1987), 74. Cf. the Victorian genre painting *Lady Jane Grey's Reluctance to Accept the Crown of England*, also by C. R. Leslie, 1828.

24. For the portrait of Victoria and Albert in their costumes for the Plantagenet Ball in 1842, see Gernsheim, *Victoria R.*, 75; for the Winterhalter, see Longford, *Victoria R.I.*, facing 193. For a discussion of Winterhalter's iconography of royal power in this painting, see Ira B. Nadel, 'Portraits of the Queen', *Victorian Poetry*, 25 (1987), 171. Even the more hostile and anxious portrayals of the Queen's startling fertility as a growing burden to the nation's taxpayers still concentrated on Victorian wifedom—the wife and mother as consumer of men's wealth. For the unfocused and anxious efforts to think Victoria as queen, see Stein, *Victoria's Year* 60–2. For some examples of hostile cartoons of the fertile Queen, see Gernsheim, *Victoria R.*, 72, 73, 77.

25. *Illustrated London News*, 1 (1842), 40.

26. See Sir Roy Strong, *And When Did You Last See Your Father?; The Victorian Painter and British History* (London, 1978), 96–7.

27. Margaret Homans, '"To the Queen's Private Apartments": Royal Family Portraiture and the Construction of Victoria's Sovereign Obedience', *Victorian Studies* (Fall 1993), 1–41: 4.

28. See Nadel, 'Portraits of the Queen,' and Gernsheim, *Victoria R.*, *passim*.

29. 'Of Queens' Gardens', in *Sesame and Lilies* (1864; 3rd edn., New York, 1888), 126.

30. J.R. Green, *A Short History of the English People* (1875; New York, 1876), 381.

31. Beatrice Marshall, *The Queen's Knight-Errant: A Story of the Days of Sir Walter Raleigh* (London, 1905), 178.

32. Anna Jameson, *Memoirs of Celebrated Female Sovereigns* (2nd edn., 2 vols., London, 1834), ii. 322.

33. Ibid. i. 296, 298, 284.

34. Homans, '"To the Queen's Private Apartments"', 4.

35. Charles Kingsley, 'Sir Walter Raleigh and His Time', in *Plays and Puritans and Other Historical Essays* (1873; London, 1879), 123.

36. William Russell, *Extraordinary Women: Their Girlhood and Early Life* (London, 1857), 82.

37. The erotics of this bedroom encounter may usefully be glossed by the gaspingly indiscreet parallel scene in William-Henry Ireland's highly coloured fantasy *Effusions of Love* (1805), in which the doomed Essex-like favourite Chatelard witnesses the undressing of the Queen of Scots and fatally betrays his infatuated presence:

> Upon your table stood the blazing tapers, whose light beamed full upon you: forth from the bandeau that enchained your hair I saw your flowing ringlets, of all art divested, hang loosely o'er your falling shoulders. . . . What a profusion of enchanting tresses wanton'd o'er your heaving bosom, seeming to kiss the thrones of bliss divested of all covering. . . . A torrent of luscious joy rush'd on my senses!—. . . I could no longer curb my raging transports—I rushed forth; then uttering thy dear name, my queen, sunk o'ercome with—* *

[William-Henry Ireland], *Effusions of Love from Chatelar to Mary Queen of Scotland. Translated from a Gallic Manuscript. . . . Interspersed with Songs, Sonnets, and Notes Explanatory . . .* (London, 1805), 121.

38. This douche of cold water to sentiment and romance had been remarked upon occasionally over the course of the eighteenth century: in 1740, noting 'the Perplexity and Irresolution with which the Queen appear'd' over deciding to execute Essex which 'has caused several Romances and Plays to be wrote, in which *Elizabeth* is represented to be struggling between Love and Anger, not knowing which of the Passions she should obey', one writer concluded sardonically that 'as she was now in the sixty-eighth Year of her Age, it seems something surprising the Motions of Love should be so very violent'. *History of the Life and Reign of Queen Elizabeth . . .* (2 vols., London, 1740), ii. 345. Horace Walpole, tongue firmly in cheek, foregrounded the same problem in an essay entitled 'On the Love of Old Women' in 1753:

I am not clear that length of years, especially in heroic minds, does not increase rather than abate the sentimental flame. The great ELIZABETH, whose passion for the unfortunate earl of ESSEX is justly a favourite topic with all who delight in romantic history, was fully sixty-eight when she condemned her lover to death for slighting her endearments.

Horace Walpole, *The World. By Adam Fitz-Adam* (No. XXVIII, Thurs. July 12, 1753), reprinted in *Fugitive Pieces in Verse and Prose* (Strawberry Hill, 1758), 121–2. Such comments, though, did nothing to displace an unembarrassedly amorous reading of the Elizabeth–Essex relationship from contemporary novels and plays: it was not until 1807 that Elizabeth Inchbald, introducing Jones's play *The Earl of Essex* in her *British Theatre* series, was able to remark that the respective ages of the protagonists might have provided material for a comedy rather than a tragedy.

39. [Mary Roberts], *The Royal Exile; or, Poetical Epistles of Mary, Queen of Scots, During Her Captivity in Scotland . . .* (2 vols., London, 1822), i. 171.

40. Walter Savage Landor, 'Queen Elizabeth, Cecil, Duke of Anjou, and De La Motte Fenélon', in *Imaginary Conversations* (1824–9), *The Works of Walter Savage Landor* (2 vols., London, 1846), ii. 177.

41. We are indebted to Dr Paul Barlow of the University of Northumbria at Newcastle for this reference: the copy of this 1860s women's magazine from which it is drawn is undated.

42. Quoted in Faberman, 'Augustus Leopold Egg', i. 151. In 1916, Beatrice Marshall, perhaps remembering this painting, relates exactly such an episode as taking place immediately after Essex's execution: 'And it was now that the Queen asked to be shown her image in a 'true mirror' without powder or paint, and started at the sight of herself as she really was, shrivelled and wrinkled by the hand of time.' Beatrice Marshall, *Queen Elizabeth* (London, 1916), 183. Although this episode is almost certainly apocryphal, there was a well-established tradition of stories about mirrors and Elizabeth, in particular a strain of anecdote that dealt with Elizabeth's dislike of mirrors after a certain age, already familiar when Ben Jonson retailed it in his cups to Drummond of Hawthornden in 1619: 'Queen Elizabeth never saw her self after she became old in a true glass . . .' *Notes of Ben Jonson's Conversations with William Drummond of Hawthornden. January MDCXIX* (London, 1842), 23.

43. See, for example, *Miss Leslie's Magazine*, 3 (Jan. 1844), 19; *New Mirror* (6 May 1843), 77.

44. Longford, *Victoria R.I.*, 195–7.
45. Kingsley, 'Sir Walter Raleigh and his Time', 124–5.
46. *Harlequin and Good Queen Bess, or, Merrie England in the Olden Time. A Grand Historical! Metaphorical!! Allegorical!!! and Diabolical!!!! PANTOMIME, performed for the first time, on Wednesday, 26th December, 1849 at the Theatre Royal, Drury Lane. Writtten by the author of 'Bluff King Hal'* (London, 1849), 9.
47. Edward Spencer Beesly, *Queen Elizabeth* (London, 1892), 123.
48. Andrew Halliday and Frederick Lawrance, *Kenilworth, or, Ye Queene, Ye Earle, and Ye Maydenne* (London, 1859), 3, 6.
49. Russell, *Extraordinary Women*, 91.
50. For a complementary reading of contemporary Victorian representations of other female monarchs as embodying anxieties about Victoria's queenship as itself excess, see Adrienne Auslander Munich, 'Queen Victoria, Empire and Excess', *Tulsa Studies in Women's Literature*, 6: 2 (Fall 1987), 265–81: see also her '"Capture the Heart of a Queen": Gilbert and Sullivan's Rites of Conquest', *The Centennial Review*, 48: 1 (1984), 23–44.
51. Longford, *Victoria R.I.*, 380.
52. The most famous example of the 'girlhood' genre is Mary Cowden Clarke's *The Girlhood of Shakespeare's Heroines* (1850–2). Other examples would include Thomas Trollope's *The Girlhood of Catherine d'Medici* (London, 1856); William Adams's *Child-life and Girlhood of Remarkable Women* (London, 1883); Jane Stoddart's *The Girlhood of Mary Queen of Scots* (1900); Katherine Cather, *Childhood Stories of Famous Women* (New York, London, 1924). These supplement innumerable examples of juvenile fiction. Paintings of childhood by Dante Gabriel Rossetti (*The Girlhood of Mary*, 1848) and Millais (most pertinently the famous *Boyhood of Raleigh*, 1870, on which more below) clearly participate also in this mode.
53. This picture was accompanied in the Royal Academy catalogue by the following quotation: 'The king's grace was well pleased to see his heir so goodly a child of his age, although the little Lady Elizabeth was considered worthy of the honour of being admitted to keep company with the young Prince Edward, her brother, her father took but little note of her.'
54. Harriet T. Comstock, *The Girlhood of Elizabeth: A Romance of English History* (London, 1914), 2.
55. *Illustrated London News*, 90 (Jan.–June 1887), 117–18.
56. de Rothschild, *Queen Elizabeth*, 45.
57. Beesly, *Queen Elizabeth*, 234–5.
58. H. C. Bailey, *The Lonely Queen* (London, 1911), 157.

59. Rudyard Kipling, 'The Looking-glass', in *Rewards and Fairies* (New York, 1910), 53–4.
60. Rudyard Kipling, *Poems: Definitive Edition* (New York, 1940), 734.

5. AN EMPRESS AND HER ADVENTURERS

1. Richard Helgerson makes this point in *Forms of Nationhood: The Elizabethan Writing of England* (Chicago, 1992), 15–16.
2. Raleigh's eventual execution under James I—supposedly at the insistence of the Spanish ambassador—had been much debated and lamented in seventeenth- and early eighteenth-century pamphlets, especially those about court favourites, but his stock as a national hero rose to unprecedented heights in the Victorian age.
3. 'A Dream of Fair Women', Alfred, Lord Tennyson, *The Poems of Tennyson*, ed. Christopher Ricks (2nd edn., 3 vols., Harlow, 1987), i. 481.
4. Tom Bevan, *Sea Dogs All! A Tale of Forest and Sea* (London, 1907), 142. This tradition found perhaps its last unburlesqued expression in a BBC Radio 4 *World History* schools broadcast of Sept. 1967, 'Drake Sails Round the World', which opens and closes its dramatized account of Drake's circumnavigation with just such cosy interviews between the bluff sea-dog and his queen. We are grateful to Penny Fielding for a copy of the gramophone record of this memorable programme (BBC records RESR 20M, 1971).
5. Robert Haynes Cave, *In the Days of Good Queen Bess* (London, 1897), p. viii.
6. A. E. Aldington, *The Queen's Preferment* (London, 1896), 14.
7. Ibid. 228.
8. Cave, *In the Days of Good Queen Bess*, 188–9.
9. Beatrice Marshall, *The Queen's Knight-Errant; A Story of the Days of Sir Walter Raleigh* (London, 1905), 216.
10. *The Gladstone Diaries* ed. M. D. R. Foot and H. C. G. Matthew (14 vols., Oxford, 1968–94), i. 45.
11. For a general overview see Edward R. Norman, *Anti-Catholicism in Victorian England* (London, 1968).
12. See also Frank James Mathew's *One Queen Triumphant* (1899), and Felicia Curtis's *Under the Rose* (1911).
13. Mrs Markham, pseud. [Elizabeth Penrose], *A History of England . . . with Conversations at the end of each chapter. For the use of young Persons* (2 vols., 3rd edn., London, 1829), ii. 81.

14. On Yonge's novel, see Jayne Elizabeth Lewis, *Many Queen of Scots* (London and New York, 1998).

15. J. A. Froude, *History of England from the Fall of Wolsey to the Death of Elizabeth* (12 vols., London, 1858–70), xi (1870). 8. This is the revised form of his *History of England from the Fall of Wolsey to the defeat of the Spanish Armada* (1856–70).

16. Ibid. xi. 9.

17. Ibid. vii (1864). 12.

18. Ibid. xii (1870). 531; and vii (1864). 425.

19. On the Hakluyt Society see D. B. Quinn, 'Hakluyt's reputation', in *The Hakluyt Handbook*, ed. D. B. Quinn (2 vols., London, 1974), ii. 147–8; also, L. E. Pennington, 'Secondary Works on Hakluyt and His Circle', *The Hakluyt Handbook*, ii. 588–9.

20. James Anthony Froude, 'England's Forgotten Worthies', originally published in the *Westminster Review* and reprinted in *Short Studies on Great Subjects* (London, 1924), 314, 315.

21. F. de Rothschild, *Queen Elizabeth* (London, 1884), 27.

22. The only earlier treatment of the New World voyages to our knowledge is John Cartwright Cross's stage spectacular *Sir Francis Drake and Iron Arm* (1800) which tells the story of Oxenham's Spanish love affair and the firing of Carthagena in a strictly heroic/romantic mode.

23. Mrs Markham, *A History of England*, ii. 122.

24. Charles Kingsley, *Westward Ho!* (London, n.d.), 352–3.

25. Charles Kingsley, *Plays and Puritans and Other Historical Essays* (London, 1873), 122.

26. Ibid. 124–5.

27. Ibid. 694.

28. A certain care is needed, however, in making this claim: John Hollins had painted his *The Circumnavigator Drake receiving the honour of knighthood from Queen Elizabeth on board his ship, the Golden Hind, in Deptford, 1581* as early as 1846, perhaps not coincidentally, in the same year as the Hakluyt Society was formed. But grand civic art seems to demand a greater popular audience than Royal Academy history-painting, and an audience which has already absorbed an implied triumphal narrative.

29. 'England's Forgotten Worthies', 337–8.

30. Leonée Ormond, 'The Spacious Times of Great Elizabeth', *Victorian Poetry*, 25 (Autumn/Winter 1987), 29–46: 38.

31. J. W. Burrows, *A Liberal Descent: Victorian Historians and the English Past* (Cambridge, 1981), 232.

32. Henry St John, *The Voyage of the 'Avenger' in the Days of Dashing Drake* (London, 1898), 367. It may be pertinent to mention here a curious artefact in our possession, apparently nearly contemporary with this novel, an approximately A4-sized card bearing, at the top, a coloured likeness of a severe-looking Elizabeth, in profile, with a halberd jutting beyond her; beneath is a picture of a stormy sea with the prows of galleons ploughing through it. Into this card are cut two rectangular holes of the same size as a standard late nineteenth-century small portrait photograph: this composite representation of Elizabeth as victrix of the Armada has apparently been designed as a matte within which to mount and frame portraits of naval ratings.

33. Respectively, Harry Collingwood, *Two Gallant Sons of Devon: A Tale of the Days of Queen Bess* (London, 1913), preface; and J. S. Fletcher, *The Remarkable Adventure of Walter Trelawney, Parish 'Prentice of Plymouth in the Year of the Great Armada* (London, 1894), 6.

34. de Rothschild, *Queen Elizabeth*, 45.

35. Burrows, *A Liberal Descent*, 231.

36. James Rennell Rodd, *Ballads of the Fleet and other Poems* (London, 1897), 47–8.

37. Rudyard Kipling, *Rewards and Fairies* (New York, 1910), 37.

38. Ibid. 42.

39. Ibid. 49–50.

40. At the same time it does not seem too fanciful to suggest that in some ways Kipling's story of the deadly Gloriana displaces some remaining anxieties about the cost of Victoria's imperial adventure, anxieties that he initially formulated in 'The Widow at Windsor' (from 'Barrack-Room Ballads') in 1898, in which the old Victoria figures as the Queen of Spades and a dreadful devouring mother to 'Missis Victorier's sons':

> Walk wide o' the Widow at Windsor,
> For 'alf o' Creation she owns:
> We 'ave bought 'er the same with the sword an' the flame,
> An' we've salted it down with our bones.

Rudyard Kipling's Verse. Definitive Edition (New York, 1940), 411.

41. Kipling, *Rewards and Fairies*, 52.

42. Cave, *In the Days of Good Queen Bess*, p. viii.

43. Kitty Barne, *Adventurers: A Pageant Play* (London, 1931), p. iii.

44. E. F. Benson, *Mapp and Lucia* (1931; New York, 1985), 3.

45. Ibid. 70, 72, 11.

46. Virginia Woolf, *Between the Acts* (1941; London, 1990), 52.

47. Virginia Woolf, *Between the Acts* (1941; London, 1990), 52.
48. Ibid. 53.
49. Robert Southey, 'The Spanish Armada', in *The Poetical Works of Robert Southey, Collected by himself. In ten Volumes* (10 vols., London, 1853–4), ii. 188.
50. Robert Anderson, *The Poetical Works of Robert Anderson* (2 vols., Carlisle, 1820), ii. 188.
51. John Thelwall, *The Trident of Albion: An Epic Effusion . . .* (Liverpool, 1805), 32, ll. 105–22.
52. *The Complete Works of Lord Macaulay* (12 vols., London, 1898), xii. 496–500.
53. Thomas Hornblower Gill, 'November 19th. The Spanish Armada', *The Anniversaries. Poems in Commemoration of Great Men and Great Events* (Cambridge, 1858). Chadwyck-Healey English Poetry data-base.
54. William Cox Bennett, 'The Armada', in *Songs for Sailors* (London, 1872), pp. viii, 66. Originally published as part of his *Proposals for and Contribution to a Ballad History of England and the States Sprung From Her* (London, 1868).
55. Algernon Charles Swinburne, *The Poems of Algernon Charles Swinburne* (6 vols., London, 1904), iii. 201.
56. Crona Temple, *Knighted by The Admiral; or, The Days of the Great Armada* (London, 1890), 95–6. This book was explicitly designed as reading for Empire Day.
57. Aubrey de Vere, *The Poetical Works of Aubrey de Vere* (London, 1884). Chadwyck-Healey English Poetry data-base.
58. Ormond, 'The Spacious Times of Great Elizabeth', 44.
59. Emily Henrietta Hickey, *Verse-Tales, Lyrics and Translations* (Liverpool, 1880). Chadwyck-Healey English Poetry data-base.
60. Robert Anslow, *The Defeat of the Spanish Armada. A Tercentenary Ballad* (London, 1888), 10.
61. W. H. Ireland, *Ballads in Imitation of the Antient* (London, 1801); Sir Henry John Newbolt, 'Drake's Drum', in *Poems: New and Old* (London, 1921).
62. James Rennell Rodd, *Ballads of the Fleet and Other Poems* (London, 1897); and the later edition of 1907, available on the Chadwyck-Healey English Poetry data-base.
63. On this film, and its perceived patriotism, see Sue Harper, *Picturing the Past: The Rise and Fall of the British Costume Film* (London, 1994), 41–2.
64. Louis Napoleon Parker, *Drake: A Pageant Play* (London, 1914), 117.
65. Rudyard Kipling, *Rudyard Kipling's Verse* (London, 1940; repr. 1977), 721.
66. A. E. W. Mason, *Fire Over England* (London, 1936), 14–15.
67. Ibid. 18.
68. Ibid. 18.

69. On the cool reception of the film of *Fire Over England* in Britain, because it was overly patriotic for the uncertain mood of the late 1930s, see Harper, *Picturing the Past*: on another Armada swashbuckler aimed at American filmgoers, Michael Curtiz's *The Sea Hawk*, see Afterword, below.

70. W. C. Sellar and R. J. Yeatman, *1066 and All That* (London, 1930), 59.

71. Caryl Brahms and S. J. Simon, *No Bed for Bacon* (1941; London, 1999), 96.

72. Ibid. 180, 182.

73. Ibid. 208.

74. Margaret Irwin, *Young Bess* (London, 1946), 24.

6. ELIZABETH MODERNIZED

1. Alfred Dodd, *The Marriage of Elizabeth Tudor* (London, 1940), pp. vii–viii. 'The truth is,' says Dodd,

   > these writers forgot the prime thing in remembering she was our greatest English Queen. They forgot that she was at heart a simple woman of primal instincts with the Eternal Feminine strong within her—that the desire for love in the most intimate sense as sweetheart, companion, wife and mother beat quite as fiercely in her breast as in the heart of the average maiden longing and dreaming of the arrival of Prince Charming who will transform all the grey hues into purple and gold. (p. vii)

   Typically for his time, Dodd claims that Elizabeth was secretly married to Leicester and bore him two children (one of them Bacon, a.k.a. 'Shakespeare': see Chapter 3).

2. See ll. 279–91 in the 'Fire Sermon' section ('Elizabeth and Leicester | Beating oars . . .'), where this allusion comes between the sordid encounter between the typist and the house agent's clerk and the laments of the dead Thames maidens, one of them 'undone' near the site of Elizabeth's own death: 'Richmond and Kew | Undid me. By Richmond I raised my knees | Supine on the floor of a narrow canoe' (ll. 293–5). *The Complete Poems and Plays of T. S. Eliot* (London, 1969), 70.

3. W. C. Sellar and R. J. Yeatman, *1066 and All That* (London, 1930), 58–9.

4. On this novel, see also Chapter 3.

5. Strachey had in fact made an early attempt to render this story in a blank verse drama entitled *Essex: A Tragedy* (1909).

6. *The Times*, 5 Feb. 1996, 3. For a sampling of other 'abnormal' Elizabeths see Ellan Calhoun Wilson, *England's Eliza* (Cambridge, Mass., 1939), 139.

7. Mrs Wilfrid Ward, *Tudor Sunset* (London, 1932), 17. On the dissemination and reception of Strachey's book, especially in America, see Barbara Hodgdon, *The Shakespeare Trade* (Philadelphia, 1998), 123–8.

8. For Woolf's views of Elizabeth and Essex see, for example, *The Diary of Virginia Woolf*, ed. Anne Olivier Bell (5 vols., Harmondsworth, 1979–85), 28 Nov. 1928; *The Letters of Virginia Woolf*, ed. Nigel Nicolson (6 vols., London, 1981), 15 Feb. 1929; *Diary*, 16 Nov. 1931; for her considered appraisal of Strachey's *Elizabeth and Essex* see her essay 'The Art of Biography'; for her discussion with Strachey in Feb. 1926, *Letters*, iii. 242.

9. See Alice Fox, *Virginia Woolf and the Literature of the English Renaissance* (Oxford, 1990); also Virginia Woolf *Orlando: A Biography* (1928; London, 1990), 11–12.

10. *Times Literary Supplement*, 30 Dec. 1909, 516, reprinted in *Books and Portraits: Some Further Selections from the Literary and Biographical Writings of Virginia Woolf*, ed. Mary Lyon (London, 1991); *The Collected Essays of Virginia Woolf*, ed. Andrew McNeillie (4 vols., London, 1986–), ii. 17; *Collected Essays*, iv. 205 ff.

11. Woolf, *Orlando*, 212.

12. Sally Potter, *Orlando: A Screenplay* (London, 1994), 9.

13. Lewis Broad, *Queens, Crowns and Coronations* (London, 1952), 173–4.

14. Benjamin Britten, *Gloriana* (1953); Plomer's libretto accompanying the CD recording of the Welsh National Opera (1993), 216 ff.

15. Lord Drogheda, *Double Harness* (London, 1976), 239–40; quoted in *Britten's Gloriana*, ed. Paul Banks (Woodbridge, 1993), 14.

16. *Coronation Glory: A Pageant of Queens, 1559–1953* (London: London Express Newspapers, 1953), 9.

17. One other New Elizabethan take on the Elizabeth-and-her-wigs motif demands citation here, a novel by 'Lozania Prole', *The Little Wig-Maker of Bread Street* (London, 1959).

18. Anne Ring, *The Story of Princess Elizabeth* (London, 1930), 6.

19. Ibid. 5–6.

20. 'A Sixteenth Century Princess Elizabeth at Hatfield, A Poem by Lord David Cecil', in *The Princess Elizabeth Gift Book*, ed. Cynthia Asquith and Eileen Bigland (London, c.1935), 135.

21. Nevill Coghill, *The Masque of Hope* (Oxford, 1948), 18–20.

22. A. L. Rowse predicted a new Elizabethan age as early as June 1942 in the *Evening Standard*. On the children's magazine see Elizabeth Longford, *The Queen: The Life of Elizabeth II* (New York, 1983), 170; Philip Gibbs, *The New Elizabethans* (London, 1953); *Daily Express*, 11 Feb. 1952.

23. Broad, *Queens, Crowns and Coronations*, 176.

24. Richard Dimbleby, *Elizabeth Our Queen* (London, 1953), 179.

25. Richmal Crompton, 'William the New Elizabethan', in *William and the Moon Rocket* (1954; London, 1991), 127–50: 127. Appropriately, their sole victim is not a true 'foreigner' at all but a retired Indian Civil Servant. The story redeems itself for a post-war, post imperial version of New Elizabethan patriotism when William and his friends find treasure during their digging—the family silver of the local grandee, buried and lost when his house was destroyed in a wartime air-raid—and persuade the grandee to surrender to nationalization by displaying it in a museum. We are grateful to Dinah Birch for alerting us to the existence of this valuable text.

26. Geoffrey Willans and Ronald Searle, *Whizz for Attomms* (1956) in *Molesworth* (Harmondsworth, 1999), 214. We are indebted to Cordelia Hall for drawing our attention to the immortal Molesworth's engagement with New Elizabethanism.

27. Eileen Murray, 'Elizabeth of England', in *Queen Elizabeth: An Anthology* (Ilfracombe, Devon, 1953), 124.

28. See the approved souvenir programme, which remarks on the coronation ring as that by which Elizabeth I had declared herself wedded to her people. *The Coronation of Her Majesty Queen Elizabeth II* (London, 1953), 29. See also *Country Life*'s coronation number, which contains an advertisement for some land agents which makes so bold as to offer an Elizabethan prayer for Elizabeth II under a facsimile of Elizabeth I's signature on page 1, and an advertisement for luxury cars topped with an Elizabethan scenario of trading English luxuries in the New World.

29. Marion Crawford, *Elizabeth the Queen: The Story of Britain's New Sovereign* (New York, 1952), 105, 5. This is the American edition of *Queen Elizabeth II* published in Britain in 1952. *Mother and Queen* is the American edition of *Happy and Glorious* published in Britain in 1953.

30. Ibid. 203.

31. See Judith Campbell, *Queen Elizabeth: A Biography* (New York, 1979), 9.

32. The Queen's Christmas broadcast, 'Christmas 1953', in *A Queen Speaks To Her People* (Inglewood, Australia, 1977), 10.

33. *Country Life*, coronation number (1953), 44.

34. Edward Abbott Parry, *England's Elizabeth, being the memories of Matthew Bedale* (London, 1904), 53–4.

35. Elswyth Thane, *The Tudor Wench* (New York, 1932), 73. The novel was published in Britain in 1933.

36. Ibid. 101.

37. Edith Sitwell, *Fanfare for Elizabeth* (London, 1946), 32.
38. Ibid. 226.
39. Ibid. 115.
40. Margaret Irwin, *Young Bess* (London, 1946), 3.
41. Ibid. 255.
42. Ibid. 437.
43. Alison Light, '"YOUNG BESS": Historical Novels and Growing Up', *Feminist Review* 33 (Autumn 1989), 58–71: 68. Light offers a fascinating essay on the ways in which the historical novel of the 1940s and 1950s kept open 'the potential for wayward subjectivities outside of the norms on offer—or differently shaped within them'. However, we would disagree with her contention that the young Elizabeth II would have appeared the polar opposite to Irwin's heroine because 'her sexuality was all but nonexistent'; any perusal of the materials surrounding the princess's wedding and coronation will find them to be suffused with romantic sexuality.
44. Sydney W. Carroll, *The Imperial Votaress* (London, 1947), preface.
45. The *reductio ad absurdum* of this notion would eventually be achieved by one of the few unabashedly pornographic treatments of Gloriana, Roger Bowdler's *The Queen's Bedfellow* (1975), which updates the apocryphal post-Essex favourite into an enormously well-endowed actor-gigolo who succeeds, unlike all other previous comers, in deflowering the Virgin Queen, to her pathetic gratitude and at some considerable physical cost to himself, bravely borne. The mildly necrophiliac buzz that this text gives off heralds the re-entry of the figure of the old Queen in the later 1970s.
46. Josephine Delves-Broughton, *Crown Imperial* (1949), 68. The only earlier version of Elizabeth's and Leicester's secret and indeed legitimate domestic bliss is provided by those initially American conspiracy theories, pioneered by Orville Ward Owen in the 1890s, that identify Francis Bacon not just as the secret author of the Shakespeare canon but as the unacknowledged son of Elizabeth by Leicester: see Chapter 3.
47. Ibid. 185.
48. Ibid. 401.
49. Master Skylark comes to sing in front of Elizabeth, and pleases her so much that she grants him one favour—her displeasure when he asks to go home is only softened by her gratification at his laudable love for his mother.
50. Little Sunbeam pleads successfully to the Queen for the release of a Scottish supporter of Mary, Queen of Scots; Perdita, this 'small, loyal subject', so engrosses Elizabeth that she chooses to be late for a ball held in her honour.
51. Alexandra Elizabeth Sheedy, *She Was Nice to Mice* (New York, 1975), 94–5.

This book's treatments of the Essex affair, of Elizabeth's relations with Shakespeare (the mice find him boring, and some of them chew up the manuscript of *Macbeth*), and especially of the Queen's death ('I nestled into her hair and cried and cried', 92), are particularly commendable. Sheedy grew up to become a Hollywood actress.

52. Evelyn Anthony, *All the Queen's Men* (London, 1960), 31.
53. Elizabeth Jenkins, *Elizabeth and Leicester: A Biography* (1961; New York, 1962), jacket blurb. This cultural formation was still alive and kicking in Silver Jubilee year; Constance Heaven's *The Queen and the Gypsy* (London, 1977), set in the first two years of Elizabeth's reign, allows Leicester, though only temporarily, to make a woman of the Queen: 'She knew then that for months, years maybe, she would have to fight him as well as herself. This night in this room was separate, apart from their ordinary lives. Here she had not been Queen, here she had known the simple joy of a woman who loves and is loved, and it must be forgotten. It could never come again. . . . She must be Queen first and woman afterwards . . .' (271).
54. Alice Harwood, *So Merciful a Queen, So Cruel a Woman* (London, 1958), 133.
55. For an alternative adventuress paired with the Queen, see Jan Westcott's treatment of Bess of Hardwick's career in *The Tower and the Dream* (1973). This amounts to the study of the interrelated fates of two sexy, wilful, liberated, politic, scheming, and hugely ambitious career women.
56. Rosalind Miles's choice of title for her first-person airport blockbuster *I, Elizabeth* (1994) wittily converts the historical icon herself back into a story-telling subjectivity by an elegantly outrageous typo supported by a strategic comma; but the narrative itself makes clear that the Queen only fully inhabits this genre of subjectivity when she's in the habit of full sex. Miles's novel, however, was not the first time the Queen narrated herself at full length; that innovation must be credited to Jean Plaidy's *Queen of this Realm* (1984).
57. Graham and Heather Fisher, *The Crown and the Ring. The Story of the Queen's Years of Marriage and Monarchy* (London, 1971), 25–6, 27. The new assimilation of the two Elizabeths in the 1970s as fellow sufferers from the cares of state is further exemplified in the American Ellen Knill's *Queen Elizabeth I Paper Dolls to Color* (Santa Barbara, Calif., 1973), which for no stated reason boasts a frontispiece (like the book's other images, a line-drawing, to be completed in crayon) depicting a dutiful, unsmiling, uniformed Elizabeth II receiving the salute at the Trooping of the Colour. On the long-running association between Elizabeth I and dolls which this popular, much-reprinted publication also exemplifies, see Chapter 1 above. Cf. the very un-New Elizabethan take on Elizabeth as a test-case in 'the

pressures and the penalties of Power . . . The impermissible sacrifice of self which Power demands and gets' offered by Robert Bolt's Elizabeth v. Mary play *Vivat! Vivat! Regina!*, first performed in 1970. Robert Bolt, *Vivat! Vivat! Regina!* (New York, 1971), p. ix.

58. A comparable official, even grandiose tone and scope marks the two big books dealing with the iconography of Elizabeth that appeared out of the academy in the mid-1970s, Frances Yates's *Astraea* (1975) and Roy Strong's *The Cult of Elizabeth* (1977).

59. She is a performer, moreover, who brings to the role not only a slightly harder-edged version of what might elsewhere make a perfect BBC female newsreader's voice, but ghosts of a much less official public past—in the form of recollections of her performances as Charlotte Corday in Weiss's *Marat/Sade*, or as the unfaithful Hampstead wife in *Sunday Bloody Sunday* or, especially, as the liberated (and occasionally topless) Gudrun Brangwen in Ken Russell's 1969 film of Lawrence's *Women in Love*. On Jackson's Elizabeth, see also Hodgdon, *The Shakespeare Trade*, 147–60.

60. A. S. Byatt, *The Virgin in the Garden* (1978; Harmondsworth, 1981), 10.

61. Ibid. 15.

62. Startling though it is, Jarman's piece is not a one-off; it crystallizes an implosion happening piecemeal in the culture at large. For while Barking Arts Council staged *Merrie England*, Edward German's nostalgic operetta about Elizabeth I, on the steps of their Town Hall in honour of the Jubilee, this doubling between the two queens seemed less resonant than that sprung at the Royal Windsor Big Top Show in May, when the Queen was confronted with a double parody of queenship and womanliness in the shape of Edna Everage impersonating her. A man impersonating a queen is not so far distant from the celebration of the perversity of the first Elizabeth.

63. On 'we are a grandmother', see Hugo Young, *One of Us: A Biography of Margaret Thatcher* (1989; rev. edn., London, 1991), 491. Many apocryphal and nearly apocryphal stories in circulation at the time made the same point: such is the story, retailed by John Pearson, for example, of 'how Mrs. Thatcher arrived at some royal occasion and was most disturbed to find that she had chosen an identical outfit to Her Majesty's': 'To avoid this happening again the prime minister's office sent a message to the Palace expressing regret, and suggesting that in future Downing Street might be informed of what her Majesty would wear when the Prime Minister was present. Back came a polite refusal, with the explanation that the queen never notices what any other ladies wear.' John Pearson, *The Selling of the Royal Family: The*

Mystique of the British Monarchy (New York, 1986), 323. On public awareness of this quasi- or would-be royalty, cf. the popular nicknaming of the pound coin the 'Maggie' on its introduction in 1982 on the grounds that it was 'brassy, and thought it was a sovereign'.

64. See Marina Warner, *Monuments and Maidens* (1985; London, 1996), who notes the role of the media in conferring on Thatcher an intimate identification with Britannia (38–42).

65. Ibid. 41. At the same time, as Hugo Young points out, she was meticulously 'feminine' about her appearance, going to the astonishing lengths of showing off her wardrobe on television and discussing even her underwear. Hugo Young, *One Of Us* (London, 1989), 307.

66. Ibid. 492.

67. John Campbell, 'After the Bombshell of Bruges', *TLS* (25 Nov. 1994), 5.

68. On cross-dressing and its many potential valences, see Marjorie Garber, *Vested Interests: Cross-Dressing and Cultural Anxiety* (New York, 1992); on Elizabeth as always-already in drag, but as an exception, see 28.

69. Richard Curtis and Ben Elton, *Blackadder: The Whole Damn Dynasty* (1998; Harmondsworth, 1999), 124.

70. Richard Morrison, 'Ruff Trade in Political Intrigue', *The Times*, 2 Sept. 1994.

71. It is no coincidence that the 1980s had already seen two plays invested in the triumph of Mary, Queen of Scots (Liz Lochhead's *Mary, Queen of Scots Got Her Head Chopped Off*, and Dario Fo's *Elizabeth: Almost By Chance a Woman*, though the first is interested in Mary, Queen of Scots as an embodiment of Scotland, and the second in her as the embodiment of Catholic Europe), not to mention a revival of Schiller's play at the National Theatre in 1997 and of Donizetti's *Maria Stuarda* at the London Coliseum in 1998.

72. Alison Weir, 'The Queen Who Still Rules Us', *Spectator*, 17 Oct. 1998, 12.

73. This post-imperial Elizabeth is anticipated or pioneered by an established line of Irish and Irish-American fictions describing the Queen's dealings with Ireland and especially with apocryphal Irish characters: the most recent example is Bill Bruehl's play *Short-Haired Grace*, which opened in Boston in early 2002, in which the Queen is confronted by a female Irish nationalist pirate called Grace O'Malley. We are grateful to Richard Burt for sending us an account of this drama. Cf. the use of the Ditchley portrait in Frank McGuinness's Shakespeare and Spenser play *Mutability* (1996).

74. Patricia Finney, *Unicorn's Blood* (1998; London, 1999), 2.

75. Ibid. 12.

76. Ibid. 236.

77. Ibid. 443.
78. Tom McGregor, *Elizabeth: Based on the Screenplay by Michael Hirst* (New York, 1998), 244.
79. Ibid. 246.
80. Hodgdon, *The Shakespeare Trade*, 143.
81. Lest all this seems far-fetched, it is pertinent to mention Mavis Cheek's *Aunt Margaret's Lover* (1994), written for a *Cosmopolitan*-oriented readership, in which the central character, a childless woman in her late thirties, takes a lover, no strings attached, explicitly on the model of Elizabeth. (Hence the use of the Darnley portrait on the paperback's cover.)
82. This diagnosis is repeated less pointedly by another Elizabeth one-woman show, allusively entitled *The Regina Monologues*, performed by Penelope Keith at the 2001 Covent Garden Festival. In this play the elderly Queen, suffering from insomnia and bad conscience in the last year or so of her life, counts her jewels in bed to comfort herself in the absence of all other forms of consolation. Astonishingly, a command performance of this monologue was chosen to form part of the Duke of Edinburgh's eightieth birthday celebrations. Like the first performance of Britten's *Gloriana*, it seems spectacularly ill-suited to the audience and the occasion. Can it really have been that the subtext of the piece—England moribund and pathetically self-congratulatory—was lost on both organizers and audience?
83. On this ballet, see Nancy Isenberg, 'Woolf's *Orlando* and the Staging of Ballet Narrative', *Textus*, 12: 1 (Jan.–June 1999), 165–84. North's ballet had its première at the Rome Opera House in May 1997. We are very grateful to Nancy Isenberg for sending us a photograph of Claudio Zaccari as Elizabeth, dancing uncertainly in her underwear around her free-standing official dress.
84. Marc Norman and Tom Stoppard, *Shakespeare in Love* (screenplay, London, 1999), 148.
85. This being Oxford, the Orator in fact spoke in Latin: both the oration and the English translation quoted here are published in *Encaenia 28 June 2000* (Oxford, 2000).

AFTERWORD

1. *The Complete Works of Anne Bradstreet*, ed. Joseph R. McElrath Jr. and Allan P. Rodd (Boston, 1981), 157–8. Like many subsequent women readers of her story, Bradstreet draws a feminist moral from Elizabeth's successes: 'Let

such, as say our sex is void of reason, | Know 'tis a slander now, but once was treason'. On women writers' repsonses to Elizabeth, see especially Lisa Gim, 'Representing Regina: Literary Representations of Queen Elizabeth I by Women Writers of the Sixteenth and Seventeenth Centuries', Ph.D. dissertation, Brown University, 1992, and '"Faire *Eliza's* Chaine": Two Female Writers' Literary Links to Queen Elizabeth I', in Susan Frye and Karen Robertson (eds.), *Maids and Mistresses, Cousins and Queens* (New York and Oxford, 1999), 183–98; Kimberly Elliott, '"Eliza's Works, Wars, Praise": Representations of Elizabeth I in Diana Primrose and Anne Bradstreet', *Women Writers: A Zine* (www.womenwriters.net), Dec. 1999.

2. For nineteenth-century examples, see Chapter 4. The Washingtons' ancestral home, Sulgrave Manor, is now owned by America and run as a museum: Harnett's novel is still in print and on sale at its gift shop. The first chapter of Harnett's romance, which talks about the family's heraldry, is called 'Stars and Stripes'. Cynthia Harnett, *Stars of Fortune* (1956; London, 1995), 1.

3. John S. Jenkins, *The Heroines of History* (New York, 1851), 320, 272–3.

4. [Samuel Langhorne Clemens] Mark Twain, *1601: Conversation, As it was by the Social Fireside, in the Time of the Tudors, embellished with an illuminating introduction, facetious footnotes, and a bibliography . . .* ([West Point, NY], 1882).

5. On Folger's buying spree see especially Anthony James West, *The Shakespeare First Folio: The History of the Book*, i (Oxford, 2001), 102 ff. On America's investment in Shakespeare see also Michael Bristol, *Shakespeare's America, America's Shakespeare* (New York, 1990).

6. See Stephen Parks, *The Elizabethan Club of Yale University and its Library* (New Haven, 1986).

7. Charles Seymour, *An Ode in Commemoration of the Four Hundredth Anniversary of the Birth of Queen Elizabeth* (New Haven, 1934). The poem's concluding allusion is to a pioneer American balloonist.

8. Anne Hollander, *Seeing Through Clothes* (1975; Berkeley, 1993), 305, 296–8.

9. Incidentally, it is a testament to how influential this story was and still is that Maxwell Anderson's play, the basis for the film, was broadcast as a *Hallmark Hall of Fame* special on NBC television in 1968, and revived as a musical in New York as recently as 1980. For a contrary reading of *The Private Lives of Elizabeth and Essex*, see Barbara Hodgdon, *The Shakespeare Trade* (Philadelphia, 1998), 130–42.

10. Martin A. S. Hume, *Sir Walter Ralegh: the British Dominion of the West* (London, 1897), p. ix.

11. Frederick Henry Koch, *Raleigh: The Shepherd of the Ocean: A Pageant-Drama*

(Ralegh, NC, 1920), 15. Cf. Pamela Bennetts, *Envoy from Elizabeth* (New York, 1973), 18: 'they grew in stature and daring, straining away from the old, outworn shackles of indifference and apathy, eager to seek a new vibrant exciting world to make their own.' It may be worth mentioning a much stranger work here, the American expatriate William Brooke Drayton's *The New Argonautica: A Heroic Poem in 8 Cantos of the Voyage among the Stars of the Immortal Spirits of Sir Walter Raleigh, Sir Francis Drake, Ponce de Leon, and Nunez de Vaca* (London, 1928), in which Raleigh posthumously laments that his utopian dreams of the New World as a site for the birth of a democratic world federalism have been betrayed by America's participation in the First World War.

12. On this play and the other Elizabethan experiences available at present-day Roanoke (including 'Tea with the Queen', a sticky-sounding fancy-dress repast with the actress currently playing Elizabeth I, which makes the same transatlantic assimilation of the two Queen Elizabeths pioneered by Ally Sheedy's Buckingham Palace mouse in *She Was Nice to Mice*), see the enterprise's website, www.thelostcolony.org.

13. Randolph Umberger, Sara Bleick, Paul Green, *et al.*, *The Lost Colony* (script and production manual) (Roanoke, 1965), 45.

14. lebame houston, *Elizabeth R: A One-woman Show based on the Character of Queen Elizabeth I* (unpublished typescript, 1994), 11–13. We are extremely grateful to ms houston and Barbara Hird for sending us copies both of this text and of *The Lost Colony*. Natalie Hays Hammond's play *Elizabeth of England*, published in New York in 1936, anticipates lebame houston's creation of an Elizabeth not too proud to visit taverns in disguise, though here she takes Leicester with her as an escort, and has come not to sound out the people but to give one of them instructions. In another American anticipation of *Shakespeare in Love*, Hammond's Elizabeth has spotted Shakespeare's talent and will henceforward send him directions on what to write, using Leicester as a messenger. She has chosen Shakespeare as her ambassador to a virile posterity:

> ELIZABETH. Long after I have lain in dust, your lines shall stand.
> SHAKESPEARE. As the nightingale doeth [*sic*] of the stars proclaim
> So may my pen transcribe your glorious reign!
> ELIZABETH (*rising*). Thus, Master Shakespeare, you shall be advised by my Lord Leycester. The good of state depends upon your wit. Myself have been most severely swayed by such romantic passion you have penned: I beg you further these, my deeds, presenting them to men.

Natalie Hays Hammond, *Elizabeth of England* (New York, 1936), 47.

15. Cf. Elizabeth's unlikely adoption of what has elsewhere been regarded as an unsuitable job for a woman, that of detective, in the American writer Karen Harper's *The Poyson Garden* (1999) and *The Tidal Poole* (2000).

❧ Acknowledgements ❧

This book has taken two lifetimes to write—specifically, the lifetimes to date of our twin daughters Elizabeth and Rosalind—and we would like first of all to thank those people who have made it possible for us to finish it by looking after the girls from time to time while we have been on research trips, presenting work in progress, or at crisis-moments in the writing. Our heartfelt thanks to our parents, Peter and Elizabeth Watson and Derek and June Dobson; Molly Kelly and her undergraduate colleagues in Evanston, Illinois; Malgorazatha Czapla; Ursula Goode; Diane Holloway; and Ivona Mihalova.

We have had a great deal of fun writing this book, and are thankful to all who have aided and abetted it. The beginnings of our research towards it were funded by a one-month American Society for Eighteenth-Century Studies/Clark Library fellowship to the William Andrewes Clark Memorial Library in Los Angeles, during which time we also visited the Huntington Library in Pasadena and the Special Collections Department on the University of California Los Angeles' main campus. A grant from the American Philosophical Society financed a subsequent visit to the great collections of Harvard and of Yale (at the former, the Widener Library, the Houghton Library, and the Harvard Theatre Collection; at the latter the Beinecke Library, the Lewis Walpole Collection, and the Mellon Center for British Art). We also received support from the American Council of Learned Societies. We are grateful to these funding bodies, and to the staffs of these libraries, together with those of the Newberry Library in Chicago, and the Folger Shakespeare Library in Washington DC (this last visited courtesy of a British Academy small grant). Back in England we have been helped by the British Library, the National Portrait Gallery Archive, the Mary Evans Picture Library, the Ashmolean Museum, and the Bodleian Library, particularly the staff of its book depository at Nuneham Courtenay.

This book has found support and encouragement in three institutions in particular: the University of Illinois at Chicago, the Open University, and the University of Surrey Roehampton (whose Research Centre in Renaissance Studies has been generous throughout). (Professional courtesy forbids us from mentioning those institutions which impeded the writing of this book, but they know who they are.) We are especially grateful to the hosts and audiences who have heard and commented upon embryonic parts of this study given as lectures and seminars: here we must thank in particular the Clark Library's Center for Seventeenth and Eighteenth-Century Studies seminar on 'Cultural Icons'; the London Renaissance Seminar; Dieter Mehl and the Deutsche-Shakespeare Gesellschaft at Weimar; Stephen Parks at the Yale Elizabethan Club; Mark Thornton Burnett at Queen's University Belfast; Ton Hoenselaars and his fellow conveners of the '*Shakespeare in Love* and the Author as Character' conference at Utrecht; David Bevington and his colleagues in the Renaissance seminar at the University of Chicago; Giorgio Melchiori and the British Council in Rome; Gisèle Venet at the Institut du Monde Anglophone in Paris; Richard Burt, Laurie Osborne, and all fellow members of the seminar they convened on 'Romancing the Renaissance' at the 2000 Shakespeare Association of America conference in Montreal; and, most memorably of all, a large auditorium full of alert and candid first-year students at Peking University in November 1999.

All sorts of friends, colleagues, and disinterested well-wishers have assisted us with leads, suggestions, help, and advice, among them: Paul Barlow; Tom Berger; Dinah Birch; Richard Burt; John Brewer and Stella Tillyard; Douglas Bruster; Frank Savage Caldwell; Michael Cordner; Tracy Davis; Barbara Everett and Emrys Jones; Penny Fielding; Elizabeth Fowler; Lisa Freeman; Marjorie Garber and Barbara Johnson; Christine Gerrard; Werner Habicht; Cordelia Hall; Susannah Herbert; Margaret Homans; lebame houston and Barbara Hird; Clark Hulse; G. K. Hunter; Nancy Isenberg; Kayla Keyser; Anne Lawrence; Catherine Loomis; Jean Marsden; Cindy McCreery; Colleen Brown McKinley; Kathleen McLuskie; Steven Mullaney and Linda Gregerson; Adrienne Munich; Michael Neill; Jean Newlin; Stephen Orgel; Marcia Pointon; Gillian Quickenden; Diane K. Roberts; Mary Beth Rose; Kathy Rowe; Liu Shusen; Sheena Stoddard; Sir Roy Strong; Hilary Taylor; Ann Thompson; Kathleen Wilson; Stanley Wells; and Georgianna Ziegler. We are grateful, too, to the staffs of the many provincial art galleries to whom we wrote in our search for nineteenth-century images of Elizabeth, some of whom went to a good deal of trouble on our behalf. We would also like to thank Jennifer Michael and Kim Baldus for running library errands for us in Evanston; and the librarian at the Lewis Walpole Collection (whose name we wrote down but have since regrettably lost) who was kind enough to provide a chaise longue on to which the pregnant Dr Watson could faint in comfort and style. We had the good fortune to research much of this book at the same time that two North American colleagues were working on related topics, both of whom were kind enough to exchange unpublished materials with us in draft, namely Jayne Elizabeth Lewis

Acknowledgements

and Barbara Hodgdon. At Oxford University Press we have been helped by Andrew Lockett, Sophie Goldsworthy, Sarah Hyland, Frances Whistler, Sandra Assersohn, and Pat Lawrence. We consider ourselves particularly lucky to have put the finishing touches to the manuscript of this book just around the corner from the home of Clare Brant, who has been conspicuous for her learning, her friendship, and her hospitality alike. We should also like to take this opportunity to acknowledge our debt to the late Thomas Heywood, who was the first writer to use the title *England's Elizabeth*, in 1631.

An early version of Chapter 4 appeared in Margaret Homans and Adrienne Munich's collection *Remaking Queen Victoria* (Cambridge, 1996), and a draft towards Chapter 3 (in Dutch) in *Feit & Fictie* (Spring 2001); work towards Chapter 3 has also appeared in *Shakespeare Survey* and *Shakespeare Jahrbuch*. We are grateful to all these publications.

Since the nature of co-written work is often misunderstood, we shall conclude here by, in effect, acknowledging each other: this is a fully collaborative book, which means that each of us and both of us planned, researched, thought out, wrote, and rewrote at least one hundred per cent of it.

M. D.
N. J. W.

Oxford, Spring 2002

❧ Index ❧

dex*

Bennett, William Cox, 'The Armada' 205

Benson, E. F., *Mapp and Lucia* 198–9

Bernhardt, Sarah 23–5

Berry, Philippa 6–7

Bevan, Tom, *Sea Dogs All!* 180–1

Bible 52, 169, 185, 206; *see also* King James' Bible

Biographica Britannica 125

Biron, Admiral 301 n. 25

'Bisley boy' legend 220

Blackadder II 253–4, plate 9

Blackmore, Sir Richard, *Eliza* 73–4

Blanchett, Cate 257, plate 12

Bloody Mary, *see* Mary I

Blount, Sir Christopher 40

Boehm, Sir Edgar 191

Bohun, Edmund, *The Character of Queen Elizabeth* 72

Boisguillebert, Pierre le Pesant, Sieur du 99

Boleyn, Anne 6, 32, 63, 84, 101, 169, 222

Bolingbroke, Henry St John, *The Idea of a Patriot King* 74, 79

Bolt, Robert 325–6 n. 57

Book of Patriotism for Empire Day, The 198

Borden, John 284

Bothwell, Earl of 36, 99, 100, 104

Bow Bells 163

Bradstreet, Anne, 'In Honour of that High and Mighty Princess Queen ELIZABETH' 270–1

Brahms, Carol, and S. J. Simon, *No Bed for Bacon* 9, 135, 144–6, 212–14, 220

Brangwyn, Sir Frank 191

Bristol, *see* Hassall, John; 'Queen Elizabeths Ghost, or the humble remonstance . . .'

Britain: and accession of James I 19, 255–6; development of national identity after Act of Union 74–5, 80–1, 84, 117ff.; and devolution 255–6, 261–2; and Elizabeth's iconography and mythology 3–4, 80, 140, 261

Britten, Benjamin, as New Elizabethan 232; *Gloriana* 29–31, 227–30, 254–5, plate 11

Broad, Lewis, *Queens, Crowns and Coronations* 227

Brooke, Henry, *The Earl of Essex* 90, 94–7

Brunton, Anne 94, 96

Bryan, Margaret, Lady 32, 169, 170

Bull, John 119

Bull Sent By Pope Pius, A 70

Burbage, Richard 123

Burghley, William Cecil, Lord 35, 41, 130, 134, 136, 148, 161, 213, 216, 300–1 n. 22, fig. 17, plate 5

Burke, Edmund 19, 21

Burney, Edward Francis 98, 164

Burns, Robert 108

Burrows, J. W. 193

Byatt, A. S., *The Virgin in the Garden* 249–50

Byron, George Gordon, Lord, *Don Juan* 154

Cadiz, sack of 40, 47

Calprenède, Gautier des Costes de la, *Le Comte d'Essex* 89

Camden, William, *Annales* 5–6, 47–8

Camden Society 7, 179

Cameron, Verney Lovett, *The History of Arthur Penreath* 194

Campbell, Hugh 154

Campbell, Lord John 155

Campion, Edmund 38

Carey, Alfred Edward, *The Dark Lady* 127

Carey, George, Lord Hunsdon 122

Carey, Robert 14

Caroline, Queen 74

Carroll, Sidney, *The Imperial Votaress* 3, 240

Casket Letters 99

Catherine of Aragon 32–3, 63, 106

Catherine the Great 154

Ender, Eduard, *Shakespeare reading Macbeth before Queen Elizabeth* 130
Eric of Sweden, Prince 35
Erickson, Carolly 32
Ermine portrait, *see* Elizabeth I, portraits
Essex, Earl of, *see* Devereux, Robert
Exclusion Crisis 69–71

Family of Henry VIII, The 33
Fielding, Henry 118–19
Finney, Patricia, *Firedrake's Eye* 256; *Unicorn's Blood* 256–9
Fire Over England (film) 212; *see also* Mason, A. E. W.
Fisher, Graham and Heather, *The Crown and the Ring* 246
Fleming, Alexander 232
Fletcher, J. S., *In the Days of Drake* 193; *The Remarkable Adventure of Walter Trelawney* 193
Fletcher, John 130, plate 5; with William Shakespeare, *Henry VIII (All Is True)* 61–5, 68, 77–8
Flynn, Errol 275–9, fig. 28
Fo, Dario, *Elizabeth: Almost by Chance a Woman* 252–3
Folger Shakespeare Library 274
Foxe, John, *Acts and Monuments . . .* 35–6, 50, 85
Francklin, Thomas, *Mary Queen of Scots* 300–1 n. 22
Fraser, Antonia 249
Frobisher, Martin 187, 188, 200, 213
Froude, James Anthony 185–7, 191, 224; 'England's Forgotten Worthies' 187; *History of England from the Fall of Wolsey to the Death of Elizabeth* 185–6
Fuller, Thomas, *Worthies of England* 38, 152

Gardiner, Stephen, Bishop of Winchester 52, 54
Gardner, Helen 249
Garter ceremonies 41, 122
Gascoigne, George 112

Gentleman, Francis 124
Gheeraerts, Marcus, the younger, *see* Elizabeth I, portraits, Ditchley
Gilbert, Sir John 130
Gill, Thomas Hornblower, 'November 19th. The Spanish Armada' 204–5
Girlhood of Queen Victoria, The 173
Girvin, Brenda, *Good Queen Bess, 1533–1603* frontispiece
Gloriana, see Britten, Benjamin
Good Queen Bess: An Extravaganza 117, 167
Goodman, Godfrey, *The Court of King James the First* 49
Gow, Mary 148
Gower, George 38, 40
Graham, J. 87
Granger, Stewart 239
Great Exhibition 151
Green, J. R. 157
Green, Paul, *et al.*, *The Lost Colony* 284
Greenwich 297 n. 48
Gregg, Tresham D., *Queen Elizabeth; or, the origin of Shakespeare* 139
Gresham, Sir Thomas 55–6, 75
Greville, Fulke 47–8
Grey, Lady Jane 33, 84, 85, 87, 101, 305–6 n. 50
Grey, Ladies Katherine and Mary 35, 103
Guy Fawkes' Day 18, 34

H., N., *The Ladies Dictionary* 84
Haier, Joseph, *Shakespeare and Queen Elizabeth* 130
Haigh, Christopher 32, 65
Hakluyt, Richard 17–18, 186–7, 188; depicted posthumously 17–18, 66, fig. 1
Hakluyt Society 179, 186–7
Hall, Peter 245
Halliday, Andrew, and Frederick Lawrance, *Kenilworth, or, Ye Queene . . .* 167